LEADERS IN PHILOSOPHY OF EDUCATION

LEADERS IN EDUCATIONAL STUDIES

Series Editor:

Leonard J. Waks
Temple University, Philadelphia, USA

Scope:

Leaders in Educational Studies provides a comprehensive account of the transformation of educational knowledge since 1960, based on rich, first-person accounts of the process by its acknowledged leaders.

The initial volume, *Leaders in Philosophy of Education: Intellectual Self Portraits*, contains personal essays by 24 leading philosophers of education from North America and the United Kingdom. Subsequent volumes are planned for history of education and curriculum studies, and volumes for other fields are under consideration. The series provides unique insights into the formation of the knowledge base in education, as well as a birds-eye view of contemporary educational scholarship.

Until the 1950s school teachers were trained for the most part in normal schools or teacher training colleges. The instructors were drawn from the teacher corps; they were not professional scholars. In the late 1950s plans were made to bring a higher level of professionalism to teaching. In the United States, the remaining normal schools initially became state colleges, and eventually state universities. In the United Kingdom, the training colleges were initially brought under the supervision of university institutes; eventually teaching was transformed into an all-graduate profession.

Commentators on both sides of the Atlantic argued that if education was to become a proper field of university study then educational scholarship itself would have to be transformed. Scholars were recruited into educational studies from social sciences and humanities disciplines to contribute to teacher education and to train a new generation of educational scholars in contemporary research methods. Under their influence the knowledge base for education has been completely transformed. In addition to major accomplishments in philosophy, history, sociology and economics of education, interdisciplinary work in educational studies has flourished. The series documents this transformation.

Leaders in Philosophy of Education

Intellectual Self Portraits

Edited by

Leonard J. Waks
Temple University, Philadelphia, USA

With a Foreword by Israel Scheffler

SENSE PUBLISHERS
ROTTERDAM / TAIPEI

A C.I.P. record for this book is available from the Library of Congress.

ISBN 978-90-8790-286-5 (paperback)
ISBN 978-90-8790-287-2 (hardback)
ISBN 978-90-8790-288-9 (e-book)

Published by: Sense Publishers,
P.O. Box 21858, 3001 AW Rotterdam, The Netherlands
http://www.sensepublishers.com

Printed on acid-free paper

TABLE OF CONTENTS

PREFACE

This volume brings together 24 personal essays by established philosophers of education, detailing their early life experiences, first encounters with philosophy, period of serious study, early professional work, and emergence as leaders. Each chapter features summaries of their bodies of mature work and reflections on the current challenges and opportunities in the field.

The need for such a work became apparent at the 2003 annual meeting of the Philosophy of Education Society (US), when a presidential panel addressed the question why leading lights in our field only a few decades ago (B. O. Smith and Paul Komisar were used as examples) were now ignored. This raised the further question why the field, as it has undergone various transitions since the mid 1950s, has failed to build effectively on its past achievements, or at least to establish these as relevant background for contemporary studies? Whatever the answer (many, none completely satisfactory, were given at that session), the field can certainly do a better job in keeping its best work alive.

This book is a means to that end. It makes available in one place summaries and bibliographies of much, if not most, of the best work in the field since the 1960s. Equally important, the essays situate this work in the lives and institutional settings of their authors. Philosophers may appeal to transcendent principles of reasoning, and seek to provide accounts of timeless concepts. Their work is nonetheless also a response to local, personal, and pressing situations, framed in the language of their times. Current and future philosophers of education will of course live in different circumstances. They will address somewhat different problems in somewhat different ways. They should, however, be able to gain greater access to the philosophical works of the last fifty years, and make greater use of their insights, when they see them as responses of flesh and blood human beings like themselves, drawing on a common philosophical tradition and sharing a common aspiration to reason.

It is a truism that 'to include is to exclude,' and so a few words must be said about how these particular authors were selected for inclusion. It would be liberating to claim that I have a proprietary formula but nothing could be further from the truth; inevitably a large element of judgment has entered the process.

After encouraging discussions about the project with Nel Noddings, Christopher Winch, Jane Roland Martin and Michael Peters, I prepared a preliminary list of possible authors residing in North America and the United Kingdom. I considered including representatives from Australia and New Zealand, but soon realized that, as I had never visited these countries, I simply did not know enough about the situation of philosophy of education there to make a selection. I checked my initial list against the tables of contents of four philosophy of education journals: *Educational Theory*, *Studies in Philosophy and Education*, *The Journal of Philosophy of Education*, and *Educational Philosophy and Theory*, and a few other education journals containing philosophical articles, to confirm that the selected authors had been active in the field over at least a quarter century. The last three mentioned journals came into existence after the analytical revolution, largely as organs of the new philosophy of education. Because *Educational Theory* was in existence prior to the revolution, I consulted every volume after 1960. This process both added some candidates to, and subtracted others from, the list. Finally I invited those on this list to contribute.

Jane Roland Martin predicted that just about everyone would agree, as they valued both the field and their own contributions, and she was right. Of those invited, only two did not accept: one declined, feeling that he had inadequate *institutional* presence in the field; the other appears to have been too busy to answer repeated emails and phone calls. The contributors also suggested others for inclusion, and some were added. However, I narrowed the field by excluding most scholars whose contributions to the field spanned less than twenty-five years as well as older scholars absent from conferences and journals in the field for many years. Essays by these younger philosophers I hope to gather in a proposed 'second series'. I wished to avoid imposing on seniors who might no longer be interested in writing for publication, or no longer find themselves in good health and able to prepare a chapter that adequately represented their contributions. Several authors urged me to ask Tom Green for a contribution despite his poor health. In the event, he died before I had the chance to ask him. Fortunately Emily Robertson has prepared a wonderful eulogy summarizing Tom's life and contributions, which appears as Appendix A. I may have passed over others who should have been included, but to the extent possible I will again attempt to rectify such omissions in a 'second series'. With these qualifications, the authors included in this volume can safely be said to be among the leading philosophers of education in the post-analytical revolution period. No claim is made or intended, however, that they are "the" leaders.

A note on the sidebars within the text

Each of the authors has contributed a list of the personal favorites among their own works. Some have also included brief lists of works which have deeply influenced them. These are included as sidebars in the chapters. For works already listed in the bibliographies, the sidebars contain only the title and year of publication. For works selected as influences but not included in the bibliographies, those possessing classical status are listed in the sidebar solely by title; others are listed with a complete citation.

Acknowledgements

I want to thank Peter de Liefde of Sense Publishers for helping me to think through the concept for this volume. In addition to providing their chapters, most contributors made useful suggestions for the volume and I thank them all. Christopher Winch helped in thinking about contributors from the UK, while John White, Patricia White and Richard Pring all answered endless questions about the background of philosophy of education there. Patricia also served as a link to Paul Hirst each time my email connection with him broke down. William Taylor prepared detailed written answers to questions about the transformation of teaching into an all-graduate profession in Britain. Paul Hirst, in addition to his encouragement and insights in emails and telephone conversations, prepared a most valuable essay on the institutional context of the flowering of analytical philosophy of education in the UK, which appears as Appendix B. Harvey Siegel saved me from some blunders in the introduction, and helped me give more coherence to my own chapter. Finally, I thank my wife Veronica and my son Sjoma for their endless understanding, support and love.

FOREWORD

I came to Harvard in 1952 under a Rockefeller grant to bring young scholars to the Graduate School of Education who had been trained not in the field of Education but in the Liberal Arts subjects, with a view to introducing new perspectives to the field. Bernard Bailyn in history and I in philosophy, both new Ph.D.s, started our teaching careers as instructors in the fall term of that year, he in history of education and I in philosophy of education. My enlightened Dean, Francis Keppel, had, however, brilliantly original ideas about how beginning instructors should be initiated into their new careers. He thought that my first semester of teaching should not be spent teaching at all. Rather, he asked me to spend that time talking individually to each one of my new faculty colleagues, whom I had not yet met, and finding out what they thought the function of philosophy of education ought to be in a School of Education and how it should be taught there.

Further, and even more radically, he expressed his firmly held belief that, contrary to the prevalent practice of assigning beginning instructors the heaviest teaching loads and gradually reducing them until the position of seniority was reached whereupon the most senior faculty members taught the lightest loads, his conviction was that exactly the reverse pattern was the most desirable. The youngest instructors, who needed to acquire an orientation to the whole area of their future teaching, and, further, to structure the courses they were going to teach, as well as the sorts of research they were planning to undertake, needed the most free time to work out their responses to these tasks in a deliberate way, and without undue pressure. By contrast, senior professors might well be assumed already to have resolved such issues to their own satisfaction and therefore to require the least time free of teaching responsibilities, hence to be assigned the heaviest loads.

The net result was that the Dean required me, following my first semester of simply consulting at my leisure with faculty colleagues, to teach just one course in the Graduate School of Education. When I asked him what sort of course that ought to be, he protested, saying that, after I had had my several talks with colleagues and pondered the possibilities, I ought to feel free to choose any course I judged to be most desirable, with no prior constraint. Quoting a racing maxim which, as I recall, he may have attributed to his father, he said, "We bet on the horse, not on the track." He indicated, finally, his realization that anyone joining a professional school with initial training in one of the scholarly disciplines would need to retain an affiliation with the discipline in question, even while developing a teaching and research identity of usefulness to the profession. The upshot was that I could, indeed should, cultivate scholarly and personal relationships with colleagues in the Philosophy Department of the Graduate School of Arts and Sciences, as well as those in the Graduate School of Education, and could welcome to my course graduate students from both schools. The prospect was that, with time, I would gradually teach additional courses, melding philosophical content with professional usefulness as my sense of what seemed appropriate continued to develop and as my research agenda matured.

The burden of this unprecedented degree of freedom was heavy indeed and I thought long and hard about how to handle it. The faculty consultations I proceeded to arrange over the next few months turned out to be quite pleasant and interesting, affording me insights into the culture of the School and the attitudes of the faculty toward philosophy of education. But they gave me no useful guidance as to what I might teach under this rubric when the next semester rolled around. The reason was that no consensus emerged from my consultations; some colleagues thought philosophers ought to promulgate values, some thought they should review the history of education, or deal with problems of American schools, or promote the ideas of John Dewey, or determine the relative merits of teaching methods or integrate the secondary school curriculum or etc. Most of these colleagues came to their positions out of earlier experiences in education as teachers, school administrators, curriculum experts, department heads, state education officers and so forth. A smaller faculty contingent came out of disciplinary areas in psychology and the social sciences, involving research of various sorts, for example, in child development, sociology, political science, economics, anthropology – but none had had more than a passing acquaintance with philosophy as an area of disciplined inquiry. Clearly I could hope for no real guidance from my new colleagues and had to decide for myself.

I had to teach out of my philosophical training; that much was clear, but what subject matter should be my focus, and how ought I to design my curriculum and mode of instruction? Philosophy is after all a many-splendored subject, reaching out in limitless directions to all corners of the universe and every aspect of life. I decided, after lengthy deliberation, to concentrate my initial efforts on ethics, as having obviously close bearings on the human procedures and effects of education, but I rejected the idea of lecturing on the history of ethics to students who could not be presumed to have had either any background in philosophy or any initial interest in learning about the development of ethical ideas, and who were, moreover, headed into quite diverse careers in education. In addition, I much preferred to teach in an informal rather than a didactic style, which would allow interaction with the multiple interests and career goals of my students, thus helping to shape my subject in making maximum contact with them while leading them, I hoped, to new intellectual levels.

The final element of my decision was based on my conviction that the best way to teach was to learn, thus keeping the process fresh and unpredictable, open to surprises at every turn -- for teacher as well as students. I had earlier, in my graduate studies, learned a fair amount about the history and landscape of ethical ideas, but I wanted an ethical focus that was new to me, accessible to a wide variety of students, and one that would require me, as well as my students, to explore novel and challenging territory. For this purpose I ended by choosing a recently published anthology of papers in analytical ethics, an area I had not earlier studied in detail – *Readings in Ethical Theory*, edited by Wilfrid Sellars and John Hospers. For each paper in this anthology, I designated a student to give a brief account of its main arguments as well as a critique thereof, then opening the floor for general discussion. The ensuing exchanges were intensive and lively, addressing serious philosophical fundamentals, but reflecting always the diverse academic backgrounds and educational aspirations of the students.

We all learned a lot in that class, not only about the intellectual bases of different approaches to ethical problems, but about the range of educational presuppositions which students brought with them to their philosophical studies. The experience was doubly beneficial to me, teaching me how to communicate with students of disparate educational backgrounds and thereby allowing me both to hear better what they were saying and to provide the new philosophical slant on education, which it was my mandate at Harvard to represent. I continued to apply what I learned thus, as I expanded the repertoire of courses I taught in succeeding years, in philosophy of science, philosophy of language, American philosophy, epistemology, symbol theory, emotion and cognition -- as well as the formats of those courses both in lecture and in seminar, and in individual reading courses too.

Early on in this development, I presented my short paper, "Toward an Analytic Philosophy of Education", in 1953, to a small session of The American Association for the Advancement of Science, which appeared not to know quite what to make of it. I had intended to help connect philosophy of education with general philosophy, then experiencing strong growth in analytic methods and applications. I certainly had no idea that my paper would have such a long life or be reckoned decades later as having helped launch a revolution.

In retrospect, I can see that my caution in advocating an analytic philosophy of education could not overcome the force of the revolutionary rhetoric. My paper began by emphasizing the ambiguity of the terms "philosophy" and "philosophy of education", acknowledging the appropriateness of various of the activities commonly denoted by these terms, including logical analysis, speculative construction, culture criticism, institutional programming, and the expression of personal attitudes toward the world. I came not to bury such activities, but rather to emphasize one such that I thought had been almost consistently ignored, namely the rigorous logical analysis of key concepts related to the practice of education. I further stressed the fact that the attempt to clarify key concepts is hardly a modern invention, being at least as old as Socrates, the current variety distinguishable largely by its greater sophistication concerning the interpenetration of language and inquiry, its attempt to emulate the empirical spirit of science, its use of new techniques in logic, and its community of investigation, unified by method rather than by theme or topic. I emphasized that this new development represented no mere doctrinal school, comprising within itself sharp differences of opinion on substantive issues.

My larger aim was to bring about closer connections between philosophy of education treated as a professional subject, and general philosophy, construed as an independent area of reflection and research. In furthering such rapprochement, I acknowledged, in my 1971 paper, "Philosophy and the Curriculum'", that the old isolated professional treatment of the subject had its own advantages in addressing issues recognizable to the educational practitioner, while the energetic push toward general philosophy had its risks as well, threatening the linkage of theory and practice in tending to scant the latter. I thus recognized the positive value and role of the old professional treatment of our subject even while trying to overcome its limitations, and suggesting new ways to develop essential links between philosophy and educational practice, thus mitigating the risks.

Despite my extended qualifications, many of my revolutionary colleagues very often adopted a more strident tone. They frequently, as a number of passages in this book will testify, described the old professional treatment of the subject to be quite worthless -- incompetent, vague, and without any redeeming virtue. They from time to time imagined themselves engaged in rebuilding the subject from scratch, as if our philosophical forebears had contributed nothing and our contemporary professionals had absolutely no material of value to impart. Moreover, ignoring the focus of analytic philosophy on method, they often supposed analysis to be restricted to early efforts to clarify key terms related to education, thereafter complaining that analytic philosophy had begun to lose its energy and needed to give way to existential, spiritual, social, political or other schools of thought, even going so far as occasionally to attack rationality itself. Ignored wholly in this trend was the fact that analysis is not a school of thought, but the application of rational methods to any subject without restriction, open to differences of doctrine by its practitioners, and hospitable to the study of any aspect or problem of education. In sum, the so-called loss of energy of analysis, of which complaints have increasingly been heard, is not a failure of analysis but a failure of the imagination of analysts. They of course need regularly to move on from initial exemplars and results, applying themselves to new issues, and designing novel intellectual techniques for dealing with them.

In my own succeeding books, what is strikingly evident is the great variety of educational problems and issues addressed, including, for example, moral, democratic, and character education, the science, art, and discipline of education, public education and the good life, religious and political education, etc. -- all treated in analytic fashion. In the Harvard Graduate School of Education where I taught, diversity of philosophical interests and training were cherished, even among newly appointed faculty members imbued with analytical spirit and verve. And thereby hangs an important tale.

My first sabbatical took me to London in 1958 and 1959, where, at a meeting of the Aristotelian Society, I for the first time met Richard Peters, then teaching at Birkbeck College. Before coming to London I had read three of his lectures published in *The Listener*, entitled Authority, Responsibility and Education, later published as a book with the same name. I had much admired those lectures for their clarity, wisdom and philosophical acumen, and was delighted to meet the author, hastening to tell him that he was, in fact, now a philosopher of education. He bristled at my description, insisting on his identity as a philosopher of psychology, and of political theory. Recalling a quip of Roy W. Sellars that there are two ways of making someone religious, one being conversion, the other definition, I told Peters that, by virtue of the authorship of his three lectures in *The Listener*, he was now, by my definition, also a philosopher of education. He then invited me to give a paper to his Birkbeck seminar and to visit his common room, and we became friends during that year.

Shortly after I returned home, my Dean asked me to meet with an official of the Rockefeller Foundation who was in town and wanted to talk with me. He asked me for my advice on what the Foundation might do to help improve the humanistic offerings of the School of Education. I conveyed both to him and to my Dean my strong recommendation that they invite Richard Peters to come as a Visiting Professor to the School of Education for an extended period, to teach philosophy of education in my Area. Thus my definition of his identity as philosopher of education was realized, at Harvard at least. He did in fact come, and I asked him to teach his own version of my Introduction to Philosophy of Education course, the focus of which was epistemology; he agreed and designed his course to address ethics and education. I thereafter offered both my course lectures and his to Scott Foresman for a series of theirs which I was editing. His book appeared in that series as *Ethics and Education*, mine as *Conditions of Knowledge*, both expressions of analytic philosophy while treating different subject matters.

Sometime later, after Professor Louis Arnaud Reid's leaving the Chair of Philosophy at the Institute of Education in London, I was invited to write a letter to the authorities there concerning Peters' candidacy for the Chair. This I was only too glad to do, and I was overjoyed that he was in fact appointed to that position, cementing his identification as philosopher of education on both sides of the Atlantic and, allied with Paul Hirst and others, leading the reform of Education in the U.K. with brilliant results. I was especially pleased that he and I could collaborate in various ways despite our different environments, exemplifying common analytic affiliations while working on different philosophical themes.

Following Peters' scheduled departure from Harvard, our School of Education continued to have senior faculty members who supplemented my epistemological interests with others of their own. William Frankena taught ethics, and contributed one of his books to my Scott Foresman series, entitled *Three Historical Philosophies of Education*, dealing with Aristotle, Kant, and Dewey. Later, Frederick Olafson joined me, concentrating on philosophy of the humanities, inclusive of history, literature and social thought. A major book of his, *Principles and Persons*, examined analytically the relations between Anglo-American ethics and the existentialism of Sartre. Once such diversity of thematic focus is seen to be compatible with analytical method, the complaint of a tired analysis is exposed for the myth that it is.

The book before us in fact destroys this myth by exhibiting the widespread accomplishments of analytic methods applied to a remarkable array of educational concerns, both theoretical and practical. The effect of analysis in our field, I believe, has been to raise the intellectual level of our deliberations, radically improving the quality of argument on topics of educational import. Of this we may justly be proud. What is needed further is the continuing and restless imagination to explore how current educational problems might be dealt with, using the best available methods to hand. What is urgently required in addition is to develop lines of thought and investigation that are consecutive, building on what has been done before, and strengthening the structural continuities of our field.

A word, finally, in praise of the design of this book, which melds the philosophical with the personal. This melding is of especial importance in the communication of large ideas, which take on special vibrancy when presented not as abstract messages alone but as products of minds, motivations, and feelings. The melding is, furthermore, urgent in our era of rampant and galloping technology, threatening to overtake every sector of life, inclusive of education. Technology is certainly essential, important and here to stay, representing the necessary transformation of our world by thought. But that thought is, as I have emphasized, powered by aspiration, and also sensitized by our emotions, responsive to dreams and memories, and disciplined by our moral sentiments. It would be a catastrophe to view analysis as enemy of the human traits we share. Like the arts, it grows from human soil and at its best brings forth its latent powers, beneficent uses, and unsuspected glories.

Israel Scheffler
Victor S. Thomas Professor of Education and Philosophy Emeritus,
Harvard University and Scholar-in-Residence, Brandeis University
October, 2007

INTRODUCTION

The Analytical Revolution in Philosophy of Education and Its Aftermath

Before the mid twentieth century school teaching, especially at the primary level, was as much a trade as a profession. Schoolteachers were trained primarily in normal schools or teachers colleges, only rarely in universities. But in the 1940s American normal schools were converted into teachers colleges, and in the 1960s these were converted into state universities. At the same time school teaching was being transformed into an all-graduate profession in both the United Kingdom and Canada. For the first time, school teachers required a proper university education.

Something had to be done, then, about what was widely regarded as the deplorable state of educational scholarship. James Conant, in his final years as president at Harvard in the early 1950s, envisioned a new kind of university-based school of education, drawing scholars from mainstream academic disciplines such as history, sociology psychology and philosophy, to teach prospective teachers, conduct educational research, and train future educational scholars. One of the first professors hired to fulfil this vision was Israel Scheffler, a young philosopher of science and language who had earned a Ph.D. in philosophy at the University of Pennsylvania. Scheffler joined Harvard's education faculty in 1952.

Scheffler's "Toward an Analytical Philosophy of Education" (1954) pointed towards a new era where the philosophical study of education would make use of the best and most current philosophical methods and thus attain recognition as a genuine branch of academic philosophy. Scheffler's article generated much programmatic discussion in education journals, and his book *The Language of Education* (1960) provided exemplary models of philosophical analyses of educational concepts for others to emulate. At the same time B. O. Smith was training graduate students in analytical philosophy of education in the college of education at the University of Illinois. *Language and Concepts in Education* (1961), co-edited by Smith and his former student Robert Ennis, added additional models of analytical philosophy of education, including articles by (among others) Smith's students Ennis, Paul Komisar and James McClellan, and Scheffler's student Jane Roland Martin. The 'analytical revolution' in American philosophy of education was launched.

Somewhat parallel developments were taking place on the other side of the Atlantic. University leaders had experienced longings similar to Conant's for up-grading the academic content of university based educational studies. Paul Hirst, a mathematics educator, took a lectureship at Oxford's department of Education in 1955 after philosophical studies with L.A. Reid at the University of London's Institute of Education. While at Oxford Hirst attended seminars and lectures of the leading Oxford philosophers: Anscombe, Toulmin, Ryle, Strawson, Urmson, Hare and Austin. Wittgenstein's *Philosophical Investigations*, published in 1953, was the topic of much heated discussion at Oxford, and Hirst's views on education

L.J. Waks (ed.), Leaders in Philosophy of Education: Intellectual Self Portraits, 1–13.

were much influenced by Wittgenstein's notion of a 'form of life'. Hirst soon returned to the London Institute of Education to take up a lectureship specifically in philosophy of education.

Meanwhile, Richard S. Peters, a prominent analytical philosopher at Birkbeck College, University of London, and head of the university's department of philosophy and psychology, was turning his attention to philosophy of education. Peters had studied philosophy as an Oxford undergraduate, and earned a Ph. D. in 1942. Like Hirst and many other authors in this book, he had spent a period of time as a school teacher before launching his academic career. Peters had recently completed two important books, *The Concept of Motivation* (1958) and (with Stanley Benn) *Social Principles and the Democratic State* (1961), when he visited Harvard as Professor of Education, and as Israel Scheffler's colleague, in 1961. The following year he returned to England to replace L. A. Reid as the head of philosophy of education at the London Institute of Education, joining forces with Paul Hirst. The analytical revolutionaries in British philosophy of education were taking possession of the field.

The revolutionaries were fully self-conscious about their insurgency. Previous teaching in the field had pitted various philosophical schools against each other: pragmatism vs. realism vs. existentialism. Which ever one of these philosophies a teacher trainee picked, it provided some sort of woolly rationale for an accepted form of teaching within the mainstream system – a kind of 'pick your own poison' substitute for serious, independent thinking. Kenneth Strike describes the situation in the United States:

> At the time philosophy of education was organized into clubs with names like "pragmatism" and "realism." It seemed like half the papers in *Educational Theory* had (or could have had) titles like "The Implications of the philosophy of Philosopher P for education" and at least half the members of the profession seemed to think that the writings of John Dewey were divinely inspired.

The analysts rejected all of this prior work as philosophically incompetent and intellectually empty. Richard Peters in the UK criticized existing work in the field as "undifferentiated mush" (Richard Pring, private correspondence). Patricia White describes it as "specialising in a kind of refined preachy woolliness". The revolutionaries thus saw themselves as re-starting philosophy of education from rock bottom. Very few of our authors, in detailing the course of their professional lives, even mention any prior work in the field, with the exception of the re-appropriation of Dewey after 1990, about which more below.

THE REVOLUTION SPREADS

The revolution was soon given additional impetus in both the United States and Great Britain. In the United States, highly critical studies of teacher education were published by James Koerner and James Conant in 1963. Their conclusions were similar, and though Koerner employed a more incendiary rhetoric, Conant's account caused the more violent reaction. Koerner's report, *The Miseducation of American Teachers* (1963), found that the courses in undergraduate teacher education programs completely "deserved their ill repute", but that the graduate programs were "even worse". Koerner found the academic content in educational graduate programs and the scholarship in educational journals "deplorable". He concluded that education courses in any institution that were derived from academic disciplines such as philosophy, history, and psychology should be taught only by persons fully qualified to teach these disciplines in the respective academic departments in the same institution. And he didn't pull back from the obvious implication: that those lacking full credentials in the academic disciplines should no longer be permitted to teach such courses. Conant's report reiterated this conclusion: effective teaching of academic content in education could only come from properly trained professors bringing to bear on educational topics the best, most current methods from well-established academic disciplines.

The Conant report was described as a "bombshell," and "the sharpest challenge to teacher education since the creation of the normal school". Given Conant's unquestioned authority as an educational leader, his report was "nothing less than insurrectionary" in aiming to free teachers from domination by educationists (Stiles, 1964). Sales exceeded 50, 000 in the first three months after publication, the book became an alternate selection by the Book of the Month Club, and received 1200 reviews in magazines and newspapers around the country. The educationists mounted a somewhat desultory defence, but driven by a public outcry about the teacher education 'crisis,' State departments of education began to call on universities to implement Conant's recommendations. Several universities, including Boston University and Northwestern, followed Harvard's lead by establishing joint graduate programs in philosophy and philosophy of education or establishing joint professorships in philosophy and education, to supply teachers of philosophy for the nation's teacher education programs. Jane Roland Martin, Jonas Soltis, and Harvey Siegel were among the graduates of Scheffler's program. Martin and Siegel, after brief periods in schools of education, eventually settled in philosophy departments. Soltis, on the other hand, became a professor of philosophy at Teachers College, Columbia University. Walter Feinberg received his Ph.D. from the Boston University joint program and soon joined the Illinois education faculty. Kenneth Strike received his from Northwestern's joint program and, after a period at Wisconsin with a joint appointment in philosophy and education, went to the department of education at Cornell.

In England, teaching was on the road to becoming an all-graduate profession after the Robbins report of 1963. At the Hull conference - jointly organised by the universities and colleges and the Ministry of Education in 1964 to explore the academic content of teacher education, Richard Peters gave voice to the longings shared by many university scholars for improvement in educational studies, and made a powerful plea for a central place for the foundational disciplines. Paul Hirst provides a full discussion of further developments in the UK in an article included as Appendix B. Undergraduate and post-graduate teacher education programs needed qualified philosophers to teach philosophy of education, and Peters and Hirst established Masters and Doctoral programs at the Institute of Education to train them. As David Carr puts it,

> Owing much to the pioneering work of educational philosophers – not least that of Richard Peters and Paul Hirst – British university departments and colleges of education were seeking to develop more professional approaches to teacher education and training grounded in better appreciation of the significance of educational theory for the effective practice of teaching. A key aim of this new conception of teacher professionalism was to raise teaching to the status of an all-graduate profession – primarily through the development of rigorously disciplined undergraduate programmes of professional education in the teacher training colleges.

Patricia White adds

> With the aim of achieving a wholly graduate teaching profession in Britain, the government established the Bachelor of Education degree. This included the disciplines seen as foundational in educational studies – sociology, philosophy, psychology and history. Peters now had the task of providing courses in philosophy of education to equip college teachers to teach the new B.Ed degree. As well as a special government-funded one year Diploma course, he had developed, with Paul Hirst, an MA in Philosophy of Education.

In addition to Carr and Patricia White, Robin Barrow and Richard Pring did graduate work at the Institute. White subsequently joined the IOE staff along with John White, who had studied with Peters at Birkbeck; Patricia White supervised Barrow's doctoral dissertation. Walter Feinberg was among the North American visitors to the Hirst-Peters program, during a sabbatical in the mid 1970s.

In the United States the training of analytical philosophers of education was initially concentrated at Harvard and Illinois. However, it soon became decentralized. Cornell, Syracuse, Temple, Stanford, Wisconsin and Northwestern, among other universities, all played important roles. Robert Ennis completed his doctorate at Illinois and took a post at Cornell; Gary Fenstermacher was among his students. Kenneth Strike, after completing his dissertation at Northwestern, went to Wisconsin and then on to Cornell when Ennis returned to Illinois. Kieran Egan, after a year of study with Leonard Waks at Stanford, completed his doctoral studies at Cornell with Strike. Hugh Petrie, a Stanford philosophy Ph.D. who had written a dissertation on learning and understanding, became one of Strike's teachers at Northwestern's joint program before joining Ennis and Walter Feinberg in the college of education at Illinois. Paul Komisar and Jim McClellan, after completing their doctoral degrees at Illinois, eventually came to Temple. Emily Robertson earned a Masters degree in their program at Temple before moving to Syracuse to

4

complete her doctoral studies under Thomas Green, who had earned his Ph.D. in philosophy at Cornell, and Paul Deitl, who had been recruited for the Syracuse education faculty from Temple. After completing his doctoral degree in philosophy at Wisconsin, Waks took a joint appointment in philosophy and education at Stanford before joining Komisar and McClellan at Temple. Denis Phillips eventually filled the position Waks vacated at Stanford and Nel Noddings, one of the many distinguished graduates of the Stanford program, soon returned to the Stanford education faculty.

While these details may be unimportant, they point to a significant difference between the development of analytical philosophy of education in the United States and the United Kingdom. Hirst and Peters were "the" unquestioned leaders in the UK, working together to construct a comprehensive philosophy of education which their students could amplify and disseminate, with Hirst leading the charge in epistemology and curriculum studies, Peters in the moral and social dimensions of education. They recruited younger scholars to work with them on a cooperative basis to build up the various elements in this philosophy. The decentralization of leadership in the United States, however, made this kind of comprehensive approach impossible. As Harvard and Illinois became less dominant, analytical philosophy of education developed in the United States more as an accumulation of loosely associated philosophical fragments than as 'a philosophy'. While the work of Hirst and Peters would remain central to subsequent efforts in the UK, Scheffler and Smith did not have, and possibly did not desire, roles as "the" on-going programmatic leaders of a coherent academic movement.

FIRST FRUITS: CONCEPTUAL ANALYSES OF EDUCATIONAL COMMONPLACES

The analytical paradigm prescribed that philosophical studies should expose, explore, clarify, critique or justify central concepts, presuppositions, and logical structures of the various areas of human endeavor: art, science, religion, morality, history, medicine, to name some main ones. When the analytical revolution reached philosophy of education in the 1950s and 1960s, the most natural first efforts tackled such educational commonplaces as: teaching, learning, subject matters, organizational settings, and social contexts, and their various inter-relationships. Studies of concepts logically related to these commonplaces -- e.g. of reasoning, explaining and indoctrinating (teaching), observation, understanding, critical and creative thinking, and intelligence (learning), aims and logical structures of subject matters (curriculum) and power and authority (organizational setting and social context) followed. To put the point crudely, these were the 'lowest hanging fruits' for the analytical program.

Because the analytical revolution was an element of a larger program of 'fixing' the broken field of educational scholarship, another important trend in early studies, unsurprisingly, focused on educational research, particularly the critique of programs, methods, and applications of empirical research. Philosophers were on the whole critical of the behaviorist and developmental research programs and intelligence testing. Drawing on work in the philosophies of the social sciences and human action, in particular on Peter Winch's *The Idea of a Social Science* (1958), they were generally skeptical about all direct applications of empirical science to educational practice.

A QUIET CRISIS AND NEW DIRECTIONS

By the mid-1970s and early 1980s new opportunities for original work along the lines of the early analytical studies were harder to come by. There were only so many commonplaces, and so many plausible analyses of them, to go around. Christopher Winch notes that his recent book-length study of learning (Winch, 200X) is the first since Hamlyn's study in 1979. Jim Garrison says that his study of the logic of teaching with Jim McMillan (1988) is arguably the last major analytical study of an educational topic to draw wide attention. While this claim may be challenged (by reference to works by Passmore, Hare, and Pearson specifically on teaching, for example) they point to something important: works concentrated narrowly on the 'logical grammar' of educational terms were going out of style. The four initial volumes Jonas Soltis's *Thinking about Education* series, on teaching (co-authored with Fenstermacher), learning (co-authored by Phillips), curriculum (co-authored with Decker Walker), and social context (co-authored with Feinberg) can then be seen as a both a cumulative summary of the analytic work on commonplaces, and a reduction of the original work to standard teachable subject matter. Meanwhile, earlier empirical research paradigms in education such as behaviorism and Piagetian developmentalism were losing their appeal; they no longer required or justified sustained philosophical critique. Many leaders in philosophy of education and their most talented students, including many authors in this volume, were moving beyond what might be seen as limitations of the analytical paradigm.

Eric Nordenbo (1979), assessing the first 25 years of the 'new' philosophy of education, proclaims that the period had witnessed the "rise and decline of analytical philosophy of education". He notes that the international student movement of the 1960s had come and gone, Ivan Illich had advanced a widely discussed broadside critique of schooling, and Paolo Friere had diagnosed conventional educational methods as a major cause of global injustice – all of this "without leaving a trace in the philosophy of education". By the end of the 1970s, Nordenbo argues, philosophers of education were suffering a "loss of faith in analytical methods," and "dissatisfaction with analytical philosophy's inability to answer normative questions".

Some evidence for this assessment is to be found in the chapters that follow. Walter Feinberg, for example, writes:

> While the analytic movement helped establish the academic legitimacy of philosophy of education, the field ... (became) increasingly distant from the immediate needs of educators. Although I was attracted to its rigor I felt that it failed to explore the larger social context of education and thus had a largely quietist

influence on the field. If I had been dissatisfied with the justification that Dewey provided for educational reform, believing as I did that it was both theoretically and practically flawed, I was even more dissatisfied with the possibility that the analytic tradition provided. At its best, it seemed to leave everything as is, in the belief that all our problems were the result of linguistic muddles. Caught between a naïve optimistic belief in progress and a similarly naïve linguistic reductionism, philosophy of education seemed paralysed.

Francis Schrag adds: "At the end of the seventies, I experienced a crisis of confidence. I … saw (analytical) ethics and social philosophy as barren." And Jane Martin, reflecting on her transition to feminist philosophy in 1980, states:

> Amazingly enough, in just two decades analytic philosophy had taken over the philosophy of education … By the time *Reclaiming a Conversation* was published, I had shed my analytic philosopher identity.

But significantly, Martin adds:

> Be this as it may, I have never turned my back on my philosophical training or renounced my earlier analytic findings. On the contrary, the training that I received at Harvard from Scheffler and others is the bedrock on which all my work rests.

Looking back with the perspective of another quarter century, and especially when drawing directly upon the essays in this volume, Nordenbo's assessment, while suggestive, can be seen as both incomplete and to some extent mistaken.

First, analytical philosophy, as Nordenbo recognises, is not a set of fixed doctrines or practices but an evolving philosophical style. When C.D. Hardie and D.J. O'Connor made their initial 'analytical' interventions in philosophy of education, philosophical analysis was still associated in many minds with British empiricism and its latter-day manifestation as logical positivism. The first analytical philosophy encounters for some of our authors were with A.J. Ayer's *Language, Truth and Logic* and, in education, with Hardie's *Truth and Fallacy in Educational Theory* (1962/1942) and O'Connor's *Introduction to Philosophy of Education* (1957). By the mid-1950s, when the analytical revolution reached philosophy of education, the links to empiricism were beginning to fray. The publication of Quine's "Two Dogmas of Empiricism" in 1951 and Wittgenstein's *Philosophical Investigations* in 1953 marked the beginnings of the end of empiricist foundationalism in Anglo-American philosophy.

In addition, by the time of the analytical revolution the unbreachable divide between the realms of facts and values was already under assault. John Rawls' "Outline for a Decision Procedure for Ethics" (1951) provided a holistic method for normative ethics closely paralleling Quine's methodological holism for science.

Alan Gewirth's "Positive 'Ethics' and Normative 'Science' (1960) showed that standard empiricist arguments for the radical separation of the two realms depended upon the biased selecting of propositions from the two fields for comparison from different levels of generality; when appropriate examples were chosen for comparison the arguments collapsed. John Searle's controversial "How to Derive an 'Ought' from an 'Is' (1964) directly challenged the unbreachable gap hypothesis; whether or not Searle's 'derivation' was successful, the conviction that normative conclusions always rested on non-cognitive normative premises, and were therefore rationally suspect, was dealt a serious blow. The rise of "applied philosophy" after 1970, moreover, brought normative and evaluative studies into the mainstream of analytical philosophy. Steven Toulmin went so far as to claim that these applied, normative inquiries had 'saved' ethics, if not philosophy.

The shift Nordenbo notes in philosophy of education at the end of the 1970s can thus be seen not so much as a move *away* from analytical philosophy as a move *within* it, not so much a "dissatisfaction with analytical philosophy's inability to answer normative questions" as a more resolute and less self-conscious taking up of such questions *within* analytical philosophy.

Second, and on a contrary note, the issue of postmodern "difference" arose in all humanities disciplines during the 1970s, stimulated in large measure by Derrida's famous talk on "Structure, Sign and Play in the Discourse of the Human Sciences" at Johns Hopkins in 1966, and its publication in *L'Ecriture et la Différence* (translated as *Writing and Difference*) in 1967 (Derrida, 1978/1967). Derrida's "deconstructive" method aimed to open a text to many new and unexpected interpretations by focusing on the binary oppositions around which the text was organized. By showing that these binaries were historically and culturally specific, a deconstructive analysis aimed to demonstrate that the text's 'meaning' was itself unstable. A new generation of Anglo-American philosophers drew upon Derrida's formulations and those of other French philosophers including Lyotard and Foucault, taking them from their specific post-1968 anti-Stalinist or 'new left' French context and applying them, in ways that were never anticipated of completely welcomed by their authors, in studies situating mainstream institutions and forms of knowledge within a hegemonic white, European culture and power-structure. These moves also characterized much of the work within the new inter-disciplines of gender studies, ethnic studies, and cultural studies in their Anglo-American forms.

After 1980 philosophers of education took up many issues involving difference: e.g., the education of women, multicultural education, the curriculum canon, and dialogue across difference. Some established analytical philosophers such as Jane Roland Martin took up these cultural issues in terms consistent with their prior works. Other philosophers of education, for the most part, those younger than the authors in the current volume, took up Derrida's method of 'deconstruction' to show that concepts like "education," "culture," "knowledge" obscured and thus served to maintain unequal power relationships and social positions. Invidious binary distinctions (male/female; developed/undeveloped; white/black) were exposed as devaluing alternative ways of seeing, knowing and valuing, and as hiding the radical contingency of accepted knowledge and values. In this development we can detect not so much a "loss of faith" in analytical philosophy by established philosophers of education, as simply the the adoption of a different style of philosophizing by some among the new generation appearing after 1980. Nor would it be accurate to account for the "postmodern turn" by reference to dissatisfaction with analytical philosophy's inability to address normative questions. Rather, the dissatisfaction of postmodernists was with the cultural certainties undergirding the normative inquiries themselves. The effect of the postmodern turn, therefore, has not been to *facilitate* normative inquiries in philosophy of education but rather to *complexify* them by exposing the contingencies with which they must contend.

A third, but related, element of the post-1980 environment was a new emphasis, influenced by Alistair MacIntyre's *After Virtue* (1984/1981), on communities and their distinct social practices. The attention paid to norms and values *within* distinct social practices, no less than the postmodern turn, challenged liberal universalist assumptions prevailing in normative ethics. Close attention to social practices and 'knowing how', as prior to propositional 'knowing that', has characterized the work of several authors in this volume, among them David Carr; it also has led Paul Hirst to revise his theory of education and knowledge that had dominated philosophy of education for decades. MacIntyre's re-appropriation of Aristotle and Aquinas also brought to the table new issues pertaining to happiness, human flourishing and the good life (John White, Nel Noddings, Robin Barrow) and the moral virtues including reasonableness (Robertson, below, but also Nicholas Burbules among others) and Care (Noddings and Martin, below, but also Ann Diller and others).

A fourth development has been the re-valuation and re-appropriation of John Dewey's philosophy of education. Francis Schrag remembers that when he entered graduate school at Teachers College in 1966 "Dewey, once considered "the" American philosopher, was a non-person so far as philosophy departments were concerned." In schools of education, however, as Ken Strike notes, his texts were often regarded as divine revelations. Walter Feinberg adds that the situation in philosophy departments in the mid-1960s was:

> very different from much of the work that I saw in the College of Education, where certain views were taken as definitive, and others judged by how well they measured up to an assumed standard. Ironically much of Dewey's writings seemed to me to be used in this way, and I had trouble with a couple of the instructors in the College of Education when they took offence when I challenged aspects of Dewey's work. Sadly the philosopher of openness had become for some the prince of dogma and the "anti-dogmatism" that Dewey advanced took on a dogmatic quality.

One result of the early analytical revolution was to dampen the enthusiasm for Dewey in educational scholarship, even though both Scheffler and Peters found much to admire in his work. Little mention of Dewey is to be found in the "new" philosophy of education of the 1950s through the 1980s. But in the 1990s several established philosophers of education (e.g., Garrison, Robertson, Pring and Waks) returned to Dewey as a source of inspiration. Several reasons suggest themselves. First, Dewey scholarship was facilitated by the completion of the Collected Works at the Dewey Study Center at Carbondale Illinois. The publication of the searchable digital edition of the works on a single CD-ROM made it relatively easy to access Dewey's ideas on any philosophical topic, as expressed in his immense body of work covering more than seventy years. Second, Richard Rorty had laid claim to the Dewey mantle in his anti-foundationalist crusade. His rhetorical gambit in *Philosophy and the Mirror of Nature* (1979) of amalgamating Dewey with Wittgenstein and Heidegger, not only as the "three greatest philosophers of the 20th century," but also as co-leaders of the anti-foundationalist revolution, compelled both Anglo-American and continental philosophers to pay heed. Third, two full length studies of Dewey's entire corpus appeared in the early 1990s (Westbrook, 1991; Rockefeller 1994), offering scholars convenient means for placing any of Dewey's works in comprehensive narratives of his life and times. Finally Dewey's cosmopolitan emphasis on cooperation and the search for a common horizon, which many philosophers had written off as either utopian or totalitarian depending upon their own leanings, found a welcome audience after three decades of deconstruction and division, as we approached the millennium, and then confronted fundamentalist terror and the limits of difference after September 11, 2001.

ANOTHER REDIRECTION? ANOTHER CRISIS?

This brings us at last to the present situation, as reflected through the chapters of this volume. Paul Hirst, one of the three initiators of the analytical revolution of the 1950s, now offers this vision for the next phase of philosophy of education:

> Academic philosophy has in the 20th Century faced the challenge of two major movements, those of analytical philosophy and post-modernism. The positive significance of both has, I consider, now been absorbed into the historical development of Western philosophy and there seems to be a slowly increasing consensus on the broad conceptual framework within which we can now best make sense of human nature and what constitutes a good life. Its major implications for educational aims and practices ... (and) their working out in much greater detail, I think, (are) the most important tasks for contemporary philosophy of education. There is in many Western societies a feeling that the upbringing of children and much institutionalised education have lost their clear sense of purpose and hence also of how best to decide their means. It seems to me philosophers of education are increasingly in a position to help significantly in elucidating those aims and practices in a way

appropriate for the institutions of modern secular and pluralist liberal democracies that are at least in principle committed to the pursuits of reason in all their affairs.

This hope for a new liberal pluralist cosmopolitan post-postmodern consensus is echoed in many of the authors in this volume; it is useful to call attention to it as one important theme in this work. I have just mentioned the re-appropriation of Dewey as reflecting new cosmopolitan leanings in philosophy. Historian David Hollinger (2005) has recently pointed to a "new wave" of cosmopolitan manifestos, declarations, and analyses, and sees this new cosmopolitanism as moving beyond the sterile disputes between liberal universalism and communitarianism. Rebecca Walkowitz (2006) has posited a 'cosmopolitan style' that is transforming literature and all humanities disciplines. Philosopher Kwame Appiah (2006) has advanced cosmopolitanism as a replacement for multiculturalism as a central organizing principle of our time.

We can see cosmopolitan trends now appearing in philosophy of education, both in the works of younger philosophers and those of the established leaders contributing chapters of this volume. To take some examples from this volume: Sharon Bailin is exploring how different cultures and cultural traditions can contribute to one another. Sophie Haroutunian-Gordon and her collaborators (including Garrison and Waks) are exploring practical strategies for enabling communicators to listen to speakers whose perspectives challenge their own. Jane Roland Martin is studying the personal metamorphoses that take place as individuals move across cultural boundaries. Nel Noddings is attending to global awareness and citizenship. Walter Feinberg is investigating the relationship between larger national societies and their various sub-groups, and working towards a cosmopolitan reconciliation of liberalism and communitarianism in which rights to religious and cultural identity are extended globally. Patricia White is studying forgiveness in the context of reconciliation after inter-ethnic brutality. Michael Peters is speaking about "deep education" as unlearning the ways of our own tribe by making our prejudices the object of our self-conscious study. Christopher Winch is studying vocational education in an international context, revealing essential national differences in the institutionalization of work but also seeking frameworks that can bridge them in the emerging European institutional order. Jim Garrison, finally, is working out a conception of "the trickster," the familiar pan-cultural character who (like Walkowitz's exemplars of transnational 'cosmopolitan style') executes his (or her) tricks both within and between existing cultural orders, poking holes in existing certainties and opening up space for new cultural inputs and the formation of bi-cultural hybrids and compounds.

However promising this sort of cosmopolitan synthesis may be from an intellectual point of view, its success will depend not merely on its intellectual resources but also on its institutional supports: government and foundation grants, university posts, foundations discipline courses required in professional education curricula. The analytical revolution in philosophy of education, after all, didn't succeed in the mid 1950s and 1960s by virtue of its intellectual superiority alone;

as we have seen above, a large institutional space was opened for it by both political and academic leaders as teacher education moved from the normal schools and teachers colleges into the universities and a proper program of studies in accord with the academic standards of the times had to be created.

Since the 1980s, however, neo-liberal state regimes in North America and the UK have inserted themselves aggressively and directly into both the schools and teacher education programs (and university programs more generally). Under such watchwords as "excellence" and "academic achievement" they have sought to transform conventional teaching practices into those that result in measurable improvements on standardized tests, converting teaching into test preparation and in the process invalidating the predictive validity of the very tests upon which they rely. They have disparaged the intellectual contributions for education of scholars in humanities disciplines, and esoteric philosophical disputes and radical formulations of post-modernist scholars have no doubt provided convenient targets for their attacks. State bureaucrats now demand that such "'useless" studies be replaced with something more "practical" – although by this they do not mean something that will *enhance* educational practice, but rather something that will *transform* it in accord with state demands. So far, protests from philosophers of education and other academics have fallen on deaf ears, and philosophy of education is losing the institutional supports it acquired in the early days of the analytical revolution. As Paul Hirst describes the situation:

> Tight control over teacher education in universities began with severe curtailment of finance for both in-service courses and for educational research, both of which were henceforth to be used almost exclusively in the service of politically determined educational policies. HMI for the first time now started to exercise a real power of quality control over teacher education courses in universities and a 1994 Education Act established a Teacher Training Agency for their detailed control under compulsory regulations. These restrictions, insisting on the direct practical relevance of all educational courses, have led to the near demise of all courses concerned specifically with the disciplines of educational theory within British universities. Recent Labour Governments have done nothing whatever to liberalise this situation.

Parallel developments to those in the UK have, once again, taken place in North America, as liberal nation states have adjusted to the demands of the emerging global economy and the increased power of transnational capital, and universities have adjusted to what Sheila Slaughter (2004) refers to as the knowledge and learning regimes of "academic capitalism". It remains to be seen whether philosophy of education can regain a favourable institutional position when the political pendulum swings away from the neo-liberal right, as it eventually will. Beyond intellectual excellence, the institutional revitalization of the field will then require strong political and organizational alliances, demonstrable contributions to practical and cultural life, and a measure of good luck.

REFERENCES

Appiah, A.K. (2006). *Cosmopolitanism: Ethics in a world of strangers.* New York: Norton.

Benn, S., & Peters, R. (1961). *Social principles and the democratic state.* London: George Allen and Unwin.

Conant, J.B. (1963). *The education of American teachers.* Carnegie series in American education. New York: McGraw-Hill. D. (1963). *The miseducation of American teachers.* Boston: Houghton Mifflin.

Derrida, J. (1978/1967). *Writing and difference*, trans. Alan Bass. London: Routledge (original publication 1967).

Feinberg, W., & Soltis, J F. (1985). *School and society.* Thinking about education series. New York: Teachers College Press.

Fenstermacher, G.D, & Soltis, J.F. (1986). *Approaches to teaching.* Thinking about education series. New York: Teachers College, Columbia University.

Garrison, J.W., & Macmillan, C.J.B. (1988). *A logical theory of teaching: Erotetics and intentionality.* Dordrecht: Kluwer.

Gewirth, A. (1960). Positive "ethics" and normative "science". *The Philosophical Review, 69*(3), 311-330.

Hamlyn, D.W (1978) *Experience and the growth of understanding.* London: Routledge and Kegan Paul.

Hardie, C.D. (1962/1942). *Truth and fallacy in educational theory.* New York: Teachers College Press (original publication 1942).

Hollinger, D. (2003) Not universalists, not pluralists: The new cosmopolitans find their way. Ch. 15 in Vertovic and Cohen, *Conceiving cosmopolitanism*, 227-239.

MacIntyre, A. (1984/ 1981) *After virtue: A study in moral theory.* South Bend: University of Notre Dame Press, 2nd edn. (originally published 1981).

Nordenbo, S.E. (1979). Philosophy of education in the Western world: Developmental trends during the last 25 years. *International Review of Education, 25*(3) 433-459.

O'Connor, D. J. (1957*). Introduction to the philosophy of education.* NY: Philosophical Library.

Peters, R.S. (1958). *The concept of motivation.* Studies in philosophical psychology. London: Routledge & Kegan Paul.

Phillips, D.C., & Soltis, J.F. (1985). *Perspectives on learning.* Thinking about education series. New York: Teachers College Press.

Rawls, J. (1951). Outline of a decision procedure for ethics, *The Philosophical Review, 60*(2) 177-197.

Rockefeller, S. (1994). *John Dewey: Religious faith and democratic humanism.* NY: Columbia University Press.

Rorty, R. (1979). *Philosophy and the mirror of nature.* Princeton: Princeton University Press.

Scheffler, I. (1954). Toward an analytic philosophy of education. *Harvard Educational Review, 24*, 223-230.

Scheffler, I. (1960). *The language of education.* Springfield MA: Charles C. Thomas.

Searle, J.R. (1964) How to derive 'ought' from 'is', *Philosophical Review* 73, (1), 43-58.

Slaughter, S., & Rhoads, G. (2004). *Academic capitalism and the new economy: Markets, state, and higher education.* Baltimore: Johns Hopkins University Press.

Smith, B. O., & Ennis, R.H. (1961) . *Language and concepts in education.* Chicago: Rand McNally.

Stiles, L.J. (1964). Dr. Conant and his critics. *Teachers College Record, 65*(8), 712-718.

Walker, D.F., & Soltis, J.F. (1986). *Curriculum and aims.* Thinking about Education Series. New York: Teachers College, Columbia University.

Walkowitz, R. (2006). *Cosmopolitan style: Modernism beyond the nation.* New York: Columbia University Press.

Westbrook, R.B. (1991). *John Dewey and American democracy.* Ithaca, NY: Cornell UP.

SHARON BAILIN

INQUIRIES ABOUT INQUIRY

Writing this chapter has provided me with a rare opportunity to reflect on my past work, to think about where it came from, how it developed, and how, and indeed whether, it all fits together. There is, within my corpus, work on creativity, critical thinking, argumentation, arts education, and theatre; dealt with from the perspectives of epistemology, aesthetics, philosophy of science, argumentation theory, and philosophy of education. It may appear, at first glance, to represent an eclectic collection of topics and issues, held together only by the fact of its authorship. Yet there is, I believe, an underlying theme which unifies this seemingly diverse collection of inquiries: the theme is that of inquiry itself. I have been exploring what it means to have good, or well justified, ideas and practices, and how we come up with new and better ideas and practices. My focus has been an examination of the generation and evaluation of the ideas, artefacts, and practices which are the hallmarks of human intellectual and practical achievement – in the arts, in science, indeed in the entire spectrum of human inquiry and endeavour.

SCHOOL AND COLLEGE

As far back as I can recall, I have had a foot planted in each of the worlds of philosophy and the arts. From childhood on, I was plagued with questions about what the world was like, why it was like it was, and what it all meant, but lacking any models or mentors, I thought that I was a weird kid with thoughts which no one else shared. Religious answers to these questions seemed to me profoundly unsatisfactory. (I grew up in a home in which Jewish tradition, loosely practiced, provided the unquestioned and unquestionable background to daily life, but this seemed to have more to do with identity (who we were and, perhaps more important, who we were not) than with seeking meaning. My one (semi) serious foray into Judaism during my youth was occasioned by a wild infatuation for a young man who was extremely observant and it was, it must be admitted, driven by passions which were not fundamentally of a religious nature.)

My encounter with philosophy as an undergraduate at the University of Toronto marked a turning point. I discovered that others before me had struggled with these concerns and their answers and ways of thinking about the questions opened up a fascinating new world of ideas. Being introduced, through philosophy, to these fundamental conversations about human existence and the nature of the world, conversations engaged in through the exercise of reason, was foundational to my future intellectual development. My conception of rationality has been developed and refined in the intervening years; it has become more generous and nuanced

L.J. Waks (ed.), Leaders in Philosophy of Education: Intellectual Self Portraits, 15–25.

and, perhaps, less utopian. Nonetheless, my abiding emotional and intellectual commitment to the life of reason and my firm belief in its rich possibilities, have been distinguishing features of my life.

My interest and participation in the arts also has a long history. My elementary school obsession for organizing plays in the schoolyard based on Classic Comic books gave way, as I grew older, to more formal participation in theatre. During my days with a Toronto theatre group, my theatrical activities included acting, painting scenery, hanging lights, driving the truck, and even shopping for costumes (I vividly recall the look of surprise on the saleslady's face at my concern that the pajamas I was purchasing might clash with the wallpaper). My particular passion, however, was, and still is directing. The exhilaration of transforming words on a page into a living vibrant work which will reach out and touch people moves me still, and inquiry into artistic creation has been an ongoing theme of my work.

TEACHING AND GRADUATE SCHOOL

After my undergraduate degree, I blithely ignored the urgings of my professors to do graduate work in philosophy. Pulled by my perennial interest in education, and succumbing to the pressures of insecurity ("am I really up to grad school?") and practicality ("it's time to get a job"), I took the plunge into teacher education. My years spent as a teacher of French and Theatre Arts at the secondary level left me with a profound appreciation for the enormity of the challenges and responsibilities of the enterprise in which teachers engage daily, as well as pressing questions about how to think about that enterprise in ways which might best further its ends and enhance its practices.

The joys and activities of motherhood put my teaching on hold 'temporarily' (or so I thought at the time). But the direct encounter with the profound and consuming experience of educating a human being from the outset had the effect of further encouraging my fascination with the educational enterprise, and the prospect of philosophizing soon trumped my desire to teach French to resistant and unruly grade 9 students. So it was off to graduate school to study philosophy of education at The Ontario Institute for Studies in Education.

PERSONAL FAVORITES

Book

Achieving extraordinary ends: An essay on creativity (1988/1994)

Articles

Critical and creative thinking (1987)
Argumentation as inquiry (1992)
The problem with Percy: Epistemology, understanding, and critical thinking (1999)
Common misconceptions of critical thinking (1999b)
Is argument for conservatives? Or where do sparkling new ideas come from? (2005b)
An inquiry into inquiry: (How) can we learn from other times and places (2006)
Culture, contamination and creativity (2007a)

I was extremely fortunate to have as my mentor in this journey my supervisor and subsequent life-long friend, Ian Winchester. My topic for exploration was creativity, an apt focus for my combined interests in philosophy, in education, and in the arts, and Ian's breadth of academic interests and expertise encouraged my investigation of this topic through a study of aesthetics, philosophy of science, epistemology and philosophy of language. (Ian did not view philosophy of education as a separate field but rather as doing philosophical work on topics of educational significance. I had the rare distinction of completing a Ph.D. in philosophy of education without ever having read R.S. Peters!) Ian was a master at guiding, provoking, and challenging, at getting his students to be clear, to question assumptions, to follow arguments wherever they lead, to take a fresh angle. His keen wit, intellectual curiosity and vitality, breadth of outlook, and generosity of spirit served as a model for me of what a philosopher could be. I attribute much of my own approach to philosophical work to Ian's tutelage and example.

ACHIEVING EXTRAORDINARY ENDS

My dissertation involved a critical examination of prevalent ideas about creativity as manifested in education, psychology, the arts, and society in general, and this work formed the basis of my subsequent book, *Achieving Extraordinary Ends: An Essay on Creativity* (Bailin, 1988/1994). In the book, I critiqued what I claimed were certain common assumptions manifested across a range of views and theories of creativity. These assumptions are: 1) that creativity is intimately connected with originality understood in terms of the generation of novelty and involving a radical break with existing traditions; 2) that the value of creative products cannot be objectively determined; 3) that creativity is a characteristic of persons irrespective of specific achievements, 4) that creativity involves a distinctive process or mode of thinking which differs qualitatively from ordinary, non-creative thinking; 4) that the rules, skills, and knowledge of specific disciplines are potentially constraining to creativity because they lock one into the prevailing conceptual framework; and 5) that creativity involves something more than skill, an imaginative element which is transcendent, irreducible, and essentially inexplicable.

The book involved a systematic critique of all of these assumptions. It began by challenging the idea that creative works display a radical discontinuity with previous products and arguing that continuities and connections with the tradition are always and necessarily in evidence. Indeed, the significance of creative works can only judged against the background of existing traditions, both in terms of how the work conforms to and how it departs from these traditions. I further argued that there are objective criteria for the evaluation of creative products and that these are provided, to a considerable extent, by the traditions out of which the works develop, including their overall aims, overarching problems and guiding methodologies. The book went on to criticize the notion that creativity is a characteristic of persons irrespective of the production of products and argued,

17

rather, that our primary ascription of creativity is in virtue of achievement. There is, however, no unequivocal empirical evidence which clearly links any particular set of cognitive or personality traits with actual creative achievement. The claim that creativity is primarily an attribute of persons rests on the belief that there is a specific process or way of thinking involved in all acts of creating, a kind of thinking which is generative, divergent, non-logical, rule-breaking and non-evaluative, but this too is a belief which I showed to be problematic. There are, rather, a variety of processes involved in creating and these include thinking which is convergent as well as divergent, logical as well as unusual, evaluative as well as generative, and rule-bound as well as rule-breaking. In fact, these kinds of thinking are not easily separated. The characterization of creativity as essentially rule-breaking was also criticized and the case was made for the central importance of knowledge, rules, skills and methods of specific disciplines for creativity. Finally, I argued that imagination and skill are intimately connected and that an understanding of this connection can go a long way toward explaining aspects of creativity which may appear at first to defy explanation.

The ideas first developed in *Achieving Extraordinary Ends* have served as foundations for a great deal of my subsequent thinking. Developing and expanding in various ways and contexts the themes laid out in the book (e.g., originality, skill, intuition, creativity in art and sciences) has formed a constant thread in my work, and although I would now be inclined to modify and modulate its arguments in various ways, I still would stand by its basic tenets.

INQUIRY AND CRITICAL THINKING

My experience amongst a pack of Popperians as a Postdoctoral Fellow in the philosophy department at York University constituted the next phase of my philosophical education, deepening my interest in philosophy of science, forging my philosophical mettle in the smithy of rigorous academic debate, and making me highly sensitive to all the possible refutations of any of my conjectures.

It was during my time teaching philosophy of education at the University of Manitoba that the next significant phase of my academic development was initiated. A chance meeting with J. Anthony Blair at a conference on thinking had the result of pointing me towards a whole new area. Tony was one of the founders of the Informal Logic movement, a field focusing on issues of reasoning, critical thinking, and argumentation. In my conference presentation, I had addressed the role of reasoning and critical thinking in creativity, and Tony prompted me to consider the reverse, i.e., the role of creativity in critical thinking. Tony's comment turned my thinking in a new direction, and through his suggestions, I was put in contact with an entire body of theoretical work on critical thinking of which I had been unaware. I also came into contact with some of the principle theorists in the area, including Harvey Siegel and Robert Ennis, and interacting with their work and ideas played an important role in helping me to develop my own positions regarding the relationship between critical thinking and creativity, and the nature of critical thinking more broadly.

One of the key papers I wrote in this regard was "Critical and Creative Thinking" (Bailin, 1987). In this paper, I criticized the sharp separation usually assumed between critical and creative thinking. According to this view, critical thinking is the means for making judgments within specific frameworks and is thus essentially analytic, evaluative, selective and highly rule-bound; it cannot, however, provide the means to transcend the framework itself. Creative thinking, on the other hand, is thought to be precisely the type of thinking which transcends frameworks and is thus, essentially generative, spontaneous, and non-evaluative, involving divergent thinking, rule-breaking, suspension of judgment, and leaps of imagination. One aspect of my critique involved reiterating my arguments that thinking critically plays a crucial role in creative production and that the characterization of creative thinking as essentially rule-breaking, non-evaluative and divergent is incorrect. The other aspect involved demonstrating that critical thinking is not merely analytic, selective, and confined to frameworks, but has imaginative, constructive aspects. Critical and creative thinking are not, then, separate and distinct modes of thinking which operate within different contexts and to different ends, but are intimately connected and both integrally involved in thinking well in any area.

The arguments regarding the critical aspects of creative production were drawn from my previous work, but the arguments regarding the nature of critical thinking constituted a new area of exploration and marked the beginning of an examination of the implications of my views about creativity for conceptualizing critical thinking. I began to focus on what I considered to be problems in the common way of conceptualizing critical thinking in terms of abilities and dispositions, and in "The Problem with Percy: Epistemology, Understanding, and Critical Thinking" (Bailin, 1999), I argued for an alternative conceptualization in terms of epistemological understanding. The latter entails an understanding of the enterprise of knowledge creation and evaluation, including the entire web of interconnected concepts, principles, procedures and purposes which constitute critical thinking, as well as the assumptions about the nature and value of reasons which ground the practice (e.g., a non-relativist epistemology, fallibilism).

My interactions with the Informal Logic community also prompted me to apply my ideas to a subfield of critical thinking, argumentation theory. I was troubled by the common perception of Informal Logic as an algorithmic, quasi-mathematical enterprise, and in "Argument Criticism as Creative" (Bailin, 1990a), I attempted to counter this perception by arguing that argument criticism has a creative dimension. Aspects of argument criticism such as the interpretation of arguments and the generation of counter-examples and counter-arguments require judgment and imagination, as do finding assumptions, envisioning potential problems in an argument, imagining alternative possibilities, and arriving at an overall assessment. The pedagogical implications included portraying the process of argumentation in the context of the larger dialectical process of inquiry of which it is part.

The theme of inquiry continued to be a focus of my thinking about argumentation. I had doubts about the primacy of the dispute-resolving model as the paradigm of argumentation, and in "Argumentation as Inquiry" (Bailin, 1992),

I argued that, from the point of view of epistemology, the process of argumentation is better conceived as a process of inquiry. It is the process whereby knowledge claims are formulated, tested, adjusted, countered, and synthesized in order to arrive at the best justified position. I further argued that stressing inquiry is important pedagogically in promoting co-operative exchange and open-minded appraisal, and in conveying to students that argumentation is a means of inquiring into what to believe and do both in the academic disciplines and in real-life situations.

I was drawn back to the theme of creativity in the context of responding to Rorty's claim that argument is inherently conservative and that philosophical progress comes from forgetting past traditions and generating 'sparkling new ideas,' not from argument. In "Is Argument for Conservatives? Or Where do Sparkling New Ideas Come From?" (Bailin, 2005b), I argued on the contrary that new ideas arise from critical reflection on problems posed by these traditions. Seeing this involves understanding traditions as modes of inquiry containing controversy and debate, with mechanisms for criticism and thus for evolution built right in. Inquiry does not, then, consist in two separate activities, one logical but unimaginative and one creative but unconstrained by critical judgment, as Rorty suggests, but rather a single activity constituted by the dynamic interplay between generation and criticism. Thus the paper argued for the importance of participating in the critical dialogues embodied by past traditions in order to further the conversation.

SIMON FRASER UNIVERSITY

Arts and Drama Education

Another turning point in my academic trajectory occurred through my taking up a position in drama education in the Faculty of Education at Simon Fraser University. As the place was brimming over with philosophers thinly disguised as curriculum specialists, I felt right at home and proceeded to further develop my ideas in the context of the arts, for example in papers on critical thinking and on creativity in drama education. (In teaching theatre to education students and in having the opportunity to direct, I was also able to get a whiff of the greasepaint once again!). Several of my pieces also engaged with some of the debates in the field of drama education, in particular the debate regarding the respective value of theatre versus the improvisational activities of creative drama. My paper, "Theatre, Drama Education and the Role of the Aesthetic" (Bailin, 1993b), argued for the educational value of drama in promoting aesthetic activity and fostering aesthetic appreciation. In "Other People's Products: The Value of Performing and Appreciating" (Bailin, 1993a), I took up the debate by arguing that viewing and performing plays can also contribute to the kind of understanding of the personal and social world that has been attributed by many drama education theorists exclusively to improvisational activities. "In the Spaces Between the Words: Play Production as an Interpretive Enterprise" (Bailin, 2001), took this argument further, arguing against the view of play production as an unreflective technical activity and elucidating the rich possibilities for educational development afforded through the creative activity of interpretation.

Critical Thinking Again

My move to Vancouver also occasioned the opportunity for a new project on critical thinking and a productive and long-term collaboration with colleagues. The Ministry of Education for British Columbia was scheduled for a province-wide assessment focusing on critical thinking, and the sudden realization that they didn't know what critical thinking was prompted the commissioning of a report on the concept. A team composed of me, Roland Case from Simon Fraser, Jerrold Coombs and LeRoi Daniels from the University of British Columbia, took on the task. We were long-standing colleagues who shared similar views about critical thinking and similar concerns about the way the term tended to be thought about and used in education, and eventually, after considerable debate, discussions with educators, and 'field testing', we produced a report entitled "A Conception of Critical Thinking for Curriculum, Instruction, and Assessment" (Bailin et al., 1993).

Roland, Jerry, LeRoi and I also produced two theoretical papers based on the ideas we developed for the report. In the first paper, "Common Misconceptions of Critical Thinking" (Bailin et al., 1999a), we critiqued several widely-held conceptions of critical thinking. We began by criticizing the idea that critical thinking involves generic skills which can be applied across contexts, arguing instead that skilled performance at thinking tasks cannot be separated from knowledge, including the background knowledge and knowledge of the concepts and principles in the particular area. Nor does the skills conception sufficiently acknowledge the central role played by attitudes in thinking critically. Conceiving of critical thinking in terms of mental processes is similarly problematic. One difficulty is that mental processes, in the sense of what goes on in the brain, are not observable, and we cannot know whether particular mental operations correlate with particular kinds of thinking. It seems, in fact, to be the case that terms such as observing, analyzing or interpreting do not refer to mental operations at all but rather to different tasks requiring thinking. The conceptualization of critical thinking in terms of a set of procedures is equally problematic. Simply carrying out a set of procedures is not sufficient to ensure critical thinking since any procedure can be carried out in an uncritical manner. Moreover, there is no one set of procedures which is necessary for critical thinking in all contexts. It is, we argued, the quality of thinking and not the process of thinking which distinguishes critical from uncritical thinking.

In the second paper, "Conceptualizing Critical Thinking" (Bailin et al., 1999b), we set out our own conception of critical thinking as a normative enterprise involving the adherence to appropriate criteria and standards. The pedagogical focus then shifts from issues relating to application of processes and the acquisition of skills to the question of what one needs to understand in order to meet the criteria of good thinking in particular contexts. In our view, learning to become a critical thinker involves the acquisition of a repertoire of intellectual resources, including background knowledge, operational knowledge of the standards of good thinking, knowledge of key critical concepts, possession of effective heuristics (strategies, procedures, etc.), and certain habits of mind. On the basis of this analysis, we elucidated three components to teaching critical thinking: 1) engaging students in tasks that call for reasoned judgment; 2) helping them develop intellectual resources for dealing with these tasks; and 3) providing an environment in which critical thinking is valued and encouraged.

The theoretical perspectives developed in these two papers formed the foundation for what has turned out to be a large scale and ongoing project of curriculum development and teacher education for critical thinking under the auspices of The Critical Thinking Consortium (TC^2). Under the direction of LeRoi Daniels and Roland Case, TC^2 has produced curriculum materials and provided workshops to teachers not only in British Columbia, but also in the rest of Canada, the United States, and around the world. It has been truly gratifying to see one's theoretical work issue in some concrete consequences in educational practice – not a common occurrence in philosophy of education.

This conception of critical thinking also formed the foundation for a good deal of my own work. I saw this conception as a way to address many of the controversies in the field of critical thinking, including debates regarding the generalizability of critical thinking, or whether critical thinking instantiates gender or cultural bias. These are issues which I took up in "Education, Knowledge, and Critical Thinking" (Bailin, 1998), as well as in other papers. In "Critical Thinking and Science Education" (Bailin, 2002), I offered a critique of approaches to fostering critical thinking in science framed in terms of the acquisition of skills and elucidated how our conception constituted a more philosophically sound and justifiable conceptualization with which to ground science education practice.

Cross Cultural Encounters

Recently my work has taken yet another turn, prompted by my encounter with different cultures during my travels. I was struck, during my trips to Bali, by the extent to which the arts suffuse all of life and are embedded in the traditions of the society. And in Italy, viewing the plethora of artworks that adorn every church, abbey, and piazza made me very aware of how misleading is our usual perception of the art of the Renaissance as the product of a few inspired artistic geniuses. Thinking about these issues in the context of my previous work on creativity led me to an exploration of views about artistic creation in other cultural contexts, an exploration which I undertook in "Invenzione e Fantasia: The (Re) Birth of Imagination in Renaissance Art" (Bailin, 2005c), "Imagination and Arts Education in Cultural Contexts" (Bailin, 2007b), and "Artistic Creativity: A Cross-Cultural Perspective" (Bailin, 2005a).

What I found was that artistic creation, in these contexts, is not understood in terms of the tenets of the contemporary Western individualistic, novelty-focused view of creativity. During the early Renaissance, for example, artistic activity was not seen as individual self-expression but rather as the making of functional artefacts; artists were viewed as craftsmen who acquired their skill through imitation and often created collectively, anonymously, and according to the specification of patrons; and the aim was not originality but increasingly the imitation of nature. Moreover, the striking innovations that took place in art during this period were based largely on the rediscovery and imitation of ancient Greek and Roman arts and were due, at least in part, to a variety of contextual influences. These included an economic boom which generated the wealth to support the arts; humanist philosophy which focused on antiquity, gave more primacy of place to the human world, and opened the way for scientific advances; and a rigorous system of artistic training based on the mastery of artistic technique through copying and imitation.

Neither are the arts seen as a matter of individual self-expression or deviation from tradition in Balinese culture. Rather, they constitute a communal activity tied to daily life, religious celebration and ritual practices. The types of objects and practices which are deemed art in Western society and set apart from everyday life are integrated into Balinese life. Nor are artists seen as imaginative geniuses set apart from society. Rather, everyone engages in some form of art-making. The passing on of the tradition is central, and the arts are learned through apprenticeship, imitation and correction.

During the course of this research, I became increasingly interested in meta-questions regarding the nature and justification of the type of cross-cultural inquiry which I had undertaken, in particular: what (if anything) can one learn from this type of inquiry that will aid one in improving one's own culture's ideas and practices? Such cross-cultural inquiry appears to have validity as a descriptive enterprise detailing ideas and practices of the groups in question. But can it help me to learn something about art and creativity which I could not find out through my traditional forms of inquiry? These questions regarding the status of my own previous investigations raise issues for me regarding cross-cultural learning more generally, i.e., what and how can we learn from the ideas and practices of other cultures? And, more generally, how do cultures learn from each other to improve their own ideas and practices and to come up with creative achievements? It was this constellation of issues which I addressed in my Presidential Address to the Philosophy of Education Society, "An Inquiry into Inquiry: (How) Can We Learn from Other Times and Places?" (Bailin, 2006). In the context of these questions, the paper ended up making an argument for the importance of openness to ideas and practices emanating from other cultures.

A possible challenge to this ideal of openness is posed, however, by those who argue for the importance of cultural preservation and fear that influences from other cultures will destroy the authenticity of particular cultures and weaken their cultural integrity. In "Culture, Contamination and Creativity" (Bailin, 2007a), my keynote address to the Philosophy of Education Society of Great Britain, I addressed some of these challenges in the context of developing an ideal of cultural 'contamination' (hybridity, mélange) as an alternative to the ideal of cultural preservation. I argued in favour of contamination on the basis of the opportunities it provides for learning, for improving our ideas and practices, for fostering creative advance, and I elucidated the role of contamination in creative achievement through an examination of a number of historical cases.

At my presentation of this paper at PESGB, I used slides of artworks to illustrate the cases: comparing Renaissance artworks with their classical antecedents, illustrating the influence of Japanese works on 19th and 20th century European art, and showing the mestizo art form which resulted from the interaction of Spanish and indigenous forms in post-conquest Mexico. I realized that this was a fairly unusual move at a Philosophy of Education meeting. But I am excited by the possibilities afforded by the history of ideas and particularly, art history and criticism, in exploring issues of culture and creativity. And my own philosophical work is becoming more interdisciplinary and hybrid as a consequence. Some of my philosophical colleagues may be inclined to view this new orientation as the manifestation of a philosophical mid-life crisis. I am inclined to view it as a fecund new direction for inquiry.

REFERENCES

Bailin, S. (1988/1994). *Achieving extraordinary ends: An essay on creativity.* Dordrecht, Netherlands: Kluwer Academic Publishers (hardcover edition); Norwood, New Jersey: Ablex Publishing Company (paperback edition).

Bailin, S. (1987). Critical and creative thinking. *Informal Logic, 9*(1), 23-30.

Bailin, S. (1990a). Argument criticism as creative. In R. Trapp & J. Schuetz (Eds.), *Perspectives on argumentation: Essays in honor of Wayne Brockriede* (pp. 232-240). Prospect Heights, IL: Waveland Press.

Bailin, S. (1990b). Creativity, discovery and science education: Kuhn and Feyerabend revisited. *Interchange, 21*(3), 34-44.

Bailin, S. (1991). Rationality and intuition. *Paideusis, 4*(2), 17-26.

Bailin, S. (1992). Argumentation as inquiry. In F.H. van Eemeren, R. Grootendorst, J.A. Blair, & C. Willard (Eds.), *Proceedings of the second international conference on argumentation* (pp. 64-69). Amsterdam: International Society for the Study of Argumentation.

Bailin, S. (1993a). Other people's products: The value of performing and appreciating. *Journal of Aesthetic Education, 27*(2), 59-69.

Bailin, S. (1993b). Theatre, drama education and the role of the aesthetic. *Journal of Curriculum Studies, 25*(5), 423-432.

Bailin, S., Case, R., Coombs, J.R., & Daniels, L.B. (1993). A conception of critical thinking for curriculum, instruction, and assessment. Report for British Columbia Ministry of Education and Ministry Responsible for Multiculturalism and Human Rights.

Bailin, S. (1998). Education, knowledge, and critical thinking. In D. Carr (Ed.), *Education, knowledge and truth* (pp. 204-220). London: Routledge.

Bailin, S. (1999). The problem with Percy: Epistemology, understanding, and critical thinking. *Informal Logic, 19*(2&3), 161-170.

Bailin, S., Case, R., Coombs, J.R., & Daniels, L.B. (1999a). Common misconceptions of critical thinking. *Journal of Curriculum Studies, 31*(3), 269-283.

Bailin, S., Case, R., Coombs, J.R. & Daniels, L.B. (1999b). Conceptualizing critical thinking. *Journal of Curriculum Studies, 31*(3), 285-302.

Bailin, S. (2001). In the spaces between the words: Play production as an interpretive enterprise. *Journal of Aesthetic Education, 35*(2), 67-75.

Bailin, S. (2002). Critical thinking and science education. *Science and Education, 11*(4), 361-375.

Bailin, S. (2005a). Artistic creativity: A cross-cultural perspective. *Childhood and Society, 1*(2), 9-26.

Bailin, S. (2005b). Is argument for conservatives? or where do sparkling new lideas come from? *Informal Logic, 1*(23), 1-15.

Bailin, S. (2005c). Invenzione e fantasia: The (re)birth of imagination in Renaissance art. *Interchange, 36*(3), 257-273.

Bailin, S. (2006). An inquiry into inquiry: (How) can we learn from other times and places? In D. Vokey (Ed.), *Philosophy of education 2006*. Urbana, IL: Philosophy of Education Society.

Bailin, S. (2007a). Culture, contamination and creativity. *Proceedings of the Philosophy of Education Society of Great Britain, 2007*.

Bailin, S. (2007b). Imagination and arts education in cultural contexts. In K. Egan, M. Stout, & K. Takaya (Eds.), *Teaching and learning outside the box* (pp. 101-116). New York: Teachers College Press.

Sharon Bailin
Simon Fraser University

ROBIN BARROW

"OR WHAT'S A HEAVEN FOR?"

I should say at the outset that I count myself fortunate to have received the education I did at the Dragon School, Westminster School and Christ Church, Oxford. It may not have made much of me in absolute terms, but it made, I am sure, as much of me as could be made. Thus, I am one of those relatively rare individuals who became an educationalist out of gratitude for rather than disappointment with their own upbringing. My schooling developed in me an enormous fascination for the sheer wonder of the world, and a huge enthusiasm for trying to understand and get inside the world of human achievement. Moving in the opposite direction to Socrates, I was initially preoccupied with the human side of things. My earliest publications, for example, were in the fields of Nineteenth Century English Literature (e.g., 1965) and Classics (1973, 1975d, 1996), and I have continued to write on aspects of the latter throughout my career (e.g., 1975c, 2006d, 2007a) both because I enjoy the study of Greece and Rome and because I am concerned to support the Humanities in our educational system. But, while my love of the Humanities remains as strong as ever, these days I find myself equally captivated by the wonders of science and the natural world.

Having read Classics and Philosophy at Oxford, I planned to teach the former in schools. I did not contemplate a university career – one advantage of having a first rate education is that one recognizes the best when one sees it, and I knew that I was not one of the best. ("Ah, but a man's reach should exceed his grasp...", and hence my title). Thus, I came to a university career by chance. While taking my P.G.C.E at the University of London, I attended the lectures of Richard Peters and Paul Hirst. Peters suggested that I should do a Ph.D. (a relative rarity in British universities at the time), working with Patricia White. Out of that work, more or less directly, came Plato, Utilitarianism and Education (1975a, see also Barrow, 1974b, 1976b & 1977), a book that I had wanted to entitle "The Liberal Democratic Dilemma" since its main thrust was against the liberal assumption that moral sense could be made out of a system involving a number of distinct principles of equal weight. The book was in many ways idiosyncratic, and, while I stand by the broad outline of my defence of Plato (to the effect that he was sincerely concerned about the happiness of all), I have since come to place myself firmly in the liberal democratic camp that I then somewhat quixotically challenged.

THE FIRST TURNING POINT: LEICESTER.

Richard Peters was also the person who suggested that I should apply for a post at the University of Leicester, and thus instigated the first of three main turning points in my career. Once there, my colleague Ron Woods and I wrote An Introduction to

L.J. Waks (ed.), Leaders in Philosophy of Education: Intellectual Self Portraits, 27–38.

the Philosophy of Education (1974) which, I am proud to say, with substantial revision along the way, and now in its fourth edition, has been continuously in print for more than thirty years.

PERSONAL FAVOURITES

Papers:
"Who are the Philosopher Kings?" (1974)
"How married are you, Mary Ann? Educating for the Real World" (1984)
"Misdescribing a Cow: the Question of Conceptual Correctness" (1985)
"The Generic Fallacy" (1991)
"Being a bit Pregnant: How philosophical Misconceptions lead to Still Born Empirical Research" (1999)
"The Higher Nonsense: Some Persistent Errors in Educational Thinking" (1999)
"Language and Character" (2004)
"On the Duty of Not Taking Offence" (2005)

Books:
Common Sense and the Curriculum (1976)
Radical Education (1978)
Giving Teaching back to Teachers (1984)
A Critical Dictionary of Educational Concepts (With Geoffrey Milburn) (1990)
Utilitarianism: a Contemporary Statement (1991)
An Introduction to Moral Philosophy and Moral Education (2007)
Plato (2007)

At that time, I met Patrick Gallagher of the publishers George Allen and Unwin in connection with editing a series of books on Classical themes for schools. In retrospect, the two books I then wrote for him reveal my struggle (now abandoned) to make my commitment to utilitarianism relevant to and compatible with my educational views. Moral Philosophy for Education (1975b) argued against the idea of philosophy of education as a distinct branch of philosophy, in favor of thinking in terms of philosophy applied to education (another view that I no longer hold). Focusing on a variety of key moral issues which also have relevance to education (e.g., equality, freedom, autonomy, respect for persons), it provides an instance of the more or less constant battle that needs to be fought against relativism under one name or another. (It is tiresome, to say the least, to meet relativists, subjectivists, sociologists of knowledge, postmoderns, etc., all of whom seem unaware that what they herald as a contemporary insight is essentially a position that was recognized and argued against by Plato). I made an attempt to reconcile my position with Kantian ethics, by pointing out that utilitarianism is concerned primarily with determining what ways of behaving are morally desirable, whereas Kant is primarily concerned with what kind of action should earn moral credit for the agent, and that his notion of a universalisable maxim is only a necessary, not a sufficient, condition of moral conduct. I argued that our acknowledged commitment to freedom and equality only makes sense on the presupposition of something like people's happiness or satisfaction. The book contains a chapter on the dangers of conducting moral debate in terms of rights, which seems to have been prescient and which anticipates a lengthier exploration of the theme in the recent An Introduction to Moral Philosophy and Moral Education. (2007c).

Common Sense and the Curriculum (1976a) is concerned with what should be taught in schools and why, which are seen as the central curriculum questions. Moral Philosophy for Education (1975b) had argued that "the task of education is... broadly speaking, to develop people in such a way that they will be enabled to take pleasure in life, while contributing to the maximization of pleasure in the community as a whole. What is educationally worthwhile is whatever will contribute to that end". In response to the criticism that anything could be educationally worthwhile on these terms, I tried to explain why that is not so, and to develop an argument for a particular curriculum. Having argued against those who would determine curriculum content by reference to contingent social values, some notion of intrinsic value, forms of knowledge or student choice, I argued for a view of the educationally worthwhile based on a recognition of the various different ways in which subjects may contribute, albeit often indirectly, to both individual and general happiness. The conclusion of the argument is that there should be a common compulsory core curriculum ("compulsion" being carefully distinguished from "coercion"), with various options in the later stages. Much of this curriculum (namely, science, maths, fine arts, history, literature and philosophy),. I would still argue is fundamental. I would not be as accommodating to religion, which I now believe should be considered through the study of history, art and philosophy and I am somewhat surprised to note my acceptance of vocational studies as a legitimate part of the school curriculum. Today I would argue that the school should be divorced from direct preparation for the world of work and that one of the problems we face is an encroachment of employment considerations into the world of education.

It is worth making the point that publishing in those days was a very different business: many firms were still family owned and staffed by individuals who cared about books, rather than simply treating them as marketable commodities, and often had a real interest in and knowledge of the fields in which they published. Furthermore, the amount that was published was of a manageable quantity: the pressure on academics to publish was minimal, at any rate in England, and, in my view, in consequence, the quality was generally higher and the significance greater. In philosophy of education in particular it tended to lead to work that was predicated on a real interest in the enterprise of education as a whole, as distinct from esoteric specialism, academic posturing or an eye on career success. I should also make the point that my relative productivity over the years has arisen mainly out of a persistent desire to sort out my thoughts about education and to express them clearly, so as to shape and share a comprehensive view of what education is all about. I have far more interest in getting things clear than in being original, which I think is often a very dangerous lure in academia. To a degree, therefore, I would accept the suggestion that in various books and papers I rework familiar territory, though I would distinguish this from simply repeating myself (others I'm sure wouldn't), and I do not see it as a hostile criticism.

From an early date I began to be concerned about misunderstandings of the nature of philosophical analysis, such as confusing it with semantics or with exclusively linguistic analysis, and with steering between the view, on the one hand, that philosophers have privileged access to an unquestionable truth and, on the other, that any opinion is as "valid" as another. (e.g., 1974a, 1981a, 1982c, 1983, 1985, 1987a, 1990a, 1992, 1995a, 1999b & c).

The essence and purpose of philosophical analysis lies in clarity and fine discrimination: noting distinctions that are there to be made. Words, of course, are not concepts, but we have little choice but to pursue the ideas through the medium of words. That any account that one may give of the concept of, say, education cannot meaningfully be said to be the true concept of education, and that any definition of the word "education" can legitimately be challenged (even though here there are certain facts about use and meaning that cannot reasonably be denied), may be readily conceded. But no such admission should get in the way of recognizing that, label them as you like, call them what you will, there are various distinct possible types of upbringing variously characterized as "education", "training", "socialization","conditioning","schooling","indoctrination", etc., and it is crucial both to note such distinctions and to grasp their various meanings fully. To that end, we need to give an account of a given concept that meets what I term the 4 Cs: Clarity, (internal) Coherence, Consistency (with one's other beliefs and values) and Completeness, this last drawing attention to the need to go on to analyse any further complex or unclear term used to explicate the original: thus no account of education is likely to be complete until one has gone on to explicate the knowledge or understanding that is an integral aspect of education.

I have also continued to argue for the great practical importance of philosophy. Connected with this, though it was something I only came to realize later, (perhaps something that only came to be later), was the perception that increasingly philosophy of education focused less and less on education. Rather, philosophers of education seem increasingly to dabble with philosophical styles and issues only tangentially related to education, and to be more interested in establishing their credentials as philosophers than as thinkers concerned about education. Thus we find many instances of preoccupation with the nature of philosophical inquiry in education that doesn't explicate any particular educational issues, of ideological explorations of educational issues, of preoccupation with a specific theoretical perspective such as phenomenology, and of focus on a single issue such as giftedness or inequality. But I would argue that you cannot make any coherent remarks about such things as giftedness or inclusion without a well worked theory of education, and that prior commitment to a school of thought or explanatory theory is alien to the essential task of trying to arrive at a reasoned defence of a particular understanding of the educational enterprise. (These concerns, of course, are connected with my current view that we should think in terms of philosophy of education rather than simply philosophy applied to education). It may be said that analytic philosophy has by its very nature tended to encourage a focus on single issues, such that some individuals confine themselves to writing about caring, creativity or critical thinking, for example. That is possibly true, but it is surely something that we should guard against: one can only go so far in analyzing a concept of caring or creativity in a vacuum, as distinct from in the context of a broad and deep understanding of the educational enterprise as a whole.

My interest in utilitarianism, with me since my undergraduate days, is something that in one respect I regret, because I think that both my interest in it and the theory itself are often misunderstood. Following Moral Philosophy for Education (1975b) and Common Sense and the Curriculum (1976a), I have increasingly tried to keep my interest in utilitarianism as an ethical theory and my educational philosophy separate. Whereas I then argued that the common curriculum would be for the common good in terms of overall happiness (and still believe that to be so), I now emphasize more the argument that to develop the mind is to develop our specifically human nature and to increase our autonomy and control over our world. In Aristotelian mode, as one might say, I argue that a certain kind of understanding constitutes our peculiar excellence, but, as reference to autonomy and control implies, I am still committed to seeing value in activity that contributes to the greater good (perhaps now in idealistic rather than purely hedonistic terms). I do not, however, associate myself with a currently popular view to the effect that education is about producing "happy individuals and useful citizens". (Such a glib phrase invites too many complex conceptual questions). Furthermore, not all values are moral values. We obviously would not countenance a view of education that systematically undermined our moral views, and as a utilitarian I would want education to increase the sum of happiness, or at least not diminish it, but the question of what is educationally worthwhile cannot be reduced to the question of what is morally good. Knowledge, for example, is an educational good, regardless of one's moral views.

So, for the most part my interest in utilitarianism as an ethical theory has nothing to do with my educational views. Plato, Utilitarianism and Education (1975a) is about Plato's educational theory rather than mine, while Injustice, Inequality and Ethics, (1982a) which attempts, unsuccessfully I now think, to look at various contemporary moral issues through a utilitarian lens, and Utilitarianism: A Contemporary Statement (1991b) are both books about moral philosophy rather than education (although the former does have a chapter on education). The recent Introduction to Moral Philosophy and Moral Education (2007c) which attempts to argue for a particular view of morality derived from a proper understanding of the nature of moral theory, is not overtly utilitarian. Happiness (1979), though entitled Happiness and Schooling in the United States, is minimally concerned with education.

THE SECOND TURNING POINT: ONTARIO

The second event to affect my career in a major way was an invitation to go to the University of Western Ontario for a year as Distinguished Visiting Professor. I'm ashamed to say that at the time I did not even know where Ontario was on the map, but it turned out to be one of the more significant moves of my life (and like all of them a matter of happenstance rather than planning). I met, amongst others, John

31

McPeck whom I persuaded to write his justly respected Critical Thinking for a series I was editing, and he introduced me to what was then the quite different academic climate of North America. (The difference has diminished vastly as British Universities more and more ape U.S ways). In particular I saw a contrast between the emphasis on sociology in Britain and psychology in North America, between the emphasis on content in the former, process in the latter, and the undercurrent of behaviourism in North America with its attendant baggage of the language of objectives, skills and empirical research. British educational theory was at that time led if not dominated by philosophical and historical research; North America was clearly in scientific mode.

I had just completed Radical Education (1978), a critique of muddled progressive thought and good-hearted sentimentality. Though in retrospect I see that I did not do justice to Rousseau in particular, I still stand by the overall line of argument. Using the term "radical" in its pristine sense of "one who wants root and branch change", the book was concerned with those who turn to nature, to student choice, to technological innovation, and even to abandoning the idea of schooling altogether as alternatives to a common core curriculum. I should say that though the tone of my writing may not have shown it at the time, I am actually much in sympathy with both some of the concerns and many of the ideals of those whose work I was criticizing: like them I dislike and fear such things as indoctrination and destroying enthusiasm in the young, and like them I want people to grow up to think for themselves in a positive and constructive way. But I believe that the answer lies in trying to improve education in something like a formal school setting, and I particularly deplored the, at best, sloppy , at worst, ideological, confused and incoherent argument frequently exhibited by a number of radical writers. I have consistently tried to battle against exaggeration, single-mindedness, dogmatism, political correctness, sentimentality and sanctimony as well as simple intellectual error and ignorance in educational debate. I came to the conclusion a long time ago that a little learning is a dangerous thing and misconception more dangerous than ignorance.

The Philosophy of Schooling (1981b) emphasized the point that while schooling may legitimately do many things besides educate, education remains something distinctive which is its prime purpose and that the question of content, in the broadest sense, remains the fundamental question in education: what is it that a well-educated person ought to understand? People do not, of course, have to attend school to become educated and some of those who do attend will not in the end be particularly well educated. But for most people, particularly those who already disadvantaged in any way, it is surely the most realistic hope of obtaining an education. To repeat my central message: to provide someone with an education is to give them something of enormous worth, quite apart from the fact that it will also increase their autonomy.

Giving Teaching Back to Teachers (1984c) was a significant publication for me, being the product of a heightened awareness of the displacement of philosophy by the coming juggernaut of technicist research into education.

I had first been awakened to the misapplication of empirical research when writing Happiness (1979). But a more immediate reason for writing Giving Teaching back to Teachers was the fact that a very large scale empirical research project into teaching was underway at the University of Leicester (O.R.A.C.L.E), which raised all manner of questions about the plausibility and coherence of such research. (O.R.A.C.L.E itself was an early product of the Americanisation of the study of education in Britain.) Argument about the nature, plausibility and prospects of empirical research into such things as teaching is now of course commonplace (though hardly, in my view, much further forward), but at the time it wasn't, and as far as I am aware the strictures and criticisms raised have never been satisfactorily contested, despite being repeated ad nauseam by myself (e.g., 1984b-e, 1986, 1991a, 1995b, 1999a, 2000, 2006c, and Barrow and Foreman-Peck, 2006) and others.

The main points of concern are these: there are so many variables that might plausibly be thought to effect relative success or failure in the classroom, and that very possibly actually do have some effect in some way, that it is difficult to see how in practice one could ever control for them all in the manner of a researcher in the physical sciences. Some factors, including some variables, are such that they cannot be directly observed themselves (e.g., lack of enthusiasm, appreciation of poetry): consequently these factors are either ignored or distorted by being defined in terms of something that is observable (e.g., appreciation of poetry is equated with a claim to appreciate poetry). There is a widespread failure to conceptualize key terms adequately; it is, for example, quite remarkable how much research on giftedness is carried out with no clear conception of giftedness itself. There is an equal reluctance to connect the research to a convincing concept of educational success; generally speaking, one is left to infer the researcher's idea of success from the instruments and tests used in the research. But what we really need to know is something about the long-term overall effects of a given type of teaching, not simply whether at the end of a course students taught in a prescribed manner score highly on a particular test, for example.

These points, taken together, imply, at best, that no empirical research-based claim about teaching should be accepted unless the research that lies behind it has itself been thoroughly scrutinized such that we can see for ourselves that it avoids these problems; at worst, they imply that in many, perhaps most, cases, the claim cannot be well-founded. This problem is frequently presented as one of the difficulty of conducting truly scientific research in the context of human agency, as opposed to inanimate matter. And so it is. But it is also possible that the reason that a scientific approach to teaching cannot yield much is that, unlike the domain of the natural sciences, there are no laws to be found in explaining human interactions. In other words, it may be that it is not simply that it is difficult to proceed scientifically in attempting to locate the rules that govern human conduct, but that there are no hard and fast rules governing it, and therefore the notion of a science doesn't make sense. Certainly, it is hard to come by any putative rule that does not admit of exceptions. It has recently been suggested that even clarity of exposition, which one might almost have thought to be a necessary aspect of successful teaching, is not always so. Presumably, the explanation of this seeming paradox is that (a) being clear is part of the definition of what most of us mean by good teaching, that (b) it is generally conducive to successful learning (an observation that hardly requires empirical demonstration in a systematic way), but that (c) sometimes some people may learn more/better when the teacher is not particularly clear (perhaps because it makes some students redouble their efforts to understand what is going on). Such an example points not to the seemingly counter-intuitive rules of teaching that empirical investigation can uncover, but rather to the fact that there are few if any such rules to be established by formal empirical inquiry.

Such points have been repudiated often enough, but they have not been refuted. I should add that of my two most recent attempts to raise this issue, I regard one (Barrow and Foreman-Peck, 2006) as rather unsatisfactory, largely due to the circumstances of publication, but the other (Barrow, 2006c) may fairly be said to represent my current position and emphasizes my increasing feeling that we simply underestimate the extent and significance of individuality in human affairs. Why should we suppose that there are any significant rules, let alone laws, that govern both A's interaction with B in relation to matter C, and X's interaction with Y in relation to Z? Why, similarly, assume that your marriage is successful for similar reasons to those of your neighbor, or that your happiness is to be explained in the same terms as mine?

I have always preferred writing books to papers: I like to place any particular issue in a broader educational context, I am more interested in general questions such as "is history worth teaching?" than in the more specific, and I am more interested in a general audience than in a purely professional one. A Critical Dictionary of Educational Concepts (1990), written with Geoffrey Milburn, I regard as one of my more useful, even valuable, books, and I think that the idea, if not always its execution, was a good one. The book, composed of a series of critical essays, attempts to explore the concepts that are central to the practice and study of education and to provide a guide to the logical and practical dimensions to and problems inherent in them. This, however, was one of the rare occasions when my general good luck with publishers did not hold. It was an early example of the now all too common practice of a publisher grotesquely overpricing a book in anticipation of a small but quick return from library sales. The result was that a book that was designed for the pocket of every student has never been seen by most.

Understanding Skills: Thinking, Feeling and Caring (1990b) attempted to outline a positive thesis against a background of a number of specific "erroneous assumptions" that, I argue, are rife in education. It also, as the title suggests, pays particular attention to the false presumption that commitment to reason is somehow divorced from concern for emotion and feeling.

Language, Intelligence and Thought (1993) presaged my preoccupation with the question of what it is to be human and, in particular, the nature of mind. Intelligence, critical thinking and various other mental concepts had been of interest to me for a long time (e.g., 1982b, 1987b, 1991a, 1995b. See also Barrow,

2004), being quintessential examples of pseudo-generic skills, but I came increasingly to feel that what is missing in educational debate is an understanding of and stress on the humanness of the human being – the uniqueness of humans. Instead, loose analogies with other animals and machines (even trees and plants) are allowed to pass unquestioned, to the detriment of a coherent philosophy of education.

THE THIRD TURNING POINT: BRITISH COLUMBIA AND ADMINISTRATION.

Then came the third major factor in my development: I became Dean of the Faculty of Education at Simon Fraser University, B.C. I do not regret this on balance, because for ten years I was able to uphold my idea of what a faculty of education should be, putting off the evil day that is now, alas, upon us – essentially a reversion to a teacher training college now trading in highly questionable graduate "field" degrees. But the job was debilitating, both literally and metaphorically, and I wrote relatively little during that period. One fascinating thing did come out of it when I was asked to edit a book on Academic Ethics (Barrow and Keeney, 2006).

The years in administration have taught me a great deal that I didn't want to know about some of my colleagues, but more still about the administration of the University. At the beginning of my first term of office, the University was small, conscientious and competent – admirable in its way. By the end of my second term the institution had more than doubled in size and had became, in my view, if not actually corrupt, at any rate self-serving, inefficient, incompetent and, above all, effectively anti-intellectual. We were (and are) simply selling qualifications so far as the reasoning of the administration goes. Academic Ethics gave me an opportunity to read and collect some of the many other troubling indictments and concerns relating to university governance.

My most recent work takes me full circle. While I was writing despairingly of the death of education (e.g. 2003, 2005a) I was asked to contribute a volume on Plato (2007a) to a new series on Educational Thinkers, which would be distinctive in that it would devote attention to the influences on the thinker in question and the subsequent effect of his ideas. This has taken me straight back to the heart of my undergraduate and graduate work and proved extremely pleasurable. I also decided to have one more (final?) go at sorting out my thoughts on moral philosophy, prompted partly by the thought that in this age of terrorism and political mayhem, the easy platitudes of postmodern relativism are intolerable and partly by the sense that people tend to lump all value questions together as moral issues, so that everything from smoking, via adultery, to recycling is seen as a moral issue, which I think is incorrect. The result was An Introduction to Moral Philosophy and Moral Education (2007c).

Future directions are hard to predict, but the immediate present sees the publication of highly critical work relating to our uncritical belief in "democracy" as the cure for all ills, educational and political (2007b), and to the latest attempt to "measure" human achievement (2006a): Charles Murray, the celebrated co-author of the Bell Curve, has claimed to measure human achievement, essentially by dint of doing nothing more than tabulating the comparative number of pages devoted to a given thinker/artist/composer in a handful of survey texts, which are themselves selected by the researcher on no publicly acknowledged principle(s). Such work seems to me, sadly, the logical conclusion of the misconceived notions of both the human mind and the social sciences that I have been concerned about throughout my working life.

On the positive side, I have recently attempted to present arguments as to why we should educate (2005b) and for a modest moral agenda for moral education (2006a). Somewhere between positive and negative comes "On the Duty of Not Taking Offence" (2005c), a determined stand against the kind of political correctness that removes our freedom to speak and renders us as a whole a tribe of victims, ceaselessly blaming others and unable to accept any personal responsibility. My next immediate project, however, is to write a book that I have been planning to do since I was a teenager. Entitled The Philosophy of Pop, it remains to be seen how educational it turns out to be.

REFERENCES

Barrow, R. (1965). "The nineties: a way of life?" *The Idler, 1*, 3-4.

Barrow, R. (1973). *Athenian democracy*. London: Macmillan.

Barrow, R. (1974a). What's wrong with the philosophy of education? *British Journal of Educational Studies, 22*(2), 133-146.

Barrow, R. (1974b). Who are the philosopher kings? *Proceedings of the Philosophy of Education Society of Great Britain, 8*(2), 200-221.

Barrow, R. (1975a). *Plato, utilitarianism and education*. London: Routledge and Kegan Paul.

Barrow, R. (1975b). *Moral philosophy for education*. London: George Allen and Unwin.

Barrow, R. (1975c). Philosophy and the classics. *Journal of the joint association of classical teachers, 5*(1), 59-74.

Barrow, R. (1975d). The teacher of classics and the teaching of philosophy. *Didaskalos, 5*(1), 59-74

Barrow, R. (1976a). *Common sense and the curriculum*. London: George Allen and Unwin.

Barrow, R. (1976b). *Plato and education*. London: Routledge and Kegan Paul.

Barrow, R. (1977). Plato and politics. *Didaskalos, 5*(3), 410-423.

Barrow, R. (1977). *Radical education*. Oxford: Martin Robertson.

Barrow, R. (1977). *Happiness*. Oxford: Martin Robertson.

Barrow, R. (1981a) Philosophic competence and discriminatory power. *Journal of Philosophy of Education, 15*(2), 229-233.

Barrow, R. (1981b). *The philosophy of schooling*. Sussex: Harvester.

Barrow, R. (1982a). *Injustice, inequality and ethics*. Sussex: Harvester.

Barrow, R. (1982b). *Language and thought: Rethinking language across the curriculum*. London, Ont: Althouse Press.

Barrow, R. (1982c). Five commandments for the eighties. *Educational Analysis, 4*(1), 49-54.

Barrow, R. (1983). Does the question 'What is education?' make sense? *Educational Theory, 33*(3 & 4), 191-195.

Barrow, R. (1984a). *Giving teaching back to Teachers*. Sussex: Harvester.

Barrow, R. (1984b). Problems in research into group work. *Durham and Newcastle Research Review,* *10*(52), 122-125.

Barrow, R. (1984c). How married are you, Mary Ann? Educating for the real world. *Oxford Review of* *Education, 10*(2), 169-175.

Barrow, R. (1984d). Teacher education and research; The place of philosophy. *Proceedings of the* *American Philosophy of Education Society.*

Barrow, R. (1984e). The logic of systematic classroom research; The case of ORACLE. *Durham and* *Newcastle Research Review, 10*(54), 214-220.

Barrow, R. (1985). Misdescribing a cow: The question of conceptual correctness. *Educational Theory.* *35*(2), 205-207.

Barrow, R. (1986). Empirical research into teaching: the conceptual factors. *Educational Research,* *28*(3), 220-230.

Barrow, R. (1987a). Conceptual finesse. *Canadian Journal of Philosophy of Education, 1*(1), 3-12.

Barrow, R. (1987b). Skill talk. *Journal of Philosophy of Education Society of Great Britain, 21*(2), 187-196.

Barrow, R. (1990a). The role of conceptual analysis in curriculum inquiry. *Journal of Curriculum and* *Supervision, 5*(3), 269-278.

Barrow, R. (1990b). *Understanding skills: Thinking, feeling and caring.* London, Ont: Althouse Press.

Barrow, R. (1991a). The Generic Fallacy. *Educational Philosophy and Theory, 23*(1), 7-17.

Barrow, R. (1991b). *Utilitarianism: A contemporary statement.* Sussex: Edward Elgar.

Barrow, R. (1992). Philosophy of Education: the Analytic Tradition. In Tortsen Huswen & Neville Postlethwaite (Eds.), *The International Encyclopedia of Education,* 2nd edition. Oxford: Pergamon Press.

Barrow, R. (1993). *Language, intelligence and thought.* Sussex: Edward Elgar.

Barrow, R. (1995a). Philosophy of education: Past, present and future. In D. Aspin (Ed.), *Logical* *empiricism in educational discourse.* Amsterdam: Butterworth.

Barrow, R. (1995b). Keep them bells a-tolling: Normal distribution and intelligence. *Alberta Journal of* *Educational Research, 41*(3), 289-296.

Barrow, R. (1996). *Greek and Roman education,* 3rd edition. London: Bristol Classical Press.

Barrow, R. (1999a). Being a bit pregnant: How philosophical misconceptions lead to stillborn empirical research. In Ron Rembert (Ed.), *From roaring boys to dreaming spires.* New York: University Press of America.

Barrow, R. (1999b). The need for philosophical analysis in a postmodern era. *Interchange, 30*(4), 415-432.

Barrow, R. (1999c). The higher nonsense: Some persistent errors in educational thinking. *Journal of* *Curriculum Studies, 31*(2), 107-119.

Barrow, R. (2000). The poverty of empirical research in education. *Journal of Moral Education, 29*(3), 313-321.

Barrow, R. (2003). In mere despair. *Prospero, 9*(4), 11-17.

Barrow, R. (2004). Language and character. *Arts and humanities in higher education, 3*(3), 267-280.

Barrow, R. (2005a). Education: The frustration. *Prospero, 11*(1), 53-59.

Barrow, R. (2005b). Why we educate. *Prospero, 11*(2), 6-13.

Barrow, R. (2005c). On the duty of not taking offence. *Journal of Moral Education, 34*(3), 265-276.

Barrow, R. (2006a). Moral education's modest agenda. *Ethics and Education, 1*(1), 3-14.

Barrow, R. (2006b). Judging the quality of human achievement. *Education and Culture, 22*(1), 7-16.

Barrow, R. (2006c). Empirical research into teaching. *Interchange, 37*(4), 300-323.

Barrow, R. (2006d). On the Teaching of Classics. In P. Brown, T. Harrison, & D. Instone (Eds.), *Theoi* *Doron.* Herfordshire: Gracewing.

Barrow, R. (2007a). *Plato.* London: Continuum.

Barrow, R. (2007b). Dictating democracy. *The Journal of Thought, 42*(1), 9-16.

Barrow, R. (2007c). *An introduction to moral philosophy and moral education.* London: Routledge.

Barrow, R. & Foreman-Peck, L. (2006). *What use is educational research? A debate*. London: Philosophy of Education Society.

Barrow, R. & Keeney, P. (Eds.). (2006). *Academic ethics*. London: Ashgate.

Barrow, R. & Milburn, G. (1990). *A critical dictionary of educational concepts*, 2nd edition. Teachers College Press.

Barrow, R. & Woods, R. (1974). *An introduction to philosophy of education*. London: Methuen (Revised Fourth Edition 2006. London: Routledge).

Robin Barrow
Simon Fraser University

DAVID CARR

PRACTICAL REASON, MORAL VIRTUE AND PROFESSIONALISM IN TEACHING

EARLY DAYS

I entered the world, towards the end of the second-world war, as the second son of working class parents in the northern English (Yorkshire) industrial town of Wakefield. Although my father was active in local politics as a labour councillor – and later became a mayor and freeman of the city – neither of my parents had received much in the way of formal education, having left school for full-time employment in their early teens. Following primary education, in the selective (11 + examination) British system of schooling of the early post-war period, I was awarded a place at an 'academic' grammar school, though most of my local friends made their way to more 'vocational' secondary schools. Like most of the other working-class children who attended the grammar school, however, I fared badly in an educational institution that was better suited to young people of rather different social background. Despite this, I have never greatly shared the bitterness and resentment often shown by others of similar experience towards the grammar school education. The educational opportunities that the grammar schools afforded were by and large admirable; but it was a difficulty that without a certain measure of what is nowadays called 'cultural capital', some children were ill equipped to benefit fully from them.

TEACHER TRAINING AND TEACHING SCHOOL

In addition, while I was preparing at age sixteen for the general certificate examination (GCE), my father died after some years of recurring illness. In view of this family loss, my own rather poor GCE results and the fact that my grammar school education had already extended a year beyond the requirements of compulsory education (since 'secondary modern' pupils usually left for work at 15), I abandoned the prospect of post-sixteen schooling and entered full-time employment in order to contribute financially to the family home in which I was still living with my widowed mother. All the same, after some years in various dead-end jobs, I came to feel the need for more satisfying professional direction to my life – and, to this end, my thoughts returned to education. Drawn to the idea of teaching, I managed to secure temporary employment as an unqualified assistant teacher in a local primary school. At the same time, however, I also set about acquiring – through 'twilight' adult education – the academic qualifications required for entry to a British College of Teacher Training. After four terms of unqualified teaching, and having managed the basic qualifications for college

L.J. Waks (ed.), Leaders in Philosophy of Education: Intellectual Self Portraits, 39–51.

entry, I was accepted for a grant-assisted three-year course at C.F. Mott College of Education in Liverpool. As this was at the height of the Liverpool 'beat boom' spearheaded by the Beatles and others, and as I was also pursuing a second course of study of blues piano and harmonica in various outfits at the Cavern, Hope Hall, Iron Door and other renowned Merseyside recreational facilities (where I shared platforms with, among others, Memphis Slim and John Lee Hooker), I cannot say that my commitment to professional education was as yet entirely total. That said, I managed to complete my teacher training on time (if with not quite flying colours) subsequently securing my first fully qualified teaching post back in my home town of Wakefield.

PERSONAL FAVORITES

Professionalism and Ethics in Teaching (2000)
Propositions negatable in three ways. (1980).
Two kinds of virtue (1984/5).
Chastity and adultery (1986).
Art, practical knowledge and aesthetic objectivity (1999).
Feelings in moral conflict and the hazards of emotional intelligence (2002).
Character and moral choice in the cultivation of virtue (2003).
Music, meaning and emotion (2004).
On the contribution of literature to the educational cultivation of moral virtue, feeling and emotion (2005).
Personal and interpersonal relationships in education and teaching: a virtue ethical perspective (2005).
On the prospects of chastity as a contemporary virtue (2005).
Moral Education at the movies: on the cinematic treatment of morally significant story and narrative (2006).

After a year back home in Yorkshire, I returned to teach in Lancashire and Merseyside schools. While some of this involved further primary teaching in Liverpool, I also worked for two years in a Lancashire secondary, teaching the two main subjects in which I had majored during my teacher training – namely Art and English. It was at college that I had begun in earnest to read classical and modern literature: I completed my final college year English dissertation on the influence of the English romantic poet William Blake on the poetry of W.H. Auden and by the time of my Lancashire teaching I was consuming the great works of nineteenth and twentieth century English and European literature at a fair rate of knots. By this point, however, it became clear to me that my interest in much of this literature was not primarily (or at any rate exclusively) aesthetic or literary: that, in short, my main interest in the novels of Dostoevsky, Tolstoy, Kafka, Camus, Mann, Joyce, Lawrence and others, was in their moral and other ideas. Indeed, it was but a short step from the novels of Mann, Camus and Sartre to the philosophical works of Camus, Sartre, Nietzsche, Kierkegaard, Bergson, Jaspers, Buber, Maritain, Marcel and others. That said, my reading was by no means confined to such writers and I was simultaneously getting to grips with Plato, Descartes, Leibniz, Spinoza and

Kant – as well as, nearer the present day, Russell, Wittgenstein and Ryle. It was also at this time that I began to feel the lack of 'proper' university education. Having also discovered that a year's employed residence in the city of Liverpool rendered me eligible for further financial assistance pending university acceptance, I decided to apply for a three-year course of full-time undergraduate study in a British Philosophy Department.

PHILOSOPHY AT LEEDS

I was fortunate to be accepted by the Philosophy Department of Leeds University (in Yorkshire again) – mainly on the basis of my professional teaching qualification, my status as a relatively mature student and (perhaps rather more) my evident passion for – as well as elementary working knowledge of – the discipline of philosophy. There can be little doubt that Leeds was one of the leading provincial departments of philosophy of the day, with several British philosophers of international reputation on the staff. Roger White, Peter Long and Timothy Potts had established reputations in the field of philosophical logic, Hugo Meynell had published widely respected work in the philosophy of religion, and U.T. Place's papers on brain-mind identity seem to have been obligatory for inclusion in any and all reputable collections of contemporary philosophy of mind. Of the two full professors in the department, Roy Holland was a leading pupil of Wittgenstein's own distinguished disciple Rush Rhees (as well as a Swansea associate of Peter Winch and a teacher of, among others, D.Z. Phillips) and Peter Geach was of course himself a leading pupil of Wittgenstein as well as distinguished spouse of the no less formidable Elizabeth Anscombe – another key disciple of Wittgenstein and Professor of Philosophy at the University of Cambridge. William and Martha Kneale, formerly of Oxford (where William Kneale was White's Professor), authors of a pioneering history of logical enquiry – *The Development of Logic* – had recently retired to the Yorkshire Dales just to the north of Leeds and were frequent visitors to the department.

That said, Leeds was the last place for anyone seeking courses in existentialism, phenomenology, structuralism or other forms of continental European philosophy. The name of the philosophical game in Leeds was linguistic analysis with a particular emphasis on more formal analytical techniques and approaches. Under the leadership of Geach and Holland, the influence of Wittgenstein was pervasive, but there was much stress on the continuity of the *Investigations* with the *Tractatus* (by contrast with other places which sometimes emphasised the discontinuity) – and, in turn, on the debt of the *Tractatus* to the logical investigations of Frege and Russell was no less emphasised. As Roman Catholics, Geach and Anscombe also acknowledged a line of philosophical descent from Aquinas, and through him Aristotle – whose role as a pioneer of formal methods was greatly highlighted. In short, while the Leeds department provided a wide-ranging programme of philosophical enquiry no less hospitable to metaphysics, aesthetics and theology than to the basics of epistemology, ethics and philosophy of mind, proper grounding in the techniques of modern formal analysis was regarded as necessary for clear progress in any and all fields of philosophical enquiry. The flourishing undergraduate led philosophy society held regular well-attended meetings that featured world class analytical philosophers – including Bernard Williams, R.M Hare, Gilbert Ryle, A.J. Ayer, Peter Strawson, J.J.C. Smart and D.Z. Phillips. My greatest coup as third year undergraduate secretary and organiser of the society, however, was to arrange a visit from Sir Isaiah Berlin – who had refused all previous overtures. One of the most memorable Leeds conferences – on the logic of Intentionality (1974) – featured Geach, Quine, Davidson, Hintikka and Follesdahl in one Olympian summit meeting.

Whatever their eventual single or combined courses of study, Leeds undergraduates were (as in other British universities) required to pursue a broader programme of three electives in their first year. In line with this requirement, I opted for courses in English Literature and the History and Philosophy of Religion in addition to the foundational course in Philosophy. The philosophy of religion was taught by Hugo Meynell (later Professor of Philosophy and Religion at Calgary), the history of religion by Professor Trevor Ling (a noted scholar and author in this field) and the first year philosophy and logic courses were taught by Roy Holland, Christopher Coope and Harry Lewis. The literature course included, among other things, a highly memorable crash course of study of a representative sample of Shakespeare's plays that utterly transformed my own appreciation of this major writer. All the same, while most philosophically interested Leeds students proceeded to combine philosophy with another subject in the second and third years of their degree, I chose – notwithstanding encouraging results in all three of my first year options – to pursue the more specialist route of single studies Philosophy. In my second year, I followed a fairly standard range of courses on ethics, ancient and modern philosophy, formal logic, philosophical logic, philosophy of science and Wittgenstein. There was rather less exposure, I recall (despite departmental interest in these topics), to aesthetics and social and political philosophy, and the history of philosophy dealt with little (even at Leeds) between Aristotle and Descartes). In my third year, in addition to continuing with the key courses for philosophical specialists on formal and philosophical logic, I was required to select two from a range of electives and to write a dissertation. In the event, I chose to study Kant with Martin Milligan and philosophy of mind with U.T. Place – but, in addition, I was also allowed to attend a remarkable (albeit demanding) programme of postgraduate seminars on the logic of intentionality by Peter Geach. I completed my third year dissertation on problems of personal identity – focused mainly around critique of Strawson, Williams and Shoemaker – under the supervision of Roy Holland.

LONDON: THE PROFESSIONAL ROAD

Looking back, there can be no doubt that my Leeds years represented nothing less than a 'Damascus' experience: that, in short, they utterly transformed my life and my view of what was from now on worth doing. But the philosophy that was now such a part of me was a very different beast from the ill-defined intellectual passion that had drawn me to the Leeds course only three years previously. In the space of a few years, I had moved from a conception of philosophy as a search for grand but vague answers to large and often ill-formed questions to the recognition that there were indeed rigorous and systematic ways in which philosophical claims and arguments might be clarified and analysed or tested for their coherence and validity. That said, I had now indulged in several further years of full time study and the question of how (if at all) I might put such studies to use in gainful employment began to assume importance. Hence, although my BA degree turned out to be good enough for me to be offered PhD funding from two different sources, I judged that I could hardly afford to devote three more years to full-time study. Instead, minded to put my recently acquired academic expertise to some practical professional use, I applied for a one-year Masters degree in Philosophy of Education at the London Institute of Education – a key programme for the wider dissemination of the new British brand of analytical philosophy of education recently pioneered by R.S. Peters. In the event, my year of MA studies in Philosophy of Education was also rich and stimulating – no less for the wider intellectual and cultural opportunities on offer in London than for the programme provided by Peters and his colleagues at Malet Street. On the London Institute programme itself I followed courses on epistemology and metaphysics by Joan Cooper, on philosophy of language by David Cooper (later Professor of Philosophy at Durham) and (not least) by R. S. Peters himself on philosophy of education – though access to such other London educational philosophers as R.F Dearden, R.K Elliott and John and Pat White was also available through their PGCE lectures. But London also afforded – not least through the marvellous intercollegiate programmes of philosophical and other lectures – direct access to the teaching of Peter Winch, David Hamlyn, David Wiggins, Richard Wollheim, Hide Ishiguro (among others) as well as to the visiting lectures of (again among others) Elizabeth Anscombe, Bernard Williams and Saul Kripke.

But now, with the end of the London masters in sight, I was looking for a job. Fortunately, however, the hour of British philosophy and theory of education seemed to have come. Owing much to the pioneering work of educational philosophers – not least that of Richard Peters and Paul Hirst – British university departments and colleges of education were seeking to develop more professional approaches to teacher education and training grounded in better appreciation of the significance of educational theory for the effective practice of teaching. A key aim of this new conception of teacher professionalism was to raise teaching to the status of an all-graduate profession – primarily through the development of rigorously disciplined undergraduate programmes of professional education in the teacher training colleges (though shorter versions of such educational discipline based programmes were seen as no less important for the professionalisation of those entering teaching via the postgraduate certificate). In short, just as (so Peters, Hirst and other had argued) general medical practitioners could hardly be considered fit for practice without some degree level theoretical knowledge of (say) physiology anatomy and biochemistry – so teachers could hardly be fit for purpose without some understanding of the psychological 'sciences' of learning, some knowledge of educational history and its role in shaping current policy and some sociological grasp of the organization and functioning of contemporary educational institutions. As philosophers, however, Peters and Hirst were also inclined to give educational philosophy a central role in the professional training of graduate teachers: first on the grounds that some grasp of (for example) ethics and epistemology was arguably needed for understanding the nature and purposes of education, the composition of the school curriculum and the wider moral and social development of young people; secondly, because the skills of discourse analysis and argumentation required for philosophy would enable teachers to detect the logical errors and fallacies of much official educational rhetoric in policy documentation and elsewhere. At all events, in large agreement with this general view of the value of philosophy for professional education – and having substantial professional experience as a former primary and secondary school teacher – I sought my first post in the field of professional teacher education.

PHILOSOPHY AND PHILOSOPHY OF EDUCATION AT DUNFERMLINE COLLEGE

I took up my first position in the education department of Dunfermline College of Physical Education in Edinburgh which was in the very process of developing its first undergraduate Bachelor of Education programme for (at that time female) physical education teachers in Scotland. In retrospect, this turned out to be not the best of career moves. At the time, the prospect appeared more appealing for various reasons. First, on a personal level, after a year in the grimy southern metropolis, I was keen to return to the north – and Edinburgh seemed a most attractive destination. Secondly, however, since there were already signs of economic downturn in the British economy and of corresponding contraction of the Robbins Report expansion of higher education of the sixties, a bird in the hand looked better than any in the bush. But thirdly, the opportunity to play a substantial role in shaping a professional teacher education programme from its inception was also far from unappealing. From a more philosophically fortuitous viewpoint, indeed, the PE focus of the new B.Ed. also promised a unique opportunity to show how some of the work that had most interested me in Leeds

---

FAVORITES BY OTHER AUTHORS:

Anscombe, G.E.M., (1959) *Intention*, Oxford: Blackwell

Campbell, J. (1982) *The Masks of God*: Vols 1-4, Harmondsworth: Penguin, 1982.

Frege, G. (1967) 'The thought', in Strawson, P. (ed) (1967), *Philosophical Logic*, Oxford: Oxford University Press

Geach, P.T., *Mental Acts*, (1957) London: Routledge and Kegan Paul, 1957

Geach, P.T. and Black, M. (eds) (1966) *Translations from the Philosophical Writings of Gottlob Frege*, Oxford: Blackwell

von Wright, G. H.(1971) *Explanation and understanding*, London: Routledge and K. Paul

Wittgenstein, L. (1953) *Philosophical Investigations*, Oxford: Blackwell

---

and London might be made relevant to the teaching of physical abilities and skills. At Leeds I had been much drawn to the efforts of such philosophers as Anscombe, Geach, Von Wright and Kenny to account for human agency in terms of a neo-Aristotelian conception of practical reason or deliberation. Von Wright, indeed, had argued that the notion of practical reason (rather than causal law) might be seen to occupy the central explanatory role in social science. However, while much of this work was clearly of some philosophical complexity, it nevertheless seemed of great potential utility for understanding the kinds of practical knowledge with which physical educationalists were directly concerned (not least in a field of pedagogical theorising in which crude causal analyses of skill largely prevailed).

(i) Practical reason and practical knowledge

At all events, after two years of settling into post and getting to grips with the teaching, I tried approaching these issues and questions from a variety of different (albeit related) perspectives. First, I sought to criticize a dominant academic tradition of curriculum thinking for its failure to appreciate (more than likely, as Ryle and others had already argued, on Cartesian grounds) the distinctive character and complexity of practical deliberation. Secondly, however, I sought to develop a distinctive theory of practical knowledge in which the pedagogical role of such deliberative capacities would be more apparent. My first published paper, 'Practical reasoning and knowing how' (*Journal of Human Movement Studies* 1978a) made a start on the second of these tasks, and my (rather less successful) second published paper of the same year, 'Practical pursuits and the curriculum' (*Journal of Philosophy of Education* 1978b) addressed the first of these concerns. However, it soon became clear that the business of understanding and explaining practical knowledge raised a host of quite technical philosophical problems that could not be confined to journals of education and teaching. My third publication 'The logic of knowing how and ability' therefore set out to address some of these more technical questions about the epistemic status of practical knowledge, and I was delighted when it was published in *Mind* in 1979. This was the first of a string of papers on practical knowledge, practical inference, the intentionality of action and theory and practice that I published over the next few years in mainstream philosophical journals (see, Carr 1980a 1980b, 1981a. 1981c, 1982, 1984).

At the same time, at the more professional end of things, I published further papers devoted to the educational or pedagogical application of these ideas (eg Carr 1981b) – including (fairly pioneering) articles on the meaning and teaching of dance (Carr 1984, 1987b; see also 1997). At all events, these attempts to understand the educational character and value of practical knowledge in terms of action theory could be regarded as making up (roughly) the first of three or four broadly connected phases or themes of my academic work in philosophy and philosophy of education. It might also be said that this work did not at the time have much impact on mainstream philosophy of education as such – although reference to it still occasionally appears, ironically enough, in the literatures of mainstream philosophy on the one hand and physical education on the other.

Indeed, despite the fact that my work on practical reason and deliberation fairly predates the educational philosophical explosion of interest in this issue of the eighties and beyond, I suspect that the philosophical technicality of the literature with which it engaged was not much to the taste of even those educational philosophers interested in raising the educational stakes of practical rationality and knowledge. That said, it seems to me that the neglect of deeper philosophical analysis of these issues in more recent work is to be regretted, and that such neglect has often led to quite superficial defences of the educational status of a variety of practical subjects – from arts and physical skills on the one hand to vocational competencies on the other.

(ii) Moral education and the virtues

The next phase of my academic work in educational philosophy – which has clear overlaps with the work on action theory – began in the early eighties and has continued more or less to the present day. One of the Dunfermline College core programmes that I developed together with philosophical colleagues was an elective on ethics and moral education in the course of which – alongside the standard fare on Plato, Aristotle, Kant, utilitarianism and emotivism – I had sought to develop a focus on neo-Aristotelian virtue ethics. This was hardly surprising given that the philosophers from whom I had (directly or indirectly) learned the philosophy of action – such as Anscombe, Geach, and Von Wright – were also key pioneers of modern virtue ethics. Once again, however, it seemed to me that any coherent work on moral education needed to be supported by serious reflection in moral philosophy and so my efforts were directed in both of these directions. At the philosophical end of things, my published work on ethics and moral philosophy – mostly but not entirely focused on virtue ethics – began in earnest with a paper entitled 'Two kinds of virtue' which appeared in the 1984/5 *Proceedings of the Aristotelian Society*. Further mainstream essays on ethics and moral philosophy appeared throughout the eighties (see Carr1986, 1987a, 1988) and have continued down to the present day (2002, 2003c). From the perspective of moral educational theory and practice, however, my publications have been numerous and wide-ranging and are therefore difficult to summarise briefly. My first publications on moral education as such seems to have been 'Three approaches to moral education' (Carr 1983) which was also the basis of my first American invitation – to a Federal government seminar on character education in Washington in 1987.

This early paper sought primarily to show the advantages and benefits of a virtue ethical approach to moral education over its cognitive developmental and other rivals. This is still very much a core concern of my work, not least in recent papers on the moral educational significance of the arts – to which I shall return. It was also the main focus of my first book – *Educating the Virtues* – published by Routledge in1991, and of a high quality and very well reviewed Routledge collection of essays that I co-authored with Jan Steutel under the title *Virtue Ethics and Moral Education* in 1999 (which included fine essays by many leading contemporary virtue ethicists and educational philosophers). But my work on moral education as such has also been part of a wider interest in values education that has also extended to religious education, spiritual education, personal and social education, sex education, education for citizenship, art and aesthetic education and values education more generally. Over the years this programme has attracted varying degrees of attention and interest – not all of it sympathetic. In this connection, it is worth mentioning my work on spiritual education (or more precisely on the educational coherence of this term) that responded fairly critically to the latter day fad for advocating a spiritual dimension to schooling. Essentially, I argued (see Carr 1981a; also Carr and Haldane 2003) that the efforts of some latter day British documentation to develop a religiously 'untethered' quasi-aesthetic notion of spiritual education were longer on vacuous (and educationally impotent) rhetoric than substance: that, in short, any serious notion of spirituality would need to be associated – in potentially problematic ways – with religion and/or religious education. This drew hostile fire from all sides – from the new age spiritualists who wanted spirituality without religious commitment, as well as from the atheists who took me to be arguing (as a theist) for a place in schooling for religious spirituality. Neither camp understood my main point which was that insofar as it was difficult to conceive any very meaningful or distinctive non-religious conception of spirituality the choice was effectively between a vacuous discourse of 'awe and wonder' on the one hand and the promotion of particular religious conceptions of spirituality which could only be problematic in contexts of public schooling on the other, In the time that has elapsed since the publication of my papers on this topic, there has been little evidence of improved critical appreciation of these issues and the flatulent rhetoric of children's spirituality has proceeded unabated in an expanding literature. Still, it may be worth mentioning that my work on ethics and sexuality has had a kinder reception in recent days with invitations (partly on the basis of an earlier *American Philosophical Quarterly* essay on the virtue ethical status of chastity) to contribute to some major philosophical collections in the fields of both sexual ethics (Carr 2005c, 2005d) and sex education.

(iii) Questions concerning teacher professionalism

A third – again not unrelated – major focus of my work has been on questions of the character of teaching, its occupational and professional status and on the grounds of professional ethics in teaching and other occupations. Once again, this interest goes back some way – at least as far as a (not notably distinguished) *British Journal of Educational Studies* paper of the early eighties. However, further thoughts on teaching and professionalism were undoubtedly spurred by concerns over the development of some rather reductive (behaviourist) models of professional teaching and other expertise – focused on teaching styles and competencies – that seemed to gain political and professional ascendancy in the late eighties and early nineties. In this regard, I published several critiques of such models (for example, Carr 1993), several articles resisting 'applied science' interpretations of the relationship of educational theory to practice and concerned to develop a non-technicist conception of this relationship (Carr 1992a, 1995b) and other papers on the grounds of professional ethics in teaching and other occupations (Carr 1992b, 1999a, 2005b, 2006a) in a variety of journals of philosophy, education and educational philosophy. I attempted to draw the ideas of these papers together into a coherent whole in my second book *Professionalism and Ethics in Teaching* which appeared in the Routledge Professional ethics Series in 2000. Much of this work has attracted professional interest and attention, I have lectured on these themes locally and internationally (and had key articles anthologised, in collections) and a good deal of it has been directed towards developing a distinctive virtue ethical conception of professional teacher expertise. A recent paper on the place of character in teaching – recently presented as a keynote to the annual Oxford conference of the Philosophy of Education Society of Great Britain and to AERA in Chicago – marks a further episode in this general enterprise.

CURRENT AND PROSPECTIVE WORK

My most recent interest in the ethical and moral educational significance of the arts – an area in which I have produced some of my most all-time personally satisfying work – is clearly continuous with my work on the ethics of moral education and teacher professionalism. In the course of arguing for the advantages of a virtue ethical conception of moral education over its various theoretical rivals I have sought to show that far from representing an autonomous mode of reflection, moral reason is (as Aristotle clearly thought) often effectively nurtured by artistic and other narratives. But, by the same token, I have also argued that if something akin to Aristotle's moral wisdom lies at the heart of effective teacher reflection then the acquisition of such wisdom cannot just be a matter of the development of context-free technical skills or competencies and may be much assisted by the broader cultural and literary initiation of teachers: that, in short, the professional expertise of teachers may stand to benefit as much (if not more) from reading Charles Dickens and D.H. Lawrence as from the perusal of books on educational psychology. Either way, there would appear to be a good case for the educational rehabilitation of the arts, which certainly seem to have suffered some educational neglect and/or curricular marginalization in recent days. At all events, I have lately explored the human significance of the arts in general and the moral, spiritual and emotional significance of such arts as literature, music, painting, sculpture and cinema in particular in articles for a wide range of journals (Carr 1999b, 2002, 2003b 2004, 2005a, 2006b; Carr and Davis 2007). Since it also seems to me that there is much more to be said about these issues, this is the direction in which I see my work proceeding in the foreseeable future. That said, while this essay has sought to show the range of my work over the years it has by no means covered everything I have done, and from this viewpoint my 2003 'introduction' to educational philosophy – *Making Sense of Education* – probably gives a better indication of the full extent of my interests over a long professional career.

RECENT AND PRESENT CIRCUMSTANCES

That career is also now much nearer the end than the beginning. The Dunfermline years are of course so much water under the bridge – though, apart from a short spell as Fellow at the St Andrews Centre for Philosophy and Public Affairs and some inevitable academic globetrotting, I have not strayed far from Edinburgh. In the late nineteen eighties Dunfermline College was 'merged' with Moray House College of Education – Edinburgh's principal institution for teacher education and training. Dunfermline College became the physical education 'annexe' of the larger institution, and I took the opportunity to transfer to the primary and secondary teacher training programmes of the latter. Shortly afterwards Moray House entered into almost a decade of semi-autonomous association with Heriot-Watt University in Edinburgh (primarily an institution of 'technical' education with no educational or teacher programmes of its own) and I was appointed to a Readership in Education under this dispensation. Towards the end of the nineteen nineties the relationship between Heriot-Watt and Moray House was beginning to show signs of strain, Moray House disengaged from this association and was in 1999 reconfigured (along with the already existing but much smaller Edinburgh education department) as the Moray House Faculty (now School) of Education of the University of Edinburgh – on the heels of which I was appointed to a personal chair as Professor of Philosophy of Education. With these various institutional and career developments, and increasing personal and family ties to Edinburgh, previous impulses to seek professional advancement beyond Edinburgh (which were quite powerful in the Dunfermline College days) have been rather overtaken by events and a move elsewhere seems unlikely (though not impossible) at this late stage in my affairs.

REFERENCES

Key Books

Carr, D. (1991). Educating the virtues: An essay on the philosophical psychology of moral development and education. London: Routledge.
Carr, D. (2000). *Professionalism and ethics in teaching*. London: Routledge.
Carr, D. (2003a). *Making sense of education: An introduction to the philosophy and theory of education and teaching*. London: Routledge/Falmer.

Edited Books

Carr, D. (1998) *Education, knowledge and truth: Beyond the post-modern impasse*. London: Routledge
Carr, D. & Steutel, J. (1999). *Virtue ethics and moral education*. London: Routledge, 1999.
Carr, D. & Haldane, J. (2003). *Philosophy, spirituality and education*. London: Routledge/Falmer.

Papers

Carr, D. (1978a). Practical reasoning and knowing how. *Journal of Human Movement Studies, 41*, 3-20.

Carr, D. (1978b). Practical pursuits and the curriculum. *Journal of Philosophy of Education, 12*, 69-80.

Carr, D. (1979). The logic of knowing how and ability. *Mind, 88*(351), 394-409.

Carr, D. (1980a). Propositions negatable in three ways. *Analysis, 40*(4), 214-219.

Carr, D. (1980b). What place has the notion of a basic action in the theory of action? *Ratio, 22*(1), 39-51.

Carr, D. (1981a). Knowledge in practice. *American Philosophical Quarterly, 18*(4), 53-61.

Carr, D. (1981b). On mastering a skill. *Journal of Philosophy of Education, 15*(1), 87-96.

Carr, D. (1981c). Practical inference and the identity of actions. *Review of Metaphysics, 34* (4), 645-66

Carr, D. (1982). Theory and practice: some analogous concepts and their disanalogies. *Metaphilosophy, 13*(3/4), 228-239.

Carr, D. (1983). Three approaches to moral education. *Educational Philosophy and Theory, 15*(2), 39-51.

Carr, D. (1984) The logic of intentional verbs. *Philosophical Investigations, 7*(2), 141-157.

Carr, D. (1984). Dance education, skill and behavioural objectives. *Journal of Aesthetic Education, 18*(4), 67-76.

Carr, D. (1984/5). Two kinds of virtue. *Proceedings of the Aristotelian Society, 84*, 47-61.

Carr, D. (1986). Chastity and adultery. *American Philosophical Quarterly, 23*(4), 363-371.

Carr, D. (1987a). Freud and sexual ethics. *Philosophy, 62*, 361-373.

Carr, D. (1987b). Thought and action in the art of dance. *British Journal of Aesthetics, 27*(4), 345-357.

Carr, D. (1988). The cardinal virtues and Plato's moral psychology. *Philosophical Quarterly, 38*(151), 186-200.

Carr, D. (1992a). Practical enquiry, values and the problem of educational theory. *Oxford Review of Education, 18*(3), 241-251.

Carr, D. (1992b). Four dimensions of educational professionalism. *Westminster Studies in Education, 15*, 19-32.

Carr, D. (1993). Questions of competence. *British Journal of Educational Studies, 41*(3), 252-271.

Carr, D. (1995a). Towards a distinctive conception of spiritual education. *Oxford Review of Education, 20*(1), 83-98.

Carr, D. (1995b). Is understanding the professional knowledge of teachers a theory-practice problem? *Journal of Philosophy of Education, 29*(3), 311-331.

Carr, D. (1997). Meaning in dance, *British Journal of Aesthetics, 37*(4), 349-366.

Carr, D. (1999a). Professional education and professional ethics. *Journal of Applied Philosophy, 16*(1), 33-46.

Carr, D. (1999b). Art, practical knowledge and aesthetic objectivity. *Ratio, 12*(3), 240-256.

Carr, D. (2002). Feelings in moral conflict and the hazards of emotional intelligence. *Ethical Theory and Moral Practice, 5*(1), 3-21.

Carr, D. (2003b). Spiritual, moral and heroic virtue: Aristotelian character in the Arthurian and Grail narratives. *Journal of Beliefs and Values, 24*(1), 15-26,

Carr, D. (2003c). Character and moral choice in the cultivation of virtue. *Philosophy, 78*(304), 219-232.

Carr, D. (2004). Music, meaning and emotion. *Journal of Aesthetics and Art Criticism, 62*(3), 225-234.

Carr, D. (2005a). On the contribution of literature to the educational cultivation of moral virtue, feeling and emotion. *Journal of Moral Education, 34*(2) 137-151.

Carr, D. (2005b). Personal and interpersonal relationships in education and teaching: A virtue ethical perspective. *British Journal of Educational Studies, 53*(3) 255-271.

Carr, D. (2005c). Abstinence. In Alan Soble, (Ed.), *Sex from Plato to Paglia: A philosophical encyclopedia*. Westport, Conn.: Greenwood Press.

Carr, D. (2005d). On the prospects of chastity as a contemporary virtue. In R. Halwani (Ed.), *Sex and ethics: Essays on sexuality, virtue and the good life*. Basingstoke: Palgrave Macmillan.

Carr, D. (2006a). Professional and personal values and virtues in education and teaching. *Oxford Review of Education, 32* (2) 171-183.

Carr, D. (2006b). Moral education at the movies: On the cinematic treatment of morally significant story and narrative. *Journal of Moral Education, 35*(3) 319-334.

Carr, D. & Davis, R. (2007). The lure of evil: Exploring the dark side of literature and the arts. *Journal of Philosophy of Education, 41*(1), 1-18.

David Carr
University of Edinburgh

KIERAN EGAN

THE MARKETPLACE OF IDEAS IS OUT OF
EVERYTHING BUT IRONY

In the screened box you will find the titles of seven books that I will refer to, along with a few others in passing. They seem to have precipitated out of the activities I have been involved in since coming to North America a long time ago to do a Ph.D. in philosophy of education. My first degree, in London (England), was in history, and, lacking any imagination about the possibilities of life, I continued in the college to do a one-year program that led to a teaching certificate.

> **PERSONAL FAVORITES**
>
> *Educational Development* (1979).
> *Education and Psychology: Plato, Piaget, and scientific psychology* (1983).
> *Teaching as story telling* (1986)
> *The Educated Mind: How cognitive tools shape our understanding* (1997)
> *Getting it wrong from the beginning: Our progressivist inheritance from Herbert Spencer, John Dewey, and Jean Piaget* (2002)
> *An imaginative approach to teaching* (2005)
> *Teaching Literacy: engaging the imaginations of new readers and writers* (2006)

Two events during my post-graduate year of teacher-training inserted the vaguest kind of definition to a small area of the vast smudge of my future. First, the program involved a course in philosophy of education, from a young woman who had recently emerged from the London Institute of Education with a Ph.D. earned while working with Richard Peters. Because most of my previous intellectual training had been in the rigorous area of empirical research called theology, I found the philosophy of education work both engaging and fairly straightforward. It did seem sensible to try to sort out what education was if one was to launch into a career doing it.

The second event was a visitation to the campus of a group from a slightly bizarre sounding organization called the Centre for Structural Communication. At the time I was fascinated by the most sophisticated technology, and interested in what the new computers could offer to schooling. I was attracted by the excited propaganda put out by the pioneers of "programmed learning" that suggested children could be enabled to learn miraculous amounts of knowledge in very little time. The visitors demonstrated a much more sophisticated "programmed" form of teaching, which was designed to engage the higher intellectual processes of students as they worked through the "study units."

L.J. Waks (ed.), Leaders in Philosophy of Education: Intellectual Self Portraits, 53–62.

STRUCTURAL COMMUNICATION

The visitors were all scientists, all the study units they had so far written were in the sciences, and they were interested in recruiting some newly graduated types to come and work with them, in Kingston-upon-Thames, to explore applying Structural Communication to humanities areas of the curriculum.

I was keen to go to the US for graduate work, to work among the humming computers of I.B.M. and Westinghouse and the rest, but also interested in pursuing possibilities in philosophy of education. My instructor recommended I write to Richard Peters and seek his advice. He kindly wrote back a long letter explaining why coming to the Institute and first doing an M.A. with him and, if he thought I showed any promise, a Ph.D. would equip me to sort the educational world out and fairly well ensure a job in a decent university.

The machines won this round, and I went to Kingston-upon-Thames for a year, writing a series of history study units using Structural Communication (S.C.) and buying a 1937 Morris 8 Tourer car for £50, from whose loss I have never quite recovered. The units were later published in book form—*The Tudor Peace*—in a series the Centre negotiated with London University Press. This looked better on my CV than the school-oriented text warranted, but who was I to complain? The Centre also negotiated a grant with I.B.M.; the firm was interested in S.C. and the sophistication of the data processing required to automate it—providing a much more interesting use of I.B.M.'s System 1500 computers than the trivial challenge involved in fitting linear and branching forms of programmed learning to them. The use of the machines for such tasks was described as providing a $100,000 page-turner. I.B.M., however, wanted someone from the Centre to work in the US on applying S.C. to their computers, and they did just happen to have someone spare.

I applied to a bundle of US universities during the year I was in Kingston, and was accepted at Stanford. I.B.M. offered a scholarship that would cover the fees—and in case any current students are reading this, I won't mention the spare-change costs in 1968—and so I was to work one day a week for I.B.M. in San Jose and later Los Gatos while attending classes at Stanford.

GRADUATE SCHOOL

My suspicion is that this volume will not have a photograph of its editor, or certainly not a photograph of how he looked in 1968. Dr. Waks was among my first instructors. His astonishing hairstyle and occasional psychedelic clothes and—shall we say?—unconventional manner disguised a deep seriousness about philosophy and a real passion as a teacher. It was the latter set of characteristics that had the lasting effect.

But apart from Len Waks, and the somewhat surreal experience of working with I.B.M. one day a week—(I had no car, so they sent to my hall of residence on campus a chauffer driven stretch Cadillac to deliver me to San Jose each week: a source of some humor and a little derision from my fellow long-haired students)—the requirements for completing a Stanford Ph.D. seemed a tad Byzantine, and took no account of people from different backgrounds. (American provincialism at the time often took my breath away; from the professor who assured me that Babe Ruth must be the best known person in the world, not realizing apparently that the rest of the world played "the beautiful game," to the "culture-neutral" GRE and other exams. I was required to take that took it for granted that US history was universally studied.) D. Bob Gowin was at Stanford on sabbatical from Cornell for the year I was at Stanford, and, seeing my mild distress at the prospect of ploughing through the pile of future courses invited me to finish my Ph.D. at Cornell. Unsurprisingly, Len Waks also left Stanford within a year for many of the same reasons that led me to depart its sunny campus.

Cornell, more like the British system I was familiar with, didn't require courses. They were available, but one only needed the signature of one's committee and one could do anything that made sense to the student and to the committee. It suited me down to the ground. I spent three happy years there, mostly in the Centre for the Humanities, taking "courses" with visitors like Hayden White and Northrop Frye, working in anthropology with Jim Siegel, and generally getting as good an education as my dedication to becoming the best pool player on campus would allow. This latter ambition was constantly frustrated by one of my fellow students, the redoubtable John Carbonell. Bob Gowin, Ken Strike, and Brian Crittenden provided a rich introduction to the culture of philosophy of education, and I graduated and came to what has been the only job I have had in academia, at Simon Fraser University in British Columbia.

SIMON FRASER UNIVERSITY

These were the years of a kind of triumphal psychology of education and the evident beginnings of the decline in influence of philosophy of education, as it began to morph into labels like "policy studies" or whatever, in generally unsuccessful attempts to make itself seem more "relevant." During the years I have been a professor of education the influence of philosophy of education has generally continued to decline, and psychology's relative success has in recent years began to waver under the repeated failure to deliver on its promise of bringing "science" to the aid of education.

The claims of educational psychology always seemed to me slightly odd, and I found the pretensions to scientific status of the articles I was reading little short of ludicrous. My job, I should mention, morphed on my arrival because someone who had planned to take a sabbatical, thus enabling the faculty to hire me, changed his mind, and so I was to be given other teaching. Given what was by then my rather diverse looking background, including a series of articles about S.C., I was asked if I would teach the introductory psychology of education class—which contained more than 300 students each semester in those days.

The work I had done on S.C. involved writing an article for the Centre's journal, *Systematics*, an account about how it could be used in teaching history. In writing this, it became clear to me that the kind of history that children could make sense of at different stages of their learning was quite different. Much of what I read simply seemed to think that children's grasp of history just became a bit more sophisticated each year. The one bright exception to this way of thinking came along with the rise in influence of Jean Piaget's theory of children's intellectual development.

This is one of those sad stories of initial love, gradually fading as you get to know the love-object better, until you finally feel cheated and repelled. Well, that maybe puts it a bit extremely. But I was cheerfully teaching my students about Piaget's theory, amongst much else, and also reading everything that I could find about applying Piaget's ideas to history. The problem in all this was that the theory and what I was reading about applying it to history seemed unconnected with my limited knowledge of students learning history, and certainly with my own experience. Quite soon I became skeptical of what I was teaching about Piaget, and then skeptical about the contents of most of the rest of the course. I began writing some articles about history, building on the model I had articulated years before for *Systematics* and also developed in my Ph.D. thesis on the move from myth to historiography in the ancient "near-east." In my Ph.D. thesis I had laid out distinctive steps in the move from mythic to historical references to the past, and then began to see how these seemed a better mirror of students' development of historical understanding than I was able to find in the Piagetian literature.

On my first sabbatical I decided I should try to gather all these ideas together and write a book. My wife had an office close to our house at the University of British Columbia, with a fabulous view up Howe Sound into the mountains beyond. I went with her to this office quite frequently. I recall sitting at a small desk at the back of the office, looking out over this stunning landscape, with a ballpoint pen in hand and a sheaf of blank yellow sheets of paper in front of me. I had a choice. I could write the book on the way historical understanding can best grow in the mind or I could generalize the theory I was developing beyond history to an attempt to articulate a quite different way of characterizing individual development in education. I wrote "Educational Development," then my name on the top sheet, and started scribbling.

I wasn't very clear at all about what I was doing, and I think that shows in the book that resulted, and a number of books I have written since. That is, it seemed clear to me that the categories in which education was generally articulated by those who participated professionally in the system failed to capture some of the most important features of being and becoming educated. What I had set about to do, in a clumsy and largely unconscious way, was to try to reformulate the categories in terms of which we might better grasp the experience of education. Yes, I know this is grotesquely pretentious, but what less is worth doing? So I tried to describe a process of education using such categories as "mythic" and "romantic" and others derived from my studies of Frye and anthropology and all the other things that floated by at Cornell and since. Within these categories I was trying to focus on smaller scale features of educational experience, and teaching and learning, and so came up with such categories as "the story", "binary opposites," "association with the heroic," and so on.

Most of the categories used to discuss education come from either psychology or philosophy, and they are categories shaped in and useful for psychological and philosophical concerns. It seemed to me that these were largely deforming education as a field of study. Maybe it isn't appropriate here to indicate that I concluded fairly early in my career that "philosophy of education" and "psychology of education" and "sociology of education" were more about the terms that proceeded the "of" in each case and not much help to the poor "education" that followed. The kinds of categories I began to work with were composed of a psychological component, an epistemological component and an emotional component—all bound up together. So my enterprise looked a bit exotic to those trained in the normal professional schools in North America. It just didn't fit, even when some of it made sense, or had powerfully positive effects in classrooms.

Categories like story, the heroic, binary opposites, jokes, the extremes of experience and the limits of reality, and, indeed, the exotic, were not familiar parts of the professional vocabularies of most educators—though "story" has become increasingly commonly used of late. Articulating a theory of education made of such "cognitive tools" and building a theory about how education can be best understood as an accumulation of a set of culturally shaped "kinds of understanding," with names such as somatic, mythic, romantic, philosophic, and ironic, was not a strategy that would sensibly be recommended to anyone trying to make a career in Education in North America in the late 20th Century.

But by chance the resulting manuscript caught the attention of an editor at Oxford University Press, and they published it. It might be all nonsense, I thought, but if it's been published by OUP it's clearly a better class of nonsense.

I was still trying to clarify what I felt was wrong with the terms in which most people in the education business talked about and thought about what they were doing. I was particularly exercised about what increasingly seemed to me the malign influence of educational psychology over the practice and thinking about education—I was also working in a teacher education program during this period. Wittgenstein seemed to sum up exactly what seemed to me especially true about educational psychology: "The existence of the experimental method makes us think we have the means of solving the problems which trouble us; though problem and method pass one another by" (Wittgenstein 1963, 232).

Lev Vygotsky (1997) made an argument similar to Wittgenstein's, which also helped me understand why so much of the work that was based on psychological theories seemed to have so little purchase on educational phenomena:

A concept that is used deliberately, not blindly, in the science for which it was created, where it originated, developed and was carried to it ultimate expression, is *blind*, leads nowhere, when transposed to another science. Such blind transpositions, of the biogenetic principle, the experimental and mathematical method from the natural sciences, created the appearance of science in psychology which in reality concealed a total impotence in the face of studied facts. (p. 280)

While that may seem an overwrought judgment about psychology in general, it captured what was bothering me about psychology's contributions to basic educational concepts, such as "learning" and "development." What was of educational importance about these concepts was lost in translation or transposition.

So I wrote the second book mentioned above. You can imagine how many friends *Education and Psychology* made me. The main thesis of the book was that no psychological theory has any implications for education. Yes, I know again— it's so patently absurd no one could take it seriously. The book suffered many reviews, some spluttering in indignation, but—no doubt my purblind idiocy—none of them seemed to take on the argument and refute it. There were some good criticisms of parts of it—particularly of my simplistic deformation of Plato's ideas into a "developmental theory," and the book is a bit of a mess. It began as an attempt to write a new kind of, and more interesting, book about "development" for education. But once I got to the chapter on Piaget, I criticized it extensively and intensively. So extensively that there really wasn't space to set about the other theories I had planned to deal with. So I made it into a book about educational theories and why psychological theories didn't fit the bill. Most of the criticisms simply asserted that I didn't understand Piaget's theory, but none of them took on any particular argument. Maybe they are right and it would have taken more of their time than it merited.

One of the central arguments of the book was that empirical research in education systematically confused two things, which I called, drawing on Jan Smedslund's work (1978), an empirical component and an analytic component. Hard to convey the argument briefly, but I was impressed by Smedslund's critique of much psychological and sociological research and, it seemed to me, it was even more impressive when addressed to educational research. Much of the difficulty of educational research--and the obvious fact we are not supposed to mention out loud that after a century of it we have yet to see any of the dramatic improvements in education that bringing "science" to its aid were supposed to deliver--is due, again, I thought, to the inadequacy of the concepts we use to think about it, derived as they are from different areas of study. Typical educational research might seek to establish an empirical connection between two independent things, like, say, the degree of order in a list and the ease with which we can memorize it. The problem with such research, and it is evident very generally, is that such studies have built into them a conceptual confusion. The independent things are never conceptually independent in fact—in this case what we find easy to memorize is clearly connected with whatever it is that makes us think of some lists as more or less ordered. So before doing our study, we are guaranteed a positive correlation. But there will also innumerable arbitrary elements that ensure that one subject finds some things easier to remember than others (if the list is of numbers and one of them is that person's telephone number, for example). The problem is that the analytic elements generalize absolutely and the arbitrary elements can't be generalized at all. By confusing the two, it looks as if we are asking a genuine empirical question and coming up with a correlation established by research between the two independent items.

The book included a number of other criticisms of current educational research as a doomed enterprise, but how could so many people be wrong for so long? Obviously my arguments could be dismissed on this ground alone. I was bemused by the response to Smedslund's work. It seemed to me that he effectively demolished a lot of the "self-efficacy" research in psychology. One of the main proponents of that work, Bandura, wrote (1978) what seemed to me an ineffectual response to Smedslund's critique. When I asked colleagues who worked in this area whether they not perturbed by Smedslund's critique, they said they were not bothered by it because it had been refuted by Bandura. (It's not that there is anything wrong with the claims of the self-efficacy research; it's just that you don't need to do the research to get to the analytic truths embedded in the research program. It's doing conceptual analysis the hard way.)

Writing critical books in education doesn't seem to get one anywhere. The book sold moderately well, but I concluded I was wasting my time making arguments that no one was really interested in thinking about and certainly had no impact on the people who made decisions about education or actually taught students. I thought I'd be better off working out my own positive theory and also writing shorter books that showed how it might be used in practice. So I wrote two theoretical books, one called *Primary Understanding* and the other *Romantic Understanding*. Both were published by Routledge. I was then going to go on and write *Philosophic Understanding* and *Ironic Understanding*, the main categories of the general theory I was trying to work out.

In *Primary Understanding* I tried to work out in much more detail the basis for my "cultural recapitulation" theory of education. I tried to show how one could make better sense of the enterprise of early education by focusing on the set of "cognitive tools" that came along with an oral language—such as story, forming images from words, binary oppositions, metaphor, rhythm and pattern, jokes, a sense of mystery, and so on—and showing how these provided the best grappling tools to knowledge available to children. I showed how such a view led to a distinctive set of procedures for teaching young children, and designed planning frameworks teachers could use, and also outlined the kind of curriculum this theory implied.

"Cognitive tools" isn't an ideal term by any means. One colleague prefers "tools of imaginative engagement," which is better but is also not ideal. I use the former in deference to Vygotky's use of the term, though the kind of category I have focused on is rather different from those identified by Vygotsky in his use of the term—in particular, that emotional component was not evident in the examples of tools that he identified.

Primary Understanding won the Grawemeyer Award, which helped sell a few copies—but not that many. There are five Grawemeyer Awards offered each year in various academic areas. They were intended to be equivalent to the Nobel prizes for areas not recognized by the Nobel prizes. Each year the musical composition Grawemeyer award is treated to a large spread in major papers, and it is a cause of national celebration for the winner's country. Hardly anyone in education even knows about the award, and the press is wholly unconcerned about the Education winner. This says something about the esteem of Education as a field of study. As Howard Gardner and I were among the first winners in North America, he suggested we should inaugurate a dinner to be held each year during AERA, which would accumulate by one person each year. This was a delightful occasion for a number of years, but then became unwieldy as the numbers exceeded a dozen. One year we went around the table discussing how easy or otherwise it was to get published the books that won the award. You would have heard of most of these books, and many are continuing strong sellers. The first person said 12 publishers had turned down her ms. before one accepted it. Everyone had a similar tale to tell. These were among the most successful people in Education in the country. We moved on to AERA proposals, and the same tale was told, even by the most famous and celebrated among the group. I had a sense of utter arbitrariness in judgments in Education. Indeed, one of the smaller pleasures now are the deferential letters from editors wondering whether I might be willing to scribble something for their journals which a few years ago were derisively rejecting the articles I had submitted to them.

Romantic Understanding—hardly a good title—sold copies to my university library, maybe my mother, but hardly anyone else. It had done much the same kind of job as the earlier book, in showing how literacy was a technology that could shape our understanding in complex ways. I tried to articulate a similar set of psychological, epistemological, and emotional categories to capture what literacy can do for us intellectually. It's not that literacy has these effects willy-nilly, but that a program of teaching and a particular curriculum can bring out the best uses of literacy in developing human minds. That was the theme of the book.

At the same time I wrote, in just over a month, a little "practical" book derived from *Primary Understanding*, called *Teaching as story telling*. It appeared first in Canada in 1986, and in the US and Britain in 1989, and has been translated into at least half a dozen languages, with some more coming in the next few years. It sold more than all my other books combined, multiplied by the number you first thought of, and continues to sell. A similar book derived from *Romantic Understanding* was called *Imagination in teaching and learning: The middle school years*. It has similarly sold very well and enjoyed some translations.

As I wrote the four books mentioned above, I was getting a clearer sense of what I was trying to do, a clearer understanding of how to articulate the sense of education that I had been groping towards. So instead of going on to write the further two volumes I had planned, and which no one would have read, I decided to try to more compactly describe the whole theory and indicate how it also had distinct implications for the way teachers should present knowledge to students at different stages of their education, and how the curriculum should be changed to accommodate to this conception of education. I had also become more familiar with Vygotsky's work during the previous few years, and some of his ideas helped me articulate some features of the theory better.

The result was a book called *The Educated Mind: How cognitive tools shape our understanding*. By chance it received a good full-page review in *The New York Times Book Review*, and, significantly as a result of this, it sold very widely, received many other reviews, has been translated into seven or eight languages, with new translation requests occurring every now and then.

This book provides the best worked out articulation of the overall theory. It tries to show how education can best be described as a series of kinds of understanding developed in our cultural history and accessible to people today. I showed how we can characterize these kinds of understanding, drawing fairly heavily on anthropological ideas, on cultural history, and on analyses of language in its various forms, culminating in a complex conception of irony, which serves as a kind of modulator of the other kinds of understanding we have access to. The book is presented as a new way to think about education. Most people in education today say that they are looking for new ideas, but it has been my observation that most people welcome a new idea with about the same enthusiasm as a crack about the head with a two-by-four. What most people mean is that they want to see new formulations of the ideas they already hold.

The concluding two chapters concern the implications of the theory for teaching and the curriculum. There was to have been a third on the institution of the school itself, but I was tired, and there seemed too much to say, so I decided I'd make that another book. The second book hasn't yet appeared; it is written and contracted with Yale University Press, and should appear soon. But I got into a mess writing it, and became too interested in the role of Herbert Spencer in influencing the school as we know it. I had to do some surgery to cut the Spencer stuff out of the book I had set about writing, and the Spencer book was published separately by Yale University Press as *Getting it wrong from the beginning: Herbert Spencer, John Dewey, and Jean Piaget*.

I did also want to keep developing ideas for how these ideas can be put into practice, so wrote a couple of books designed mainly for teachers: *An imaginative approach to teaching*, and *Teaching literacy*. I think educational philosophy can too easily become a rather idle activity. The usual criticism of the analytic tradition tended to be along the lines of: "Well, now you've got clarity—so what do you do with it?" I have also formed a research group, whose main activities include developing the theory and also developing materials for teachers to enable them to use the practical implications in their classrooms. We have a number of publications, research projects, and an intergalactic network in formation (www.ierg.net).

Theory generating seems to me a wholly neglected activity in philosophy of education. And even more neglected is working out the practical implications of one's theorizing. If one is trying to sort something out about education, the results of one's work must be able to impact the actual education of children. I do have colleagues who feel that their job is done when they finish their theorizing. I sometimes unkindly ask them who they think is going to come along and do the heavy lifting now that they've done their work. The answer for pretty well all educational theorists, of course, is "No one."

So the work I have tried to do is generate a theory of education that best expresses my sense of what the enterprise is about, defend it against the kind of dominant discourse that it is currently incompatible with, show why that incompatibility redounds to the disfavor of the dominant discourse, and then show that in practice the theory I have articulated works and works better than pretty well everything else that is being done to children in the name of education. Again, no point trying to do less, eh? I have mentioned "scribbling" away and gradually moving towards articulating an idea of education that seems in some sense to have been there from the beginning. Where do such ideas come from?—Philip Larkin asked, and replied "beats me" (Larkin, "Dockery and son," from *The Whitsun Weddings*, 1964). It has been a generally pleasant occupation, facing the blank pages and trying to fill them with something closer to some image that resides somewhere in one's consciousness. It sometimes seems as though that image just came with one into consciousness, but no doubt it was shaped by endless others' scribbling in the past and one's experience, and the hard part of the scribbling is trying to be honest to this flickering and shifting image, and recognizing, ironically, that the words in which we try to capture our ideas are always inadequate to the image they seek to lay out on the blank pages.

REFERENCES

Bandura, A. (1978). On distinguishing between logical and empirical verification. *Scandinavian Journal of Psychology*, *19*, 97-99.

Egan, K. (1979). *Educational development*. New York: Oxford University Press.

Egan, K. (1983). *Education and psychology: Plato, Piaget, and scientific psychology*. New York: Teachers College Press, 1983; London: Methuen, 1984.

Egan, K. (1986). *Teaching as story telling*. London, Ontario: The Althouse Press, 1986; London: Routledge, 1989; Chicago: University of Chicago Press, 1989; Lisbon: Dom Quixote. 1994; Madrid: Ediciones Morata & el Ministerio de Educación y Ciencia. 1994; Stockholm: Runa Forlag. 1995; Oslo: Ad Notam Gyldendal, 1996.

Egan, K. (1997). *The educated mind: How cognitive tools shape our understanding*. Chicago: University of Chicago Press, Rio de Janeiro: Editora Bertrand Brasil, 2002; Barcelona & Buenos Aires: Ediciones Paidos, 2000; Copenhagen: Gyldandal, 2003; Stockholm: Bokförlaget Daidalos, 2005; Athens: Atrapos, 2006; Professia: St. Petersburg, 2006; Tel Aviv: Sifriat Poalim, 2007; Korean and Romanian, in press.

Egan, K. (2002). *Getting it wrong from the beginning: Our progressivist inheritance from Herbert Spencer, John Dewey, and Jean Piaget*. New Haven: Yale University Press.

Egan, K. (2005). *An imaginative approach to teaching*. San Francisco: JosseyBass.

Egan, K. (2006). *Teaching Literacy: engaging the imaginations of new readers and writers*. Thousand Oaks, CA: Corwin Press

Smedslund, Jan. (1978). Bandura's theory of self-efficacy: A set of common-sense theorums. *Scadinavian Journal of Psychology, 18*, 1-14.

Vygotsky, L. S. (1997). *The collected works of L. S. Vygotsky*. Rieber, R. W. & Wollock, J. (Eds.) (vol. 3). New York: Plenum.

Wittgenstein, L. (1963). *Philosophical investigations* (G. E. M. Anscombe, Trans.). Oxford: Blackwell.

Kieran Egan
Simon Fraser University

WALTER FEINBERG

THE CONSTRUCTION OF A SOCIAL PHILOSOPHER OF EDUCATION

INTRODUCTION

At the time that I entered Boston University (BU) as an undergraduate in the late 1950s, all juniors in the liberal arts college were required to take two semesters of philosophy, and I selected a course from Peter Bertocci who had a reputation as a stimulating demanding teacher. Bertocci was an exciting undergraduate lecturer and addressed issues that I had privately pondered without guidance in high school about the character of truth, and the difference between truth and illusion, about the nature of the good life and the "real" meaning of success, about the existence of God in a world where evil can thrive. By the time I decided to major in philosophy the Department was expanding its orientation beyond its original Personalism, which developed out of the Methodist tradition, and now included in addition to Personalists, Marxists, Pragmatists, Existentialists and Positivists.

BU had traditionally been strong in the history of philosophy and philosophy of religion, and during the 1950s professors like Peter Bertocci, John Lavely and Richard Millard joined with Professors in the College if Education to develop a role for the Department in philosophy of education. They secured funds from the Federal Government for graduate students in philosophy who wished to focus some of their work on education. I had been dissatisfied with my own high school education, feeling that it emphasized the importance of grades and getting into the right college to the neglect of something deeper, and I was pleased when I was offered one of the three Fellowships.

LEARNING TO BE A PHILOSOPHER

In graduate school I learned how to address the questions of others and began to take small steps towards formulating my own questions by interrogating the arguments of established philosophers. We were taught that an internal criticism— one that took an argument on "its" own terms—had priority over an external one—a criticism that took an argument on "our" own terms. I do not recall being told really why this insistence, nor do I recall questioning the assumed boundaries between external and internal, or the relative authority this gave to the text over the reader—all considerations that might be raised today. Nevertheless the priority was an important component of our training and it communicated a deep respect for the works of historical and contemporary thinkers. It required that we hard work to suspend our own perspectives and initial judgments as we tried to enter into the systematic thought of philosophers.

L.J. Waks (ed.), Leaders in Philosophy of Education: Intellectual Self Portraits, 63–80.

PERSONAL FAVORITES

Reason and Rhetoric (1974)
Understanding Education: Toward a Reconstruction of Educational Inquiry (1982)
Japan and the Pursuit of A New American Identity: Work and Education in a Multicultural Age (1993)
On Higher Ground: Education and the Case for Affirmative Action (1998)
Common Schools/Uncommon Identities: National Unity and Cultural Difference (1998)
For Goodness Sake: Religious Schools and Education for Democratic Citizenry (2006)
Liberalism and the Dilemma of Public Education in Multicultural Societies (with K. McDonough) (2003)

INFLUENTIAL WORKS BY OTHERS

Callan, E. *Creating Citizens* Oxford University Press, 1997
Dewey, J. *Democracy and Education*
Freire, P. *Pedagogy of the Oppressed*
Glover, *Humanity: A Moral History of the Twentieth Century* Yale University Press, 2000
Habermas,J. *Knowledge and Human Interest*
Hegel, G. *The Philosophy of Right*
Kymlicka, W. *Liberalism, Community and Culture* Oxford University Press, 1991
MacIntyre, A. *After Virtue*
Peters, R. S. *Ethics and Education*
Rawls, J. *A Theory of Justice*

This training was not much different than that of many others who graduated with a Ph.D. from philosophy departments in the US in the mid 1960s in philosophy, but it was very different from much of the work that I saw in the College of Education, where certain views were taken as definitive, and others judged by how well they measured up to an assumed standard. Ironically much of Dewey's writings seemed to me to be used in this way, and I had trouble with a couple of the instructors in the College of Education when they took offence when I challenged aspects of Dewey's work. Sadly the philosopher of openness had become for some the prince of dogma and the "anti-dogmatism" that Dewey advanced took on a dogmatic quality.

There were also gaps in the BU philosophy curriculum, and some important works in modern philosophy were slighted. For example, while I had seminars in Quine, Whitehead, Hegel, Alexander, and Bergson along with the rationalists, and empiricists, BU did not offer a seminar in Wittgenstein or Austin and it had very limited offerings in the growing area of conceptual analysis. Moreover, while we were expected to cut our philosophical teeth by close textual readings of the "historical" greats, there was little opportunity to explore some of the contemporary issues, or the concepts used to describe them. Hence while I was trained well as expositor and critic I was not encouraged to explore issues of the day philosophically.

For example, while the Free Speech Movement was beginning, and while the civil rights marches had already begun, there were no seminars exploring issues of speech, even as it was developed by Austin, and the idea of a philosophical seminar examining issues of race was unheard of—even though BU's now most famous alumni, Martin Luther King, was then leading the Civil Rights movement.

I was fortunate that later in my graduate career I received a Fellowship in the interdisciplinary Human Relations Center where, under the leadership of Kenneth Benne, a prominent philosopher of education who had studied under Dewey, many of these issues were topics of consideration. Ironically, the one issue that concerned Benne most directly—homosexuality-- remained unspoken until decades later, but at the time, no one asked and he didn't tell.

At that time the distinction that is now common between teaching and research universities was less developed. However, if there had been such a classification BU would have been viewed as a teaching university. The Graduate Program in philosophy stressed teaching and every Ph.D. student was expected to take one course in teaching philosophy before completion. And, while I thought it might be nice to publish something at some later time in my career, my efforts and my thoughts were focused on studying philosophy in order to teach it at the college level. The emphasis on teaching was reinforced by the message that we earned the right to criticize a position only after we had represented it fairly. The ideal was to present an argument even better than the original, and some like Richard Millard did a masterful job of advancing different position over the students' attempts to puncture them.

Graduate seminars involved explication and critique with students sparing with the professor over the internal coherence of the text. For me the pedagogy served three purposes. First, it provided a first hand understanding of significant texts and a familiarity with the complex structure of a philosophical argument. Second, it helped to hone my own critical skills, and to gain some ability to address arguments on their own terms and third, as my own skills developed, I began to overcome my own painful shyness, and to develop a higher level of self-esteem. Self-esteem, not to be confused with over-confidence, is critical to any intellectual work. It is the sense that you have the capacity to improve on your latest effort and that a single mistake is not a sign of an inability to improve. Because self-esteem requires the ability to recognize one's own errors, it is very different from over-confidence in which errors are overlooked or their significance minimized.

However, the pedagogy requires a shared understanding that critique and argument are not intended to diminish students, but to engage them in an intellectual quest. Many philosophy students do understand this, but as I was to learn when I began to teach in schools of education, where a kinder, gentler climate seemed to prevail, it is not universal and should not be taken for granted, and if this shared understanding is not present, blunt critique can be counter productive.

The pedagogy was limited from another standpoint. It was, in education jargon, heavily teacher-centered with the instructor explicating the texts, the students raising issues and the instructor responding to further explicate or defend the text. Hence discourse flowed from text to teacher to student to text, to teacher, to another student, etc. It rarely, if ever, flowed from student to student or from student to text to student. The method was Socratic in more ways than one. The student dialogued with the teacher (Socrates) but only the teacher was acknowledged as the repository of Wisdom. When I began teaching I found this to be a foreign approach for many students in education, and needed to adjust my pedagogy considerably.

The pedagogical style of the philosophy department was complemented by a friendly, but formal ambience. I do not recall ever passing a philosophy professor without being pleasantly greeted, but greetings were formal, Mr. Feinberg, Dr. Millard, or Professor Lavely, etc. (While the faculty at B.U. had hired one woman just before I left, it was, like most philosophy departments, dominated by white men, although there were some outstanding women graduate students.) The Human Relations Center, which I will discuss shortly, was governed by a very different pedagogy and a much more informal ambiance.

During my senior year, I took a course with Marx Wartofsky in American philosophy. Wartofsky, a Marxist and a Jew could not find an academic job after graduating from Columbia in the early 1950s because of the Red Scare, until he was hired by the then President of BU, a Methodist minister, Harold C. Case. Wartofsky was an enormously talented person, an accomplished violinist who spoke a number of languages and had worked as a machinist while biding his time during the McCarthy era. Given my own background—Jewish with both parents originally from New York—and given that my own political socialization began in grade school when my mother's cousin, James Wechsler, the editor of the then liberal New Your Post, was interrogated on Television by Senator McCarthy, it was easy to relate to Wartofsky

I had entered Boston University with a vague idea of attending law school as one way to effect social change. While I hardly knew James Wechsler, his experience before the McCarthy Committee, together with the army McCarthy hearings were for me lessons in the abuse of power. I followed the hearings intensely, began to buy the Post when I could get a hold of it at the newsstand at Harvard Square, read the editorial pages and, mostly left, columnists. While I was still in public school I had ordered the record of these hearing and tried to figure out the subtleties of certain remarks or innuendoes.

My encounter with Wartofsky, and later Kenneth Benne a professor in philosophy of education, suggested that I might be able to pursue both my interests in philosophy and my interests in social change together. Both had come to BU under unusual circumstances. As I mentioned Wartofsky had been hired by Case after his black listing from other Universities for his earlier political activities while Benne had been fired from University of Illinois after he was outed as a homosexual and then hired by BU. When he came to BU he was ill and stayed with Case until he recovered.

Benne was an amazingly creative and energetic man who used his training in philosophy of education and pragmatism to inform his pioneering work on organizations and small groups. Likely without McCarthy witch hunts, Wartofsky would have remained in New York, teaching at Columbia, NYU or CUNY, where he went after retiring from BU and if it were not for the homophobia in Champaign/Urbana, Benne, who Dewey in his letter of recommendation to Illinois[i] described as the most talented graduate student he had had in decades, would have remained at Illinois to help develop what at the time was fast becoming the most prominent philosophy of education program in the country. Ironically, because of the courage and integrity of President Case, I was the beneficiary of two witch-hunts. After the three years I was given a fellowship in the Human Relations Center to work with Benne.

B.U. was always seen as a poor relation to its counterpart across the Charles, but it is somewhat ironic that while Harvard, the bastion of liberalism, was hiring "the best and the brightest"—Kissinger, Bundy, the architects of Vietnam, the Methodist Minister who served as President of B.U., was hiring, much to my later educational benefit, homosexuals and Marxists, as well as renegades from Soviet oppression in Eastern Europe. (Wartofsky once told me that in his job interview Case asked him to tell him *everything* about his political activities. When he was finished Case thanked him and explained that he wanted this information so that if he were ever asked whether he knew of Wartofsky's past when he hired him, he could answer that he did.)

Although Wartofsky kept his politics out of his teaching much in the same way most of the B.U. Personalists left their own religious views out of the classroom, I began to get the idea that philosophy might be more than an intellectual exercise and might well have a role to play in improving people's lives.

The rich mix in the philosophy department, Personalists, Existentialist, Pragmatist, positivists, and Marxist was the result of the academic openness of Case and of those Personalists in the Philosophy Department who had followed its founder, Borden Parker Bowne (1847-1910), in their willingness to entertain unpopular views. (At one point Bowne was the object of a heresy trial by the Methodist Church.) Sadly, after I left and after the University hired its first non-Methodist Presidents and later, with philosopher John Silver as President, this climate of openness was severely strained.

Having been socialized into this formal atmosphere of the Philosophy Department, the informal ambience of the Human Relations Center was very disconcerting. Here everyone regardless of rank--students, secretaries and faculty--was called by their first name. It took a considerable amount of time before I could call "Dr. Benne" by his first name and he never suggested that I do so. However, that was the norm and so I went out of my way to avoid calling him anything for a year or so, but later I conformed to this non- conformist climate and called him Ken. The pedagogy practiced in the Human Relations Center was also a stark contrast to that in the philosophy department. Instead of the professors occupying center-stage, here they faded into the background as students engaged with one another. The object of study was the interactions of the group and too much intervention on the part of the professor would interfere with the dynamics of the group.

I still maintained formality when in the philosophy Department until the day I received my Ph.D. when I also received a license to call my philosophy professors, Peter, Dick, John and Marx. I now understand that the difference in ambience is more than simply a matter of personality, although it was that as well. It was related to the different ideas about the purpose of education and the role of scholarship in the two fields. Although I tend toward the informal with my students, I have come to appreciate (or perhaps overly romanticize) the way the use of formal titles can enable work to continue with students and colleagues alike even when personal relations get bumpy. Nevertheless, I have come to prefer the style of the Human Relations Center, not that of the Philosophy Department. However, it is often useful for me to recall just how difficult it was to enter into an informal mode with my professors, especially when I am working with more traditional students from Korea or Japan. There is a lot more that could be said about each of the two "styles" and the assumptions about the goals of education and the understanding of autonomy that they rest on, but for a student studying philosophy of education it was useful to experience them both.

The Human Relations Center was involved in applied social science research about organizational change. Among its major activity was the running of T-groups, a practice modelled after the work of Kurt Lewin and pioneered by Benne and a few others. The T-group was supposed to be a laboratory in human relations and democratic leadership where the facilitators, as they were called, took a non-directive role and created opportunities for members of the group to reflect upon the dynamics and interactions among them. The members of the groups came from a variety of backgrounds, business, education, religion, but almost all were liberal in their orientation.

While I had reservations about the philosophy behind the T group idea, and questioned whether it could work under conditions of unequal power, I found the groups personally rewarding. They provided insight into some of my own characteristic ways of responding in group settings and provoked certain adjustments. For example, I tended to hesitate or not to advance a hunch for fear of being wrong. Part of this came about because of family history where "mistakes" could be lamented for a lifetime, but part came from the philosopher's caution to get the argument right. The T group ideal is that truth is approximated best through engagement and dialogue, and that hunches need to be expressed if the idea is to work. This is especially true when many of those hunches involve the meaning of the gestures, involuntary expressions, postures or ideas. The same situation may also apply in schools and classrooms where the written text delivers only part of the picture.

The two fields served different needs, but both were important in my development. Philosophy--austere, distant, rational, systematic, and intellectual-- was useful for a young scholar trying to hone his analytical skills and gain intellectual confidence. The Human Relations Center with its commitment to social justice and its direct involvement in schools, churches and the civil rights movement, and the discourse that it encouraged across disciplines, grounded my studies in philosophy and provided a practical outlet for it.

By the time I entered the Human Relations Center, I had written a Masters' thesis on Hegel's concept of property.[ii] The thesis was an examination of the nation state as an institution for liberal ideals. At the time, the status of German philosophy in the United States was very low, and Hegel was completely out of fashion in most high prestige departments. One reason was that a stigma on anything German carried over from the War Years, but another was the growing influence of analytic philosophers who disparaged the German system builders as obtuse, meaningless and philosophically irrelevant. Wartofsky, along with the Personalists went against this trend and, for different reasons, had a deep interest in German philosophy. Thus both encouraged this project.

When a draft of the thesis was completed, Wartofsky returned it unmarked, except for three words pencilled in red at the end—"opaque, turgid and completely incomprehensible". Even though it was a thesis on Hegel, himself, pretty opaque, turgid and, at times, incomprehensible, coming from Wartofsky these marks were not meant as high praise. (Thirty-five years later I though of the perfect come back—"Come now Marx, surely you must know that if it is opaque it cannot be *completely* incomprehensible". Yet by that time he had passed away.)

Since this was also a time when my father became sick and had to give up his small store, I questioned whether I should continue in graduate school, but having few options stayed and spent the summer rewriting the thesis. When it was finished Wartofsky sent it over to his former teacher, Herbert Marcuse, then at Brandeis, who asked to see me and praised the work very generously. The visit was short, but very important and helped validate my growing sense of competence. I have shared Wartofsky's response to the draft thesis with my own graduate students when they get discouraged about their progress hoping that it can help them understand graduate education is a process where honest but painful criticism serves a productive role. I try to be careful, however, to make my own criticisms less caustic and more detailed than Marx's had been, and rarely write in red.

The thesis on Hegel helped to shape the issues that would define much of my career. In Hegel's own work, and especially in those who followed him on the left, I began to glimpse a tension in liberal thought between the concern for some kind of national coherence and identity and a concern to allow friction and to acknowledge differences. While Hegel presented this tension in terms of Civil Society, he believed that it was reconciled by the emerging modern state. Some years after my thesis was completed, I began to see the tension in cultural terms and to relate it to problems of schooling in liberal, democratic societies.

In my dissertation,[iii] I attempted to address this problem through a comparison and analysis of the work of a British Hegelian, Bernard Bosanquet and John Dewey. Bosanquet argued that the state is a natural outgrowth of human development and not, as the liberal tradition would have it, the artificial result of a contract that arises out of a state of nature. It should thus not just serve to resolve conflicts, but to harmonize human needs and desires. As such Bosanquet argued that the state is the condition for the ethical fulfilment of the individual.

Although Bosanquet advanced his argument before the Third Reich made a mockery of the idea of the state as the ethical fulfilment of the individual, I thought that there were elements in the argument that were worth salvaging and that Bosanquet could be seen as providing not a political program that would subsume the individual to the state, but rather a standard by which to judge the state where the flourishing of the individual would be a measure of its goodness. Dewey, while much more circumspect about the role of the state shared with Bosanquet a concern to harmonize human interest and desires through voluntary associations. The state was important in constraining the adverse indirect consequences of private acts and, through education, in encouraging the development of new interests and associations. While I thought Dewey's understanding of the state was superior to Bosanquet's because it provided for the development of individual interests and associations, I was critical of his ethical theory and this criticism was to shortly play a large role in both my reassessment of Dewey and of philosophy itself.

EARLY CAREER

When I finished my degree I had a choice of entering a philosophy department or of teaching philosophy of education at Oakland University, in Michigan. I chose Oakland, a new dynamic institution aided in its founding by the cooperation of labor and industry. I felt that it would allow expression to both my philosophical and practical bents. Oakland was founded with the participation of both Walter Ruther, the former Head of the automobile workers and Matilda Wilson, an heiress to the Dodge motor company fortune, and is located just outside of the industrial city of Pontiac. The idea was to provide a first class liberal education for the children of workers and first general college graduates. The appointment came at a time when most intellectuals and many leading politicians believed that education alone could solve the nation's racial problems and lift people out of poverty, and Oakland was an expression of that hope. At Oakland I worked with two colleagues, Henry Rosemont and Marc Briod, to establish a tutorial in the city of Pontiac. The tutorial was one of the few places where students at the University could interact with African American children inner city children. It survived the riots of the late 1960s and was still functioning many years after I left Oakland for Illinois in late 1967.

Very early one Saturday morning toward the end of my first year teaching at Oakland I received a call from the Chairman of the Department of History and Philosophy of Education at the University of Illinois asking if I would be interested in coming there for an interview. Although Illinois had perhaps the most renowned program in the Country, having been socialized in a philosophy department, I knew only two things about the University—that it had fired a biology professor for advocating free love and it had a famous classicist on its faculty who was a member of the John Birch Society and who accused Dwight Eisenhower, a moderate Republican president, of being a front for the Communist party—I was not inclined to go, but I told the Department Head that I would talk to my wife and I asked him to call in a few days. Having lured my wife to the heartland of Michigan, I was uncertain how she would react to the prospect of moving to Champaign/Urbana, cities that as provincial Bostonians, neither of us had heard of before the phone call.

By the time the Chair called back, however, we had spoken to Rosemont, who had been an undergraduate at the University of Illinois, and he advised me to accept their invitation for an interview. I spent a day on Campus, much impressed by its quad, the fantastic library, and many of the people that I met, and at the end of the visit I was offered the position and a couple of weeks later, I accepted it.

Graduate Students and Faculty today would see this entire procedure as odd and much of it would now be illegal. I never applied for the position, I had not published, and I was not asked to teach a sample class or to give a paper. Although the actual reason Illinois approached me is unclear, it is likely that Ken Benne or Richard Millard, my undergraduate honours advisor, both of whom had close friends in the Department, had been asked to recommend someone, and that they recommended me. Often when the issue of affirmative action comes up today in my class I used this experience to shock some students into an awareness of just what white privilege meant, how invisible it can be and how much it can be taken for granted. Given that by and large *only* other white males were in the pipeline, it is almost impossible to tell what a truly open search might have secured.

THE UNIVERSITY OF ILLINOIS

During my first year at The University of Illinois, Martin Luther King was assassinated, and race dominated the discussions in my class. Two events stand out. The news of King's assassination came as I was teaching an evening course and many in the class were stunned, but one older white student muttered to me after I dismissed the class: "he got what he was asking for!" The other event involved an African American who, a couple of years after the assassination, had been appointed as the first Black Principal of one of the elementary schools in the area, and told me that in his desk was a bible that had been donated by the KKK in 1948. Even though Boston had lots of racial tension, especially around bussing, I was still stunned to confront these issues in such a direct and raw way.

One of the things that is difficult to comprehend these days is the fact that there were almost no African American students on Campus, and also just how much that absence was taken for granted on the even the most liberal of Northern Campuses. People who would decry forced segregation in the South often did not even take note of the absence of Black students at their own universities. At Oakland we thought we were doing a good deed by bringing white Oakland students into the inner city and not until our Christmas party did it hit me that all of the tutors were white and all of their pupils were Black. When I arrived at Illinois there were more students from Taiwan on Campus then there were African Americans. Moreover, there was not one Black faculty member in the Education College, and I believe that there were only two in the entire university. There were, however, at least two graduate students, one of whom, James Anderson is now my Department Head and another, who came a few years later, Mildred Griggs, recently served the College as its Dean. However, at the time few seemed to notice this absence or see it as a problem.

Protest and Change

As a consequence of the assassination and the riots that followed, the University agreed to admit 500 additional Black students by the fall. I proposed to my College that we develop a consciously integrated "Alternative Teacher Education" program (ATEP) that provided students with small seminars and coordinated their freshman courses together with an early in-school experience. In ATEP we worked with students to accommodating them to the requirements of the University while we introduced them to the world of schools. The program was organized around small seminars. The instructors worked on reading and writing skills and connected the student's assignments to their classroom observation in the public school. Of the 500 Black students admitted to the different programs in the University, the retention and graduation rate among the hundred or so students in this program was by far the highest.

Scholarship and Research

During my involvement with ATEP I began to do the research for my first book, *Reason and Rhetoric*[iv]. At first I saw this work as paralleling the work in my dissertation and drawing on the largely philosophical concerns that were addressed there. My dissertation focused strictly on philosophical texts, exploring as good philosophy gradate students might, the meanings, arguments, ambiguities and contradictions that I found in Dewey and Bosanquet. However, I also later read a report Dewey had written during World War One and submitted to the War Department on the Polish community in Philadelphia.[v] The report, marked confidential questioned the loyalty of the leaders of the community and suggested that the government keep a close surveillance on them, proposing such illiberal ideas as government infiltration of their membership. I was both bothered and puzzled that until this time the study had been overlooked by virtually every Dewey scholar, including me, and this was so even though it was described in the then most authoritative bibliography of Dewey's works[vi]. I also began to see this event in light of the more abstract criticism that I had made of the conflict between intelligence and community in Dewey's ethical theory[vii].

   In reflecting on my oversight, and why I had not given more significance to this episode earlier, I began to question aspects of my philosophical training, and some of the pedagogical assumption it entailed. For example, close textual reading, exposition and internal criticism assumes that meaning of the text remains stable over time. Yet in the case of my reading of Dewey, subsequent historical events and understandings began to influence what to count as the "meaning" of the text? The war in Vietnam certainly influenced the fact that the Polish Study came into focus as part of the Dewey canon and this in turn illuminated parts of his other works. While writing my dissertation, I was largely interested in the *philosophical* works of Dewey, and his study of an American Polish Community was not philosophy in the usual sense of that term. It did not lend itself easily to the form of internal criticism I was taught to prize. Yet that internal criticism was important allowing me to see this study as a result of an important ambiguity in his ethical theory. And, it brought many other issues into play—what is the appropriate line between truth and power, scholarship and effectiveness, National unity and cultural identity—themes that would enter into my later work.

Prior to the Vietnam War many on the progressive left were largely unconcerned with cooperation between the university scholar and the National government with many liberals believing that there was a progressive and benign quality to such cooperation. They believed, with some justification, that in many areas, such as Civil Rights, the Federal government must serve a crucial partner in advancing a progressive agenda. I shared this assumption, and thus initially ignored the citation and quite full description of this work that was published in the definitive Dewey bibliography mentioned earlier. Given the assumption about the benign quality of cooperation with the national government I likely dismissed it as rather unremarkable.

Vietnam altered my consciousness, and so Dewey's involvement in this episode took on a larger significance. The change was not in Dewey, however, but in a social norm and in my view about how much citizens ought to trust their government. Dewey rightly held that moral norms are human creations that have proved useful to the evolution of the species, but the Polish study was a dangerous violation of those historical lessons, made easier because of his moral theory was less sensitive than it might have been to the way coordinated government power could be abused in the name of an important cause.

Still, the close reading and internal criticism of Dewey allowed me to view the Polish study in a wider context and to see both benefits and costs of his evolutionary conception of ethics. Dewey's evolutionary view of ethical theory placed the highest value on coordination and cooperation and in his view the Poles were not adequately cooperating in the war effort. Yet the view of ethical development as increased coordination placed pragmatic limits on the development of a moral vision that could have constrained his understanding of the rights of Poles in the United States and his willingness to recommend to the War Department that it intrude on them. The other side of this, however, is that his evolutionary view of ethics does allow for growth and development in our collective moral understanding, and it is this growth that allows us to now reflect back and to question Dewey's engagement with the War Department on ethical grounds.

I became interested in the fact that Dewey scholars, myself included, had ignored this involvement for so long. It was only when Vietnam provoked protests about government and academic co-operation that the spot light focused on his involvement with the Polish Community. Reports of government infiltration of anti-war groups during Vietnam were foreshadowed by Dewey's report to the War Department on the loyalty of Polish American Americans. Certainly Dewey's involvement exemplified my criticism that his moral theory limited the scope of moral vision, but it also eventually led me to see both an evolutionary and a tragic quality to much moral deliberation.

The Vietnam War marked a change in the zeitgeist and in the way the rights of members of minority groups is understood. The melting pot ideal, once the default position of liberal theorists, has given way to a more refined understanding of the significance of cultural identity. And while we can only speculate, I would like to believe that had this understanding been available to Dewey in the way that it is to us that he would have conducted his study more openly and drawn different conclusions. Certainly, as Kevin McDonough and I have pointed out, the philosophy of liberalism has taken a different turn since Dewey's time and is developing more awareness of the importance of cultural factors to individual development, a move which we call affiliational liberalism[viii]. However, if this speculation is correct it also reinforces Dewey's views about the potential evolutionary quality of ethical ideals, and allows that there can be progress in our understanding of social justice.

PHILOSOPHY OF EDUCATION

Unfortunately, and in violation of his own critical spirit, Dewey had become an icon for many educators. His influence on philosophy however had already waned by the 1950s to be replaced by the analytic school and shortly after, a number of American and British educational philosophers began to follow the analytic movement. The model for education was actually laid down by Charles Dunn Hardie in his 1942 book[ix], but Hardie's book came out during the war and did not receive any significant attention in the United States until it was republished in 1960. Hardie applied the then new method of analytic philosophy to education. His concern was not to reform education directly, but to bring clarity to the muddle that he thought often passed as meaningful discourse about education. After the war, this movement was lead by people who were educated in Departments of philosophy and included, among others, Israel Scheffler at Harvard, Richard Peters at the London Institute of Education and Paul Hirst at Cambridge. They were joined by newly minted Ph.D.s in some of the high profile programs in education such as the University of Illinois and Columbia Teacher's College.

This period was marked by considerable collaboration between Departments of philosophy and some of their colleagues in philosophy of education and it was marked by considerable intellectual vitality. New journals were initiated, and bright graduate students were attracted to the field directly out of undergraduate college. The changes were also visible in the Philosophy of Education Society, (PES) where the older ways of classifying philosophies of education—essentialism, pragmatism, perenialism, reconstructionism, etc-- were dismissed by the young Turks as too broad, too vague and too uncritical. Within perhaps ten years the analytic style of doing philosophy came to dominate PES and it remained in control until the early 1980s, when a series of different voices began to be heard and the influence of Marxism, feminism and post structuralism was felt.

While the analytic movement helped establish the academic legitimacy of philosophy of education, the field moved away from the work of schools becoming increasingly distant from the immediate needs of educators. Although I was attracted to its rigor I felt that it failed to explore the larger social context of education and thus had a largely quietist influence on the field. If I had been dissatisfied with the justification that Dewey provided for educational reform believing as I did that it was both theoretically and practically flawed, I was even more dissatisfied with the possibility that the analytic tradition provided. At its best, it seemed to leave everything as is, in the belief that all our problems were the result of linguistic muddles. Caught between a naïve optimistic belief in progress and a similarly naïve linguistic reductionism, philosophy of education seemed paralysed. Some analytic philosophers of education, such as R.S. Peters,[x] tried to smuggle a normative perspective into their analysis of language, (in this case Kant) but Peters' attempt to marry analytic philosophy and Kant was transparent and unsuccessful.

One of the mistakes of the analytic movement was to act as if concepts had an independent existence and that one could thus understand them by mapping out the conceptual terrain in which they are imbedded (as, for example, with the analysis of the concept of indoctrination) or to show how a concept is used given certain conditions (Austin). Missing was a history of the development of the concept itself, and an understanding of how that history influences the debate over education. An example is the concept of "racism". The concept first appeared in the middle part of the twentieth century as an appendage to a Webster dictionary. Yet here its meaning referred largely to the attitudes of people of different white nations towards one another. "Racialism", a rather benign term, was more often used to describe the attitude of whites toward blacks and "racism" had to wait decades before it was fully born, and used to counter the racist reproduction process and the social "scientific" explanations—racial differences in IQ; cultural deficit—that served to reinforce it. The development of the concept of racism, in contrast to the earlier and morally neutral concept, racialism, allowed the discourse to explore institutional patterns rather than just individual attitudes. The analytic movement largely ignored the birth process and took concepts as born fully formed. Yet when the history of a concept is considered educational philosophy can reach beyond itself and engage with concepts developed by other disciplines as they influence the debate about the direction of social reproduction.

I began to develop this insight in my 1982 book, *Understanding Education*[xi] where I argued that educational philosophy had a critical agenda-- to use philosophical analysis to critically examine the educational consequences of the ambiguities and taken for granted normative assumptions of social science and their educational research programs. For example, I analysed the claim "IQ tests measure intelligence" and showed why that claim is ambiguous and how that ambiguity is used to promote a conservative social agenda. In addition, *Understanding Education* offered a positive task for educational philosophy and proposed a conception of educational study where its object would not be reduced to fit into some other field such as psychology or sociology.

I proposed that education as an institutional practice involves the conscious the reproduction of skill clusters, or roles, and forms of inter-subjective understandings. Together these produced a more or less coherent social identity. The role of educational scholarship, as I saw it, was to probe processes of reproduction so that it would be possible to evaluate the hierarchies that resulted in relation to the functions they served or the opportunities that they disregarded. Given this view, then the practice of educating had a normative aim—to enable students to become critically aware of the ways in which skills are clustered and common meanings are produced to shape a shared identity. The practice of educating thus involves not only the reproduction of skills and identities, but also the development of a critical consciousness that should enable students to be mindful of a given social arrangement. The corollary for educational research, as my colleague Eric Bredo and I argued in our *Knowledge and Values in Educational Research*,[xii] was to develop research programs that highlighted these constraints and opportunities and thus fostered critical engagement.

Following the publication of *Understanding Education* I became interested in examining specific instances of social reproduction and as a result in some of my work I began to incorporate observations and interviews as a part of my discussion of social issues. Sometimes I used these interviews to create virtual dialogues between different participants in the social reproduction process. At other times I used them to probe the limits of understanding across cultural and religious boundaries and to probe the appropriate responses to these limits that are available to those who are committed to a liberal conception of justice. Broadly speaking the earlier studies[xiii] focused on inequality and the more recent ones on identity. However, there is no single point where one receded and the other became more dominant and I continue to address issues of equality.[xiv]

The transition from a focus on inequality to a focus on identity came in my study of the relationship between Japanese schools and the practices of Japanese industry. I began the study in response to the claim made in the early 1980s that American schools are responsible for the decline in American industry and in the loss of its competitive edge, especially to Japan. While the claim itself is obviously simplistic (as proof, witness the decade long recession in Japan in the 1990s) it was an occasion to explore just what schools reproduce when they function in radically different societies, such as Japan and the United States. The result was an extended essay on the philosophies of individualism and communitarianism and the way in which they are incorporated into schooling and work in the two countries.[xv]

While I use the term philosophical ethnography[xvi] to describe these studies they are not to be confused with the more descriptively comprehensive studies of anthropology. "Ethnography light" is perhaps a more accurate qualifier. For example, I visited but did not live in Japan; the observations and interviews were not as extensive as they would be if conducted by a professional ethnographer, and they begin not with the question "what is going on here", but rather with a focal concern such as in a recent study of religious schools, *For Goodness Sake*[xvii] — "how do these educators understand the relationship between religious instruction and moral education?" Moreover, the focus is always some normative issue and the immediate object of these ethnographic studies is to engage participants in a philosophical discussion that will illuminate the reasons for their educational decisions, and will probe other possibilities. While the method has its limitations, it is an important tool for philosophers of education to use when appropriate and in this age of social engagement where the idea of a single, hermetically closed thing called "a culture"[xviii] is no longer appropriate and where engagement across different normative frames of social reproduction is increasingly common a philosophical "ethnography light" method will be a needed tool for philosophers of education.

MY RECENT WORK

When Dewey reported on the Polish community, he was concerned about the incorporation of a non-democratic group into a democratic society. He seemed here, in contrast to the tone of much of his more theoretical writings, that democracy justified extraordinary means of incorporation, including government surveillance. Whatever one may think about Dewey's role in this event, the question of the relationship between the larger society and its subgroups--cultural, religious and others-- remains one of the most important issues for modern philosophers of education to address, and these concerns continue to be the focus of my most recent scholarship, from my defence of affirmative action[xix] in *On Higher Ground* to my argument that public schools have an obligation to some cultural subgroups to enable them to maintain a cultural identity; in *Common Schools/Uncommon Identities,*[xx] to the exploration of the idea of affiliational liberalism in the introduction to Kevin McDonough and my anthology, *Citizenship in Liberal-Democratic Societies*; to my examination of the conflict between pluralism and liberalism as it is expressed in religious schools in *For Goodness Sake*. In these works I explore the roots of philosophical liberalism and argue that considerations of race, class, religion, gender and sexual identity are consistent with the liberal educational ideal of promoting individual growth and autonomy. In my two most recent works, *For Goodness Sake* and "The Dialectic of Parental Rights and Social Obligation"[xxi] (forthcoming) I show how the public's interest in social justice and equity, the child's interest in an open future and autonomy, and the parents' interest in advancing their own children's life chances and shaping their religious beliefs can be reconciled.

The Future of Philosophy of Education in a Global Context

Most of my work has been done within a North American and specifically US context. Even the work in Japan was undertaken with educational reform in the United States as the primary concern. Yet today in an ever shrinking world, flattened out by rapid transportation and instantaneous communication, in a world in which a sneeze in an elevator in Hong Kong can initiate an epidemic in Toronto, where a half an once of pressure on the return key of a computer can send a billion dollars flying at the speed of light from one part of the world to another with thousands of jobs following it; where a seed designed in a laboratory in Illinois can be developed in China and save thousands of lives in the Sudan, where a movement begun in India can inspire a letter on rights issued by a minister sitting in a Birmingham jail and where that letter can lend sparks to a revolution in Johannesburg and Soweto, in such a world we have no choice but to address the aims of education and the process of reproduction not just as citizens of nations but as the planetary species with the recognition that we alone have the responsibility for survival of all life that dwells here, with us.

The problem for the new philosophers of education in addressing and shaping norms of intersubjectivity will be to do so in ways that extend individual identity globally without destroying the sense of self so often associated with being located within a specific place and with belonging to a coherent community. To address this challenging problem philosophers of education will not be able to draw solely on the material and inspiration of one nation or one intellectual tradition, but will need to function as normative ethnographers, translating one community to another while engaging the forms of understanding and norms that are imbedded in each.

When the new philosophies of education are written some will not be from the standpoint of the nation state with clear national boundaries, with singular cultural and linguistic preferences and sharply defined loyalties. Rather they will be written from the standpoint of a citizen in an ever-interdependent world, one where childhood represents the emergence not from dependence to independence, but as Dewey thought from dependence to interdependence where education involves learning to reconstruct self and desire conscious of finite resources and of other peoples.

Post Script

Recently I have been invited to serve as the co-founder of Fudan University's School of Philosophy's Institute of Philosophy of Education. Fudan is located in Shanghai China and the hope of my Chinese colleagues and myself is to infuse educational research in China, and perhaps eventually elsewhere, with an understanding of the role that philosophy can play in opening up new visions for education and providing ways to extend horizons of meaning across global barriers.

NOTES

[i] John Dewey, reference letter for Kenneth Benne, University of Illinois Archives, Benne file.

[ii] Walter Feinberg, *Hegel's Conception of Property*, Unpublished Master's Thesis, Boston University, 1962.

[iii] Walter Feinberg, *A Comparative Study of the Social Philosophies of John Dewey and Bernard Bosanquet*, Boston: Boston University unpublished Doctoral Dissertation, 1965.

[iv] Walter Feinberg, Reason and Rhetoric: The Intellectual Foundations of Twentieth Century Liberal Educational Reform, New York: John Wiley, 1974.

[v] John Dewey, Confidential Report: Conditions Among the Poles in the United States, Washington: 1918.

[vi] Milton Halsey Thomas, *John Dewey: A Centennial Bibliography*, Chicago: the University of Chicago Press, 1962.

[vii] Feinberg, W. "The conflict between intelligence and community in Dewey's educational philosophy". *Educational Theory*. 19 (3), Summer, 1969. 236-248.

[viii] Walter Feinberg and Kevin McDonough, " Liberalism and the Dilemma of Public Education in Multicultural Societies" in Kevin McDonough and Walter Feinberg (eds.) *Citizenship and*

Education in Liberal-Democratic Societies: Teaching for Cosmopolitan Values and Collective Identities, Oxford: Oxford University Press, 2003, pp. 1-22.
ix C. D.Hardie, *Truth & Fallacy in Educational Theory.* (New York: Bureau of Publications, Teachers College, Columbia University), 1942/1962
x R. S. Peters, *Ethics and Education,* USA: Scott Foresman, 1967.
xi Walter Feinberg, *Understanding Education: Toward a Reconstruction of Educational Inquiry,* Cambridge: Cambridge University Press, 1982.
xii Eric Bredo and Walter Feinberg, *Knowledge and Values in Social and Educational Research,* Philadelphia: Temple University Press, 1982.
xiii Walter Feinberg and Suzanne R. Langner, " The Other Face of Competition" in Evan M. Melhado, Walter Feinberg and Harold M. Swartz, (eds.) *Money, Power and Health Care,* Ann Arbor, Michigan: Health Administration Press, 1988.
xiv Walter Feinberg, *On Higher Ground: Education and the Case for Affirmative Action,* New York Teachers College Press, 1998. A. Belden Fields and Walter Feinberg, *Education and Democratic Theory: Finding a Place for Community Participation in Public School Reform,* Albany, New York, SUNY Press, 2001
xv Walter Feinberg *Japan and the Pursuit of A New American Identity: Work and Education in A Multicultural Age,* New York: Routledge, 1993.
xvi Walter Feinberg, "Philosophical Ethnography: Or How Philosophy and Ethnography Can Live Together in the World of Educational Research" in *Educational Studies in Japan: International Yearbook, No. 1, 2006,* Japan: Japanese Educational Research Association, 2006. pp. 5-14.
xvii Walter Feinberg, *For Goodness Sake: Religious Schools and Education for Democratic Citizenry,* New York: Routledge, 2006.
xviii Walter Feinberg, "Culture, Class and Nation: An Educator's Reconstruction" Unpublished Butts Lecture: American Educational Studies Association, Charlottesville, VA November 2005.
xix Walter Feinberg, *On Higher Ground: Education and the Case for Affirmative Action, New York, Teachers College Press,* 1998.
xx Walter Feinberg, *Common Schools, Uncommon Identities: National Unity and Cultural Difference,* New Haven: Yale University Press, 1998.
xxi Walter Feinberg, "The Dialectic of Parental Rights and Social Obligation" in Walter Feinberg and Christopher Lubienski, (eds.) *School Choice Policies and Outcomes: Empirical and Philosophical Perspectives,* SUNY Press (forthcoming).

REFERENCES

Bredo, E. & Feinberg, W. (1982). *Knowledge and values in social and educational research.* Philadelphia: Temple University Press.
Feinberg, W. (1962). Hegel's conception of property, Unpublished Master's Thesis, Boston University.
Feinberg, W. (1965). A comparative study of the social philosophies of John Dewey and Bernard Bosanquet, Boston: Boston University unpublished Doctoral Dissertation.
Feinberg, W. (1969, Summer). The conflict between intelligence and community in Dewey's educational philosophy. *Educational Theory, 19*(3), 236-248.
Feinberg, W. (1984). *Reason and Rhetoric: The intellectual foundations of twentieth century liberal educational reform.* New York: John Wiley.
Feinberg, W. (1982). *Understanding education: Toward a reconstruction of educational inquiry.* Cambridge: Cambridge University Press.
Feinberg W. & Langner, S. R. (1988). The other face of competition. In Evan M. Melhado, Walter Feinberg, & Harold M. Swartz (Eds.). *Money, power and health care.* Ann Arbor, Michigan: Health Administration Press.
Feinberg, W. (1993). *Japan and the pursuit of a new American identity: Work and education in a multicultural age.* New York: Routledge.
Feinberg, W. (1998). *On higher ground: Education and the case for affirmative action.* New York: Teachers College Press.

Feinberg, W. (1998). *Common schools/uncommon identities: National unity and cultural difference.* New Haven: Yale University Press.

Feinberg W. and Odeshoo, J. (2000). Educational theory in the fifties: The beginning of a conversation Educational Theory, *50*(3), 289-307.

Feinberg, W. (2006). *For goodness sake: Religious schools and education for democratic citizenry,* New York: Routledge.

Feinberg, W. (2006). Philosophical ethnography: Or how philosophy and ethnography can live together in the world of educational research. In *Educational studies in Japan: International yearbook, No. 1, 2006* (pp. 5-14). Japan: Japanese Educational Research Association.

Feinberg, W. (forthcoming). The dialectics of parental rights and social responsibility, in Feinberg, W. Lubienski, C. (Eds.), *School choice policies and outcomes: Empirical and philosophical perspectives.* SUNY Press

Feinberg W. & McDonough, K. (2003). Liberalism and the dilemma of public education in multi-cultural societies. In Kevin McDonough & Walter Feinberg (Eds.), *Citizenship and education in liberal-democratic societies: Teaching for cosmopolitan values and collective identities* (pp. 1-22). Oxford: Oxford University Press.

Fields, A. B. & Feinberg W. (2001). *Education and democratic theory: Finding a place for community participation in public school reform.* Albany, New York: SUNY Press.

Hardie, C. D. (1942/62). *Truth & fallacy in educational theory.* New York: Bureau of Publications, Teachers College, Columbia University.

Peters, R. S. (1967). *Ethics and education.* USA: Scott Foresman.

Thomas, M. H. (1962). *John Dewey, A centennial bibliography.* Chicago: The University of Chicago Press.

Walter Feinberg
University of Illinois

GARY D FENSTERMACHER

IN SEARCH OF AGENCY FOR CLASSROOM TEACHERS

What would teaching and learning look like if it accorded with the highest ideals of which the human species is capable? If there is one question that has followed me for most of my career, that is the one. As it stands, it is certainly robust and complex enough to provide challenge to the philosopher of education. Yet it becomes even more complicated when asked in the setting of the modern American public school. That is, what would teaching and learning *in the context of contemporary public schooling* look like if it accorded with the highest ideals of which we are capable? This second phrasing quickly leads to another question: Is the school as we know it an impediment to undertaking teaching and learning in ways that accord with our highest ideals? Indeed does the modern school even exist to aim at pursuing with the young the noblest moral and intellectual ends that can be conceived by the human race?

While the career of scholarship that is described in this chapter does not always come directly to grips with these questions, it is certainly motivated and sustained by them. It is a career intent on working out what these most noble ideals might be and how they might be pursued in the setting of the school as we know it. These are not uncommon aspirations for philosophers of education; they have motivated the likes of Plato, Kant, Rousseau and Dewey, as well as most if not all of the philosophers who write for this book. What gives this particular career an orientation different from many others is its preoccupation with working out the ways empirical research bears on the pursuit of high ideals in education. Much of the work described here is rooted in the belief that good empirical research can be enormously beneficial to systematic, formal education. It may also do considerable harm when improperly interpreted or applied.

Given this interest in empirical research, another question, correlative to those posed above, comes to the fore: Just how and where does social science, particularly psychology, fit into conceptions of the relationship between education and human flourishing? No adequate answer to this question can be fashioned by philosophy of science alone. The reason is that an adequate answer must be more than logically and conceptually defensible. It must also have some practical utility; it must carry clear and coherent implications for what educators might do differently in order to more closely approach the highest ideals of which we are capable. Furthermore, it must include a description of and justification for the high ideals that enable human flourishing. This joining of philosophy and education makes the study of the several questions raised above both fascinating and risky. Fascinating because the terrain of inquiry is so vast and so replete with opportunities as to be enthralling; risky because one's knowledge and skill are

L.J. Waks (ed.), Leaders in Philosophy of Education: Intellectual Self Portraits, 81–92.

seldom sufficient to resolve the complexities and nuances of so extensive a domain of inquiry.

The pages that follow describe how I came to address these questions and the efforts made to contribute to their resolution. The journey begins in graduate school because that is where I discovered my philosophical interests and learned how to pursue them.

GRADUATE SCHOOL

Though nominally admitted to a doctoral program in education, the five of us matriculating in 1963 to the specialization in history and philosophy of education were expected to devote a year of study in Cornell University's departments of history and philosophy. Believing that I would prefer history over philosophy, I enrolled in two history courses and one philosophy course. When the semester concluded I was completely captured by the philosophy course. It was a course on philosophy of mind (sometimes also called philosophy of psychology) taught by a brilliant but moody professor named Norman Malcolm.

ELEVEN MILEPOSTS IN MY SCHOLARSHIP

(2005). On making determinations of quality in teaching. (with V. Richardson)

(2001). On the concept of manner and its visibility in teaching practice.

(2004). *Approaches to teaching* (4th edition) (with J. Soltis).

(1997). On restoring public and private life

(1994). The knower and the known: The nature of knowledge in research on teaching

(1993). The elicitation and reconstruction of practical arguments in teaching (with V. Richardson)

(1990). Some moral considerations on teaching as a profession

(1986). Philosophy of research on teaching: Three aspects

(1985) Determining the value of staff development (with D. Berliner)

(1983). The interests of the student, the state and humanity in education (with M. Amarel)

(1979). A philosophical consideration of recent research on teacher effectiveness.

At the time, no small part of Malcolm's fame rested on his close relationship with Ludwig Wittgenstein. One quickly senses just how close when reading Malcolm's memoir (Malcolm, 1958) of Wittgenstein, which is widely regarded as a remarkable example of the genre. But it was not Malcolm's connection to Wittgenstein that attracted me. It was his deep interest in the philosophy of mind (which, of course, explains no small part of the connection between Malcolm and Wittgenstein). Another three courses or seminars with Malcolm provided a thorough acquaintance with such topics as intention, free will, determinism, motivation, explanation, consciousness, the mind-brain relation, folk and scientific psychology. A key legacy of study with Malcolm was the profound importance of intentionality for understanding human behavior.

The rapidly expanding literature in philosophy of mind in the 1960s was highly attentive to distinguishing reasons from causes for human behavior—with the differences between accounting for behavior on the basis of external stimuli or internal neural synapses, on the one hand, or on the basis of intentions, plans, and motives of the behaving agent, on the other. Much was made of the distinction between behavior and action. The most frequently proffered example was the difference between an arm going up (behavior) and waving one's arm or signaling (referred to as an "action" because it expressed the intention of the behavior). Behavior (in contrast to action) might be interesting as an artifact, but its meaning is what is critically important; this meaning can only be assessed by understanding the intention of the behaving person (or "agent," as philosophers referred to the intentional actor).[i]

In that time and place, one could not acquire an education in philosophy without simultaneously learning a way to do philosophy. Variously named concept analysis, ordinary language analysis, or analytic philosophy, the emphasis was on the linguistic and logical features of concepts central to the multitude of topics in philosophy of mind. The meaning of key words (such as 'reason', 'motive', and 'intention') was presumed to reside in their usage, and analytical tools were devised for the deep exploration of usage. At the same time, a rigorous logic emerged as the standard for argument. Clarity of language and coherence of logic were the desiderata of this approach to doing philosophy, an approach that was, to an extent, being propelled by a desire to accomplish in philosophy what scientific method was accomplishing in chemistry and physics.

For reasons that I did not grasp at the time, and still do not fully understand, philosophy of mind and the analytic method held great appeal for me. I found the topics in philosophy of mind fascinating and embraced the precision of language that was demanded in writing and discussion. The idea that one could be clear about where and how one was confused was somehow hugely satisfying. The possibility of critiquing a colleague's work by metaphorically crawling inside its logic and its language offered a means not only to critique that colleague's work but also advance one's own studies. Graduate school and Norman Malcolm in particular laid the groundwork for the vast majority of scholarly work I would do over the ensuing 40 years. At the time, however, I gave nary a thought to what it all had to do with education. No one in the philosophy department appeared interested in so mundane a topic. It would not be until three or four years into my first professorial appointment that I would begin to see any connection. Once again, a special person would come to the fore to assist with finding those connections.

UCLA

Following a brief stint as an instructor at New York University, where I took an oath that I would never again live in a big city, I accepted a position at the University of California, Los Angeles. The lure of Southern California in the late sixties simply overpowered any loathing I had for urban life. The campus was more beautiful than any I had seen before and the glamour of Westwood and the Sunset Strip proved irresistible to this small town boy from Pennsylvania. It was only after accepting the position and looking for a place to live that I discovered that L.A., like all cities, had an "other side of the tracks." As it turned out, an inability to afford (or even aspire to) a home near that beautiful campus would not be my only disappointment.

A year and half into the position I faced up to the fact that I was not getting much enjoyment from being a philosopher of education and teacher of educational foundations. I had no sense that what I was doing would make any difference to much of anything that mattered. My efforts seemed artificial and excessively abstract, far removed from what was happening all around me. In retrospect, harboring such feelings at the time may not have been all that unusual, for this was the era of the war in Viet Nam, continuing struggles for civil rights, hippies and free speech, helicopters spewing tear gas over the protesters on the UC Berkeley campus, and the student shootings at Kent State. In addition to these momentous events, the state of California was forever reforming education. Hardly a day passed without an article about the L.A. schools or California education appearing in the *Los Angeles Times*. In the midst of these tectonic cultural shifts it was hard to believe that I was engaged in relevant, worthwhile work. These feelings were aggravated by the fact that I had not a clue how to make my graduate studies in philosophy relevant to the work of educators. Not knowing how to handle my frustration, I made an appointment with the dean of the education school to see if he had some advice for me. His name was John Goodlad and he was about to succeed Norman Malcolm as my muse.

Goodlad was a superb mentor to junior faculty. In my case, he correctly presumed that I knew far more about philosophy than I did about education, either its theory or its practice. He arranged for me to work with teachers at the University Elementary School, a K-6 laboratory school on the university campus. At the same time, he invited me to assist him with an effort to restructure teacher education at UCLA. I knew next to nothing about teacher education but was so flattered by this invitation to become involved in the initiative that I agreed without hesitation. As I observed and worked with teachers in venues ranging from the UCLA lab school to the inner city schools of Los Angeles, I developed an ever-increasing appreciation for their skills, their dedication, their problems, and their shortcomings. As this appreciation deepened, it exposed an opening for philosophical notions acquired in graduate school.

Classroom teachers and teacher educators are, in varying degrees, agents. Their conduct can be fully understood only by attending to descriptions of their intentions and plans. The work of teaching is not, as the dominant educational psychology of the time suggested, some complex series of behaviors with yet-to-be-discovered causal connections to student learning. Rather, it is a rich, ever-changing palette of hopes, plans, and appraisals of what it is possible to accomplish with these particular students in this context at this time. As I sat as an observer in teacher team meetings at the lab school it became increasingly easy to perceive what was taking place there as a powerful instantiation of the concepts of intention, motive, and agency.

This connection would have been far less obvious had I not also, in the role of teacher educator, spent time in a number of elementary and secondary public schools in Los Angeles County. The differences between the UCLA lab school and many of the L.A. public schools I worked with became apparent when viewed from the perspective of philosophy of mind: The lab school teachers were true agents in the sense that they framed and acted on their plans and intentions, while many (but by no means all) L.A. county teachers I encountered appeared to teach according to scripts prepared elsewhere. That is, one had the sense the L.A. teachers had little sense of efficacy deriving from the freedom to carefully ponder prior actions and present circumstances in order to formulate revised plans, then carry out these plans in accordance with their own deliberations. To put the matter in somewhat more philosophical terms, the lab school teachers acted more like fully autonomous agents while many of the L.A. teachers acted more in accord with plans and procedures that were less the result of their own deliberations and more the result of mandates, conventions, and the often less-than-subtle imposition of what might be called "the culture of accepted practices in urban schools."

These observations of teacher practice, while lacking in nuance and sufficiency of evidence, did offer hope that my graduate school studies could be used to gain a better understanding of the work of teaching and teacher education. Teachers, I reasoned, should be treated as autonomous agents, not as automatons, else how can they be expected to foster independence of mind and action in their students. Note the entry here of one aspect of high ideals: Independence of mind and action. Where did it come from? Most likely it came from a group of British philosophers writing in the 1960s and '70s, including R.F. Dearden, P.H. Hirst, and R.S. Peters (see, for example, Dearden, Hirst & Peters, 1972). Although not personal acquaintances like Malcolm and Goodlad, their impact on my thinking was profound. They, too, were students of philosophy of mind, but unlike me they possessed a remarkable grasp of the potential synergy between philosophy of mind and normative theories of education. Among their more significant contributions was the uniting of a profoundly Enlightenment conception of the aims of education with conceptions of human agency being developed in the philosophy of mind. As such, their writings addressed an extensive array of high educational ideals, from critical thinking, rationality, and wonder, to autonomy, moral virtue, emotional sensibility, and aesthetic appreciation.

It was from these writers that I learned not only how to use analytic philosophy to explore the larger aims and ends of education, but also how these ends connected to many of the core concepts in philosophy of mind. Still, I had no idea how to channel these understandings into a scholarly program of work that I could call my own. That would happen after encountering a small community of researchers engaged in the study of teaching.

THE RESEARCH ON TEACHING COMMUNITY

In the late 1960s, the state of California undertook one of its many massive restructurings of teacher education law and policy. This time, the upshot was the California Commission for Teacher Preparation and Licensing, a new state regulatory commission given authority to grant, suspend and rescind licenses to teach, as well as the authority to approve programs for the education of teachers.

Many of the newly appointed members of the Commission wanted a full-scale overhaul of teacher preparation. To accomplish this reform they sponsored, with federal assistance, one of the largest studies of teacher effectiveness ever undertaken, the Beginning Teacher Evaluation Study (B.T.E.S.). As an ex officio member of the Commission (yet another consequence of my association with Goodlad), I became involved with the researchers working on B.T.E.S. as well as the much broader community of educational researchers seeking a better grasp of how teachers can be more effective in promoting student learning.

As in the case of getting to know teachers better in their work settings, getting to know researchers better in their settings led to perspectives on their research quite different from what one typically acquires merely from reading articles and texts. Personal contact illuminates the deeper hopes, the troubling doubts, and the internal debates that are seldom encountered when one's sole contact is through the completed literature. An upshot of this contact, for me, was a growing respect and admiration for the work underway. At the same time, there was a gnawing frustration with the absence of both a fundamental regard for the agency of the teacher and a robust sense of the grander aims of education.

Many of the researchers appeared to presume that if they discovered which teacher behaviors (processes) yielded significant gains in student achievement (products), it would then be possible—and appropriate—to stipulate that all teachers employ these behaviors. Some of the researchers expressed skepticism about how directly one could proceed from finding relationships between process and product to mandating processes that produced the desired products or outcomes, but this skepticism was typically framed as the result of shortcomings in research design and method, not as morally questionable tactics for improving teaching. In other words, many researchers believed at the time that if they did indeed succeed in isolating the determinants of good teaching, then governing authorities—be they school boards, state or federal governments—could legitimately require teachers to enact these determinants (see Gage, 1977, for one of the more persuasive arguments of this kind).

This view struck me as a potentially huge restriction on the intentionality of teachers and teacher educators, as well as their students. If these researchers were successful in realizing their agendas, a likely consequence would be the marked diminution in the role of intentionality in the activities of teachers. Teacher plans and timetables, expectations for student work, and learning outcomes would likely be developed in venues external to the classroom, and then imposed from without. Among the downside consequences of this loss of intentionality would be a loss in the teacher's sense of efficacy; a lack of due consideration for the larger, more noble aims of education; and a diminished ability on the teacher's part to model for the student what it means to be an autonomous agent. Under such circumstances, about the only way a teacher might lay claim to agency is as a kind of classroom-level guerrilla fighter. It seemed absolutely wrong-headed that the upshot of otherwise potentially valuable educational research would be to force teachers into so defensive a posture.[ii]

In what can only be described as yet another stroke of good fortune, I had many opportunities to discuss these concerns with some exceptional researchers and theoreticians, most notably David Berliner and Lee Shulman. Berliner was the lead researcher for the primary phase of B.T.E.S., bringing him into frequent contact with members of the Commission. Shulman was one of the major theoreticians within the research on teaching community as well as a founder and principal investigator of Michigan State University's newly formed Institute for Research on Teaching. Both of them showed considerable interest in issues of teacher autonomy and high educational ideals. In many hotly debated conversations with them, their thoughtful consideration of my concerns and well-mounted defences of their research gradually forced reconsideration in my view of the problem. I began to see that quite often it is not the research itself that jeopardizes agency on the part of teachers and students. It is the manner of its implementation.

To be clear about this last point, there are indeed a host of philosophical challenges in the design, methods and conduct of behavioral research. These more or less internal difficulties are frequently addressed in philosophy of mind and philosophy of social science (including the work of a number of other authors appearing in this book). At the same time, there are clear benefits to such research, as findings on such topics as wait time, time on task, advance organizers, opportunity to learn, teacher expectations, reinforcement, and scaffolding clearly demonstrate. Urged on by the exchanges with Berliner and Shulman, I wondered whether there might be a way to capitalize on such benefits without diminishing agency—even in cases where the research itself is inattentive or oppositional to agency. This inquiry opened a new line of study on the place and purpose of practical reasoning in teaching.

THE PRACTICAL ARGUMENT PHASE

Suppose we "unpacked" teacher agency as a form of practical reasoning. Perhaps then there might be a way to take account of relevant research findings by somehow incorporating them into the plans being considered by the teacher, much as Aristotle incorporated certain facts (e.g., "Light meats are easily digested") into his notion of the practical syllogism.[iii] This notion did not amount to much more than mental tinkering on my part until encountering Thomas Green's 1976 presidential address to the Philosophy of Education Society (Green, 1976). In that address, Green asked what competencies a teacher required in order to be successful in instruction. Answering his own question, he replied, "the competencies needed are simply those that, within moral restrictions, are required for a teacher to change the truth value of the premises of the practical argument in the mind of the child" (p. 249). There was the notion I was searching for: "the practical argument in the mind of the child."

However, it was the teacher, not the child, who was the object of interest. Suppose we treated the findings of research as either (1) bearing on the truth value of premises that formed the practical argument of the teacher, or (2) as becoming one or more of the premises in that practical argument. To adapt Green ever so slightly, we would then identify "what is required to change the truth value of the premises of the practical argument in the mind of the [teacher], or to complete or modify those premises, or to introduce an altogether new premise into the practical argument in the mind of the [teacher]" (p. 252). This approach offers two benefits: (1) the agency of the teacher is preserved, and (2) relevant research is given a place in the teacher's consideration of instructional activity. If this view is correct, then there is no need to mandate the use of research results or coerce teachers into practices consistent with these results (unless, of course, one is unwilling to allow the teacher the option of deciding against the use of practices implied by the results of research).

The only way I could figure out how to explore this notion was after the fact; that is, to examine the teacher's reasoning following instruction. In brief, this amounted to video taping a volunteer teacher for many hours, then editing the tape to isolate one or more episodes of instruction that suggested a pattern of practice. The teacher and I would then view the tape together.[iv] At some point, I would stop the tape and ask, "That was an interesting episode. What were you doing there?" After some exploration to ensure that the teacher and I were "looking at" the same thing, I would ask, "Why did you do that?" or "What were you hoping to accomplish there?" Often hesitantly at first, but soon gaining confidence, the teacher would offer an account of what we were viewing. As this account unfolded, I would try, as graciously as possible, to fashion the emerging account into a kind of argument that the teacher might use to explain, and perhaps defend, his or her practice to another person. As the argument was formed, it provided the opportunity to raise a series of questions. For example, one question might be, "As you were waiting for your students to respond to you, did you reflect on the notion of wait time?" Another might be, "I noticed that when teaching math, you use a fair amount of seatwork for the students while you work at your desk. Have you had a chance to observe how many of your students remain engaged with their worksheets while you are working at your desk?[v]

Note how these queries serve as an interrogation to the initial practical argument in the mind of the teacher. What is taking place here is an example of what Green described as the competencies for successful instruction, wherein the teacher is reconsidering "the truth value of the premises of the practical argument" or completing or modifying those premises, or introducing "an altogether new premise into the practical argument." In my case, I was attempting to introduce the findings of research on teaching to validate or seek a change in teacher practices. If any changes actually occurred, it was a result of the teacher's own decision to make them. That would likely happen only when the teacher found the revised practical argument he or she had formulated—the one that included an account of the bearing of the research on action—an advance over the prior practical argument. Any intervention of a more compulsory nature risked diminishing agency.

Over the next decade, Virginia Richardson, my primary collaborator in this work, and I expanded the notion of practical argument, turning it into more of an analytical device for teasing out the moral, empirical, theoretical, and stipulative aspects of teaching practice.[vi] The expanded version provided a means to intervene in teaching practice to foster increased consideration of high educational ideals and promising results from educational research.[vii] As we pushed away on this enlarged version of practical argument, it was soon apparent that the findings of research on teaching were not the only missing consideration in the practical reasoning of many teachers. The moral dimensions of teaching were largely absent as well. This discovery took both of us off onto an entirely different line of inquiry.

THE MANNER IN TEACHING PROJECT

How might a philosopher attend to the moral dimensions of a teacher's practice without setting off alarms that one was now either (1) intruding into a highly personal domain that was none of the philosopher's business, or (2) taking a particular moral position within a realm (the public school) that was presumed to be more or less neutral with regard to moral values? Simply using the word "moral" in the public school context often meant long, tedious explanations of what one was trying to do. Moreover, I was not so much interested in determining whether what the teacher was doing was morally good or bad; instead my interest was in the moral features of just about anything the teacher did in relation to his or her students. These features range all the way from simple considerations of fairness in providing access to classroom resources to differential displays of caring as the teacher's attention moves from student to student. I sought a term that would connote the moral freight carried by these everyday pedagogical activities. "Manner" became that term.

The concept of manner is intended to differentiate certain features of teaching from those that typically fall within the notion of method. As findings from research on teaching and the various subject matters work their way into practitioner handbooks and school staff development programs, everyone's attention appears to be on instructional methods—on the skills, techniques, and devices that would make instruction more efficient and effective. Little attention is typically given to the underlying traits and dispositions that define and structure the relationships between teachers and students. For example, to what extent were the exchanges between teacher and student even-handed, nurturing, respectful, intellectually sustaining, or, on the other hand, mean-spirited, humorless, showing favoritism, or intellectually vacuous. The "display" of such dispositions on the part of the teacher could be described as that teacher's manner.

An awkward and not altogether accurate way of explaining the notion of manner is to compare the expressive aspects of teaching to radio waves. A radio wave is fundamentally a carrier wave. We have all "heard" such waves, as they are quiet "dead" spots we encounter when tuning a radio. This carrier wave is then modulated to produce information in the form of voice, music, and data. In my crude analogy, manner is the carrier wave, while method is the modulated wave. That is, all the time the teacher is presenting information (the modulated wave), he or she is also simultaneously expressing personal characteristics, such as honesty, hubris, fairness, meanness, compassion, and so on (the carrier wave). The expression of traits does not occur independently from the presentation of content, but part and parcel with it. Moreover, what the students "pick up" from teaching is more than the information alone; they also grasp, in ways varying from elementary to sophisticated, the manner of the teacher.

The notion of manner thus becomes more than a device for Richardson and me to peer into the moral conduct of the teacher. It is also a low-threat, novel way to engage teachers in a discussion of the moral and intellectual features of their conduct in the classroom. Thus, as we explored with teachers the practical arguments that we co-constructed with them, the concept of manner provided us a way to venture into the moral and intellectual realms of their pedagogical conduct. Indeed the notion became so fascinating that we set aside further work on practical argument so that we might focus exclusively on manner. A sizeable grant from the Spencer Foundation enabled us to work with eleven teachers in two very different school settings to explore how teachers' traits and dispositions gain expression in the everyday activities of the classroom and how such expression might foster or impede the students' own development of morally and intellectually worthy traits.

Over three years of the Manner in Teaching Project we learned much about manner and its dynamic, complex interactions with method.[viii] One of the more surprising results was the way their involvement in the study reinforced the teachers' views of the centrality of the moral in the work of teaching, and, in a number of instances, helped them to become more comfortable in their moral "skins." This is not to say that the teachers became moral tutors or proselytizers for their own moral views. Rather it is to say that the teachers gained greater recognition of and appreciation for how their normal, everyday engagements with students carry moral and intellectual freight. As they considered this aspect of their pedagogy, they searched for ways to enhance traits and dispositions they believed furthered the breadth and depth of the education they provided, while also seeking to de-emphasize traits that appeared to be impediments to realizing valued moral ends.

The findings from this work were extremely gratifying to us because they offered yet another perspective on how teacher agency might be enhanced. Considerations of manner open a path for discussion with teachers not only about agency, but also about the more noble ends of education. As teachers' awareness of the multiple dimensions of their pedagogy expand, their ability to manage these dimensions increases. When this happens, we are a few steps closer to answering the question that opened this chapter: What would teaching and learning look like if it accorded with the highest ideals of which the human species is capable?

CONSIDERATIONS BY WAY OF CONCLUSION

As I step back from the various phases of my career it looks to me to be fashioned from a desire to give classroom teachers as much control over their pedagogy as possible, consistent with philosophical notions of agency and intentionality, while simultaneously holding this authority accountable to high ideals, relevant empirical research, coherent practical reasoning, and a manner expressive of worthy moral and intellectual traits. At least, this is what I hope might be the bottom line assessment of my philosophical career. That, however, is a judgment that must be made by others.

Another aspect of this career, when viewed in hindsight, is the great, good fortune of encountering remarkable colleagues and nurturing contexts along the way. It began in graduate school with Norman Malcolm, continued on to UCLA with John Goodlad, through the research on teaching community where David Berliner and Lee Shulman offered healthy criticism and superb support, then on to the practical argument and manner phases where I had the benefit of many endlessly engaging encounters with Tom Green. In over 20 years of exchanges with Tom I am still not sure whether he thought I was on the right track, but he never hesitated to ride that track with me.

Finally, my collaboration with Virginia Richardson has been especially engaging, for she is the person who took many of the philosophical ideas I was trying to work out in my head and turned them into research agendas. In the course of our trying to understand what it would mean to study these ideas in the context of teacher practice, in natural classroom settings, we learned so much more about the ideas themselves. There is, I believe, such great potential in collaboration between educational philosophy and educational research. This work has been immensely invigorating for me. So invigorating, in fact, that it led to a marriage. But that is a story for another chapter.

NOTES

[i] Norman Care (1996) offers a conception of agency that fits well with the way the term is used in this chapter. Agency, for Care, refers to "one's capacity to live one's own life so that what takes place in it is seen by one as flowing from or resisting what one views as one's own choices and decisions" (p. 2).

[ii] This argument is worked out in detail in several of my writings, particularly in Fenstermacher, 1979, and 1986..

[iii] *Nicomachean Ethics*, chap. VII, Book VI.

[iv] It was the edited tape we viewed together. However, the teacher was always given copies of all taping that occurred in his or her classroom.

[v] This question is an invitation to consider the research on time on task (as described in Fisher & Berliner, 1985).

[vi] See, in particular, Fenstermacher & Richardson (1993). For a critique of the early work on practical argument, the Fall, 1967 (37:4) issue of *Educational Theory* includes six articles in reaction to my work on practical argument.

[vii] For an example of how this might be done, as well as an illustration of the success that can be realized from the approach, see Richardson 1994.

[viii] Not all of these findings have been published, although some of the early results are available See *Journal of Curriculum Studies*, 33(6), 2001, 631-735, for a series of six articles on the work of the Manner in Teaching Project.

REFERENCES

Aristotle, Nicomachean ethics.

Care, N. (1996). *Living with one's past: personal fates and moral pain.* Lanham, MD: Rowman & Littlefield.

Dearden, R.F., Hirst, P.H., & Peters, R.S. (1972). *Education and the development of reason.* Boston: Routledge and Kegan Paul.

Fenstermacher, G. D (1979). A philosophical consideration of recent research on teacher effectiveness. In L. S. Shulman (Ed.), *Review of research in education* (vol. 6, pp. 157-185). Itaska, Illinois: F.E. Peacock.

Fenstermacher, G. D & Richardson, V. (1993). The elicitation and reconstruction of practical arguments in teaching. *Journal of Curriculum Studies*, *25*(2), 101-114.

Fenstermacher, G. D (1986). Philosophy of research on teaching: Three aspects. In M. C. Wittrock (Ed.), *Handbook of research on teaching* (Third Edition) (pp. 37-49). New York: Macmillan.

Fenstermacher, G. D (1979). A philosophical consideration of recent research on teacher effectiveness. In L. S. Shulman (Ed.), *Review of research in education* (vol. 6, pp. 157-185). Itaska, Illinois: F.E. Peacock.

Fenstermacher, G. D (1986). Philosophy of research on teaching: Three aspects. In M. C. Wittrock (Ed.), *Handbook of research on teaching* (3rd ed.) (pp. 37-49). New York: Macmillan.

Fenstermacher, G. D (1990). Some moral considerations on teaching as a profession. In J.I. Goodlad, R. Soder, K. A. Sirotnik (Eds.), *The moral dimensions of teaching* (pp. 130-151). San Francisco: Jossey-Bass.

Fenstermacher, G. D (1994). The knower and the known: The nature of knowledge in research on teaching. In L. Darling-Hammond (Ed.), *Review of research in education 20* (pp. 3-56). Washington, D.C.: American Educational Research Association.

Fenstermacher, G. D (1997). On restoring public and private life. In J. I. Goodlad & T. J. McMannon (Eds.), *The public purpose of education and schooling* (pp. 55-71). San Francisco: Jossey-Bass.

Fenstermacher, G. D (2001). On the concept of manner and its visibility in teaching practice. *Journal of Curriculum Studies*, *33*, 639-654.

Fenstermacher, G. D & Amarel, M. (1983). The interests of the student, the state and humanity in education. In L S. Shulman & G. Sykes (Eds.), *Handbook of teaching and policy* (pp. 392-407). New York: Longman.

Fenstermacher, G. D & Berliner, D. C. (1985). Determining the value of staff development. *Elementary School Journal*, *85*(3), 281-314.

Fenstermacher, G. D & Richardson, V. (1993). The elicitation and reconstruction of practical arguments in teaching. *Journal of Curriculum Studies*, *25*(2), 101-114.

Fenstermacher, G. D & Richardson, V. (2005). On making determinations of quality in teaching. *Teachers College Record*, *107*(1), 186-213.

Fenstermacher, G. D & Soltis, J. (2004). *Approaches to teaching* (4th edition). New York: Teachers College Press.

Fisher, C. W. & Berliner, D. C. (1985). *Perspectives on instructional time*. New York: Longman.

Gage, N. L. (1977). *The scientific basis of the art of teaching*. New York: Teachers College Press.

Green, T. F. (1976). Teacher competence as practical rationality. *Educational Theory*, *26*(3), 249-262.

Malcolm, N. (1958). *Ludwig Wittgenstein: A memoir*. New York: Oxford University Press.

Richardson, V. (Ed.). (1994). *Teacher change and the staff development process*. New York: Teachers College Press.

Gary D Fenstermacher

JIM GARRISON

THE EDUCATION OF ONE
PHILOSOPHER'S EROS

A decade ago, I began a book titled *Dewey and Eros* by claiming: "We become what we love. Our destiny is in our desires, yet what we seek soon comes to possess us in thought, feeling, and action." (Garrison, 1997, xiii) I believe that now more than when I first wrote it. What follows is a love story; one about loving ardently if not well. It is about being possessed more than about possessing. Thus far it is a five part story involving the attraction to philosophy and later philosophy of education, my early years in the profession, the allure of the pragmatic philosophy of John Dewey, mistakes made, and my fascinations over the last five or six years. I conclude with some speculations about the future.

Like all re-membering, the parts are assembled according to present needs, desires, and interests as well a what I have forgotten about the past and what I hope for in the future. Many write the stories of their lives, at least their professional lives, as if they had a rational life plan with a clear teleology. For my part, I went were my passions and imaginaries took me, although I did try to educate my *eros* along the way.

EARLY WORK

Like many, I entered academic philosophy when degrees in other academic disciplines (humanities, physics, and psychology in my case) failed to satisfy my vague desires. I have been an interdisciplinary scholar with broad interests from the beginning, which I now realize is not good for professional focus and career development. I entered doctoral study in philosophy primarily because at the time I passionately believed science was the great evil of our age. After taking a Ph. D. in the history and philosophy of science and mathematical logic, I came to think it was not science as much as scientism that is the disaster.

I was educated in the analytical tradition that even today holds sway in many philosophy departments, although it has almost vanished from the philosophy of education. After taking my Ph. D. in 1981, I bummed around for a couple of years working in a warehouse, driving a truck, and running a mathematics tutorial laboratory at a community collage, before serving as a junior investigator for two years (1983-1985) on an NSF grant in mathematical logic; specifically, the logic of questions and answers (i.e., erotetic logic). It was during this time that I made the switch to philosophy of education. The grant had both a philosophy of science and a philosophy of education component. Mentoring is immensely important and having the opportunity to work with a first rate philosophical logician (Jaakko Hintikka) and an equally outstanding philosopher of education (C. J. B. Macmillan), who, unfortunately, I only met at the very end of my graduate studies,

L.J. Waks (ed.), Leaders in Philosophy of Education: Intellectual Self Portraits, 93–100.

provided me with the very best mentoring imaginable. Both were renowned analytical philosophers. The late Jim Macmillan and I were especially close personally and I learned much about life from his mere presence. Over the years, I have come to believe that the people that have ideas and ideals are more important than the ideas and ideals alone and that we learn best when we live in communities of shared wonder, care, and inquiry.

The grant concentrated on the role of questions and answers in learning. A question put to nature (e.g., an experiment) is much like any other question. Early in my career, I published a number of papers on the logic of questions and answers in history of science, epistemology, and educational journals. Along the way, I came to believe that if we had a rich theory of learning we would not much care about epistemology anymore. Such a stance led naturally to a career in the philosophy of education when the time came to choose. I also felt that I could do things in the *field* of education that I could not do in the *discipline* of philosophy, and I was right.

Oftentimes young scholars execute the research program defined by their dissertation; I was no exception. My dissertation was on theory-ladenness in early modern physics; it mixed the history of science with the philosophy of science and allowed me to address other topics like value-ladenness and methodological constraints in inquiry. In addition, erotetic logic supplemented it nicely. For example, we may think of experiments as questions put to nature. The presuppositions of the question control the conditions of answerhood. The presuppositions are the concepts of the theory. Nature can only answer the question posed. If the presuppositions are improper, then the answer will prove partial, misleading, or simply incorrect. Similar remarks hold for questions put to persons in statistical or ethnographic research in the social

---

PERSONAL FAVORITES

Papers

The Paradox of Indoctrination: A Solution.(1986).
Realism, Deweyan Pragmatism, and Educational Research. (1994)..
Dewey's Philosophy and the Experience of Working: Labor, Tools and Language. (1995).
A Deweyan Theory of Democratic Listening. (1996).
John Dewey, Jacques Derrida, and the Metaphysics of Presence. (1999).
An Introduction to Dewey's Theory of Functional "Trans-Action": An Alternative Paradigm for Activity Theory. (2001).
Toward a Transactional Theory of Decision Making: Creative Rationality as Functional Coordination in Context (with S. Mousavi) (2003).
Reflections on Whitman, Dewey, and Educational Reform: Recovering Spiritual Democracy for Our Materialistic Times (with E. J. O'Quinn) (2005).

Books

Dewey and Eros: Wisdom and Desire in the Art of Teaching. (1997).
The Erotetic Logic of Teaching. (with C.J..B Macmillan) (1988).
Teaching, Learning, and Loving. (eds., with D. Liston) (2004)

sciences. For some typical examples of my work in the philosophical journals during this period, see Garrison 1986a, 1987, and 1988a; for similar work in education, see Garrison 1986b, 1988b, and Macmillan and Garrison, 1986.

In the tenure earning years (1985-1989) and promotion to full professor (1989 1992), I relied on what I had; so, I published largely on the philosophy of science as it applied to education (especially science education and educational research) and, with Jim Macmillan, erotetic logic as it applied to teaching and learning. Eventually, Jim Macmillan and I published *The Erotetic Logic of Teaching* (1988), arguably the last major work of analytic philosophy of education to gather wide attention. There we defined teaching as follows: "It is the intention of teaching acts to answer the questions that the auditor (student) epistemologically ought to ask, given his or her intellectual predicaments with regard to the subject matter." (32) This definition ignores the embodied, impassioned, and noncognitive dimensions of teaching. While I no longer believe this is a complete definition of teaching, it does offer an exhaustive study of the cognitive dimension of teaching by demonstrating that teaching does not imply learning, although teaching does require making logical contact with the presuppositions of the students' often tacit questions. As far as I am aware, teaching remains undefined; I can assure you it is among those tasks that appear easy as long as you do not think about it very hard. I still believe any satisfactory definition of teaching, as distinct from learning, will incorporate aspects of Jim and my definition, or at least the reasoning that went into it.

DEWEY STUDIES

Once they achieve tenure, some young scholars make a dramatic turn into something new. For my part, I had been trying to escape my academic "skill set" for some time. I first encountered Dewey by chance when I came across *Experience and Nature* in my philosophy department library while on the NSF grant in logic; impressed, I went on to read *Democracy and Education* and some essays. With only this limited exposure, I had nonetheless published on Dewey in philosophy (see Garrison 1985) and in education (see Garrison and Shargel, 1985) as early as the mid-1980s, although I did not begin to read him intently until about 1990. Like others that fail to come to grips with the architectonic of Dewey's philosophy, my early papers had many important omissions. When in 1992 I began signing my papers Jim Garrison instead of James W. Garrison, it released me from my former self, and Dewey became the focus of my research program.

At first, I was timid and approached Dewey in terms of his theory of inquiry (Garrison, 1994, 1995a, 1995b). Increasingly, however, the less cognitive aspects of his work attracted me. The aesthetic reading of Dewey evidenced by many of the contributors to Garrison (1995c) was significant. Dewey's emphasis on pre-cognitive intuition, "qualitative thought," imagination, and so on especially interested me; indeed, many of my critics claim I ignore the cognitive aspects of Dewey, which I find to be a great irony. Feminist readings of Dewey, especially their emphasis on embodiment, emotions, differences, and oppression also influenced me (see Seigfried, 1996). Finally, from my first publication on Dewey

(Garrison, 1985), I have been interested in his metaphysics. In philosophy of education (Garrison, 2002) and in traditional philosophy (Garrison 1999a), I have been able to show that like Jacques Derrida, Dewey completely rejects almost the entirety of Western metaphysics (the ideas of fixed essences as the perfect *telos* of all inquiry that departs from some indubitable foundation). Dewey criticized the very notion of ultimate foundations; for him, all essences (including personal and species identity) are contingent and constantly evolving, but not toward any ultimate end. This means almost all the criticisms of his metaphysics are irrelevant.

My most recent work on this topic (Garrison 2005) includes an extensive discussion of Dewey's theory of universals, which I hope will silence some of my critics who think I fail to do justice to the cognitive aspect of Dewey. Actually, explicit, mediating, cognitive (or significant) meanings and intuited, immediate, qualitative (sense) meanings are intertwining moments of any developing experience.

Reading Dewey eventually led me to conclude that the real problem of our age is an excessive confidence in the cognitive, knowing dimension of human experience. Our primary relation to reality is an affair of qualitative having, doing, enjoying, suffering, and enduring before, and after, it is a matter of knowing. Further, intellectualism tends to elevate the scientific value sphere of culture to the detriment of the aesthetic and ethical value spheres. Indeed, the diremption of cultural value realms into the scientific, aesthetic, and ethical is part of the problem; each interpenetrates the other two. The consequence of only one dimension of human experience dominating the philosophical conversation is that enormous gaps go unnoticed. Since my concern with these fissures and omissions has accounted for much of my work over the years, I will return to it later. Part of my attraction to the philosophy of Dewey is that he sees these gaps as gashes in the cultural conversation and attempts to eliminate them. Philosophy itself has ceased to be the friendship (*philia*) of wisdom (*sophia*) and has become "philoepisteme." I attempt to read Dewey as a friend of wisdom who discerns the good while realizing wisdom depends on knowledge. This is the stance taken in Garrison (1997).

Dewey is a difficult philosopher to grapple with; most grossly underestimate him. He is intricate, organic, and holistic; each part depends functionally on every other. Dewey often complained that his critics only interpreted him after they have discarded different parts of his thought; in this regard, things have changed little over the years. Since the 1930s, most of those in philosophy departments in the U. S. have dismissed Dewey. There has been a renaissance in pragmatism in the academy at large since the publication of Richard Rorty's (1979) *Philosophy and the Mirror of Nature*, which uses Dewey extensively to take on some of the most difficult problems in contemporary philosophy. These include not only the correspondence theory of truth, but also the very idea of epistemology, the notion of absolute fixed foundations, the idea of pure reason, the mind versus body dualism, and a host of other pseudo-problems that Dewey too decried. The trouble, well known to Dewey scholars, is that Rorty's reading of Dewey is incomplete, often confused, or dramatically at odds with Dewey's own position. For instance, having taken the linguistic turn, Rorty entirely dismisses Dewey's theory of experience. For Dewey the domain of language always assumes the larger domain of experience. There are things in experience that we feel and respond to yet cannot articulate. We have and are such experiences, but cannot speak them; if we could, we might gain power over them. Of course, Dewey is aware that when children become linguistic beings, it alters their experience, and that becoming a linguistic being affects all realms of experience; nonetheless, the ineffable remains and it may move us. Immediate, consummatory aesthetic or religious experiences are Dewey's two prime examples. If you have ever had an experience of the numinous, it seized you, and whatever you may have to say about it later, even the best of poets know it comes short of the actual experience. Rorty also prefers Dewey's connections between philosophy and poetry and the arts while dismissing the many associations he makes between philosophy and technology. This stance helps Rorty defend his nominalism, which is not so easy to do against the universal laws of science (e.g., the law of gravity). This is important to my own work because I often note the many places where Dewey says that science is a creative art. Indeed, Dewey reminds us that for the classical Greeks, the object of knowledge for *techne* (skilled know how and knowledge of production) is *poiesis* (making, creating, calling into existence and not just metered words that rhyme). Rorty needlessly traps himself in a subtle science versus the arts dualism; a cultural wound Dewey sought to assuage. Nonetheless, Rorty's readings tend to drive the dominant interpretations of Dewey in philosophy and sometimes in education as well. There has been a tremendous flowering of Dewey studies in recent years, much of which had to work itself out from under Rorty.

Meanwhile, those in education departments have been reading Dewey all along, but naturally confined themselves mostly to his educational works. While I still believe this is the best entry into Dewey, his educational works often omit important details. Further, with the exception of Dewey's (1938/1988) short *Experience and Education* and Dewey's (1929/1984) even shorter *The Sources of a Science of Education*, most educators do not read anything after Dewey's (1916/1980) *Democracy and Education*, which is a middle period work. Dewey's *Collected Works* are divided into the Early, Middle, and Later Works. We find not only his most enduring books, but also the sheer bulk of Dewey's writings in his Later Works, which educators largely ignore. Understandably, few educators have the training or time to master such a massive corpus. Moreover, Dewey remained an icon in education even in the years when philosophers forgot about him. This leads some to cite his work as an almost dogmatic authority while others, understandably, believe his authority blocks the road of inquiry. In addition, many in and out of education assume post-modernism/post-structuralism has rendered him outdated. However, anyone who rejects western metaphysics will not find post-modernism intimidating, or even especially original.

I believe much of Dewey's philosophy remains poorly understood and that he was far ahead of his time—and ours, although Dewey does require reconstruction. Given he was a philosopher that argued for the continuous cultural reconstruction and reconstructed his own thinking in major ways throughout his career, no doubt he would have reconstructed himself many times by now. Personally, I believe there are as many valuable reconstructions of Dewey as there are thoughtful people willing to execute them. It is my belief, however, that reconstructive projects should start from a solid understanding of Dewey's position so that we may avoid serious misunderstanding. My major philosophical mistake in the last half-decade is that instead of actively carrying out my own version of one such possible reconstruction, I got caught up in battles with some very capable people over the correct reading of Dewey (see 2000a, 2000b, and 2001). I should have let confusion reign, trust the field to work it out for themselves (including the possibility that I am mistaken), listened to my critics better, and then played with the possibilities. This paragraph has been difficult for me to write; as I said, mine is a story about loving ardently if not well. Much of the education of *eros* lies in learning to find direction after misdirection.

CLOSING ARTIFICIAL GAPS

As indicated earlier, I am concerned with the artificial separation of science from aesthetics and ethics with the accompanying tendency to laud the former to the detriment of the latter two. I also worry about the allied tendency to celebrate knowledge and the known to the detriment of being, having, and doing; we should consider thinking, feeling, and acting as equally significant sub-functions of the unified function of living. We tend to say too little about embodiment, emotions, imagination, and much more, while we sometimes say too much about knowing and the known, although I do not doubt the latter are profoundly important. A colleague and I began to address these issues in a co-edited work a decade ago (see Garrison and Rud, 1995). Contributors examined such topics as emptiness, moral luck, hospitality, privacy, and personal style. More recently, another colleague and I have co-edited a collection of essays that look specifically at the relation between teaching, learning, and loving (see Liston and Garrison, 2004). Another topic that is a gap in the educational conversation is listening (see Kimball and Garrison, 1996; Oliver and Garrison, 1996; Garrison 1996, and Garrison 1999b). Listening is the other and far more neglected half of communication, both linguistic (symbol meanings) and nonlinguistic (natural signs and the like). Nonlinguistic communication we share with other animals and we almost entirely ignore it.

I continue to work on listening with my colleagues (e.g., Rud and Garrison, 2007) while pursuing gaps and gap creators. If one worries about gaps long enough, they will eventually come upon the figure of the Trickster. Trickster is one of the most pancultural of all mythological characters. Often he is associated with the creation of language or its interpretation. He is Krishna among the Hindu. Among the Greeks and within the tradition of western thought, he is the god Hermes, from which we derive the word hermeneutics, the art of interpretation. He was the messenger of the Greek gods mediating between heaven and earth, the guide of mortals to the underworld after death, and the patron of thieves. The divine trickster figure among the Yoruba of West Africa is Esu who mediates between the divine and mundane worlds. He is the ancestor of "Signifying Monkey," who we encounter in contemporary hip-hop (11). As female, trickster tends to live in folktales rather than high cultural myths; a fact calling for more study. In all incarnations, trickster's ploys are linguistic, tropic, and treacherous. He works inside and outside any structure, set of regulations, or codified standards. His "logic" is that of paradox, contradiction, and harmonized, if unreconciled, opposites. We encounter the trickster at borders, crossroads, and liminal spaces. He not only moves through doors, windows, and portals of all kinds, but also creates them. He pokes holes in the most impervious of perfect sanctuaries. Tricksters execute their tricks inside and outside the existing *logos* that structures the approved actions of a given culture breaking laws, defying categories, and bending standards. I am currently working on a book titled *Teacher as Trickster*. Simultaneously, A. G. Rud and I are beginning preliminary work on a book on *Reverence and Education* in hopes of bringing a sense of the numinous and holy into the educational conversation without becoming caught up in dogmatic religion, or religion at all (reverence has had naturalistic as well as religious associations since antiquity). Reverence leaves one in a state of holy dread, wonder, and awe before the incomprehensible mystery of existence. False reverence arises from hubris, from thinking we know the divine plan in detail; it occurs when we confuse our finite ego with the ways of the infinite and inexhaustible. False reverence arrogantly asserts self-serving cultural structures, rules, and standards under the guise of obeying divine dispensation (it often does not matter whether the putative privilege come from science or religion). Trickster's seeming irreverence is often more reverent than such supercilious pieties, sense it acts to break the bounds of oppressive structure and once again reveal the infinite plenitude of existence beyond. Nonetheless, intelligent, wise, and perceptive irreverence will engage in careful inquiry. Cognition is always important, even though wisdom lies beyond it.

I do believe our destiny is in our desires, which is why the education of eros to desire the good remains the highest aim of education. Here, I have portrayed the education of my passions into the present as best I can and, from here, I have tried to project future possibilities. Of course, we may never know our fate in advance, and the end is always near.

REFERENCES

Dewey, J. (1916/1980). Democracy and education. In Jo Ann Boydston (Ed.), *John Dewey: The middle works,* Volume 9. Carbondale: Southern Illinois University Press.

Dewey, J. (1929/1984). The sources of a science of education. In Jo Ann Boydston (Ed.), *John Dewey: The later works,* Volume 5 (1-40). Carbondale: Southern Illinois University Press.

Dewey, J. (1938/1988). Experience and education. In Jo Ann Boydston (Ed.), *John Dewey: The later works,* Volume 13 (1-62). Carbondale: Southern Illinois University Press.

Garrison, James W. (1985). Dewey and the empirical unity of opposites. *Transactions of the Charles S. Peirce Society, 21*(4), 549-561.

Garrison, James W. (1986a). The paradox of indoctrination: A solution. *Synthese, 68*(2), 261-273.

Garrison, James W. (1986b). Some principles of postpositivistic philosophy of science. *Educational Researcher, 15*(9), 12-18.

Garrison, James W. (1987). Newton and the relation of mathematics to natural philosophy. *Journal of the History of Ideas, 48*(4), 609-627.

Garrison, James W. (1988a). Hintikka, Laudan and Newton: An interrogative model of scientific inquiry. *Synthese*, 74(2), 145-171.

Garrison, James W. (1988b). The impossibility of athoretical educational research. *Journal of Educational Thought*, 22(1), 21-26.

Garrison, James W. & Shargel, Emanuel I. (1985). Precognitive knowledge and the acquisition of meaning in Ryle and Dewey. *Philosophy of Education 1985: Proceedings of the Forty-first Annual Meeting of the Philosophy of Education Society*, 317-326.

Garrison, Jim. (1994). Realism, Deweyan pragmatism, and educational research. *Educational Researcher*, 23(1), 5-14.

Garrison, Jim. (1995a). Deweyan pragmatism and the epistemology of contemporary social constructivism. *American Educational Research Journal*, 32(4), 710-740.

Garrison, Jim (1995b). Dewey's philosophy and the experience of working: Labor, Tools and language. *Synthese*, 105(5), 87-114.

Garrison, Jim, ed. (1995c). *The new scholarship on Dewey*. Dordrecht: Kluwer Academic Publishers.

Garrison, Jim. (1996). A Deweyan theory of democratic listening. *Educational Theory*, 46 (4) 429-451.

Garrison, Jim (1997). *Dewey and eros: Wisdom and desire in the art of teaching*. New York: Teachers College Press.

Garrison, Jim (1999a). John Dewey, Jacques Derrida, and the Metaphysics of Presence. *Transactions of the Charles S. Peirce Society*, 35(2), 346-372.

Garrison, Jim, (1999b). The political theory of John Dewey and the importance of listening in education. In Jürgen Oelkers and Fritz Osterwalder (Eds.), *Die Neue Erziehung. Beiträge zur Internationalität der Reformpädagogik*. Bern: Peter Lang, 371-394.

Garrison, J. (2000a). A response to James Scott Johnston. *Educational Theory*, 502) 275-276.

Garrison, J. (2000b). A response to McCarthy and Sears. *Educational Theory*, 50(4) 542-543.

Garrison, Jim (2001). Dewey and eros: A response to Prawat, *Teachers College Record*, 103(4), 722-738.

Garrison, Jim (2002). Dewey, Derrida, and "the double bind." *Educational Philosophy and Theory*, 35(3), 349-362. Reprinted in *Derrida, deconstruction and education*, Oxford: Blackwell, pp. 95-108.

Garrison, Jim (2005). Dewey on metaphysics, meaning making, and maps. *Transactions of the Charles S. Peirce Society*, 41(4), 818-844.

Garrison, Jim (2006). Hegelian continuity in Dewey's theory of inquiry. *Educational Theory*, 56(1), 1-37.

Good, James A. (2006). *A search for unity in diversity: The "permanent hegelian deposit" in the Philosophy of John Dewey*. Lanham, Md.: Rowman & Littlefield Publishers, Inc.

Kimball, Stephanie L. & Garrison, Jim. (1996). Hermeneutic listening: An approach to understanding in multicultural conversations. *Studies in Philosophy and Education*, 15(1 & 2), 51-59.

Liston, Daniel & Garrison, Jim (Eds.). (2004). *Teaching, learning, and loving*. New York: Routledge.

Macmillan, C. J. B. & Garrison, James W. (1986). Erotetics revisited, *Educational Theory*, 36(4), 355-361.

Macmillan, C. J. B. & Garrison, James W. (1988). *The logic of teaching*. Dordrecht: Kluwer Academic Publishers.

Oliver, Kimberly L. & Garrison, Jim (1996). Kinesthetic istening: The other half of the dance. *Journal of Physical Education, Recreation & Dance*, 67(6), 37-39.

Rorty, R. (1979). *Philosophy and the mirror of nature*. Princeton, NJ: Princeton University Press.

Rud, A. G. & Garrison, Jim (Forthcoming). Reverence and listening in teaching and leading. *Learning Inquiry*, 1(2). Special Issue on Listening and Reflecting, Leonard J. Waks (Ed.).

Seigfried, Charlene Haddock. (1996). *Pragmatism and feminism: Reweaving the social fabric*. Chicago: The University of Chicago Press.

Jim Garrison
School of Education
Virginia Tech

SOPHIE HAROUTUNIAN-GORDON

PHILOSOPHY FOR THE FUN OF IT[1]

INTRODUCTION

Philosophy in Poetry?—I'm sure I'm not the first.
Perhaps you would not see it in the writings of Paul Hirst.
Remember, please, Jean-Jacques Rousseau—his novels and confessions;
He brought philosophy to art to manage his obsessions.

A poem is very helpful in mining the unexpected.
Surprising thoughts always emerge, though some must be rejected.
But in amongst the rubbish will be diamonds in the rough.
And if you polish them with care, you'll have important stuff.

My life as a philosopher began when I was born.
My name is Sophie, so to wisdom seeking I was sworn.
My father first taught me the craft—a theologian he
And put into my hands a volume authored by Dewey.

Yes, *Human Nature and Conduct*-- I read it in high school.
While other kids might find it dull, to me it was too cool!
I thought I understood it and explained it to my father.
He said I grasped it, so I felt it was worth all the bother.

In college, it was Heiddegger, and Sartre, Merleau-Ponty.
Of course I wrestled Hegel, and let's not forget Nietzche.
I fell in love with logic—the square of opposition!
But Aristotle did compete with Sophie, the musician.

Before I tackled Dewey, I was playing the piano
And when I got to college, I began to sing soprano.
So I pursued both passions--I could not give up either.
Music and philosophy—I chose to omit neither.

I finished Cornell –Iowa-- in 1965.
But cultivating passions had not taught me to survive.
So I pursued a master's – in planning and instruction.
To teaching as my life's career, that was the introduction.

L.J. Waks (ed.), Leaders in Philosophy of Education: Intellectual Self Portraits, 101–112.

I wrote a master's thesis—and returned to Aristotle:
I argued sixth grade reasoning was beyond coo and coddle.
Those kids could tell a syllogism valid or invalid
Informal reasoning they grasped—hummed through it like a ballad.

While teaching sixth grade students, I reached insight number one:
I like to do philosophy because it is such fun!
To read and do philosophy are really not the same
The former tackles mostly books, the latter-- many game.

For one can <u>do</u> philosophy with books or films or art
Or many other things – if ambiguity's a part.
To do philosophy, I ask: Does X mean that or this?
In answering that question, I try hard to not miss

A piece of telling evidence that opens up the meaning.
For if I miss it then perhaps I'll trade the truth for seeming.
Yes, find and study evidence; that's how my time is spent.
And when I think I've seen it all, I make an argument.

But more about my craft to come. For now, it's history.
I taught sixth grade for five great years, then went to U. of C.
Chicago give me Toulmin, Schwab, and Dunkel every day
But mostly I spent time translating works by Piaget.

PIAGET

You see, sixth graders' thinking left a very deep impression.
I hoped to grasp their thought though class had ceased to be in session.
Piaget talked of stages and about assimilation.
He spun a theory, oh so grand, he called "equilibration."

He said that babies quickly form some structures cognitive.
With them, the babies learn about how things in this world live.
When information that they get defies what they believe
The structures must accommodate, lest the child be deceived.

The permanence of objects – hallmark of the child's first stage.
Move an object where you will, she'll stay on the right page.
She knows that if she saw it go from one place to another
She'd better look under the last—forget the bright, first cover.

Then next, pre-operations, lasts from ages two to five.
The child will get distracted by most things, dead or alive.
She'll watch the water pour from one container to another
She'll think the short, fat glass has less -- give it to little brother!

Arriving at age seven, so-called "concrete operations,"
She is not fooled by different shapes, or colors, or gyrations.
She knows the content only changes if you take away
So pour the water where you will, its quantity will stay.

Piaget described stages in so very much detail.
His careful observation of performance did not fail.
But as I waded through the pages I became perplexed:
How was it that the children moved from one stage to the next?

Piaget's answer? Watch and see structures accommodate
And change their features 'til the thought becomes more accurate.
Assimilate, accommodate, those two must be in sync
Until structures equilibrate so that the child can think.

I felt Piaget's story was not satisfactory.
There were too many holes in his elaborate theory.
Let's take accommodation: to just what does it refer?
Do features of the structures change? And how does that occur?

Or is it that one structure is selected to replace
Another in some circumstance, because it can't keep pace?
In that case, features do not change—both structures do exist.
The one was substituted for the job from a long list

Of possibilities that sat in the child's repertoire.
It seemed to me that explanation did not go too far.
But Piaget did not give up—"No, I'll elaborate.
From Waddington I can learn to explain "accommodate."

"From him, I'll simply borrow a most useful metaphor
Assimilation genetic: How could I ask for more?
His great story about chreods, likewise, is heaven-sent
As with it I can now explain how the environment

"Can have an impact on the changes that the structures make."
I argued that his story, although lengthy, was half-baked.
For in the end, like Chomsky, he owed much to nativism.
And let's remember that as we applaud constructivism.[2]

WITTGENSTEIN

But now I had a problem that I needed to resolve:
Piaget failed, so what should the new story now involve?
Into my life came Wittgenstein, and clearly saved the day:
With dialogue he showed one could put structures clean away.

Do not posit them at all; we won't ask how they change.
Instead, invite us now to play another language game!
Just take a look at language in some context, if you please.
You'll find you can explain what's learned with even greater ease

Than you had first imagined. Now, this really sounded good!
Give up equilibration? At last, I thought that I could!
Yes, Wittgenstein suggested new tasks for philosophy:
Why talk in terms of mental states? Try anthropology!

As in his *Philosophical Investigations*, I
Decided to try dialogue to see what it could buy.
I'd seen sixth graders change their minds within a conversation
I saw Herr Wittgenstein do same—it was a revelation.

He liked to talk with Augustine, who said we first learn names.[3]
Their dialogue shows everyone how we learn the language games.
We do learn names—that's one of them, but there are plenty more:
We learn to report, speculate, and order from the store.[4]

We learn the games while playing them with others who engage us:
Connect the word "book" with a sound they make while we turn pages.
We come to see the word "book" does not fit some situation:
When we said "book," pointing to cow, we caused a violation.

The meaning that "book" has for us does change as we do use it.[5]
And how we use it follows rules --or else we do abuse it.
We may not think about the rules, or then again, we may:
To draw a line one foot in length, our ruler shows the way.

People use words, says Wittgenstein—for us, a form of life.[6]
Which means we do it naturally—much as man takes a wife.
"But if it's natural, why do we say it follows rules?"
For us, it's natural to construct rules to use as tools.

And one who knows the rules is likewise the one who can use them.
That one has mastered a technique and so will not confuse them.[7]
Given conditions of the game, that one will now go on
And tell us "2,4,6, . ." is followed by: " 8,10, and so on."

"'[I] Understand a word': [it is] a state. A *mental* state?"[8]
Grammatical investigation shows it does not rate.
Compare "When did your pains get less" with all the words that follow:
"When did you [cease] to understand that word?"—See, it is hollow.

The problem is that mental states like pain have a duration.
One can say when they start and stop—arrive and leave the station.
And in between they are continuous, we can attest.
But I can't say when I ceased to know words learned for a test.

In sum, to explain change in thought, said Ludwig Wittgenstein
Forget about a process which you say occurs in time.
Instead, look for conditions that will justify the claim:
She showed the fly the way out of the fly-bottle again![9]

PLATO

Okay, I was on the right track at last, it seemed to me:
Observe how people learn new language games –like a,b,c.
One way of learning them, I had seen, was through a dialogue—
A process, though not mental, which could lead up from the bog.[10]

And so I turned to Plato, and his famous *Republic*.
I watched how Socrates conversed with others for a kick.
I saw how he did turn the souls so they looked where they should
And when they did, lo and behold, they sometimes glimpsed the Good!

Thrasymachus—a case in point—thought little of the just.
In fact, he thought the unjust had the good life, full of lust.
But when he talked with Socrates, at last he did admit:
The unjust are unlearned and bad—so that's the end of it.[11]

The other interlocutors, as well as Socrates,
Through conversation changed their minds, although by slow degrees.
They learned that justice was not the advantage of the stronger
Rather: each mind your own business and we will all last longer .[12]

I sought out cases where a child did learn through conversation.
I looked, for instance, at the slave boy on Meno's plantation.[13]
One sees how Socrates did teach geometry through talk:
He asked the slave some questions, and quickly the slave did balk.

"I cannot tell you, Socrates, how long the side must be
In order to get twice the size of the square we now see.
By doubling each side, we get a square for times the size.
I thought I knew the answer but I see I was not wise."[14]

"Observe, Meno" says Socrates, "his stage of recollection:
At first he thought he knew the length, now he's lost all direction.
Although he's very confused and has much perplexity
I say that he is better off: he'll now search willingly."[15]

Indeed, the slave boy answers the new questions put to him.
And in so doing, sees the square in a new relation
Looking at its diagonal—a line he had ignored
The boy sees the solution—and Meno gets the reward.

For Meno, in his dialogue with Socrates, had asked:
What do you mean by "recollect?" Remembering the past?
Why do you call that learning? That's what I want to know.
The conversation with the slave boy was the perfect show.

Both slave and Meno learned new language games from Socrates:
The slave learned to observe the square in new ways—now he sees
Perspective can change everything! The geometric figure?
Extend the lines and see it as a part of something bigger.

And Meno learned to think of learning in a brand new way:
It is called "recollection" since it puts new thoughts in play.
New thoughts arise from slumber in the face of some questions:
Queries draw out one's reasoning –work just like suggestions.

When people hear a question, they may see how to go on
That is, if they have learned the rules to follow to respond.
So asking the right question is perhaps most critical:
If it is clear it draws out thought nearing veridical.

GADAMER

The language game of dialogue—that is the game I study.
I consult cases outside books to help clear up the muddy.
I have had many questions about the rules of the game.
To answer them, I often turn to classrooms once again.

One time, I looked at students who were working in high school.
And there I found them reasoning about two in a duel.
I watched two groups who questioned *Romeo and Juliet*
I saw it happen, day by day, it moved like a duet.

The teachers, just like Socrates, asked questions to the groups.
Some students, like Thrasymachus, played games and jumped though hoops.
And tried to make the conversation like a circus act
While others did join in an investigatory pact.

They sought to make interpretations seemingly correct
They read and re-read passages, their meanings to dissect.
But how should I describe the very nature of their game?
The rules for arbitrating when their meanings weren't the same?

I needed help and so I turned to Hans-Georg Gadamer.
Without his *Truth and Method,* I would not have got too far.
In terms of the first question, Gadamer gave one word—play:[16]
To-and-fro motion without goal--What transpires on the way?

The text the students studied was a play and play they did.
And as they put their questions to it, found its meaning hid.
Preparing for discussion, they wrote questions next to lines.
They'd then review the questions and pick some of them as primes.

These questions were the ones for which they most desired an answer.
The text seemed non-definitive—'twas darting like a dancer.
Their play began when they found points of ambiguity
If evidence conflicted, they faced incongruity.

They came to the discussion with questions doing a burn.
In such state, said Socrates, they would be ripe to learn.
Toss out the hot coal—give others your genuine query
If they find it of interest, they'll help solve the mystery.

I watched discussants play with possibilities and plans:
They scrutinized the evidence—like sifting through the sands.
Once one made a decision—answer X because of Y
One picked the road and started down, the chance for change gone by.[17]

For players there is no choice: play by the rules of the game.
The rules say once the answer's picked, one must support the claim.
So answering involves a risk—the answer must make sense.
That is, it must be the best claim, given the evidence.

And now, we come to question two—that of disagreement.
Suppose two people disagree in tones truly vehement.
Again, I found that Gadamer had much wisdom to offer
The game will master players-- will show them what to proffer.[18]

The question that all wish to answer—it shows the route out
It transforms evidence and teaches what the text's about.
Continue conversation, 'til its object does emerge--
'Til the truth finds its question, which permits it then to surge.[19]

DEWEY

At last, I saw how Gadamer and Plato come together.
Though writing centuries apart, they're birds of the same feather.
Both believed remembering belongs with dialectic.
Conversation draws out truth that can persuade a skeptic.

"One cannot have experience except as one has questions,"[20]
Said Gadamer—and from Plato one does not hear objections.
And Wittgenstein , too, might agree, given his predilection
For dialogue with Augustine and others, real or fiction.

But having watched how dialogue can turn the soul,[21] I learned:
It's critical to cultivate some questions 'til they burned.
How could I help the teachers help their students with this feat?
I had another question from which I could not retreat.

By now, I did teach teachers, so I could not just conceal
My ignorance—indeed I had a problem very real.
I taught them at Northwestern –a fine university.
I felt the answer should help where there was diversity.

One day into my office walked two teacher candidates
They offered me a project that was surely in the fates.
They wished to lead discussions with two fourth grade groups in school
And hoped the conversations would teach kids to be less cruel.

One group was in the city, and the other way outside.
The texts, they said, should come from different cultures, far and wide.
I let them do the project, but with one clear proviso:
I would help them cultivate the questions—to revise so

That finally they had before them questions that were clear.
Agreeing thus, we started out together without fear
That we would have much trouble, and indeed we got on well.
And all that work on questions grew less difficult to sell.

The candidates led ten discussions on five different texts.
I questioned all their questions 'til they knew not what came next.
They had to do revisions, and they tried the best they could.
One week I had to be away, that's when they became good.

They pushed each other just as I had done-- to clarify.
They grew intolerant of vagueness – stopped it slipping by.
They replaced terms quite technical with meanings they intended.
The failure to express their deepest points of doubt had ended.

For the last two discussions, they did recombine the groups:
Brought some to city, some to suburbs, thus formed two new troops.
Diversity of background faced both leader and discussant--
Would they converse in a society that says they mustn't?

"Democracy," writes Dewey—"More than form of government.
It is a mode of ...living"[22] that Americans were sent
By wise forefathers who foresaw life as association—
And thus proposed democracy with which to bond the nation.[23]

From Dewey, we got inspiration and reaped the rewards
For hours clarifying questions: students dropped their swords.
Together, cultivating queries they cared to resolve--
I watched as differences helped their ideas to evolve.

CONCLUSION

So, *Cultivating Questions*[24] tells the story of the project
It shows fourth graders find a Gadamerian object.
It gives some credit for success to the fine co-leaders.
And shows us all developing—becoming good readers.

With watching conversations, came my insight number two:
The way I do philosophy teaches me something new.
What did I learn—or better yet, what did I recollect?
To question is most critical; to listen-- more so yet.

Until I analyzed the transcripts of the ten discussions
I thought good questions stayed asleep until the talk did rush on.
But posing a good question will depend on what one hears
How to improve that hearing? Once more, I had to change gears.

And I returned to Plato, once again to *Theaetetus*[25]
I thought a very simple case would help me to complete this
Study of dialogue. But I was wrong—it was the start
Of a new line of inquiry from which I could not part.

The *Theaetetus* brought me to some new hypotheses
About the kind of listening that brings one to one's knees,
To have the will to listen to a challenging perspective--
To use it to allow one to become much more reflective.

I put forth the hypotheses to those in P.E.S.[26]
I said that based upon one case, all I could do was guess.
It seemed to me, however, listening began with question
One listened, then, to get some help and overcome congestion

Congestion did occur when hearing clashed with a belief.
Has one just been mistaken? Listen hard to get relief.
Perhaps, although quite challenging, the point of view has merit.
Perhaps, indeed, that perspective would be good to inherit!

I tested the hypotheses –they did fit Socrates.
The next step was to try them out in real life, if you please.
And so I go about that task, although not all alone
For others now do work with me, and they help me to hone

My thoughts, so for example, they have given me instruction
They helped me to direct attention toward the interruption—
The interruption that occurs before new turns are taken
Down other roads, perhaps to fix the ideas found mistaken.

Now, I have many colleagues who write about listening
They look at different topics—from silence to pretending
To listen when the listening is not so very good.
Sometimes it's best to make believe that one has understood.[27]

And so the work goes forward, and I look at more cases.
I'm still convinced that questioning is found in most all places.
While some colleagues[28] aver the opposite, I disagree
And so I end the present poem with insight number three:

Philosophy is so much fun—at least the way I do it.
It always shows me something new—although perhaps I knew it.
Philosophy is most at home where dialogue is sure
And poetry helps listening to reach a form more pure.

NOTES

[1] The poem that follows is divided into seven sections, each with twelve verses. Each verse consists of two rhyming couplets. The basic meter is iambic septameter, and the lines are "fourteeners"— fourteen iams per line. Richard Strier points out that fourteeners was the dominant Elizabethan verse form before iambic pentameter, and that a fourteener was a long line put together from two shorter lines which are the basic psalm meter in English (8's and 6's they are called). Thanks to Richard and to Julie Johnson for their comments on an earlier draft and to Julie for help with the meter.

[2] Haroutunian-Gordon, S. (1983). *Equlibrium in Balance: A Study of Psychological Explanation.* New York, Springer-Verlag.

[3] Wittgenstein, L. (1958). G.E.M. Anscombe (trans.). *Philosophical Investigations* (3rd ed.). New York, The Macmillan Company, I:1.

[4] PI I: 23.

[5] PI I: 20.

[6] PI I: 19

[7] PI I: 151.

8   PI I: 151 (a).

9   PI I: 309.

10 Plato. (1958). A. Bloom (trans.). *The republic*. New York: Basic Books, 533d.

11 Plato, *Republic*, 350d.

12 Plato, *Rebublic*, 433a-b

13 Haroutunian-Gordon, S. (1987). Evaluating teachers: The case of Socrates. *Teachers College Record*, 89(1), 117-132.

14 Plato. (1956). W. K. C. Guthrie (trans.). *Meno*. New York: Penguin Books, 84a.

15 Op. cit.

16 Gadamer, H. G. (1985). Sheed and Ward, Ltd. (trans.). *Truth and method*. New York: The Crossroad Publishing Company, p. 92.

17 Ibid., p. 95.

18 Op. cit.

19 Gadamer, *Truth and method*, p. 101-2; 325-6.

20 Gadamer, *Truth and method*. p. 325.

21 Haroutunian-Gordon, S. (1991). *Turning the soul: Teaching through conversation in the High School*. Chicago: University of Chicago Press.

22 Dewey, J. (1916). *Democracy and education*. New York: The Free Press (Macmillan), p. 87.

23 Op. cit.

24 Haroutunian-Gordon. (forthcoming). *Cultivating questions: A focus for schooling in the twenty-first century*. New Haven, Connecticut: Yale University Press.

25 Plato. (1961). F. M. Cornford (trans.). *Thaetetus*. In E. Hamilton and H. Cairns (Eds.), *ThecCollected dialogues of Plato*. Princeton, New Jersey: Princeton University Press.

26 Haroutunian-Gordon (2004).

27 Burbules (in preparation)

28 E.g., the papers by Garrison and Waks (in preparation). The role of questioning in listening is further explored in a special journal issue, Listening and Reflection, L.J. Waks, ed., *Learning Inquiry* 1(2) 2007.

PERSONAL FAVORITES

Equilibrium in the Balance: A Study of Psychological Explanation (1983)

"Evaluating Teachers: The Case of Socrates" (1987)

"Explaining Change in Psychology: The Road not Taken" (1988)

"Teaching in an Ill-Structured Situation: The Case of Socrates" (1988)

From Socrates to Software: The Teacher as Text; the Text as Teacher (1989; ed.)

"Socrates as Teacher" (1989)

"Statements of Method in Teaching: The Case of Socrates" (1990)

Turning the Soul: Teaching through Conversation in the High School (1991)

"Listening—to a Challenging Perspective" (2004)

Cultivating Questions: A Focus for Schooling in the Twenty-First Century (forthcoming)

BIBLIOGRAPHY

Burbules, N. (in preparation). Pretending to listen. In S. Haroutunian-Gordon & L. Waks (Eds.), *Listening in context: Challenges for Teachers.*

Dewey, J. (1916). *Democracy and education.* New York: The Free Press (Macmillan).

Gadamer, H.G. (1985). Sheed and ward, Ltd. (trans.). *Truth and method.* New York: The Crossroad Publishing Company.

Garrison, J.W. (in preparation). Compassionate listening in teaching and learning. In S. Haroutunian-Gordon & L. Waks (Eds.), *Listening in context: Challenges for Teachers.*

Haroutunian-Gordon. (forthcoming). *Cultivating questions: A focus for schooling in the twenty-first century.* New Haven, Connecticut: Yale University Press.

Haroutunian-Gordon, S. (1983). *Equlibrium in balance: A study of psychological explanation.* New York, Springer-Verlag.

Haroutunian-Gordon, S. (1987). Evaluating teachers: The case of Socrates. *Teachers College Record, 89*(1), 117-132.

Haroutunian-Gordon, S. (2004). Listening – To a challenging perspective. In K. Alston (Ed.), *Philosophy of Education Yearbook 2003.* Urbana, Illinois: Philosophy of Education Society.

Haroutunian-Gordon, S. (1991). *Turning the soul: Teaching through conversation in the high school.* Chicago: University of Chicago Press.

Plato. (1956). W. K. C. Guthrie (trans.). *Meno.* New York: Penguin Books.

Plato. (1958). A. Bloom (trans.). *The republic.* New York: Basic Books.

Plato. (1961). F. M. Cornford (trans.). *Thaetetus.* In E. Hamilton & H. Cairns (Eds.), *The collected dialogues of Plato.* Princeton, New Jersey: Princeton University Press.

Waks, L. J. (in preparation). Two types of interpersonal learning. In S. Haroutunian-Gordon & L. Waks (Eds.), *Listening in context: Challenges for Teachers.*

Wittgenstein, L. (1958). G. E. M. Anscombe (trans.). *Philosophical investigations* (3rd edition). New York: The Macmillan Company.

Sophie Haroutunian-Gordon
Northwestern University

PAUL H. HIRST

IN PURSUIT OF REASON

HOME AND RELIGION

From my very earliest years I was surrounded by a family fiercely focussed on education and teaching. My father seemed to be for ever studying and attending evening classes in foreign languages at the local 'technical college'. He had intended to go to university and become a teacher but World War I meant he was called up for military service, registered as a conscientious objector and after a brief spell in prison became an office clerk dealing with foreign correspondence. His older brother fulfilled his military service, then trained as a teacher, eventually becoming the headteacher of a local high school. My maternal grandmother, who lived near us, had also trained as a teacher and spent spells in high school teaching while a housekeeper helped bring up her seven children, six of whom went on to university and two of whom also became high school teachers. It was taken absolutely for granted that my sister and I would do well at school, go to university and probably become teachers. We both did exactly that.

But education and teaching were nevertheless of very secondary importance in my upbringing. My father, dissatisfied by the religious teaching in his own protestant upbringing, had become a serious Bible student learning Latin, Greek and Hebrew so as to get to 'the truth' more fundamentally than he thought the current 'King James' English translation of the Scriptures could deliver. He had then joined the Plymouth Brethren, a fundamentalist evangelical sect whose teaching he judged to most accurately follow Biblical doctrines and amongst whom he became the local Senior Brother and a nationally known preacher. Following above all the teaching of St.Paul he came to see the whole of God's creation, including the whole of human society and human understanding, if extraordinary manifestations of Divine glory and wisdom, nevertheless as deeply corrupted by evil and sin and destined for final destruction. Personal salvation through the sacrificial death of Christ could however save us individually from that end by our commitment to Christ as personal Saviour and our starting now a life devoted to the spiritual service of God in obedience to His will, forsaking the satisfying of all natural personal desires. My father sought to live that life himself in everything including the upbringing of his children, seeing all advancement in education and in society as justified only as promoting one's own and others spiritual development. Knowledge and understanding he saw as good and necessary for a deep appreciation of profound spiritual truths but, as pursued for their own and worldly ends, doomed to lead only to the further corruption of life and society.

This view of life both implicitly and then increasingly explicitly shaped almost the whole of my existence from birth until when aged seventeen, in 1945, I literally

L.J. Waks (ed.), Leaders in Philosophy of Education: Intellectual Self Portraits, 113–124.
© 2008 Sense Publishers. All rights reserved.

left home to go to university. Until then my father made it plain he was the divinely appointed indisputable head of his family though he delegated all domestic and daily responsibility for us children to our mother. He dealt directly only with our discipline and our regular religious activities. No display of emotions, even affection, was acceptable ever, and 'love' it was made clear must be understood as simply concern for the good of others irrespective of any personal 'feelings'. Love of God was a strictly spiritual experience bestowed by His grace. Believing that one's work should be only the means to promoting the spiritual life for himself and his family my father never sought nor accepted any advancement in his clerical job. He devoted all his spare time to his religious studies and the service of others in Brethren communities. We lived very simply and had few toys as children, leading lives largely dissociated from other children except for the few amongst the local Brethren. I felt isolated, different, rarely joyful or happy, feelings only reinforced by my having several spells of quite serious illness. But life like this I learnt was to be expected as a child of grace in a sinful world.

SCHOOL AND MATHEMATICS

With little by way of non-religious activities available at home I not surprisingly found school work more interesting than almost anything else in life. There were even no non-religious books available at home except language books, an atlas and, for some undeclared reason, the works of Shakespeare. There was available to me no daily newspaper or even radio until I was fifteen when I learnt in school science how to build a simple 'crystal set' that I listened to on head phones in my bedroom. Working hard at school I was fast-tracked so that from fourteen I studied almost exclusively mathematics and physics. Under the tuition of a brilliant mathematics teacher I then did sufficiently well to gain entry to Cambridge with scholarships adequate to finance me there.

By the time I left school however the first seeds of philosophical questioning had been sown in my mind above all by that same mathematics teacher. He made me not only adept at solving mathematical problems but aware also of the enormous power of mathematical truths as established by deductive proof and their crucial difference from the empirical truths established experimentally in the physical sciences. What, I went on to ask myself, is the equivalent basis for the truths of the religious beliefs about God set out in the Bible? Their internal claims to be true by revelation seemed to need some further justification and the claim to some private experience of 'salvation' I found mysterious and unsatisfactory. I had no such significant experience myself and was strong enough in my questioning to quietly but firmly resist all suggestions that I should formally join the Plymouth Brethren by baptism. Protected though I was from close relationship with all adults outside the Brethren other than my teachers, and explicitly from even several members of our wider family who had now clearly no religious affiliation, I nevertheless came to know enough about life in the world at large to find it hard to believe that many things denied to me were sinful and that those enjoying them were all personally destined for eternal damnation. The power of religion for good in the life of my parents, and its importance in society at large I nevertheless did not seriously question and felt sure that when I got to university I would have chance to discover adequate justification for at least certain basic religious and moral truths on which I might personally live a wise and good life.

CAMBRIDGE AND PHILOSOPHY

Once at Cambridge I was not surprisingly shaken to discover the extreme narrowness of my background intellectually, culturally and socially and soon set about trying to remedy that. My mathematical studies caused me little problem so for my undergraduate years I used all the immense facilities of the place to get something like the liberal education that had so far been denied me. Philosophically I was mesmerised by hugely popular lectures by Bertrand Russell. But it was all way over my head, and in my amateurish way I learnt very much more from his already classic *The Problems of Philosophy* (1912), his soon to be published *A History of Philosophy* (1946) and his early book on logic and mathematics *The Principles of Mathematics* (1903). That last book and Max Black's *The Nature of Mathematics* (1933) got me thinking seriously about philosophers' hugely different accounts of the nature and truth of mathematical propositions. In religious terms, I was surprised to find a strong Christian Union of evangelical students holding to a theology amazingly close to that of the Plymouth Brethren but neither amongst them nor anywhere else did I encounter any robust answer to my questions about the basis of religious truth claims. It was in fact my encounter with Ayer's notorious *Language, Truth and Logic* (1936) that most strongly influenced both my religious and more general philosophical thinking. Not because I readily accepted all that he argued but because he forced me to think about the relationship between the 'meaning' and 'truth' of propositions. The 'verifiability principle' - that 'the meaning of a proposition lies in the method of its verification' – I thought brilliantly clear and correct about the nature of mathematics and the sciences. His dogmatic assertion that all religious claims are 'meaningless' and all moral principles merely 'expressions of emotion', however, I thought manifestly false. What seemed to me to follow was that religious claims and moral principles must be at least putative forms of propositional understanding for which the methods of verification must be carefully elucidated and critically examined. By the time I left

---

PERSONAL FAVOURITES

Educational Theory (1966).
Knowledge and the Curriculum (1974).
Moral Education in a Secular Society (1974).
Education and Diversity of Belief (1985).
The Theory-Practice Relationship in Teacher Training. (1990).
Education, Knowledge and Practices (1993).
The Demands of Professional Practice and Training (1996).
The Nature of Educational Aims (1999).

Cambridge I'd got no further forward on the truth criteria of religious propositions but was impressed on moral issues by G. E. Moore's 'intuitionism' in *Principia Ethica'* (1903). By then too I had however also at least tried to read a strange book called *Tractatus, Logico-Philosophicus* (1922) by Ludwig Wittgenstein, a reclusive Fellow of Trinity who was said to have once worked closely with Russell, quarrelled seriously with him and was now developing a radically new approach to questions of language, meaning and truth with a group of brilliant young colleagues and students though as yet none of this work was available in print.

TEACHING AND EDUCATIONAL STUDY

As a new graduate in a post war Britain desperately short of mathematics teachers, I went immediately into high school teaching and, modelling myself on my own old teacher, quite readily settled to preparing able pupils for university entrance. But then on the basis of my reading in Cambridge I started puzzling over how school mathematics syllabuses and teaching might be changed to more explicitly convey to pupils a grasp of the true nature of mathematics and its intellectual significance and power. A brief return to Cambridge on leave from teaching to take a basic professional educational qualification only encouraged me in such ideas and contacting the University of London Institute of Education, where I knew Max Black had taught, I soon found myself as a part-time doctoral student under the joint supervision of their Professor of Philosophy of Education, Louis Arnaud Reid, and a psychologist who had done research on the development of children's mathematical abilities using Russell's analysis of mathematical concepts and principles as a basis.

In this new context I started attending postgraduate seminars in philosophy of education in general and, though far from sympathetic to the Wittgensteinian ideas now increasingly spreading amongst academic philosophers, Professor Reid encouraged me to explore them widely. The earliest published work of this kind was not at all obviously related to particular educational questions but Gilbert Ryle's *Concept of Mind* (1949) was different. He saw philosophy as centrally concerned with a form of analysis that seeks to clarify the meaning of concepts by showing how the superficial features of our language mislead us. We mistakenly take nouns like 'mind' or 'number' to designate 'entities' with 'properties' even if 'immaterial', we take 'thinking' to be an 'activity' if 'inner' and independent of what is 'outer'. But what was more he used such methods to explore most illuminatingly educationally important concepts like those of propositional and practical knowledge, intelligence, dispositions and teaching. Soon after, R. M. Hare's *The Language of Morals* (1952) was a similar work with direct implications for moral education. And one year later came Wittgenstein's epoch making book *Philosophical Investigations* (1953), full of complex arguments that were already provoking fundamental reconsiderations in many branches of philosophy and whose major implications for thinking about education I wanted to explore more systematically. By 1955 I was wondering if I might move out of school teaching into educational research when a new lectureship in the teaching of mathematics in the University of Oxford Department of Education was advertised for which I somewhat presumptuously applied. My interview for the post in fact took up my wider interests in philosophy of education and when I was given the job it was on the understanding that I would not only work with new graduates going into mathematics teaching but also start up an optional seminar course in contemporary philosophy and education.

OXFORD AND ANALYTICAL PHILOSOPHY

What my move to Oxford was in fact to give me was the unique opportunity to immerse myself in the revolution in British philosophy taking place at that time. With much the largest group of philosophy students in the Country studying at Oxford many of Wittgenstein's followers from Cambridge were now appearing as teachers in Oxford and greatly influencing the work there. Whenever my own teaching duties permitted I was therefore able to attend lectures and seminars by such luminaries as Anscombe, Toulmin, Ryle, Strawson, Urmson, Hare, and Austin. I also took the opportunity to do something to overcome my lack of study of the history of philosophy and was particularly swept off my feet by careful reading of Kant's Critiques of Pure and Practical Reason. It was in fact to Kant that I now began to look for a view of reason which would provide for me personally, as well as for my developing view of education, a defensible justification of moral principles as well as an overall grasp of the place of theoretical knowledge in human life. But it was from Wittgensteinian work that I took two major theses that influenced me profoundly. First, that philosophy is fundamentally concerned with helping our understanding in all forms of discourse by carefully mapping the relationships between the concepts embedded in our use of language and secondly, that Wittgenstein's 'private language argument' shows forcefully that all understanding is dependent on agreement in the application of concepts in public discourse and in particular that all our knowledge of our own as well as of other minds cannot be intelligibly based simply on episodes of individual private experience. What I did not begin to find in any of the new work in analytical philosophy however, including that specifically in philosophy of religion, was any account of how religious propositions might come to have any defensible rational justification. I was slowly in fact becoming clearer about the autonomy of moral understanding from all religious beliefs and at the same time losing much of my personal early confidence that religious claims could be given any adequate rational basis. Within a few years I was in fact to reach the sceptical conclusion that though the quest for religious understanding might be a justifiable human aspiration there seem to be no justifiable grounds for holding that any propositional beliefs about any transcendent entities can be known to be true. That education must for everyone be centrally concerned with the development of reason however was becoming a prime concern for me and having to devote so much of my time to the particular matters of the teaching of mathematics was becoming irksome. When, therefore, after four years in Oxford, Professor Reid invited me to move to London to a new lectureship specifically in philosophy of education, I was keen to accept even though it meant leaving behind all the philosophical riches available in Oxford.

LONDON AND RICHARD PETERS

My move to the London Institute of Education was however fortuitous, for when a few years later Professor Reid retired he was replaced as Head of Philosophy of Education by Richard Peters, with whom I was to start a collaboration which was to shape the whole of my academic future. Peters had studied philosophy first at Oxford, then in London, was head of a Department of Psychology and Philosophy in the University of London, had written an important book on the concept of motivation, then jointly authored a major work, *Social Principles and the Democratic State* (Benn & Peters, 1959), and had spent a sabbatical year at Harvard with Israel Scheffler, the first major American philosopher of education already developing an 'analytical' approach. Our areas of philosophical interest complemented each other and his position on many matters was even more Kantian than mine. He had both a strong scholarly background in classical studies and a firm grasp of the history of philosophy both of which I seriously lacked. But above all his firm critical confirmation of my increasingly stridently propositional approach to all knowledge and understanding gave me the confidence to explore the implications of such a view for many fundamental issues in educational theory and practice. Under his strong leadership we worked together for some 10 years basically launching the philosophy of education within the UK as a major distinct area of academic study being given the opportunity when national government decided to make school teaching an all graduate profession and all professional preparation the responsibility of universities.

At a national conference of universities convened to clarify the future shape of educational studies under their aegis, Peters arranged for me to give the lead paper analysing the nature of educational theory and for him to follow with a paper on the contribution of philosophy of education to that theory. This was only the second major paper I wrote for publication (Hirst, 1966) and in it I argued that educational theory is concerned with the formulation of the principles of educational practice, principles whose rational justification can come only from the findings of work in contributory academic disciplines such as philosophy, psychology, sociology and history. There is no unifying theory that seeks to integrate the work in these disciplines, I suggested, other than the formation of the principles whose significance can then only be seen in the results of practice based on them. The inadequacies of this account I recognised, but not how deep seated they are. By contrast Peters' own paper set out the task of philosophy of education in what I still regard as a classic statement when he outlined how it raises and seeks to answer questions about the concepts used in our understanding and conduct of the practices of education, examines the forms of justification for what is advocated and what is done, and calls in question the presuppositions that are made in these processes (Peters, 1966). But the whole problem of the nature of educational theory and of philosophy of education's contribution to it is one of the two major themes to which I have repeatedly returned over the years and which still dominate my philosophical work.

The other major theme I have constantly returned to has been that of what the most fundamental aims of education ought to be and how they should be embedded in school curricula. In my first paper on this issue, Liberal Education and the Nature of Knowledge (Hirst, 1965), I argued that the most fundamental good for us individually is the development of our naturally given mental capacities in achieving knowledge and understanding which constitute the good that the mind seeks and which is necessary for our each leading a good, a rational, life. I argued that in human history we have so far progressively developed some seven logically distinct if inter-related forms of knowledge and understanding by means of which alone we can make sense of ourselves and our world and into which a liberal education should seek to initiate us all. By a form of knowledge I meant a developing body of true propositions justified by appeal to agreed public truth criteria whose distinctive concepts, logical structure and criteria we must each seek to master. The existing forms of knowledge I suggested are mathematics, the physical and biological sciences, the human and social sciences, history, moral understanding, literature and the arts, philosophy and 'putatively' religion.

Over the ensuing years I sought to refine this thesis exploring its implications for curriculum construction and analysing the nature of teaching it implies (Hirst, 1974a). But my personal interests led me to explore particularly the nature of the three most controversial areas of such an education, those of moral education (Hirst, 1974b), religious education (Hirst, 1974a and 1985), and education in the arts (Hirst, 1974a). In these areas particularly I increasingly became aware of the significant problems I had to face stemming from my long held presupposition that all rationally defensible beliefs, actions and emotions must necessarily be anchored in propositional truths. Yet I failed to give sustained attention to these difficulties for some 10 years as I progressively became involved in matters of university administration first in London, then as Head of the Department of Education in the University of Cambridge and additionally with numerous national bodies as a major expansion of the universities took place.

MACINTYRE AND PRACTICAL REASON

When in due course I had opportunity to devote sustained attention once more to my philosophical interests it was to discover how profoundly Wittgenstein's influence had transformed academic philosophy and how inadequately I had taken on board the real messages of his *Philosophical Investigations*. There was important work now by others like that of Habermas in his *Knowledge and Human Interests* (1972) and Rorty in *Philosophy and the Mirror of Nature* (1980). But it was the work of MacIntyre in *After Virtue* (1981) and *Whose Justice? Whose Rationality?* (1988), followed by Dunne's impressive *Back to the Rough Ground* (1993), that particularly led me to radically rethink the whole character of reason, its place in human life and hence its proper place in education. First, I slowly came to the conclusion that, bemused by positivism and then by Kant, I had totally failed to appreciate the importance of Aristotle's distinction between theoretical and practical reason. Reformulating that distinction in contemporary terms I came to see a crucial difference in these two exercises of our rational capacities. The exercise of reason in a theoretical sense results in our achieving bodies of propositions about whose truth we can agree and which thereby satisfy our natural intellectual desires for knowledge and understanding. But we are capable also of the exercise of reason in achieving actions and practices which we can agree constitute our moral and social good in their satisfying our practical, material and emotional needs and desires. What it is rational to do in practice is however not something we can work out theoretically first in terms of propositional principles and then act on accordingly. The nature of action is such that what it is rational to do can be discerned only in action itself and its consequences. The exercise of practical reason has to be developed as practical wisdom that discerns what in specific particular situations and circumstances will best achieve the satisfaction of our needs and desires. The use of discourse in this situation can at best indicate what action has in the past been found good in general as a guide to our discerning what now it is good to do in other complex circumstances. But provoked by MacIntyre I secondly came to see far more clearly than I had ever before that we are not constituted as the individual persons we are simply by nature and what we add to that by way of knowledge and understanding.. Rather we become who we are only by the exercise of our individual capacities in relating to others and by participating in, or reacting to, all manner of socially constructed practices of which we are the heirs. All that we are as persons publicly and privately we become by way of our response to features of our publicly shared social world of languages and practices.

Not surprisingly these two major shifts in my thinking led eventually to my taking a much more clearly neo-Aristotelian view of the good life for each of us. If human societies are seen as ever more complex structures of social practices developed for the articulation and satisfaction of our naturally given, inter-related needs and desires, this leads readily to the concept of a good life for each of us as a life which flourishes by maximising the development and satisfaction of our desires across the whole trajectory of a life within the social contexts available to us. Such a good life is thus a life of practical reason conducted in response to the most rationally developed practices in our context. And such a life is of course only possible for us if we fully recognise our necessary inter-relatedness with and dependence upon others with differing natural capacities and who are equally seeking a good life in the social contexts we share. In that sense our good lives depend on our living in a good society. What this new view means of course is that I still hold the good life to be a rational life but now that it is one grounded above all in the development and exercise of practical reason rather than theoretical reason though the two are necessarily interrelated in complex ways. And if that is how the good life for each of us is to be understood then the most fundamental aims of education can no longer be conceived as in my earlier notion of a liberal education.

EDUCATIONAL THEORY AND THE AIMS OF EDUCATION

Throughout the period of re-examination of certain of my fundamental philosophical beliefs I wrote nothing for publication on specifically philosophical issues. Being much involved in matters concerning the professional education and training of teachers however, I nevertheless wrote several papers in which I considered the issue of the nature of educational theory and its relationship to practice. Prior to my detailed study of the writings of MacIntyre I wrote a major paper (Hirst, 1983) which shows how the influence of other philosophers was already helping to steer me firmly away from my original rationalistic account of the practices of education as the application of rationally justified propositional principles. By 1990 (Hirst, 1990) I was describing teaching much more in MacIntyre's language as engaging in a body of developing social practices into which student teachers should be critically initiated and by 1996 (Hirst, 1996) was exploring this approach in more analytical detail. More generally I came to see that the knowledge and understanding of education that professionals need has to be understood as discourse embedded in the existing practices of education into which successive generations of teachers need to be critically initiated and in which alone they can develop the complex personal qualities of practical reason that their work demands. What philosophy of education as a theoretical propositional form of understanding and knowledge can then do is promote the critical examination of the conceptual apparatus used in educational discourse and practices, of the forms of justification of what is done and advocated, and of the presuppositions made in these processes.

By 1991, I felt clear enough about the implications of my new philosophical position for re-characterising the fundamental aims of education to give an invitation paper to the annual conference of the Philosophy of Education Society in America on that theme (Hirst 1991). A more considered version appeared two years later (Hirst, 1993) and my clearest formulation of the aims in 1999 (Hirst, 1999). The position for which I argue is that if a good life for each of us is a life of practical reason as I have outlined it then our upbringing and education must consist of our progressive initiation into those social practices in response to which we can each find our greatest satisfaction and fulfilment over the trajectory of our whole life. In any given social context there will be practices that are clearly necessary for any good life and which must therefore figure in the education of all. Many will relate to naturally given needs and capacities, physical, psychological and social, in the management of oneself in one's environment, the establishing and sustaining of personal and other social relationships and the conduct of effective communication. Others will relate to more complex and sophisticated needs and interests that have emerged to do with say, finance, law, and politics. Beyond these are practices which are desirable according to personal differences and social circumstances, such as those of the arts, sports, different occupations and of intellectual and religious pursuits. Wide opportunity to discover those practices of significance for each individual is crucial, at first under the guidance of parents and later with the help of teachers but leading on to individual personal choice. Initiation too must cover for every practice the full range of its significant elements in the concepts, discourse, activities, judgements, knowledge, principles, skills and dispositions it involves. What matters most in the practicalities of the structuring and conduct of such an education is that it be determined throughout by the exercise of practical reason by those who are themselves adequately equipped in the practices for which they are the initiators.

THE PRESENT AND THE FUTURE

For a considerable time now I have been aware that in my published work I have never given sufficient attention to spelling out fully enough the concept of human nature presupposed by my view that human beings are distinctively marked out by their capacities for practical and theoretical reason. The position I have come to take on this is that shared by an increasing number of philosophers who have worked in the analytical tradition and is perhaps best exemplified in books by Strawson (1992), Kenny (1989) and MacIntyre (1999). Drawing on both philosophical and empirical work this view sees us as the latest natural entities in an evolving sequence of distinctive types of entities ranging from the inorganic, through to the organic entities of plant life, thence to those of animal life and finally to the entities of human life. In this process of evolution the entities of each later stage possess newly emerging characteristic properties and capacities that presuppose certain distinctive properties of the preceding stages. The result of this approach is that our major inter-related distinctive human capacities are seen as those for concept formation, language use and propositional reasoning plus those for intentional agency, self-conscious affective awareness of our mental states, and practical reasoning. It is these capacities that make possible our intellectual achievements of knowledge and understanding and our practical achievements of personal and social good lives. Upbringing and education are then the intentional enterprises that seek such distinctive ends as appropriate for every child.

In this fundamentally philosophical view of each human life and its possibilities there is however no longer any significant place for the religious beliefs and practices that dominated so comprehensively my early upbringing. In this picture all that we can intelligibly know as true and discern as morally good is of its nature the product of, and is limited by, our rational capacities. The analysis on which it rests sees all our concepts of entities, their existence, character and qualities as inextricably dependant on our bodily capacities for observation and intentional behaviour. The notions of transcendent entities and their characteristics are then in principle elusive in so far as the very notion of their transcendence withdraws the criteria of meaning for the concepts being employed. What it means for an entity to have mind, intelligence or knowledge, be spiritual or capable of love, are all notions that can be given content only by virtue of our experience as essentially limited and constrained, embodied beings with the relationships we have to other such beings. For a being without our publicly shared capacities we have no way of cashing their significant application. That God exists as the cause of everything that exists is a confused or indeed contradictory notion unless the concepts of cause and existence are changing from their ordinary meaning when applied to God. But to what are they then changing? At best their meaning is in some sense analogical or metaphorical but they are then being used without the elements of non-metaphorical underpinning that all our clearly intelligible use of metaphor requires (Kenny, 2004). Similarly the notion that faith or trust can ever itself justifiably be the basis of a legitimate claim to truth or to morally good action is simply to cease to use the concepts of truth and moral good as these have coherent meaning in our basic discourse. This is not to deny that we may justifiably marvel at our existence or puzzle over our inability to coherently ask let alone answer these metaphorical questions. Nor is it to fail to recognise that we might find great support and comfort in life from religious interpretations of human experience. But it is to insist that truth and goodness can only justifiably be found elsewhere in the conclusions reached in the exercise of practical and theoretical reason. It is to insist too that religious interpretations of experience to be acceptable at all must be consistent with the achievements of theoretical and practical reason and that even then their intelligibility and validity as accounts of transcendent entities and events are from a rational point of view at best elusively analogical. It is indeed to be religiously agnostic.

Academic philosophy has in the 20th Century faced the challenge of two major movements, those of analytical philosophy and post-modernism. The positive significance of both has, I consider, now been absorbed into the historical development of Western philosophy and there seems to be a slowly increasing consensus on the broad conceptual framework within which we can now best make sense of human nature and what constitutes a good life. This I have briefly sketched above primarily from the analytical point of view within which I have worked. Its major implications for educational aims and practices I have however so far only outlined in the most general terms and their working out in much greater detail I think the most important task for contemporary philosophy of education. There is in many Western societies a feeling that the upbringing of children and much institutionalised education have lost their clear sense of purpose and hence also of how best to decide their means. It seems to me philosophers of education are increasingly in a position to help significantly in elucidating those aims and practices in a way appropriate for the institutions of modern secular and pluralist liberal democracies that are at least in principle committed to the pursuits of reason in all their affairs. Little such work has so far been done in any detail but in their recent writings John White (2002, 2005) and Patricia White (1983, 1996) have given many of us an exemplary lead. Over the years I have changed some of my basic philosophical beliefs and I think for good reasons. But as I have argued in my most recent comments on the topic (Hirst, 2005), I have no doubt whatever that Richard Peters (1966) was quite right that philosophy of education is that historic academic theoretical pursuit whose task it is to seek to clarify the concepts we use in our understanding and practices of education, the forms of justification we use for what we do and the presuppositions we make. To those ends as pursued within our contemporary context I remain completely committed.

REFERENCES

Ayer, A. J. (1936). *Language, truth and logic.* London: Faber.
Benn, S. I., & Peters, R. S. (1959). *Social principles and the democratic state.* London: George Allen & Unwin.
Black, M. (1933). *The nature of mathematics.* Cambridge University Press.
Dunne, J. (1993). *Back to the rough ground.* Indianna: University of Notre Dame Press.
Habermas, J. (1972). *Knowledge and human interests.* London: Heinemann.
Hare, R. M. (1952). *The language of morals.* Oxford University Press.
Hirst, P. H. (1965). Liberal education and the nature of knowledge. Reprinted in Hirst P. H. (1974a).
Hirst, P. H. (1966). Educational theory. In J. W. Tibble (Ed.), *The study of education.* London: Routledge
Hirst, P. H. (1974a). *Knowledge and the curriculum.* London: Routledge.
Hirst, P. H. (1974b). *Moral education in a secular society.* London: Hodder & Stoughton
Hirst, P. H. (1985). Education and diversity of belief. In M. C. Felderhof. (Ed.), *Religious education in a pluralist society.* London: Hodder & Stoughton.
Hirst, P. H. (1990). The theory-practice relationship in teaacher training. In M. Booth, J. Furlong, & M. Wilkin (Eds.), *Partnership in initial teacher training.* London: Cassell.
Hirst, P. H. (1991). Educational aims: Their nature and content. In *Proceedings of the Philosophy of Education Society.* U.S.A. 1991.
Hirst, P. H. (1993). Education, knowledge and practices. In R. Barrow & P. White (Eds.) *Beyond liberal education.* London: Routledge.
Hirst, P. H. (1996). The demands of professional practice and training. In J. Furlong & R. Smith (Eds.), *The role of higher education in initial teacher training.* London: Kogan Page.
Hirst, P. H. (1999). The nature of educational aims. In R. Marples (Ed.), *The aims of education.* London: Routledge.
Hirst, P. H. (2005). Philosophy and education – A symposium. A response and a rejoinder to Wilfred Carr. *Journal of Philosophy of Education, 39*(4), 615-632.
Kenny, A. (1989). *The metaphysics of mind.* Oxford University Press.
Kenny, A. (2004). *The unknown god.* London & New York: Continuum.
MacIntyre, A. (1981). *After virtue.* London: Duckworth.
MacIntyre, A. (1988). *Whose justice? Which rationality?* London: Duckworth.
MacIntyre, A. (1999). *Dependent rational animals.* London: Duckworth.
Moore, G. E. (1903). *Principia ethica.* Cambridge University Press.
Peters, R. S. (1966). The philosophy of education. In J. W. Tibble (Ed.), *The study of education.* London: Routledge.
Rorty, R. (1980). *Philosophy and the mirror of nature.* Oxford: Blackwell.
Russell, B. (1903). *The principles of mathematics.* Cambridge University Press.
Russell, B. (1912). *The problems of philosophy.* London: Williams and Norgate.
Russell, B. (1946). *A history of philosophy.* London: Allen and Unwin.
Ryle, G. (1949). *The concept of mind.* London: Hutchinson.
Strawson, P. F. (1992). *Analysis and metaphysics.* Oxford University Press.
White, J. (2002). *The child's mind.* London: Routledge.
White, J. (2005). *The curriculum and the child.* London: Routledge.
White, P. (1983). *Beyond domination: An essay in the political philosophy of education.* London: Routledge.
White, P. (1996). *Civic virtues and public schooling.* New York and London: Teachers College Press.
Wittgenstein, L. (1922). *Tractatus logico-philosophicus.* Trans by C. K. Ogden. London: Routledge.
Wittgenstein, L. (1953). *Philosophical investigations.* Oxford: Blackwell.

Paul Hirst
University of Cambridge

JANE ROLAND MARTIN

IT'S NOT ON THE LIST

I was the student without a paper topic. My high school friend Heather had no problem finding one. An aspiring lawyer, she reported first on The Egyptians and the Law, next on The Greeks and the Law, then The Romans and the Law, and after that it was smooth sailing. My friend Mary had no trouble either. Hoping to become a farmer, she wrote on The Egyptians and Agriculture, The Greeks and Agriculture, etc. etc. But I had no such dreams. No occupation called out to me, no subject captured my interest. Even the topic I finally settled on for my senior year research project at our Dewey-inspired school -- The History of Progressive Education--meant nothing to me at the time.

In college I had the presence of mind to avoid courses with papers and I tried to pursue the same policy when, after drifting into school teaching, I enrolled in a master's program in education so as to receive pay raises. And then, because it was the only class that met in the late afternoon, I found myself in "Research on Teaching" where on the very first day the instructor read a long list of research topics from which we were obliged to choose.

For the first time in my life a paper topic spoke my name. I rushed up to Dr. Cogan after class and told him with a certain amount of pride, "I want to write on the case method of teaching." He looked at me, shook his head in wonder, and said, "It isn't on the list." Thinking him extraordinarily obtuse I replied, "What do you mean it isn't on the list? I just heard you say it." "I'm sorry," he said, "it isn't on the list. You can write on it if you really want to. But it isn't on the list."

Looking back some fifty years later I see this moment as pivotal, for I think it fair to say that not being on the list is a metaphor for my life in the philosophy of education. Although I did not know it at the time, in deciding to go with the case method of teaching I was laying the groundwork for my future career.

When I enrolled in Dr. Cogan's course I had no idea that such a thing as educational research existed. I still remember where I was sitting the day I realized that some people actually spend their lives doing this work, and I can recall my excitement. When I tried to picture myself running experiments, collecting data, doing statistical analyses, however, my imagination failed. It was then that Jack Easley, one of Israel Scheffler's first doctoral students, urged me to take a course with his mentor. "Analytic philosophy," he told me, "is the key to everything." The next semester I signed up for a group reading course with Scheffler--it was the last class I took for my master's degree--and soon thereafter I left school teaching to be a fulltime graduate student.

Before I immersed myself in analytic philosophy I was deeply troubled by the mindless 5th grade curriculum of my Massachusetts public school: social studies as a set of unconnected concepts; math as a set of unrelated facts and techniques;

L.J. Waks (ed.), Leaders in Philosophy of Education: Intellectual Self Portraits, 125–134.
© 2008 *Sense Publishers. All rights reserved.*

music as songs to be sung in solfege. When, however, I tried to design better curricula, I was brought up short by the arbitrariness of my attempts. What justified my thinking that this social studies curriculum was better than the one in place? On what basis was it legitimate to decide which content to include? Once I discovered analytic philosophy, I knew that to answer my own questions I would have to continue my studies.

The trouble was that the further I traveled into philosophy, the more distant seemed the problems that had once exercized me. Before long, debates about the structure of historical explanation loomed larger on my horizon than discussions of the school curriculum. Insofar as I thought about education at all, definitions of teaching and learning commanded my attention. When some four decades later I wrote in *Coming of Age in Academe* (2000) that the academy's admission fee includes estrangement from the real world and its problems, I was speaking from experience. By 1961, the year I received my PhD, I had thoroughly internalized the lesson that the greater one's distance from one's object of study, the better one can understand it. I had become convinced that, intellectually speaking, there was no higher good than clarity. I had been persuaded that philosophers qua philosophers were not qualified to make value judgments. And I had learned to view with suspicion those few philosophers who wrote and spoke in a language that everyone could understand. My first published paper, originally written for one of Scheffler's seminars, illustrates the distance I traveled from the schoolroom during my graduate studies. "On 'Knowing How' and 'Knowing That' (1959) was a discussion of one man's critique of another man's analysis of the verb "to know."

Thanks to Gilbert Ryle's *The Concept of Mind*, the knowing how/knowing that distinction was very much on the analytic philosophy list when in 1960 I went to my first meeting of the Philosophy of Education Society--a meeting attended by only one other woman. But analytic philosophy was not on the philosophy of education list; in fact, analytic endeavors were not allowed on the program and the few analytic philosophers in attendance had to meet in someone's room each evening to read and discuss each other's papers. I owe a great debt to Bob Ennis

---

PERSONAL FAVORITES

Books

Reclaiming a Conversation, (1985)
The Schoolhome (1992)
Changing the Educational Landscape (1994)
Coming of Age in Academe (2000)
Cultural Miseducation (2002)
Educational Metamorphoses (2007)

Articles

Science in a Different Style, *American Philosophical Quarterly,25* (1988), pp. 129-140

Another Look at the Doctrine of Verstehen, _British Journal for the Philosophy of Science_ (1969), pp.53-6. Reprinted in Michael Martin and Lee C. McIntyre (eds,) *Readings in the Philosophy of Social Science* (Cambridge, MA: MIT Press, 1994), pp. 247-258.

Basic Actions and Simple Actions, *American Philosophical Quarterly* (1971) pp.59-68.

---

with whom I had corresponded about his article on neutrality. Not only did he invite me to contribute a chapter to the groundbreaking book he was editing with B. Othaniel Smith. (Martin, 1961) He made sure that these "young Turks" welcomed me into their small circle.

That was the first of two heady counter-cultural experiences I have had in my career. The second time I found myself in the company of people so enthusiastic, so intellectually excited, and so willing to learn from one another was when I started to inquire into the place of women in educational thought. As I immersed myself in the feminist literature and got to know a number of the pioneering authors of what was then called "the new scholarship on women," I once again felt in the vanguard of a revolution in scholarship.

My work on women was launched in 1980 when I received a fellowship from the Bunting Institute of Radcliffe College. I am eternally grateful for the Bunting's gift of time, an office of my own, and the opportunity to work closely with psychologist Carol Gilligan and her associates. In addition to sharing her ideas with me and providing invaluable feedback on mine, Gilligan enlarged my understanding of my own research program immeasurably. Not the least of her contributions was to point out to me that in a matter of months my question had shifted. After discovering early on that women had practically no place at all in that area's subject matter, I had begun asking, What happens to educational thought when women are brought into it?

My immediate reason for applying to the Bunting Institute was to write the Presidential Address to the Philosophy of Education Society that I delivered in April of 1981. In the event, I completed four papers that year (1994, ch. 1-3; 1982) that formed the basis for *Reclaiming a Conversation* (1985). Reconstructing a philosophical conversation over time and space about women's education, this book established that when women are brought into educational thought everything changes. Naturally, the question arises of how to educate girls, but that is the least of it. Standard interpretations of central historical texts such as Plato's *Republic* and Rousseau's *Emile* have to be reconsidered; commonly accepted beliefs about the function of education, the nature of school, and what it means to be an educated person must be rejected; and the assumption that whatever is considered to be an appropriate education for boys is adequate for both sexes turns out to be mistaken.

Needless to say, my new topic was not on the list. Amazingly enough, in just two decades analytic philosophy had taken over the philosophy of education list. But in 1980 the study of women was no more on its agenda than it was on any other mainstream one.

I must confess that when I published my Bunting Institute findings about the place of women in the subject matter of my discipline--or rather, our lack of place as either the subjects or the objects of educational thought--I had no idea what the consequences of this "off-list" excursion would be. I never dreamed that colleagues would excoriate my work, accuse me of no longer doing philosophy, or say that women educational thinkers did not qualify for the canon and that the whole subject of women's education was out of bounds: all of which amounts to their saying that my topic was off the list and so was I. Yet they did. Nor did I know how eager many, many women and some men across the United States and around the world were to talk about the taboo subject of women. But to my great surprise they were.

With hindsight I realize that colleagues may have been troubled not only because I was writing about women but also because I had made a culture crossing. By the time *Reclaiming a Conversation* was published, I had shed my analytic philosopher identity. It had never been an entirely comfortable fit, for as my own research on women showed, the traits composing it were gendered in favor of males; which is another way of saying that they were evaluated negatively when exhibited by people like me. Be this as it may, I have never turned my back on my philosophical training or renounced my earlier analytic findings. On the contrary, the training that I received at Harvard from Scheffler and others is the bedrock on which all my work rests. Moreover, *Reclaiming a Conversation* (1985) and the books that followed are informed by my early discussion of the relationship between the disciplines of knowledge and the curriculum, my analysis of the concept of a hidden curriculum, my critique of the received theory of liberal education, and my inquiry into the nature of the educational basics.

Still, in working with classic texts and with long neglected works like Mary Wollstonecraft's *A Vindication of the Rights of Woman* and Catharine Beecher's *A Treatise on Domestic Economy*; in taking seriously the new scholarship on women; in drawing on the insights of literature and biography; in attending to the social, political, and cultural contexts in which statements are made and practices pursued; and in addressing real life problems of education: I was abandoning many of the analytic mores I had once embraced.

Despite the transformation of both me and my work, a close reader will find continuity between my "pre-feminist" and post-analytic writings (see Mulcahy, 2002). He or she will also discover that these latter follow one upon the other in what might almost be considered a straight-line progression. No sooner did *Reclaiming a Conversation* appear in print than a colleague informed me that her students wanted to know what I meant when I said in the last chapter that education must give "the reproductive processes of society" their due. It took me seven years to figure out what I meant and *The Schoolhome* (1992) represents my answer.

The Schoolhome takes as its point of departure John Dewey's great insight that when home changes radically, so must school; otherwise, an important part of children's education will be at risk of extinction (Dewey, 1956/1900). It was 1899 when Dewey said this and he was keenly aware that the Industrial Revolution had moved manufacture out of the private home and into the public world. Because children acquired a host of valuable traits in the course of participating in that manufacture, he proposed that the school curriculum be transformed and work be placed at its center. In effect, he envisioned school as in this respect a functional equivalent of home.

By the late 1980s when I began addressing the question that *Reclaiming a Conversation* left hanging, I had become deeply concerned about the violence that children in the U.S. were experiencing both at home and in the world. And then it struck me that in the last decades of the 20th century home was once again undergoing a transformation and its teachings were at risk. This time, however, the problem was not that work had been removed from the home but that a domestic vacuum had developed in children's lives because women as well as men were now going out to work. (Many women left home to go to work in the past, but most women returned home when they had children.) Harking back to Maria Montessori's Casa dei Bambini, the solution I proposed in *The Schoolhome* was to turn school into "a moral equivalent of home."

Needless to say, the basic idea of *The Schoolhome* was off the list. Dewey notwithstanding, late 20th century philosophers seemed loath to explore the idea or concept of school. That my new conception of school drew upon Montessori's work did not help matters for of course she was not on the list. Nor did it improve the situation that I went beyond stressing the importance of home's curriculum in the 3Cs of care, concern, and connection to propose that home could be a model for school. Because of its location in the so-called private sphere of society and its close association with women, home was certainly not thought to be a bona fide subject for the philosophy of education.

After publication of *The Schoolhome* I was again greeted with mixed messages. Even as some colleagues called my ideas essentialist, classist, and racist, teachers told me they were trying to do in their classrooms the very things I said needed to be done, Montessori educators told me I had gotten her philosophy right, and a young woman undergraduate in Tokyo thanked me saying that now she knew that she could marry, have children, and follow her dream of working in banking.

History also repeated itself with the appearance of *The Schoolhome* in that I again found it necessary to take up questions I had left open. In particular, having called for an inclusionary rather than an exclusionary school curriculum in this book, I at long last felt compelled to address the problem that had sent me into philosophy--namely that there is too much to teach; or, as I was beginning to conceptualize the problem, that there is a superabundance of cultural stock. In addition, queries from colleagues and students made me see that in my eagerness to establish home as a bona fide partner in the education of a nation's young, I had slighted the numerous other educational agents in our midst. Religious institutions, neighborhood gangs, the media, the military, governmental groups, local businesses, non-profit organizations: once one agrees that the stock a culture passes down from one generation to the next encompasses far more than "high" culture or the "higher" learning, the list of educational agents becomes well nigh endless.

This time it took me ten years to deal with the gaps in my text. The end result was *Cultural Miseducation* (2002) a book based on my 1995 DeGarmo Lecture to the American Educational Research Association (1996), my 1996 John Dewey Lecture, and a 1998 lecture to the U.S. Philosophy of Education Society (1999).

How is a culture's wealth to be defined? Who is qualified to contribute to it? How can we preserve a culture's assets for the next generation? How can we minimize the transmission of cultural liabilities such as violence, poverty, greed, mendacity, and hatred of other races, religions, genders, ethnicities, and sexual orientations? In *Cultural Miseducation* I developed a "cultural wealth perspective" that allows one to ask basic questions about education that do not appear on

129

philosophy of education's list. They do not because the dominant perspective of Western educational thought has been that of the individual. Of course, the education of individual people--and, by extension, groups of individuals--is of the utmost importance. I hoped, however, to supplement the standpoint of the individual with one that is equally valid and in so doing also make clear how important education's unintended aspects often are.

Just as the educational landscape is transformed when women enter, everything changes when a cultural wealth perspective is brought into it. View education in this light and the realities of multiple educational agency can no longer be ignored. The whole wide range of a culture's groups and institutions can in plain view be seen transmitting cultural stock to young and old alike. One can also then see that this stock includes cultural liabilities as well as assets, that the portion of stock that the culture expects schools to pass down is relatively small, and that the transmission of stock is as likely as not to be unintended and unwitting. With these new perceptions comes the realization that cultural miseducation is a fact of contemporary life. And with this discovery comes the understanding that what in *Cultural Miseducation* I called "the new problem of generations"--namely, how to maximize the transmission of cultural assets while minimizing the transmission of cultural liabilities--is one of the most pressing that our or any culture faces.

Given that *Cultural Miseducation* is not specifically about women, it may be wondered how it can possibly represent a point on a straight line progression from *Reclaiming a Conversation*. The fact that it addresses very general questions that a book which sought to answer the question *Reclaiming a Conversation* left open testifies, however, to the validity of my discovery that when women enter the educational realm, the whole landscape is transformed. Furthermore, *Cultural Miseducation* provides a language in which to describe--or, if you will, a conceptual framework with which to understand--what I was doing in its predecessors, namely make a case for the preservation and transmission to future generations of valuable portions of this culture's wealth: in the one instance, the ideas of Plato, Rousseau, Wollstonecraft, Beecher, and Gilman about women's education; and in the other, the knowledge, skills, attitudes, values, practices, and world views that the culture has historically associated with the private home and family.

The straight-line progression does not end with *Cultural Miseducation* for the book I am now writing--tentatively entitled *Education as Change*--addresses the question of whether the perspectives of the culture and the individual can be joined together. The answer I give is that they can be, but it is only because I deviated from the straight and narrow that I have been able to see how this can be done.

In the 1970s, largely because I was teaching at the University of Massachusetts, Boston, I began collecting stories from fact and fiction of what I eventually came to see as case studies of educational metamorphoses; that is, whole person transformations due not to drugs or the wave of a wand but to education. When I sent *Cultural Miseducation* to the publisher, I had every intention of moving directly on to its unanswered question, but my case studies chose that very moment to assert themselves. Thus it was that when the American Educational Studies Association invited me to give their 2002 Kneller Lecture (2004), I decided to talk about them. In the event, the lecture all but wrote itself and when I was done I knew that I had a chapter outline for a book. And so against my better judgment, for I firmly believed that I was getting sidetracked, I took time away from my mainline project to write *Educational Metamorphoses*. (2007)

Upon finishing *Educational Metamorphoses* my first surprise was that what I had all along considered a digression led me directly to the solution of how to unite the two perspectives. One of the book's main theses is that the whole person or identity transformations that every single one of us undergoes in a lifetime are also culture crossings. This is most easily seen in the case of Minik, the small Inuit boy who after being brought to New York City by explorer Robert Peary turned into an All American boy. But it is also apparent in the metamorphoses experienced by G. B. Shaw's Eliza Doolittle, Victor the Wild Boy of Aveyron, Malcolm X, and the many other cases I discuss. Another central theme is that practically everyone undergoes a series of such metamorphoses/ crossings in a lifetime. When on the completion of *Educational Metamorphoses* I returned to my self-imposed challenge, I realized that because of their size, these radical transformations serve, as it were, as magnifying glasses through which one can more clearly see education at work.

My second surprise was to discover how fruitful the idea of educational metamorphoses is. While my book about them was still in press I had occasion to write an essay for a volume on education for democratic citizenship and another one for a volume on women in higher education. In both instances my recent inquiries allowed me to see, as I would not have done otherwise, that a whole person transformation/culture crossing constituted the heart of the matter. My study of the relevant literatures also disclosed that these two problems are seldom, if ever, constructed with this in mind.

Educational Metamorphoses was actually my second deviation from the straight and narrow. My first occurred when I took time off from working on *Cultural Miseducation* to write a book about women in the academy. As *The Schoolhome* was a product of my concern about the violence in U.S. society, *Coming of Age in Academe* was the result of my alarm about the direction in which feminist scholars in the academy appeared to be heading. Based on two long theoretical papers that were published in the journal *Signs* and a keynote address I gave at a conference at Duke University, (1994b, 1996, 1997) this book investigated the price that women scholars were paying for membership in academia. Offering an immigrant interpretation of women's several entrances into higher education, it asked what kind of transformation of the academy is needed for women to feel at home as students and professors without losing sight of their mothers, daughters, sisters, half-sisters, female cousins, and aunts.

Perhaps because I saw *Coming of Age in Academe* as a digression, it took me a while to realize that its conceptualization of women as immigrants to the academy fed directly into my idea that whole person transformations are culture crossings. Finally, however, it dawned on me that on my first off-the-course junket I had discussed a special case of the phenomenon whose general contours I outlined on my second such adventure.

CONCLUDING REFLECTIONS

If there is anything I have regretted in the course of my off-list career it is that I did not teach graduate students and did not have access to the facilities that a major research university would have provided for I would have liked to set in motion some of the research projects that in my writings I said were needed. On the other hand, had I not in 1972 become a member of the Philosophy Department at the University of Massachusetts in Boston, I might never have found my way back from the ivory tower.

My trip home from pure philosophy began in the 1960s when student protests about the irrelevance of academic learning resuscitated the Deweyan beliefs about education that I had breathed in with the air as a child and that my doctoral studies had nearly extinguished. Should school be divorced from the world? Should theory and practice be rent asunder? I had once known better. Remembering that my reason for leaving teaching was that I hoped eventually to improve educational practice, I started then and there to mend my ways.

The return journey was far more difficult than I anticipated for no one had taught me how to apply my philosophical training to everyday experience. It helped more than I can say to join a faculty where I was surrounded by colleagues with similar concerns and a department that soon took the radical step of making it part of its mission to convince students that philosophy does bear directly on human affairs.

My subsequent decision to study the place of women in educational thought also hastened my return from the ivory tower. In 1980 a fundamental premise of feminist scholarship was that academic learning should illuminate the lives and experiences of women past and present in all corners of the earth. My new inquiries thus put me in touch with the world as I, a mother of two sons, knew it. With items such as marriage, mothering, domesticity, sex role stereotypes, a gender based division of labor, and women's double-binds now on my list, I was at long last able to identify with my subject matter. After hearing me respond to a lengthy attack on the papers I wrote at the Bunting Institute, a man who had once voiced the concern that if I married and had children I would abandon my career said, "You are a different person. What's happened to you?" I replied, "I finally know what I am saying."

Have I never regretted going off the list? Had I done so in response to momentary whims and fancies, I might well have rued the day for a person who goes off-list can feel very lonely and one who stays off-list is apt to be treated as an outsider. But my reasons were not so arbitrary.

Let me say parenthetically that I have always assumed that my not being able to find a paper topic was a serious defect and that the fault was in me. It was only as I was starting to write the last paragraphs of this chapter that it occurred to me that perhaps the fault resided not in me but in an unspoken culture wide list that ruled out the very topics that might have gripped a young girl. I will never know the answer to this conundrum but I do know that in my lifetime the philosophy of education list has been relatively short and has excluded any number of topics of great moment for both men and women.

Although my scholarly work has undergone at least one major transformation over the years, certain constants run through it, perhaps the most striking of which is an inclusionary impulse. Long before I documented the missing women in educational thought and called for our inclusion I challenged the thesis that the disciplines of knowledge have the ruling hand in what is and is not taught in school, saying that the disciplines constitute one way of life or form of human activity among many and that the many deserve a place in the educational scheme of things. I criticized the received view of liberal education as the development of rational mind for being too narrow, saying that liberal education needs to be understood as the development of persons who think and act and in whom reason and emotion are inextricably bound together. I also argued for a broadly inclusive conception of school subjects while questioning the dogma that there is a short list of bona fide school subjects and an even shorter list of what can qualify as an educational basic.

Once I started to bring women into educational thought philosophy of education's exclusionary tendencies became even more evident than they had been. For better or worse, we women carry with us a great deal of cultural baggage. Thus, when women are missing from the educational realm, so is the private world of home and family; which is to say that the tasks, duties, activities, and responsibilities that cultures assign us are missing as well as the traits they attribute to us. Small wonder the landscape changes dramatically when women enter it. And small wonder that educational thinkers today are apt to welcome women into the educational realm but want us to leave our cultural baggage behind.

The inclusionary impulse that motivated both my Bunting Institute papers and *Reclaiming a Conversation* can also be seen at work in *The Schoolhome* for there I challenged the assumption that home and family belong to the private sphere and are not, therefore, the business of education. In *Cultural Miseducation* and *Educational Metamorphoses* I in turn rejected narrow definitions of education that limit it to processes that are consciously intended and whose outcomes are valuable.

In citing some of the list's omissions I do not mean to understate the difficulties of going off-list, of which loneliness is merely an example. It has, however, been my good fortune to have in Michael Martin a philosopher husband with whom I have been able to talk through all my ideas and who has supported my work at every step of the way. I have also been lucky enough to belong to Phaedra, a small group of philosophers who have read and critiqued almost everything I have written. Moreover, and I cannot stress this enough, I am a product of--or rather, a beneficiary of--the experiment in education that took place in the U.S. in the early decades of the 20th century. Interviews with my classmates have made me realize that one of the things our progressive school taught us was that it is all right to be different and very important to speak out when you encounter something in your world that needs changing.

In my case, moreover, the rewards of not being on the list have far outweighed the penalties. What greater happiness can there be for someone who never knew what to write about than to spend her days delving into problems that fascinate her? What greater joy than to know that she is writing about issues that matter? What greater satisfaction than to discover that an exploration of the off-the list topics to which she seems to have been drawn ever since that fateful moment in Dr. Cogan's classroom can sometimes illuminate and occasionally even transform on-list concerns? And what greater delight than to be served a fortune cookie the night before completing this chapter whose message read: "Do not follow where the path may lead. Go where there is no path...and leave a trail."

REFERENCES

Dewey, J. (1956/1900). *The school and society*. Chicago: University of Chicago Press (originally published 1900).

Roland, J. (1959). On 'knowing how' and 'knowing that' *The Philosophical Review, LXVII*, 379-388.

Roland, J. (1961). On the reduction of 'knowing that' to 'knowing how'. In B. Othaniel Smith & Robert H. Ennis (Eds.), *Language and concepts of education* (pp. 59-71). Chicago: Rand McNally & Co.

Roland, J. (1982). Sex equality and education: A case study. In Mary Vetterling-Braggin (Ed.), *'Femininity,' 'masculinity,' and 'androgyny'* (pp. 279-300). Totowa, NJ: Littlefield, Adams & Co.

Roland, J. (1985). *Reclaiming a conversation: The ideal of the educated woman*. New Haven: Yale University Press

Roland, J. (1992). *The schoolhome: Rethinking schools for changing families*. Cambridge: Harvard University Press.

Roland, J. (1994a). *Changing the educational landscape*. New York: Routledge.

Roland, J. (1994b). Methodological essentialism, false difference, and other dangerous traps. *Signs, 19*, 630-657.

Roland, J. (1996). Aerial distance, esotericism, and other closely related traps. *Signs, 21*, 585-614.

Roland, J. (1996). There's too much to teach: Cultural wealth in an age of scarcity. *Educational Researcher, 25*(2), 4-10, 16.

Roland, J. (1997). Bound for the promised land: The gendered character of higher education. *Duke Journal of Gender Law and Policy, 4*(1), 3-26.

Roland, J. (1999). The wealth of cultures and the problem of generations. In S. Tozer (Ed.), *Philosophy of education 1999* (pp. 23-38). Urbana, IL: Philosophy of Education Society.

Roland, J. (2000). *Coming of age in academe: Rekindling women's hopes and reforming the academy*. New York: Routledge.

Roland, J. (2002). *Cultural miseducation: In search of a democratic solution*. New York: Teachers College Press.

Roland, J. (2004). Educational metamorphoses, *Educational Studies, 34*(1), 7-24.

Roland, J. (2007). *Educational metamorphoses: Philosophical reflections on identity and culture*. Lanham, MD: Rowman & Littlefield.

Mulcahy, D. G. (2002). *Knowledge, gender, and schooling: The feminist educational thought of Jane Roland Martin*. Westport, CT: Bergin & Garvey.

Jane Roland Martin
University of Massachusetts, Boston

NEL NODDINGS

A WAY OF LIFE

This chapter is organized around my chief philosophical and educational interests. The work described has been inspired by several great loves: my husband, Jim— my best friend since age fourteen; ten wonderful kids who never accused me of neglecting them, although I'm sure I did sometimes; an exciting and supportive institution, Stanford University; and the world of ideas and books. Here's part of the story.

THE ROOTS OF CARING

From the age of seven or eight, I knew that I wanted to be a teacher. In third grade, as we stood for the daily pledge of allegiance, I could see the red roofs of Montclair State Teachers College where I would some day go to prepare as a teacher. (It would become Montclair State College while I was there and is today Montclair State University.) Grades one to six were spent in a wonderful, progressive public school to which I was devoted. Then my parents moved us to the Raritan Bay area of New Jersey and, after a period of desperate homesickness, I fell newly in love with the salt air of the Jersey shore. Not only that, I fell in love with my high school. For me, school was a second home; indeed, sometimes it was my main home. I hated the end of a school year in June and couldn't wait for its opening in September. Deeply influenced by my high school math teacher, I decided to major in math and become a secondary school math teacher myself. Interest in mathematics has never left me.

However, there were other influences on my life's direction. My future husband, Jim, was also in those high school math classes; we shared that experience. I rushed through college in three years, and he served two years in the army. Then we married and moved to a community in southern New Jersey. My first teaching job was a self-contained sixth grade class. It was an unexpected but wonderful experience. I had an opportunity to teach all the things I had so enjoyed in my own elementary school years. Jim and I engaged in all sorts of activities with my students--"our kids"-- who became like younger brothers and sisters. These kids and I stayed together for three years—by mutual consent. Fifty years later, at a reunion in our old school, I told "our kids" that it was there, with them, that the ethic of care began for me.

The second experience that inspired my work on caring was motherhood. We had five children in a few short years, and I had settled into teaching math at the high school level—at the high school from which Jim and I had graduated. These were good years but far too busy. I received an NSF fellowship to do my master's in math, Jim had a good job as an engineer, and we adopted several more children. I

L.J. Waks (ed.), Leaders in Philosophy of Education: Intellectual Self Portraits, 135–144.

chaired the math department, served as assistant principal, and taught as an adjunct at Rutgers. Then an opportunity came my way that I resisted. Jim had a terrific job offer in California. I was not happy about this, but we left for California at the end of the school year in June.

PERSONAL FAVORITES

Books

Caring (1984)
Women and Evil (1989)
The Challenge to Care in Schools (1992)
Educating for Intelligent Belief or Unbelief (1993)
Happiness and Education (2003)
Critical Lessons (2006)
When School Reform Goes Wrong (2007)

Articles/Chapters

On Community, 1996.
An Ethic of Care and its Implications for Instructional Arrangements, 1988.
Does Everybody Count? 1994.
A Skeptical Spirituality 2003.
War, Critical Thinking, and Self-Understanding, 2004.

What was I to do? Fortunately, I was always an outstanding test-taker. I took the GRE special in June or July, got exceptional scores, and was admitted to Stanford that fall. A whole new life opened up. Because I wanted a broader view of education than math provided, I decided to study curriculum broadly. However, in my first term, I stumbled upon philosophy, and that changed everything. I loved it. And at Stanford, philosophy and math came together beautifully.

This brief biographical account helps to explain what I have done as an educational philosopher and writer. When I had finished my doctoral studies (once more in a rush--completing my course work and dissertation in the same term) and had obtained a faculty position at Penn State, I started out writing analytical articles with titles such as "Teacher Competency: An Extension of the Kerr-Soltis Model" (1974); "Competence Theories and the Science of Education" (1974); "A Pedagogical View of 'Knowing That' and 'Knowing How'" (1975); "'Reasonableness' as a Requirement of Teaching" (1976). My interest in math continued with "Developing an Elementary School Problem Solving Curriculum in CAI" (1979); "Dangers of Formalism" (1980); "Word Problems Made Painless" (1980); "Facilitating Symbolic Understanding of Fractions" (with Priscilla Chaffe-Stengel, 1982); and "Formal Modes of Learning" (1985).

In 1977, after spending a year as Director of the Laboratory Schools at the University of Chicago, I returned to Stanford as a faculty member. In the 1990s, I served for two years as Associate Dean and for two more years as Acting Dean, but my mind and heart were caught up in ideas. I was, and still am, lost (and found) in thought. Over the years, I've published 16 books and more than 200 chapters and articles, and my work has so far been translated into 10 languages.

CARING GROWS

Sometime in 1979, I actually sat down to think about what I was doing. I asked myself how I could bring the two parts of my life together—the philosophical skills I had acquired in doctoral studies and the commitment to caring induced by motherhood and those three wonderful initial years of teaching. Philosophy had become—and still is—a way of life for me. The result was my first paper on caring, presented at a meeting of the California Association for Philosophy of Education. This was followed by another presented at the John Dewey Society meeting in Houston (1980); a paper generated by these presentations was published in *Foundational Studies* and in the *Journal of Curriculum Theorizing*. In none of these presentations and papers was there any mention of gender. It was Bill Pinar, at the JDS meeting, who suggested to me that there was a gender aspect to my work.

The generous response of readers and critics to these early papers encouraged me to write *Caring: A Feminine Approach to Ethics and Moral Education* (1984; 2nd edition, 2003). The word *feminine* in the title plagued me for years. For a while, I regretted using it, but now I am convinced that it was necessary. I was trying to develop a picture of moral life that arises from centuries of female experience—experience in caring not only for children, the sick, the elderly, but also , more generally, in responding to the expressed needs of those we encounter. This approach to moral life centers on *natural caring*, the impulse and capacity to respond as carer to the needs of the cared-for without the intercession of abstract principles and rules. It focuses on attention, response, and relation. It is caring out of love or inclination. Immanuel Kant described women as behaving well or being "good" out of "inclination"; they tend to be "nice," he said. But such niceness earns no moral credit. To receive moral credit, from Kant's perspective, one must act in obedience to principle.

Most of my work over the past twenty years has been devoted to overturning that judgment. Even when the inclination to care fails and we must summon ethical caring by reflecting on our best selves-as-carers, our aim is to restore natural caring, not to surmount it. I have addressed this theme in *Women and Evil* (1989), *Starting at Home* (2002), and in a succession of articles and chapters. In current work, I point out that even the Golden Rule is rephrased: Instead of "Do unto others as you would have done unto you," we say, "Do unto others as they would have done unto them." This different perspective offers powerful suggestions for human encounters at every level.

Work on care theory exhibits an interesting example of simultaneous creation. I had just completed the manuscript of *Caring* when Carol Gilligan's *In a Different Voice* came out (1982). I had referred to her earlier paper, "Woman's Place in Man's Life Cycle" (Gilligan, 1979) but could do little more than add the new book to my list of references. Gilligan was working from the perspective of developmental psychology, and her book quickly became a classic in both psychology and feminism. My own work had been influenced by Martin Buber's relational ethics, Milton Mayeroff's book on caring, and my own experience as a

137

mother and teacher. However, I soon learned that others were thinking about caring and related concepts—Kari Waerness in sociology, Jean Watson in nursing, Catherine Keller in religion, Sara Ruddick in feminist philosophy, and several Jungian feminists. By the 1990s, we were aware of each other's work, and care theory grew rapidly. We also learned about important work that preceded our own—for example, that of Simone Weil and Iris Murdoch on the topic of receptive or loving attention.

In 2002, *Starting at Home: Caring and Social Policy* was published. A question had arisen as to whether *caring* should be considered a "domestic ethic," one with little or no application in the public sphere. I wanted to show that care theory could be effectively used to guide public policy, and in this book I discussed its application to problems of homelessness, deviance, and social policy generally. It is in *Starting at Home* that I introduced a distinction I have since used repeatedly— that between *expressed* and *inferred* needs. I'll say more about that important distinction in the following discussion of caring in education.

CARE THEORY AND TEACHING

Philosophical work on care theory has carried over into my work in education. *The Challenge to Care in Schools* was published in 1992, and it (like *Caring*) has been translated into several languages. It, too, has generated a substantial list of articles and chapters. My interest in math education has not been lost, and many examples in that book and related articles are drawn from the teaching of mathematics. Accepting the commitment to care—to listen and respond to the expressed needs of students—leads us to reflect upon and question everything we do as teachers. It has led me to reject competitive grading (or any grading when I can avoid it) in favor of continuous, constructive feedback; teacher and student should work together to produce results that are satisfactory in an objective sense and satisfying to both teacher and student. It has also led me to question the wisdom of organizing whole courses and programs around pre-specified objectives. Teachers intend to produce learning, of course, but that learning often emerges in shared experience. Moreover, creative teachers frequently intend to induce awareness, not specific learning, and sometimes we simply intend to share matters that may interest students and lead some of them to deeper learning.

There is a history of analytic work on the nature of teaching. In graduate school, I was steeped in this literature, including that of Bob Gowin, Paul Komisar, Jim Macmillan, R.S. Peters, Israel Scheffler, B. O. Smith, and Jonas Soltis. Central to the debate at that time was the question: Does teaching imply learning? The question was inspired by lines in Dewey's *How We Think*: "Teaching may be compared to selling commodities. No one can sell unless someone buys....There is the same exact equation between teaching and learning that there is between selling and buying" (1933, pp. 35-36). Most of the philosophers who addressed this issue in the late 1960s-early 1970s rejected the proposition that teaching necessarily implies learning. I found that work fascinating and was delighted to co-teach a seminar on teaching with Phil Jackson at the University of Chicago. My own conclusion was then (and still is) that Dewey was right—teaching does imply learning—but the proposition should not be interpreted to mean that teaching must produce learning of exactly and only the material pre-specified as objectives, nor does it mean that a particular effort to teach X to a class will result in every student's learning it. In addition to teaching for some common, pre-specified objectives, teachers rightly offer a world of learning opportunities from which students may construct their own learning objectives. I've emphasized this again in *When School Reform Goes Wrong* (2007).

How does care theory contribute to the analysis of teaching? In recent work, I've contrasted two approaches to caring in teaching: relational caring and virtue caring (Walker & Ivanhoe, 2007).This work has been partly inspired by conversations with Michael Slote, who has tried to convince me that care ethics is a branch of virtue ethics. Care ethics and virtue ethics certainly share several characteristics. Most important, both de-emphasize the role of principles in ethical conduct; both turn instead to something in the moral agent—in virtue ethics, character; in care ethics, an ethical ideal constructed through caring encounters. The essential difference lies in care ethics' emphasis on the caring *relation* and the contribution of both carer and cared-for to this relation.

In teaching, the difference between virtue caring and relational caring can be dramatic. Virtue carers are often highly conscientious teachers who work largely on the basis of inferred needs. From the study of their subject, curriculum theory, and pedagogy, they infer the needs of their students and work hard to meet them. There is strong backing in educational theory for this approach. Ralph Tyler (1949), for example, discussed "the learners themselves" as a source of learning objectives, but Tyler referred to learners as groups—for example, fifth graders or children in a particular city. In contrast, when Dewey spoke of learners, he directed our attention to individuals and their particular interests. In agreement with Dewey, care theory puts emphasis on the *expressed* needs of individual students. Relational carers, in contrast with virtue carers, concentrate on uncovering the intrinsic motives of their students, listening to their interests and concerns, and co-planning their courses. The establishment of caring relations is primary.

Caring teachers of either sort are concerned with the development of whole persons; that is, they feel some responsibility to encourage moral, aesthetic, and social development as well as intellectual growth. As part of my work in care theory, I've devoted considerable time to moral education from the perspective of relational caring (which unless otherwise stated is always what I mean by *caring*). In *Caring* and again in *The Challenge to Care in Schools*(1992, 2005), *Educating Moral People* (2002), and a number of articles and chapters, I've suggested a four-part model for moral education: modeling, dialogue, practice, and confirmation. Caring teachers show what it means to care in their own interaction with students. They engage students in substantive dialogue, using that dialogue to learn more about their students and to direct moral thinking. They provide opportunities for their students to practice caring in small group work, cross-age tutoring, and service learning. And, as they come to know their students, they confirm them; that is, they recognize and affirm the better selves struggling to be realized in each student.

This model contrasts sharply with many character education programs organized around the explicit teaching of specific virtues, and I've criticized character education in several articles. However, there are a few very attractive, thoughtful programs in character education, and I've taken note of these, too. It seems entirely appropriate, for example, to designate a virtue each month for discussion, but it is absurd to suppose that we can inculcate a virtue per month in our students. Here again, there is a long history of fascinating philosophical work dating back to Socrates. Is it possible to teach virtues? Probably not. But since we are not born virtuous (pace Rousseau), teaching must have something to do with the production of moral people. Describing and justifying this "something" is a continuing challenge for philosophers of education.

PROFESSIONAL INTRUSIONS

It is deeply satisfying to be engaged in intellectual work—to think, write, and be challenged by one question after another. However, to be employed as a professor, one must accept other professional responsibilities. For me, teaching never interfered with my research; I found the two tasks synergistic, but I have always had a relatively light teaching load. Other tasks, however, might get in the way.
There are organizations to join. Starting as a member, I eventually served as president of the Philosophy of Education Society, Far West Philosophy of Education Society, California Association for Philosophy of Education, the John Dewey Society, and the National Academy of Education. I was honored to accept these positions, but they did take time.

Some writing tasks were even more time consuming. I think it is a professional responsibility to accept some assignments to write handbook chapters and reviews, but such assignments do distract us from the development of our own ideas. Over the years, I have written chapters for the *Review of Research in Education* ("Feminist Critiques in the Professions"), the *Handbook of Research on Teaching* (4th ed.) ("The Caring Teacher"), the *Handbook of Research on Curriculum* ("Gender in the Curriculum"), and the *Handbook of Research on Mathematics Teaching and Learning* ("The Professional Life of Mathematics Teachers"). Recently, I have written a chapter for the *Encyclopedia of Social and Cultural Foundations of Education* ("Philosophy of Education") , one for the *Handbook of Moral and Character Education* ("Caring and Moral Education"), and one for the *Cambridge Companion to John Dewey* ("Dewey's Philosophy of Education").

These are time-consuming tasks, but they are ultimately rewarding in forcing us to review and extend our knowledge. I have taken on each such task somewhat reluctantly but, fortunately, have found myself immersed in topics and issues that I might easily have forgotten. Their great value to the writer is in recalling, organizing, and evaluating material as a foundation for both teaching and further research. I have occasionally even found them useful for the generation of new ideas.

For similar reasons, I have not been excited about writing formal textbooks. I have done one, *Philosophy of Education* (1995; 2nd ed. 2006). The best part of the experience was sharing the text in manuscript form with students at two universities. Their questions and comments drove revisions that enhanced the clarity and organization of my writing. As writers, we can learn much from our readers.

Reviewing manuscripts for journals and book publishers is another task that, at first, seems to intrude on one's own writing time. But this too is a learning experience, a way to keep up with what others are thinking. It is also a way to give anonymous advice to young scholars, and that can be satisfying. When the manuscripts under consideration involve my own work, I often learn something that assists me in revising or clarifying my work. I guess the lesson here—one that I keep forgetting—is to limit the number of such assignments one accepts and to use those accepted to enrich one's store of knowledge.

CARING CONNECTIONS

As a result of the work on caring, I have had opportunities to work in several disciplines as well as across areas within education. The connection to feminist philosophy is obvious. In addition to *Caring* and *Women and Evil*, I have published articles in *Hypatia, Signs, Journal of Social Philosophy,* and *Midwest Studies in Philosophy*. My work within education also reflects feminist interests. At present, I am outlining a chapter on feminism and education for the *Oxford Handbook of Philosophy of Education*. I am also planning a book that extends *Caring* and will look at an alternative approach to moral philosophy built on evolutionary concepts. Over several years, I have been pleased to work with nursing groups and nurse-theorists. Collaborations with groups outside of education seem to come in cycles and, although it is obvious that I cannot work in all of these areas continuously, I always regret the lapses in connections. In addition to chapters in several books, I've published articles in the *Journal of Clinical Ethics* and *Theoretical Medicine and Bioethics*. In *Starting at Home*, I addressed ethical issues associated with drug use and addiction. *Caregiving*, a volume co-edited with Suzanne Gordon (a journalist) and Patricia Benner (professor of nursing), appeared in 1996. It is the product of collaboration among nurse-theorists, philosophers, physicians, sociologists, writers, and educators.

Another important connection has been one to religion and religious education. *Women and Evil* is a study of evil from the perspective of women's experience. It is highly critical of Judeo and Christian traditions that have created elaborate mystifications of evil. These traditions have raised blaming the victim to an art; women, the victims of male domination, have been blamed for the existence of evil in the world. If I were writing the book today, I would include Islam in my criticism. But the book is not all critical. In discussing moral evil, I identify three basic forms: the deliberate infliction of pain, separation, and helplessness. The book concludes with recommendations on ways to educate for what Carl Jung called a "morality of evil." I was pleased to have an excerpt from *Women and Evil* included in an anthology, *The Problem of Evil* (Larrimore, 2001). Feminism and religion came together again for me in a chapter, "A Skeptical Spirituality," (Groenhout and Bower, 2003).

In 1993, *Educating for Intelligent Belief or Unbelief* was published. It is an expanded version of my 1991 John Dewey Lecture. In it, I argue for a balanced and expansive approach to religious understanding. Public schools should not advocate for or against religion, but they should not ignore an area of thought that has had enormous influence on human culture. We should introduce students to important thinking that supports religion and to some that opposes it—to C. S. Lewis and to Bertrand Russell. I show in this book how topics on religion can be addressed in every disciplinary subject.

This is a topic of continuing interest. I believe we cannot claim to educate when we refuse to provide our students with material that should enable them to make intelligent decisions about their religious orientation and to address their basic spiritual longing. I have included chapters on religion or spirituality in *Happiness and Education* (2003) and in *Critical Lessons* (2006), and I have recently presented a paper, "Understanding Unbelief as part of Religious Education," in which I argue that high school students should come to some understanding of deism, agnosticism, atheism, and secular humanism.

THE AIMS OF EDUCATION

Three of my recent books concentrate on the aims of education, and they were inspired in part by troubling trends in current schooling. With the increased emphasis on college for all, it sometimes seems as though the only aims of education are economic—financial success for individuals and competitive supremacy for the nation. In *Happiness and Education*, I argue that such thinking is leading to a disastrous course of action in education. We too often disregard the contributions of hosts of citizens whose work does not require a college education and, because we now force "academic" study on everyone, we have eliminated much intellectual content from our academic courses. There is more to a good life than making and spending money. Moreover, there is much essential work in our society that does not require a college education. Opportunity to go to college should be open to all qualified students, but they should not be told—explicitly or implicitly—"go to college or be nothing." Our democracy depends on a respectful recognition of interdependence, and all honest work should be appropriately rewarded. I have argued that the intellectual integrity of both academic and vocational studies by maintained.

In *Happiness and Education,* a full chapter is devoted to aims and aims-talk. Talking, reflecting, and debating about the aims of education are not idle pursuits for arm-chair philosophers. Every generation must undertake such discussion or risk abandoning the next generation to mindless mental labor. What are we trying to accomplish in education? Do our efforts on behalf of individuals impede or enhance the welfare of our nation? How? What is the meaning of terms—e.g., *self-actualization*—that we use so easily?

I started *Happiness and Education* by noting that most of us confess a desire to be happy. Why, then, does *happiness* seldom appear as an aim of education? Aims, in contrast to goals and objectives, are not always pursued directly; rather, they serve as guides to all we do. I do not argue that we should simply make students happy. Rather, I recommend that we share with students some of the best thinking on happiness—its nature and sources. Accordingly, chapters address suffering and unhappiness, needs and wants, making a home, places and nature, parenting, character and spirituality, interpersonal growth, preparing for work, and community and service. The book concludes with a chapter on happiness in schools and classrooms. *Happiness and Education* is a reflection of my belief in philosophy as a way of life. It has already been translated into five languages.

Critical Lessons covers some of the same topics from a different perspective. Most schools list *critical thinking* as an aim of education but, paradoxically, they avoid discussion of controversial or critical issues, and I argue that it is essential to discuss critical issues if we hope to induce critical thinking. The book takes Socrates seriously—understanding ourselves is the foundation for all meaningful knowledge. Students should be encouraged to gain critical knowledge about themselves as individuals and about the groups to which they belong. When a topic is controversial, students should be exposed to the best thinking of reasonable people on all sides of the issues. The message throughout is: Think! Topics include understanding one's own learning habits, the psychology of war, house and home, parenting, animals and nature, advertising and propaganda, making a living, gender, and religion. Some topics are very controversial, but I have tried to avoid giving answers. Instead I present views and urge people to think about them.

My latest book, *When School Reform Goes Wrong* (in press as I write this), is an essay that invites readers to think about school reform and, in particular, to reflect critically on the mandates of the No Child Left Behind act (NCLB). In this book, I critically examine terms such as *equality, accountability, standards, proficiency,* and *testing.* I question the moral justification for using methods that depend on threats, pernicious comparisons, and penalties. I point out that NCLB demands the impossible, and trying to meet those demands may actually make matters worse. I defend the comprehensive high school. While recognizing mistakes in its implementation, I commend it as a reform that made it possible for the majority of American children to attend and to graduate from high school. In this book, I *do* draw conclusions and make specific recommendations.

What is so wonderful about working in philosophy of education is that there are always important and fascinating questions to tackle. I've done some work recently on global citizenship (2005) and hope to do more on peace education. Educating for a love of place is another topic of continuing interest. Chapters on this topic appear in *Happiness and Education, Educating Citizens for Global Awareness*, and *Critical Lessons.* Foremost in my mind right now is an extended argument for the ethic of care based on ideas from evolutionary science. I can't imagine running out of ideas.

REFERENCES

Dewey, J. (1933). *How we think.* Chicago: Henry Regnery.

Gilligan, C. J. (1979). Woman's place in man's life cycle. *Harvard Educational Review, 49*, 431-446.

Groenhout, R. E. & Bower, M. (Eds.). (2003). *Philosophy, feminism, and faith.* Bloomington: Indiana University Press.

Larrimore, M. (Ed.). (2001). *The problem of evil.* Oxford: Blackwell.

Noddings, N. (1984). *Caring: A feminine approach to ethics and moral education.* Berkeley: University of California Press (2nd edition, 2003).

Noddings, N. (1988). An ethic of care and its implications for instructional arrangements, *American Journal of Education.*

Noddings, N. (1989). *Women and evil.* Berkeley: University of California Press.

Noddings, N. (1992). *The challenge to care in schools.* New York: Teachers College Press. (2nd edition, 2005).

Noddings, N. (1993). *Educating for intelligent belief or unbelief.* New York: Teachers College Press.

Noddings, N. (1994). Does everybody count?" *Journal of Mathematical Behavior, 13.*

Noddings, N. (1995). *Philosophy of education.* Boulder, CO: Westview Press (2nd edition, 2006).

Noddings, N. (1996a). *Caregiving.* (Ed. with S. Gordon & P. Benner). Philadelphia: University of Pennsylvania Press.

Noddings, N. (1996b). On community, *Educational Theory.*

Noddings, N. (2002a). *Starting at home: Caring and social policy.* Berkeley: University of California Press.

Noddings, N. (2002b). *Educating moral people.* New York: Teachers College Press.

Noddings, N. (2003a). *Happiness and education.* Cambridge: Cambridge University Press.

Noddings, N. (2003b). A skeptical spirituality. In Groenhout, R. E. & Bower M. (Eds.), *Philosophy, Feminism, and Faith.* Bloomington: Indiana University Press.

Noddings, N. (2004).War, critical thinking, and self-understanding, *Phi Delta Kappan.*

Noddings, N. (Ed.). (2005). *Educating citizens for global awareness.* New York: Teachers College Press.

Noddings, N. (2006). *Critical lessons: What our schools should teach.* Cambridge: Cambridge University Press.

Noddings, N. (2007). *When school reform goes wrong.* New York: Teachers College Press.

Tyler, R. W. (1949). *Basic principles of curriculum and instruction.* Chicago: University of Chicago Press.

Walker, R. L. & Ivanhoe, P. J. (Eds.). (2007). *Working virtue: Virtue ethics and contemporary moral problems.* Oxford: Oxford University Press.

Nel Noddings

MICHAEL A PETERS

ACADEMIC SELF-KNOWLEDGE AND SELF-DECEPTION

A Brief Excerpt from a Personal History of Prejudice

SCENE 1507

Rousseau begins his *Confessions* by assuming an intimacy with the reader, preferring a direct form of address that has all been written out of academic discourse but remains still in the genre of autobiography and the memoir. The standard academic article based on its group style to us late moderns appears a timeless and culturally stable form yet it is only a few hundred years old. Growing up with the institutionalization of the young sciences the article of the periodical only came into existence with the development of the scientific periodical dating from the *Philosophical Transactions of the Royal Society* established by Henry Oldenburg in 1665 whose reports read like the experiments of a boys-own science club. This theme of the changing mode of scientific communication is the subject of my latest work.

Against Rousseau's colorful self-observations the standard grey academic article seems to drain the text of any personal reference like a catheter taking off excess fluid from a fresh corpse. Rousseau not only assumes a kind of complicit relationship with his readers—friends, family, and close associates—but also enters into the active and generative fiction that he can tell the truth about himself, without leaving anything out of his account. As someone nurtured on a range of textual models and modes of criticism I know this to be one of the powerful fictional principles that underlies the form and is demanded by it. In a strong sense it is part of the necessary illusion on which it rests (as Nietzsche might argue). Even the chronological order that accompanied the rise of the novel, echoing 'events' generally beginning with the birth of the hero or heroine and ending with his or death, masks an obvious untruth about time, about the accumulation, selection and editing of facts and their arrangement in a temporal narrative crafted about the self and its awareness of its own historicity. We could say that this is a necessary lie—a deceit—that makes the genre productive. Hayden White, the great American poststructuralist historian, in his magical little text 'History as literary artefact' draws the distinction between fact and narrative, chronicler and historian, in a way that preserves the integrity of both. The chronicle records events and the sequence of events and this reportage of events is susceptible of verification as fact, even if we have difficulty of establishing the meaning of 'fact'. The historian does not

L.J. Waks (ed.), *Leaders in Philosophy of Education: Intellectual Self Portraits*, 145–158.

PERSONAL FAVORITES

Education and the Postmodern Condition, 1995
Wittgenstein: Philosophy, Postmodernism, Pedagogy, 1999
Poststructuralism, Marxism and Neoliberalism; Between Theory and Politics, 2001
Poststructuralism and Educational Research, 2004
Building Knowledge Cultures: Education and Development in the Age of Knowledge Capitalism, 2006
Knowledge Economy: Development and the Future of Higher Education, 2007
Saying and Showing: Wittgenstein as a Pedagogical Philosopher, 2008
Derrida, Politics and Pedagogy: Deconstructing the Humanities, 2008
Foucault, Truth and Subjectivity: Education and the Culture of the Self, 2008

WORKS THAT INFLUENCED ME MOST

Wittgenstein, L. *Tractatus Logico-Philosophicus* (1922).
Wittgenstein, L. *Philosophical Investigations* (1953)
Nietzsche, F. *On the Genealogy of Morals and Ecce Homo.*
Nietzsche, F. *Beyond Good and Evil*
Nietzsche, F. *The Will to Power*
Heidegger, M. *Nietzsche, Vol. I: The Will to Power as Art.* (1979)
Foucault, M. *Essential Works of Foucault, 1954-1984*, 3 volumes, edited by Paul Rabinow, New York: The New Press. . (1997-9)

have the same license as the novelist in that she must try to account for the facts, that is, she must construct a narrative that weaves the facts together as a coherent account or interpretation. This interpretation is an active process of making meaning through principles of contextualization and bringing new facts to light that necessarily involves a set of literary conventions concerning representation, among other things. Wittgenstein might say 'The past is everything that was the case'-- an infinite world of facts and sub-facts existing in a network of relationships of causes and actions.

The narrative and styles of narrative—even the study of narrative and its various forms, so-called 'narratology'—is a philosophical and literary problem that anchors the place of the former in the concerns of the latter; not just the question of time and its representation in terms of subjectivities but also the historical narrative. Indeed, this problem in oblique ways motivates my readings of Wittgenstein (Peters et al, 1999, 2007), Nietzsche (Peters et al, 2001) and Heidegger (Peters, 2002). These 'prophets of postmodernity' I found the most interesting to read—diagnostic, deeply analytical, ethical—although I also enjoyed the rigor and robustness of Frege, Russell and the early Wittgenstein.

In our culture, as Paul Ricoeur (1984, 1985, 1988) remarks in his landmark three volume study *Time and Narrative*, there are two main forms of narrative: narratives as 'fiction' that even if based in real events and characters, depart from reality as an exercise of imagination; and, historical narratives which while unable to do without composition seeks methodologically to attain a degree of objectivity as form of social inquiry. It is with Ricoeur that narrative attains its centrality to understanding the connections between narrativity, identity and time. Narrative is the discourse that frames the agent's experience and gives expression to the complex historical present that represents the agent's actions in a sequence and context and thus becomes a condition of temporal existence. It also is a mode for transforming historical time into human time understood as a public time in which generations and lives can be located and predecessors can be determined. Narrative also thus forms the basis for a narrative conception of identity, drawing actions into a 'plot' with a temporal span, emplotting actions and providing a story-like unity to give characters depth as persons who can initiate action in response to events, actions that have an ethical dimension in so far as they involve mutual recognition and responsiveness to others, and therefore can be morally evaluated.

SCENE 1008

Consider then the case of autobiography and its relation to philosophy and education. It contains all the difficulties of confession and narrative with the added problem of a kind of self-reflection, even self-knowledge that springs from hindsight and from a commitment to the norms of truth-telling. This self-knowledge is a species of historical self-reflection borne of experience and a willingness to risk telling the truth, even when the result may picture oneself in a poor light. The autobiography combines truth-telling with courage and frankness, as Foucault would say of parrhesia—it is also a little confessional machine. It only takes place against the possibility of knowledge in general and claims against the possibility of self-knowledge. Is the self, even with hindsight, transparent or forever opaque? Is the self a book to be read? If so, what are the forms of reading the self and to what extent do these forms constitute something different from reading a book? Is there a radical alterity of the authorial self, as Proust indicated? Is the self structured like a language (with apologies to Lacan)—not the unconscious but the fully rational conscious self? How easily can we read our own motivations? Can we really penetrate below the social conventions of self structuring to read and understand our motives, choices, and intentions? Both Barthes and Foucault entertain doubts about the 'author-function'. 'What matters who's speaking, someone said, what matters who's speaking' Samuel Beckett writes in *Texts for Nothing*. The subject is not the author of its language but is authored by language. So I must begin with skepticism not only of the form of the personal reflection and its hidden technology of time that helps to create the professional narrative but also with the explicit warning that even with the greatest sincerity, honesty, frankness and attention to detail my account will inevitably and inescapably harbor the prejudices that like a gigantic cultural force field constrains the choice of words, the metaphors and structures the form.

SCENE 71

A working class boy growing up in Wellington, New Zealand, I was the cultural hybrid and mobile subject of an Italian immigrant family on my fathers' side (though he was born in New Zealand) and a mother of an English and Irish descent--a 'warbride'. My parents married in Stranroa and settled in late 1940s New Zealand after the war taking up the opportunity of rehabilitation loans to servicemen and women to establish themselves as poultry farmers. I did not think much of my origins, situation, or, indeed, class position throughout my career. Only in retrospect have I understood the significance of the fact that books were largely absence in the family home, and never discussed in the household, as they are in middle class homes. I was a poor reader anyway, slightly dyslexic I discovered much later, and infinitely preferred outdoor activities and sports of all kinds. In fact I regarded readers with heavy inarticulate suspicion and associated kids that wore glasses with a kind of book-worm personality, permanently withdrawn and frightened of life.

SCENE 78

At home I read first my mother's magazines looking at the pictures of mature women in their corsets and enjoying the brevity of magazine pieces that discussed all manner of things concerning 'beauty'--becoming more beautiful, beautifying the home--and little stories of relationships written mostly by women about relationship problems. In my early teens I graduated to my sister's romantic fiction—*Forever Amber*—that I had to read secretly, alone, furtively, and mainly for the passages concerning romantic sexual longings. My reading history was thus both vicarious and voyeuristic--I was reading material aimed at a differently gendered audience—and I came to reading through a feminine perspective and through the female body. This is true also of learning to read, for me no more than a kind of word recognition and familiarity, and functional literacy that I never went beyond until my late teens. Then I thought reading was a 'girlish' activity. I associated it with long periods of sitting still and I never had the discipline myself to sit still enough for long enough to read much that was worthwhile. I do not remember reading anything in my early years that made a lasting impact. I did like being read to--I enjoyed stories read aloud and, often in the story-teller tradition I used to tell my younger brother stories at night time when we were tucked up in bed and too wide awake to go to sleep easily.

SCENE 83

The other source of my early reading material was comics. I read them enthusiastically and swapped with other kids in the neighborhood—pocket war comics, and the superhero comics, *Superman, the Phantom,* and *Marvel Man.* These I loved. After television my interest in comics sharply declined. This is an odd combination—women's romance and boy's comics—and I think the combination was probably significant in shaping a romantic and 'heroic' subjectivity in my teens that influenced my reading preferences and later dictated certain kinds of philosophy I found more interesting than others—the philosophy of the subject, the autobiography as philosophy, and interplay between philosophy and literature that marks out the work of Stanley Cavell as one of the most interesting living philosophers. Already my subjectivity as a reader was formed. I detested dry school textbooks that promised little except sheer repetition and preferred oral discussions where it was possible to joke, to act, to ad lib and to play the fool. I was the class clown. I made jokes at the teacher's expense. I was a 'smart alec' but I couldn't help myself. The logic of performance encouraged me to play up; to spurt out a string of one-liners and to act out. I didn't mind being a fool if the class laughed with me. It was a working class attitude to reading and to learning; to the idea that anything learned from books was not real nor worth the candle. The investment of time was not warranted because it returned so little. It was certainly not to be considered 'work' and, by contrast, I preferred making things, drawing, dancing, sports, and playing. I lived for the playground. (A note to myself to be careful not perpetuate the romantic sociology of the working class that Paul Willis' work dismantled, portraying the tragedy of working class youth who through their resistance ended up on the shop floor like their fathers).

SCENE 1003

I now realize that the role of the fool is also a romantic fiction and that the structure of the fool's discourse is comprised of paradoxes, riddles, jokes, semantic contradictions, conundrums, and puzzles that plot linguistic limits and yet speak the truth through these deep tautologies. (Rather like Wittgenstein). Shakespeare's fool, the bard-trickster, the jester, the stand-up comedian can regularly get away with saying things that most of us only think in our most creative moments though never get the chance to utter. Not just the fool but the madman too who speaks to us in strange and unfamiliar terms. The fool, the madmen, and maybe also the child, not yet linguistically socialized, or the Other — the primitive other of Wittgenstein's tribal languages permitted only a handful of words. Philosophy has always struck me as a form of madness (one form of academic pathology in general) that needs a cure—a very Wittgensteinian point. Philosophy (and psychoanalysis) is, as Karl Kraus and Wittgenstein would say, both a disease and its own cure. We must learn to know when to stop doing it and how to cure ourselves from idle words games that often amount to mere cleverness. (Puzzles for their own sake have never interested me, nor the standard tests of intelligence). The disease comes about from an embedded metaphysics—'deep disquietudes' about mind/body dualism or imagining a ghost, demon or devil who constantly deceives or tricks us with his magnificent illusions. Philosophy takes place against a source of skepticism that takes us to the limits of sense against which and through extraordinary examples and clever argument we might be brought back home again—to ordinary language and to the everyday—from irrationality to rationality, from unreason to reason, from madness to sanity. (I cannot but help myself. Descartes, Wittgenstein and Cavell, Foucault and Derrida, Beckett, Joyce, Magritte inhabit this landscape. The philosophy and theatre of the absurd.)

SCENE 81

I was scallywag at primary school who used to break out in beads of sweat every time the class was made to read aloud. The anticipation of my turn was killing. I dreaded the prospect of stumbling haltingly across words and trying to make the sounds my lips and tongue seemed naturally to resist. (I was never fluent). I have a clear memory of reading my first book ever when I was in my first year of high school. It was called *Seven Years in Tibet* and it took me almost seven months to read. I thought you had to read every line and start each page, left to right, faithfully word by word, and proceed from top down. If you did not read every word you were cheating. I did not realize that meaning is a creative process of anticipation, of imagination, of assembling word meanings, and of active construction. Each book was a little confessional treadmill for me and, even so, it seemed to me a terrible waste of time; it was an activity that rendered very little by comparison with the world of action and everyday life. I never knew the meaning of 'reading for pleasure'. Reading was a task; it never gave me pleasure except in the sense of reading those sexy passages in my sister's romantic novels.

SCENE 97

When I was 15 or sixteen, after watching Maigret, a British TV series about a French detective, I took to eating large quantities of strange smelling cheeses, pickled onions (I don't know why I considered these French), and smoking cigarettes (endlessly), which I did self-consciously with a particular set of affections that I also learned from TV: the art of holding a cigarette, the games with inhaling smoke, letting it drift out of the nose, or blowing smoke in a continuous stream with the head tilted back. I was learning to be cool. I am still caught in the net of those pretensions and sophistications. At about the same time, in the early 1960s I have a vivid impression of myself (is this a sense datum?) where I was posing in a coffee bar 'reading' Sartre's *Words*. (I think I read it.) It was the first significant philosophy book, even though it was an autobiography, that I had read and I became wistful about an imaginary grandfather who could know me well and read to me and take an interest in my development.

SCENE 70

I do not mean to imply that I lacked all spurs to the intellect in my family environment. My father was a dreamer and I learned from his powerful sense of self-romance. He had great sense of personal style, modelled, it now seems to me, on the popular movies of the war period. He was better looking than Ronald Reagan and had a Hollywood quality of the leading man about him. He was also as a young man a successful boxer and knew how to look after himself, and his life was like a Hollywood movie--lying about his age to join the air force, training in Canada, manning the giant Sunderland flying boats as a tail gunner, and flying surveillance and reconnaissance aircraft around the African coast. I got the distinctive impression that he considered *that* to have been his life and the family life that came later was sort of incidental. My mother by comparison was much more analytical and in argument always had the better of him. She was tenacious to the point of madness and family dinner time conversations became free-for-alls that started with the unwritten law that anyone could hold the floor. Interruptions were common and these undisciplined conversations often ended in the reassertion of parental authority and tears or angry outbursts by us children who recognized that illicit power techniques were used in the last instance. I certainly learned to assert my views early and also learned some of the basic skills of argument on my feet, so to speak. It might be better to say that I learned the tricks of persuasion and to recognize illicit forms of argument that played on the audience, although I could not recognize them then as examples of common fallacies.

SCENE 1031

I want to say how important formal State education has been for me. It has, in the language of pedagogy, transformed me, created me; it has shaped my preferences and defined my interests and continues to do so, every day. I can not even imagine what I would be or have become without 'an education', even if it also inculcated many bad habits and opinions to keep a gaggle of experts busy for a generation of remediation. The education I received in New Zealand schools and universities so completely manufactured or accounted for a kind of subjectivity it is hard to think of any set of beliefs that have not been changed, refined, arranged or reassembled over time. I was lucky as a pupil and student that not of my choosing I grew up in a country that defined itself through its welfare distributions. And while there were selection mechanisms, gate-keeping and cut-off points, examinations and educational testing, somehow I made it through them to a point at least where I became slowly and bit by bit educationally independent and self-determining. Little by little I gained confidence in my ability to think and to trust my own judgment, my own appraisals of situations, people and texts. I should say that there were many individual teachers who were inspiring and committed—whose lives clearly depended upon their vocation to teach. So I was lucky, a fact of history and political economy. I would not call it moral luck so much as the historical luck of simply being born in 1948 at the height of the establishment of the welfare state in New Zealand, a country that led the world in terms of its commitment to a social experiment in equality.

SCENE 1247

I am beholden in more ways that I can name to a system that placed so much emphasis on equality even if it was sometimes misplaced or wrongly allocated or badly distributed (for example between Maori and pakeha). I owe my self and my livelihood to that creaky, pastoral and centralized bureaucratic system. It gave me a structural class advantage I would never had had; it also imbued an ideological sense of opportunity and equality; it paid for my schooling and a scholarship at university that meant I could afford to drink copious amounts of alcohol and sit around talking earnestly about the issues of the day; it gave me an inherent sense of fairness, together with an optimistic view of human nature as socially transformable through education. In short, it provided what educational historians call 'educationalization' (an ugly word), a kind of normalization as a welfare subject that I carried through to my training as a teacher and later in the seven years I spent teaching in various secondary schools in Christchurch and Auckland. Its patina has not faded. The welfare ethos has become a kind of politics for me worth defending and, as I became more aware of different welfare regimes with the collection of rights they ascribed, I became a defender of the welfare state, critic of the New Right reforms enacted ruthlessly in New Zealand in the 1980s and 1990s, and later more a considered student of comparative social policy analysis.

SCENE 137

Even fast-forward has its glitches. 'Going to university' was a result of the most determined attitude on my part. My mother threw me out of school during the preparatory year, saying that I was leading the 'life of a gentleman' (I was bunking lots of classes). When she threw me out I worked in a food factory producing pies for the remainder of that year and decided that I could not face factory life of constant drudgery and hard, repetitive, work even though I like the mateship. It touched me. I understood this solidarity even if I was above it and able to get out. University seemed a good postponement of having to get a job. And having 'fluked' (a lucky accident) School Certificate and University Entrance, to me a remarkable coincidence (and an event that was tied up in a personal proof for the nonexistence of God),

SCENE 142

I went to Victoria University of Wellington (named after Queen Victoria) to begin my education, again. This time I desperately wanted to succeed and I approached it systematically as a problem. I knew in principle what you had to do; sit in lectures and take notes—you simply summarized what the lecturer was saying. It was a memory game and the rules stipulated that you tried to get everything down, preferably in the words that were spoken. I learned also by copying behavior—sometimes, occasionally, I inserted my own thoughts in the notes; sometimes I used different colors to distinguish between my thoughts, the text, and those of the lecturer. I always headed up the notes with the date of the lecture.

SCENE 1489

Only much later did I come to think about 'notes' as a pedagogical and philosophical form in conjunction with Wittgenstein. He seemed to write nothing else. His *Notebooks* are of course famous and they record almost an ethnography of himself and his own ruminations at specific times of his life. Not only notes by

Wittgenstein himself but those of his students have been published as reconstructions of Wittgenstein's course of lectures given at Cambridge. Wittgenstein's composition and re-composition of his notes, his endless activity of trying to find the most satisfactory order for expressing his thoughts, seemed to me the most intensive thinking I had ever witnessed. Notes in this context take on a theoretical component as an expression of style and a theory of thinking. The aphorism was considered the best form for capturing insights that come to us not as a continuous stream of thought but in fragments that require ordering and sequencing and further reflection. They are, so to speak the first stage of the expression of thought, sometimes never superseded and permitting of endless task of composition. Wittgenstein's' philosophy is a philosophy of notes and that says something very significant about his style and his seriousness, as well as his preferred method of working, of composing philosophy and writing it like poetry. Yet there was little formal instruction or workshops about note-taking. I learned through practice and by copying the behavior of others. Eventually I evolved this practice into a very sophisticated form of learning with a kind of distinctive personal shorthand that left some time for reflecting on what was being said.

SCENE 1480

Copying has never received its rightful place in pedagogy; it has never been theorized properly in my view as the perfect learning machine it is. I don't mean simple repetition, although here too much goes unnoticed. I mean the sing-song chants of the tiny-tots who learn to speak in unison and learn their time tables through oral repetition. The essence of copying has such an honored place in the preservation, storage and retrieval of manuscripts. Copying is a significant part of the history of the scribe and scribalism; it is part of the social life of the medieval library; a foreshadowing of the book; and aspect of language learning. Copying is never machine repetition but also involves reiteration that wanders, that makes mistakes, that is self-correcting, that impinges upon the conscious mind to solidify meanings. It requires the discipline of a disciple; a follower—someone who emulates the master in order to become the master. It is inescapable in all learning, the ordinary and the everyday; the routine, the ritual petition, the phatic communion.

SCENE 156

I was lucky to have some superb university teachers, it happens all professors and all male: a Maoist geographer, Keith Buchanan, who wrote on African 'underdevelopment' and poetically about the transformation of the Chinese landscape; a historiographer and philosopher called Peter Munz, who was a student at one time of both Wittgenstein and Popper and saw the moral choice that confronted us in the twentieth century; and Don McKenzie, a Shakespeare expert who provided an original interpretation of *Timon of Athens* based on understanding the importance of medieval astrology. All were passionate about their subjects; all

153

of them were highly entertaining and brilliant lecturers, aware of their audiences and intent on explanation, exposition, and the work of clarification and interpretation. I benefited immensely from being close to those people even though class shyness prevented me from getting too close.

SCENES 1009-1520

I am to skip over the sheer drudgery and repetition that routinizes daily life. Only in the word, in study, in conversation, in collaboration, did it seem to me possible to move beyond this repetition. During my experience as a secondary school teacher in New Zealand, someone who taught both geography and English literature, I became interested in philosophy and was given my first formal introduction when I began a Philosophy of Science degree at the University of Canterbury, beginning with Frege, Russell and the early Wittgenstein and ending with the Popper/Kuhn debate. Philosophy soon became an all-consuming passion. All my teaching was transformed. Every classroom question was probed and prodded, unmasked and exposed. I incited my students to uncover the presuppositions and underlying assumptions of every statement. The excitement of critique has never worn off. I decided to return to philosophy full time, after seven years of teaching and being somewhat disillusioned, I gave up teaching and became a full time philosophy student pursuing a Masters at the University of Auckland and completing papers on Kant, Wittgenstein, Philosophy of Mathematics, Philosophy of the Social Sciences, and Political Philosophy.

SCENE 1058

One of my first and significant lessons in the history of prejudice occurred when I was in my second year of my philosophy Masters. I was sitting a round a table with a group of students in the graduate room to decide with the professor which courses would be offered and what our interests were. In response I piped up and said: 'I'm interested in the question of cultural relativism in the later Wittgenstein' to which the professor replied 'Relativism! How could anyone be interested in relativism? It is such an undergraduate doctrine!' He was angry. I persisted and he eventually supervised a paper with only two students that spent the entire year reading Plato's *Theatetus*. In the term paper I took the position of Protagoras against Socrates, arguing that the classic self-refutation objection did not go through. I had passed all other papers with flying colors and also had taken an additional paper for fun. In all I did not receive less than a 'A' grade. For this paper while I toiled and read the secondary literature, restyling the essay many times I received the exact same grade that he had assigned on the first reading of the draft. I understood something very deep and troubling about the nature of the university and philosophy that stood me in good stead thereafter. It was part of my unofficial education in the history of prejudice and as I progressed through my career from completing the PhD *(On the Problem of Rationality in the Later Wittgenstein)*, to gaining my first academic position, to being appointed to a Personal Chair at

Auckland, and various professorial positions at the Universities of Glasgow and Illinois (at Urbana-Champaign) I increasingly came across different kinds of prejudice and also learned that like everybody else I was not immune.

SCENE 1243

I miss out the PhD experience and the beginnings of a writing relationship with Jim Marshall that lasted more than twenty years. I miss also a form of collaboration that I learned a great deal from and at close quarters. I miss out the enjoyable aspects of Denis Phillips' sabbatical at Auckland, who as my external assessor read and commented on everything I wrote and encouraged me to continue. I miss out the fact and experience that brought me to the subject of education rather than philosophy per se and how I received my second political education in an Education Department working with a group of scholars in Cultural and Policy Studies that as it happens turned out to be an extraordinary group of thinkers and scholars—Jim Marshall, Roger Dale, Alison Jones, Colin Lankshear, Susan Robertson, Linda Smith, Eve Coxon, Peter Roberts, Graham Smith, Gary McColluch and many others—all of whom both individually and collectively influenced my thinking. Certainly, the influence of sociology of education against my own prejudices had a lasting effect upon me as did Kaupapa Maori philosophy. One of the most valuable aspects of any of my abilities was that of 'acting out of character' and of changing my mind especially on the basis of argument or evidence. Increasingly I have found this process of unlearning liberating and exciting even when it means that I have to step outside my identity and assume new positions.

SCENE 1312

I remember coming across Jean-Francois Lyotard's (1984) *The Postmodern Condition* shortly after completing my PhD thesis in 1984. Reading Lyotard was like a revelation. I had come across the book accidentally and found it interesting because of its playful appropriation of Wittgenstein's work. I like Lyotard's playful and innovative reading of Wittgenstein; it provided a political interpretation. Later I struggled to read his essay 'After Wittgenstein' in the original French and began to realize how insightful his positioning of Wittgenstein was in relation to the question of European nihilism but also to the question of the purity of language and its breakup after the collapse of the Hapsburg Empire. The happy and accidental conjuncture of Lyotard and Wittgenstein set me on a path which I am still traveling. On reading Wittgenstein during my years of PhD studies I read also Heidegger and Gadamer, then under the influence of my colleagues more and more the founders of Critical Theory, and later again Lyotard, Foucault, Derrida, all of whom I have written books about.

SCENE 1412

I was offered my first job by Professor Warwick Elley at the University of Canterbury. This rescued me as I was self-employed for seven years working mostly as a researcher and consultant mostly for government departments. Warwick offered me my first academic job and I taught at Canterbury for two years before returning to a position in Auckland that was offered almost immediately after going to Canterbury. A friend of mine, one of a small group of Marxist scholars who befriended me and gave me my third political education, suggested that I write a book given that I had already written so many papers. He said: 'Michael, have you ever thought of writing a book?' I did not need any further encouragement and began immediately almost instantly writing to Lyotard to ask him if he would write a foreword. He wrote short handwritten letters always in French. I corresponded with him for over a year and with his inspiration put together a collection entitled *Education and the Postmodern Condition* which was published in 1996. The study of Lyotard also put me in touch with a range of scholars including Bill Readings who invited me to Montreal to present a paper in the seminar program that later became *The University in Ruins,* still a powerful book.

SCENE 1509

The label 'postmodern' and 'postmodernism' has followed me around since my Canterbury days in 1990. It has stuck to me irrespective of attempts to treat its symptoms and to diagnose the condition. I arrived at Canterbury to find a cartoon pinned on my door that advertised 'Foucault flakes, a new cereal that was more real than any other cereal'. At Auckland my appointment to a personal chair was derailed because of ideological interference, so my Vice-Chancellor said. He had to start the process again because the moderator was openly ideologically hostile to a perceived 'postmodernism'. Again, on arriving in Glasgow I was asked by the then head of Senate, an Australian physicist, 'What's all this nonsense about Foucault?' I replied: 'I'm happy to talk about Foucault, what texts have you read?' It became instantly apparent that he had not read any but this did not stop him from having an opinion and one that dismissed Foucault completely on the basis of hearsay or, perhaps, more charitably, on the basis of secondary texts or commentaries. This has been a characteristic of university life and it continues to amaze me; the extent and frequency with which hard and fast battle-lines are drawn up prior to reading, study or discussion. I come across this kind of prejudice in students who are otherwise outstandingly competent; I come across it among faculty, junior as well as senior professors. It most often takes the form of prejudice against thinkers and authors, rather than texts.

SCENE 1510

In his philosophical hermeneutics Hans-Georg Gadamer ascribes an important role to the positive rehabilitation of prejudice. Our prior hermeneutical situatedness involves an anticipation of completeness that opens us up and allows what is to be interpreted to be understood in a preliminary manner. Prejudices understood as pre-judgments are an indispensable part of understanding for Gadamer but then they are also revisable and as we become aware of them they too can be made the object of our attention and questioning in a way that fundamentally alters our own self-understanding. This is definitely a process of 'deep education' that is ultimately 'spiritual' and I would describe it in Wittgensteinian therapeutic terms or in Derridean deconstructive terms or in Foucaultian genealogical terms as beginning the process of *unlearning*, unlearning the manners of the tribe and the prejudices that form us and our subjectivities.

REFERENCES

Lyotard, J-F. (1984). *The postmodern condition: A report on knowledge,* trans. Geoff Bennington and Brian Massumi, Manchester: Manchester University Press.
Peters, M. A. & Besley, Tina (A. C.) (Eds.). (2007). *Why Foucault? New directions in educational research.* New York: Peter Lang.
Peters, M. A. & Besley, Tina (A. C.). (2006). *Building knowledge cultures: Education and development in the age of knowledge capitalism.* Lanham, Boulder, NY, Oxford: Rowman & Littlefield.
Peters, M. A. & Biesta, G. (2008). *Derrida, politics and pedagogy: Deconstructing the humanities.* New York, Peter Lang (forthcoming).
Peters, M. A. & Burbules, N. (2004). *Poststructuralism and educational research.* Lanham, Boulder, NY, Oxford: Rowman & Littlefield.
Peters, M. A. & Marshall, J. D. (1999). *Wittgenstein: Philosophy, postmodernism, pedagogy.* Westport, CT. & London: Bergin & Garvey.
Peters, M. A. (Ed.). (1995). *Education and the postmodern condition,* Foreword by Jean-François Lyotard. Westport, CT. & London: Bergin & Garvey.
Peters, M. A. (1996). *Poststructuralism, politics and education.* Westport, CT. & London, Bergin and Garvey.
Peters, M.A. (2001). *Poststructuralism, Marxism and neoliberalism: Between theory and politics.* Lanham, Boulder, NY, Oxford: Rowman & Littlefield.
Peters, M.A. (2002). (Ed.). *Heidegger, education and modernity,* Lanham, Boulder, NY, Oxford: Rowman & Littlefield.
Peters, M. A. (2007). *Knowledge economy: Development and the future of higher education.* Rotterdam: Sense Publishers.
Peters, M. A., Burbules, N., & Smeyers, P. (2008). *Saying and showing: Wittgenstein as a pedagogical philosopher.* Boulder: Paradigm (forthcoming).
Peters, M. A., Lankshear, C., & Olssen, M. (Eds.). (2002). *Critical theory and the human condition: Founders and praxis.* New York: Peter Lang.
Peters, M. A., Marshall, J., & Smeyers, P. (Eds.). (2001). *Nietzsche's legacy for education: Past and present values.* Westport, CT. & London: Bergin & Garvey.
Reading, B. (1996*). The university in ruins.* Harvard: Harvard University Press.

Ricoeur, P. (1983, 1984, 1985). *Time and narrative*, 3 vols. trans. Kathleen McLaughlin and David Pellauer. Chicago: University of Chicago Press, 1984, 1985, 1988.

Trifonas, P. & Peters, M. A. (Eds.). (2005). *Deconstructing Derrida: Tasks for the new humanities*. New York: Palgrave.

Michael A. Peters
University of Illinois at Urbana-Champaign

HUGH G PETRIE

BLIND VARIATION AND SELECTIVE RETENTION

Over 50 years ago I sat in the living room of my home in a small town in Colorado where the Dean of Admissions of the California Institute of Technology was interviewing me for freshman admission to their engineering program. As we spoke, the dean said that many intelligent students in small town high schools gravitate toward science and mathematics courses, because these are often the only ones that such students find intrinsically interesting. Without excellent teachers in the humanities and social sciences, such students may not realize the intellectual attractions of those fields.

A "BROAD" UNDERGRADUATE EDUCATION

I was ultimately admitted to Caltech and MIT as well as to the University of Colorado. Because I was awarded a very generous scholarship to Colorado, I enrolled there, but, heeding the words of the Caltech dean, I naively thought I would expand my horizons by entering a joint five-year engineering and business program! It was the beginning of blind variation and selective retention although I could not have put those words to it at the time.

Fortunately, after my first two years at Colorado I discovered that I could also sit in on general honors courses, and, eventually, I became the first engineering student at Colorado to enroll full-time in that program. In my first honors seminar I read Descartes. "Cogito, ergo, sum!" Wow! That dean was right; there was a whole new intellectual world in the humanities. By then, however, I was so far along in my applied mathematics and business studies that I decided simply to finish them rather than shifting at that time to my newfound love of philosophy. My advisors also told me that since analytic philosophy was the intellectual fashion of the day, my work in mathematics would stand me in good stead. I received a Fulbright Fellowship to Manchester University to study mathematics and philosophy for a year and then I took up Woodrow Wilson and Danforth Fellowships to study philosophy at Stanford.

As befitted the vogue in philosophy in the early 60s, I was thoroughly indoctrinated at Stanford into the reigning forms of linguistic analysis. However, I had always been interested in educational issues, and, in particular, in how we learn and come to know what we know. I gravitated to epistemology in my studies and I was particularly influenced by Israel Scheffler's *The Language of Education* (1960). Scheffler's later book, *Conditions of Knowledge* (1965) was copyrighted the same year as my doctoral dissertation, *Rote Learning and Learning With*

L.J. Waks (ed.), *Leaders in Philosophy of Education: Intellectual Self Portraits*, 159–172.

Understanding, and the philosophical resonance between the two is really quite remarkable.

At Stanford, I also established a relationship with Larry Thomas, the senior philosopher of education at Stanford's School of Education. I was able to assist him in a couple of summer courses in philosophy of education (a bit more blind variation).

EVOLUTIONARY EPISTEMOLOGY AND PERCEPTUAL CONTROL THEORY

Following my doctoral work at Stanford, my first academic position was in the philosophy department at Northwestern University. There I made the acquaintance of Joe Park, the philosopher of education in the School of Education, who encouraged my early research and writing in philosophy of education, mostly an elaboration of the analytic epistemological themes drawn from my doctoral dissertation (Petrie, 1968, 1969, 1970).

PERSONAL FAVORITES

Why has learning theory failed to teach us how to learn (1969).

Can education find its lost objectives under the street lamp of behaviorism? (1975).

Do You See What I See? The Epistemology of Interdisciplinary Inquiry (1976).

Evolutionary rationality: or can learning theory survive in the jungle of conceptual change? (1977).

The Dilemma of Enquiry and Learning (1981)

Metaphor and learning (with R. Oshlag) (1993).

Petrie, H.G. From 'my work' to 'our work' (1998).

It was also at Northwestern that the major influences on my intellectual development occurred. During my first year as an assistant professor, I was visited by Donald Campbell, the social psychologist, innovative social science methodologist, and "closet" philosopher of science. It is from Campbell's work in evolutionary epistemology that I have drawn the title, "Blind Variation and Selective Retention," for my contribution to this volume. That phrase, as I will elaborate in what follows, sums up not only my intellectual autobiography, but also my views on how we come to know what we know.

Campbell was going on sabbatical during my first year at Northwestern, but he had heard that the philosophy department had hired an epistemologist and philosopher of science, and he wanted to ask me to co-teach a standard course he offered the next year when he returned. The course was entitled, "Knowledge Processes," and I said I would be happy to do so as long as my chair agreed. (Interestingly, it was this experience with Don Campbell that later encouraged me as a dean to encourage joint teaching experiences by my faculty, even if it didn't quite constitute a "regular" teaching load.)

It was during that course that I was first introduced to Thomas Kuhn (1962), Stephen Toulmin (1963), Karl Popper (1965), N. R. Hanson (1958), and, of course, to Donald Campbell. In the course, I read early drafts of his landmark "Evolutionary Epistemology" (1974). However, it took me awhile to selectively retain all the wonderful blind variations I was introduced to during that course. In fact, as a newly minted Ph.D. (does anyone know more than brand-new Ph.D.'s?), I was amazed that this well-known and highly respected full professor could be making so many elementary epistemological mistakes; mistakes that I had learned to refute during my graduate studies in analytic philosophy. So we had a number of robust discussions in the course about the theses Campbell was presenting. The students, quite naturally, loved the back and forth between the professors. After several months of Don Campbell's patient explanations of his position and questioning of my arguments, I began to think that maybe this full professor knew more than I had originally assumed. By the time we co-taught the course several times in the following years, I was beginning to see the outlines of how evolutionary epistemology might just be able to solve some of the continuing vexing philosophical questions of how we know and how we come to know. Over the years, I continued to keep in touch with Don Campbell and read all that he published on evolutionary epistemology.

The other major influence on my intellectual development also occurred at Northwestern, and, once again, was the result of blind variation and selective retention. The blind variation came from my attending a series of informal luncheon get-togethers organized by Don Campbell. At those luncheons, I made the acquaintance of William Powers. Powers was a true iconoclast. He earned his bachelor's degree in physics, and then enrolled in a doctoral program in psychology to pursue his interests in the connections between certain engineering concepts and human behavior. He left without finishing his degree in psychology in disgust with the reigning behaviorist ideology in psychology.

When I met Bill Powers, he was working as an engineer at a research facility at Northwestern and attempting to pull together his insights about human behavior into a book. At several of our luncheon meetings, he gave demonstrations of what he came to call perceptual control theory. These demonstrations served both as striking refutations of stimulus-response psychology and as incredibly compelling illustrations of perceptual control theory. (For the interested reader, some of these original demonstrations, others developed later, and a general introduction to perceptual control theory can be accessed through the home site of the control systems group at www.perceptualcontroltheory.org. Also see Powers (1998) for a basic introduction to perceptual control theory.)

I was fascinated by this initial brief exposure to Powers' work and I determined to learn more about it and to try to give it a broader exposure. Consequently, I asked him to co-teach a graduate seminar with me on his work. Only about a half dozen Northwestern students signed up, but it was a mind-bending experience for all of us. Bill had us read draft chapters of the book he was working on, showed us many more demonstrations, and engaged us in the most exciting intellectual experience I had ever had. Those chapters later became his seminal book, *Behavior: the Control of Perception* (1973).

LINGUISTIC ANALYSIS

My earliest work at Northwestern was still largely influenced by my doctoral training in analytic philosophy. Even in these writings, however, there were glimmers of the more full-blown emphasis on conceptual change, knowledge acquisition, perceptual control theory, and a naturalized, evolutionary epistemology which came to dominate my later work. In "The Strategy Sense of 'Methodology'" (1968), I used the language of logical analysis to argue for the importance of the processes of obtaining knowledge and not just analyzing states of knowing or knowing how. In "Science and Metaphysics: A Wittgensteinian Interpretation" (1971a), I was already propounding the continuity of science and philosophy, as opposed to the linguistic analysts who held that philosophy was all about grammar. This lengthy book chapter used that paradigmatic linguistic philosopher, Wittgenstein, as a source for hints as to what I and others later came to call naturalized epistemology.

Don Campbell's influence was already apparent in another one of my early papers still couched primarily in the idiom of logical analysis. "A Dogma of Operationalism in the Social Sciences" (1971) argues that the behaviorist's beloved concepts of reliability and validity as exhibited in operational definitions are actually relative to what we take as an observation language. Contrary to the beliefs of most behaviorists, it is simply unsupported dogma to believe that there is some a priori set of observational terms, e.g., atoms of behavior, to which we can always unproblematically refer.

EPISTEMOLOGICAL AND PSYCHOLOGICAL THEMES AND THEIR IMPLICATIONS FOR EDUCATIONAL PHILOSOPHY

In 1971 I moved to the School of Education at the University of Illinois at Urbana-Champaign as a philosopher of education. By then my work was beginning to reflect not only the influences of my time at Northwestern, but also my increasing interest in setting my work in educational contexts. I began to consider how topics such as the theory-ladeness of observation, critiques of behaviorism, the epistemology of interdisciplinary inquiry, metaphor, conceptual change, naturalized evolutionary epistemology, and perceptual control theory have important educational implications.

The Theory-ladeness of Observation and Critiques of Behaviorism

"Why Has Learning Theory Failed to Teach Us How to Learn" (1968) applies the relativity of observational languages to stimulus-response learning theorists on the one hand and educational practitioners on the other. The former use behavioral observational categories and the latter mentalistic action categories. The two camps pass each other in the night. "Theories Are Tested by Observing the Facts: Or Are They?" (1972), expands considerably on the learning theory article. In particular I argue there that non-behavioral approaches in educational research cannot simply be ignored and that an eclectic "functionalism" in educational research is bound to try to compare apples and oranges and, hence, end up being incoherent. Only fully articulated Kuhnian paradigms can fruitfully be compared in terms of educational research. "Can Education Find Its Lost Objectives Under the Street Lamp of Behaviorism?" (1975) applies the lessons of "Dogma" (1971) to a thoroughgoing critique of the educational policy of utilizing behavioral objectives as the panacea for all, or almost all, educational ills.

Interdisciplinary Inquiry

Perhaps my best-known, and most reprinted, article relies heavily upon the theory-ladeness of observation. Early in my career at Illinois, I was invited to join a group of engineers, natural scientists, social scientists, and humanists who were funded by the Sloan Foundation to explore, in an interdisciplinary way, the role of the social sciences and humanities in an engineering curriculum. The method was to hold interdisciplinary seminars of all the faculty participants. Each seminar was led by an expert in a different discipline, engineering, humanities, social science. The faculty member of the moment attempted to answer the question, "How does my discipline view the world?" If ever there was a real-life exploration of the theory-ladeness of observation, this was it! It formed the impetus for my work in the epistemology of interdisciplinary inquiry and led to my most widely published paper, "Do You See What I See? The Epistemology of Interdisciplinary Inquiry" (1976a). In this paper, I argued that truly interdisciplinary inquiry can proceed only if there is at least a rudimentary understanding of the observational categories, and, hence, theory, of the various disciplines involved. This explains why interdisciplinary work is so hard. You almost have to acquire a new discipline. A later reflection on interdisciplinary education can be found in "Interdisciplinary Education: Are We Faced with Insurmountable Opportunities?" (1992a).

Metaphor

So, are we faced with insurmountable difficulties because we have to learn the concepts and observational categories of the new discipline? Not quite. From the seminars, I learned that well-chosen and elaborated metaphors can at least begin to provide the insights necessary to understand one's partners in an interdisciplinary effort. This realization was strengthened by my Illinois colleague, Andrew Ortony. His extensive work on metaphor (1975, 1979, 1993) is a gold mine for the student who wishes to pursue this line of work. I was also influenced by my truly remarkable graduate students at the time who helped me refine my thinking on metaphors and conceptual change. These students included Ralph Page, Robert Halstead, Felicity Haynes, Eric Weir and Graham Oliver, among others. It was from attempting to solve the problem of how we learn new conceptual schemes that my work on metaphor emerged.

Of course, the interesting implication for education is that students learning a new discipline are in the same position as the participants were in the interdisciplinary seminars. They all need to learn the theory-laden observational categories of the discipline without the benefit of any a priori neutral set of observations. Students do, however, have a teacher and good teachers are able to use well-chosen metaphors to help bridge the gap between the common sense observational categories of the student and the observational categories to be learned in the discipline. I argue these points in "Metaphorical Models of Mastery: Or, How to Learn to do the Problems at the End of the Chapter of the Physics Textbook" (1976). I believe that Kuhn's (1974) notion of "exemplars" i.e., exemplary problem solutions, is part of what allows the metaphors to be successful. I also suggest here that the scientist involved in conceptual change at the frontiers of the discipline is, in many ways, analogous to the student. Both need to try out new observational categories with the help of metaphors. The student has the teacher to help weed out bad interpretations by guiding the student through the new field with demonstrations, lab exercises, homework, and the like. The scientist has "nature" as teacher. Experiments are performed and they help weed out incorrect predictions, hypotheses, and observational categories. My most detailed account of how metaphors work for both the student learning something new and for the scientist on the frontiers of knowledge can be found in "Metaphor and Learning" (1979a) and in the revision of that book chapter with Rebecca Oshlag (1993).

FAVORITE WORKS OF OTHERS

Campbell, D.T. Evolutionary Epistemology (1974).
Hansen, N.R. *Patterns of Discovery* (1958).
Kuhn, T. *The Structure of Scientific Revolutions* (1970)
Popper, K. *Conjectures and Refutations: The Growth of Scientific Knowledge* (1965).
Powers, W.T. *Behavior: The Control of Perception* (1973)
Powers, W.T. *Making Sense of Behavior: The Meaning of Control* (1998).
Toulmin, S.. *Foresight and Understanding.*(1963)

Conceptual Change and Naturalized Evolutionary Epistemology

Returning to my first theme at Illinois, I eventually came to see that a naturalized evolutionary epistemology was necessary to encompass all of these insights — the theory-dependency of observation, the growth of knowledge, conceptual change, metaphors, and critiques of behaviorism. And the key slogan for that epistemology provides the title to this chapter, "Blind Variation and Selective Retention." I adopt this phrase from Don Campbell's brilliant piece, "Evolutionary Epistemology" (1974). There is no way that I can fully elucidate this idea in the short space I have available here, nor can I begin to deal with the numerous "standard" objections to a variation and retention view of evolution, whether biological or conceptual. Campbell does a wonderful job, and I devote considerable space to this topic in my book, *The Dilemma of Enquiry and Learning* (1981). For now let me simply say that "blind" does *not* mean "random." Rather it means that although *what* is being varied, e.g., concepts, theories, even organisms, does not know beforehand what will be encountered, these variants, because they have survived thus far, already contain a good deal of at least partial wisdom about the environment. We don't start from scratch varying "atoms." Furthermore, selection need not involve the complete elimination of some variants. There are "vicarious" selection mechanisms at work too, e.g., generally accepted common sense theories, other scientific theories not at the moment subject to examination, long-standing common sense observational categories. None of these are a priori infallible, and each may be questioned in its turn, but they at least have worked tolerably well up until now. Finally, although we can never have direct access to "reality as it really is," there is a role for a reality that forms the basis against which we test, change, and test again our representations of it. I am a realist.

My first, short account of how evolutionary epistemology can deal with conceptual change is to be found in "Evolutionary Rationality: Or Can Learning Theory Survive in the Jungle of Conceptual Change?" (1977a). In this paper I argue that given the theory-dependency of observation a philosophical concern for truth cannot be taken simply as some sort of direct correspondence between our observations and conceptual schemes on the one hand and "reality" on the other. Rather, we must consider how our observational categories and conceptual schemes as a whole allow us to deal with the world in terms of all of the human purposes, social and individual, that we have. Thus, although I read very little Dewey or James or other pragmatists, I believe that I echo some pragmatic themes in my work. This relation to pragmatism becomes even more evident in "Science and Scientists, Technology and Technologists, and the Rest of Us" (1977b). In this book chapter I explicitly consider the relationship between evolutionary epistemology and pragmatism. Specifically, I argue that evolutionary epistemology can assist pragmatism with several of the traditional challenges to its justification of science. Evolutionary epistemology can help locate sources of values in science while still allowing for the "objectivity" of science and technology that is found in the disciplinary aspects of science. It can, by taking an appropriately long-term and expansive view of the development of science help defend the value of science and technology from isolated counterexamples in which science and technology have not led to humane results. Finally, evolutionary epistemology can help pragmatism deal with the objection that inappropriate social power distributions might capture the social arrangements of the disciplines. This can happen here and there, e.g., in "scientific" objections to global warming funded by industry. But the fact that the scientific disciplines often find other social arrangements to further their work, e.g. universities, "green" organizations, suggests that the discipline will continue to evolve and answer our basic human purposes.

Perceptual Control Theory

Just what is "Perceptual Control Theory?" Unfortunately, I can hardly explain it adequately in the limited space available here. I again refer you to the web site

165

mentioned above where you can explore a number of different introductions to the theory, along with on-line demonstrations. In brief, perceptual control theory (PCT) explains how entities control what happens to them and illustrates the relationships between actions and goals, perceptions and actions, and perceptions and reality. Furthermore, it does so within a single, testable concept of how living systems work. The most important insight is that human beings employ negative feed back systems to control their *inputs*, i.e., their *perceptions*, rather than their outputs, i.e., their behaviors. Behavior is used to control our perceptions of our environment and these perceptions are compared with what we want to see, i.e., our purposes and intentions in acting. We then vary our outputs, not with any sort of detailed "plan", but almost automatically. These outputs affect the world which in turn affects out perceptions, bringing them closer to what we want to see in the case of well-adjusted control systems. Think of driving a car. We don't calculate which way to turn the wheel when the road turns or a crosswind takes us out of the lane; we just automatically turn the wheel until we perceive the car where we want it to be in conjunction with the road.[*]

My first attempt at introducing PCT to educational audiences was "Action, Perception, and Education" (1974). It fell stillborn from the press. I followed this attempt to present the whole of PCT in one article with a number of more pointed educational implications. In "A Rule by Any Other Name is a Control System" (1976c) I argue that any number of problems with the analysis of rule-following in psychology can be solved by treating rule-following as the operation of control systems rather than as some mysterious and complicated associationist view of habits.

In "Against 'Objective' Tests: A Note on the Epistemology Underlying Current Testing Dogma" (1979) I show how "objective" tests as they are understood in the evaluation literature are sorely limited in how much they can actually tell about the competence and knowledge of those who are being tested. On the other hand, "subjective" tests are much more nuanced and capable of revealing the depth of understanding of the person being tested. All of this follows from a principle of PCT, "the test for the controlled variable." The test for the controlled variable is a method for finding out just what perceptions someone else is actually controlling for with their behavior. The test proceeds by introducing what would be disturbances to the hypothesized variable that one thinks the person is controlling and seeing what they do to counteract those disturbances. Thus, it is no accident that one of the most intellectually challenging tests we have, the Ph.D. oral, allows for the examiners to vary their questions to explore just what the candidate really has in mind. Even doctoral prelims are typically of an essay variety where the candidate can counteract the disturbance introduced by the questions. We certainly do not give Ph.D. candidates "objective" true-false or multiple choice tests. My most elaborate exposition of how PCT helps us ground testing is to be found in my Philosophy of Education Society Presidential Address, "Testing for Critical Thinking" (1986).

In "Program Evaluation as an Adaptive System," (1982) I apply the notions of PCT and adaptive systems to argue that in order for program evaluation to be integrated into an institution's structure rather than resisted by it, both the evaluation scheme and the institution must be viewed as adaptive systems which control their perceptions. I also suggest in "Purpose, Context, and Synthesis: Can We Avoid Relativism?' (1995b) that evaluation specialists who insist that evaluation research must be tied to the context and the purposes of the evaluation can, nevertheless, reach warranted conclusions. They do not need to retreat to positivism or be branded as relativists. Indeed, human beings, conceived of as control systems, are able to achieve consistent results in a constantly changing environment. Thus in evaluating how they do that, we <u>must</u>, as evaluators, look at both what the actors are trying to achieve and at how the context in which they are doing this is changing.

THE DILEMMA OF ENQUIRY AND LEARNING

Clearly the most comprehensive and detailed analysis I give of the various themes encompassed in my philosophical work is to be found in my book, *The Dilemma of Enquiry and Learning* (1981). In this work, I take Plato's Meno dilemma seriously. The dilemma says that we can neither inquire into anything which we know nor into anything which we do not know. For if we already know something, we have no need to inquire, but if we do not know something, we cannot inquire, for we would know neither where to begin nor when we had reached knowledge of what we do not know. In short, the Meno dilemma seems to pose the Kantian question, "How are inquiry and learning possible?"

In brief, my solution to the Meno dilemma (after extensive exposition and argument) is that we must step between the horns of the dilemma by giving both of them their due. One of the major preconditions for stepping between the horns is to argue that we must focus on knowledge *processes* rather than knowledge *structures*. "Knowing" and "learning" are the fundamental notions rather than "knowledge and "what is learned." If we focus on knowledge process, we can see that even what I called the "old knowledge" horn of the dilemma is really quite sharp. Just because we "know" something in the sense of having acquired a knowledge structure it does not follow that we automatically know how to apply that structure in a constantly changing environment to achieve consistent results. Recall the example of driving a car. Almost everyone already "knows" how to drive. Yet each time we are on the road, even on our well-worn route to the office or the grocery store, we are faced with different circumstances with which we must cope in order to get where we are going. The behaviorist and even traditional cognitivist psychological approaches to explaining our continuing successes in such situations face insurmountable difficulties.

In the book I call the knowledge process that accounts for our ability to utilize existing conceptual frameworks in changing circumstances, "assimilation," and while the term is similar to Piaget's use of the same language, I do not give it a Piagetian elaboration. Rather, I present perceptual control theory and show how it transparently shows how conceptual structures conceived as perceptual control systems and hierarchies of control systems explain our ability to achieve consistent results in very different environments.

Of course, the "new knowledge" horn of the dilemma is very sharp as well. Occasionally, we really do need to radically change our conceptual schemes, whether we are scientists on the frontiers of knowledge or students just learning a brand new discipline that is incompatible with our existing beliefs. I call the knowledge process that accounts for radical conceptual change, "accommodation," although again the concept is not the Piagetian one. I argue that the blind variation and selective retention mechanism elaborated in a naturalized evolutionary epistemology is what is needed to account for successful processes leading to new knowledge structures.

The way between the horns of the dilemma lies in recognizing a reflective equilibrium between assimilation and accommodation. In dealing with the world we almost always try to assimilate new situations by means of our existing knowledge processes. However, if we continuously fail to be successful, we may need to try new structures. These new trials are best understood as metaphors that have to be tested against the world through whatever observational categories we happen to be using. Gradually, both metaphors and observations are brought into a kind of equilibrium, at least for the moment.

Educationally, I argue that we seem not to recognize the need for both assimilation and accommodation. Still less are we aware of when one ought to be stressed and when the other. In any educational situation we need to carefully analyze whether we are trying to get a student to refine an existing knowledge process or when we are trying to get the student to acquire new knowledge processes. We must always be striving for a reflective equilibrium between assimilation and accommodation in both our classroom practice and our educational policy making.

The book brings together in one place almost all of my thinking about educational epistemology. It utilizes themes from conceptual change, the centrality of metaphor, a focus on knowledge processes, the new psychology of perceptual control theory, and a naturalized evolutionary epistemology.

TRANSITIONS

During the year's in which I was writing *Dilemma*, I was also undertaking a number of new blind variations in both my personal and professional lives. I divorced and remarried. I have now been married for 28 years to my wife, Carol Hodges. During this period, some of my writing on accountability and evaluation as well as my work in interdisciplinarity came to the attention of the higher administration at Illinois. I was asked to take over as the director of the campus-wide program evaluation system at the university. Since it was just about my turn to assume a term as chair of my department, I blindly decided that the university-wide administrative position would be more interesting and probably less challenging than departmental politics. I was certainly wrong about the latter assumption. However, the opportunity to utilize my expertise in interdisciplinary inquiry to assist a blue ribbon campus committee of professors from different disciplines pass evaluative judgments on their colleagues' departments was one of the high points of my administrative career. And all of this was going on while I was writing my book!

The next blind variation came with our decision to move to Buffalo. Since Carol was a Ph.D. graduate of the University of Illinois, she was only able to teach there for several years on soft money and we were constantly on the lookout for a place where we could both obtain academic positions. By 1981 I had completed my stint as a campus-level administrator, but there were almost no openings for a philosopher of education, at least at institutions that also were looking for a reading and elementary education professor. So I started looking for administrative positions and in 1981 Carol accepted a faculty position at State University College at Buffalo and I accepted the deanship of the school of education at the State University of New York at Buffalo—both SUNY institutions, but separate.

A PHILOSOPHER DEAN

Thus began my 16 year tour of duty as dean, followed by two years back as a professor before retirement. During my tenure as a dean, my professional interests turned largely to educational policy issues, although still strongly influenced by my philosophical beliefs. There were several strands in my work during this period. In 1987 a number of colleagues and I founded the journal, *Educational Policy*. A number of the "themed" issues from the journal were fleshed out and became edited books (Weis, L. et al. *Crisis in Teaching: Perspectives on Current Reforms*. 1989a), (Weis, L. et al. *Dropouts from School: Issues, Dilemmas and Solutions*. 1989b), (Altbach, P.G. et al. *Textbooks in American Society: Politics, Policy, and Pedagogy*. 1991a), (*Weis, L. et al. Critical Perspectives on Early Childhood Education*. 1991b), (Petrie, H.G. *Professionalization, Partnership, and Power*. 1995). A second focus emerged from my role as one of the founders of the institutional educational reform movement known as the Holmes Group (see the Holmes trilogy, *Tomorrow's Teachers* (1986), *Tomorrow's Schools* (1990), and *Tomorrow's Schools of Education* (1995). Although the Holmes Group as an organization is no more, the ideas it propounded have had a significant impact on teacher education. Extended preparation programs, a strong liberal arts education, a rejuvenation and strengthening of professional training, the concept of professional development schools as a joint project of real schools and schools of education, an emphasis on more practice-oriented research by education professors in research universities—all are now part of the educational landscape in one form or another.

I wrote on extended preparation and the liberal arts in teacher education (1987a, 1987b), strengthening professional preparation (1990), and professional development schools (1995a). I also continued to utilize my interests in educational epistemology in my policy writings. In "Knowledge, Practice, and Judgment" (1992b), I argued that we must substitute a notion of teacher judgment for that of "applying" research to practice. The latter depends for its justification on discredited views of knowledge processes, while the former takes full account

169

of the view of knowledge processes I describe in *Dilemma*. Finally, in "From 'My Work' to 'Our Work'," (1998) I reflected on my experiences as a dean in trying to encourage changes to the faculty culture in schools of education in research universities. Instead of the faculty viewing themselves as more or less independent intellectuals who happen to have a mailing address and email account at a university, I tried over my years as a dean to encourage more collaborative teaching, research and outreach activities with the rest of the education profession—a shift from "my work" to "our work." At best, I had modest success.

CONCLUSION

Nevertheless, as I suggested in my valedictory address to the last group of students who graduated under my deanship, our efforts in the academy, whether teaching, research, service, or administration, are all a work in progress. As an education profession we refine our knowledge here and there and occasionally, blindly stumble across something quite new. Once in awhile, those blind variations are selectively retained and our profession lurches forward. The best each of us can do is make our own individual contributions and hope that some will "stick." That is what I have tried to do since my first encounter with that dean of admissions from California Institute of Technology over 50 years ago. I have undertaken one blind variation after another, starting with "broadening" my undergraduate education to include business as well as engineering. As it turns out my undergraduate business degree stood me in good stead as a dean 30 years later. I stumbled onto Don Campbell and Bill Powers and they changed my intellectual life in the most profound ways. I participated in an interdisciplinary seminar and became fascinated with the topic. I became a campus level administrator to avoid being a chair and was then able to find employment as a dean so that my wife and I could pursue joint careers in education. As a dean I put my philosophical background to work in furthering the cause of educational reform. I varied a lot of things, the outcomes of which I certainly could not have predicted in advance. But I used my knowledge and experience and values to select and retain what I hope were the best of those variants. I can only hope that others will carry on the work in progress that is educational philosophy.

NOTE

* Those familiar with the educational literature will recognize that William Glasser has written extensively in education utilizing a concept he calls "control theory." Although there are superficial similarities to Powers' perceptual control theory, Glasser completely fails to appreciate that what is controlled are perceptions, not actions or behaviors. This renders Glasser's version of control theory no more insightful than most other cognitivist theories in psychology.

REFERENCES/BIBLIOGRAPHY

Altbach, P.G., Kelly, G.P., Petrie, H.G., & Weis, L. (Eds.). (1991). *Textbooks in American society: Politics, policy, and pedagogy.* Albany, NY: SUNY Press.

Campbell, D.T. (1974). Evolutionary epistemology. In P.A. Schilpp (Ed.), *The philosophy of Karl Popper. The library of living philosophers, vol. 14.* LaSalle, IL: Open Court.

Hansen, N.R. (1958). *Patterns of discovery.* Cambridge: Cambridge University Press.

Holmes Group. (1986). *Tomorrow's teachers: A report of the Holmes Group.* East Lansing, MI: Author.

Holmes Group. (1990). *Tomorrow's schools: A report of the Holmes Group.* East Lansing, MI: Author.

Holmes Group. (1995). *Tomorrow's schools of education: A report of the Holmes Group.* East Lansing, MI: Author.

Kuhn, T. (1970). *The structure of scientific revolutions.* Enlarged Edition. Chicago: University of Chicago Press.

Kuhn, T. (1974). Second thoughts on paradigms. In F. Suppe (Ed.), *The structure of scientific theories.* Urbana, IL: University of Illinois Press.

Ortony, A. (1975). Why metaphors are necessary and not just nice. *Educational Theory, 25,* 45-53.

Ortony, A. (Ed.). (1979). *Metaphor and thought,* First edition. Cambridge: Cambridge University Press.

Ortony, A. (Ed.). (1993). *Metaphor and thought,* Second edition. Cambridge: Cambridge University Press.

Petrie, H.G. (1965). *Rote learning and learning with understanding* (Ph.D. Dissertation). Stanford University.

Petrie, H.G. (1968). The strategy sense of 'methodology'. *Philosophy of Science, 35*(September), 248-257.

Petrie, H.G. (1969). Why has learning theory failed to teach us how to learn. *Proceedings of the Philosophy of Education Society, 1968.* 163-170. (Reprinted in Broudy, H. S., Ennis, R. H., & Krimerman, L.I. (Eds.) (1973), *Philosophy of educational research.* New York: John Wiley and Sons, pp. 121-138.)

Petrie, H.G. (1970). Learning with understanding. In Martin, J.R. (Ed.), *Readings in the philosophy of education: a study of curriculum* (pp. 106-121). Boston: Allyn-Bacon.

Petrie, H.G. (1971a). Science and metaphysics: A Wittgensteinian interpretation. In Klemke, E. (Ed.), *Essays on Wittgenstein* (pp. 138-169). Urbana: University of Illinois Press.

Petrie, H.G. (1971b). A dogma of operationalism in the social sciences. *Philosophy of Social Science, 1.* 145-160.

Petrie, H.G. (1972). Theories are tested by observing the facts: or are they? *Philosophical redirection of educational research, National Society for the Study of Education yearbook, 71*st Yearbook (pp. 47-73). Chicago: University of Chicago Press.

Petrie, H.G. (1974). Action, perception, and education. *Educational Theory, 24,* 33-45.

Petrie, H.G. (1975). Can education find its lost objectives under the street lamp of behaviorism? In Smith, R. (Ed.), *Regaining educational leadership: essays critical of PBTE/CBTE* (pp. 64-74). New York: Wiley.

Petrie, H.G. (1976a). Do you see what I see? The epistemology of interdisciplinary inquiry. *Educational Researcher, 5*(2), 9-15 (Republished in (1976a) *The Journal of Aesthetic Education, 10*(1) 29-43; Reprinted in (1986). Chubin, D. E., Porter, A. L., Rossini, F. A., and Connolly, T. (Eds.), *Interdisciplinary analysis and research* (pp. 115-130). Mt. Airy, Maryland: Lomand.)

Petrie, H.G. (1976b). Metaphorical models of mastery: or, how to learn to do the problems at the end of the chapter of the physics textbook. In Cohen, R. S., Hooker, C. A., Michalos, A. C., & Van Evra, J. W. (Eds.), *PSA 1974* (pp. 301-312). Dordrecht, the Netherlands: D. Reidel.

Petrie, H.G. (1976c). A rule by any other name is a control system. *Cybernetics Forum, VIII,* (Fall/Winter), 103-114.

Petrie, H.G. (1977a). Evolutionary rationality: or can learning theory survive in the jungle of conceptual change? *Proceedings of the Philosophy of Education Society, 1976,* 117-132.

Petrie, H.G. (1977b). Science and scientists, technology and technologists, and the rest of us. In LaBrecque, R. & Crockenberg, V. (Eds.), *Culture as education* (pp. 79-100). Dubuque, Iowa: Kendall-Hunt.

Petrie, H.G. (1979a). Metaphor and learning. In Ortony, A. (Ed.), *Metaphor and thought* (pp. 438-461), First Edition. Cambridge: Cambridge University Press.

Petrie, H.G. (1979b). Against 'objective' tests: A note on the epistemology underlying current testing dogma. In Ozer, M.N. (Ed.), *A cybernetic approach to the assessment of children: Toward a more humane use of human beings* (pp. 117-150). Boulder, Colorado: Westview Press.

171

Petrie, H.G. (1981). *The dilemma of enquiry and learning.* Chicago: University of Chicago Press.

Petrie, H.G. (1982). Program evaluation as an adaptive system. In Wilson, R. (Ed.), *New directions for higher education: designing academic program reviews, no. 37* (pp. 17-29). San Francisco: Jossey-Bass.

Petrie, H.G. (1986). Testing for critical thinking (Presidential Address). *Proceedings of the Philosophy of Education Society 1985,* 3-20.

Petrie, H.G. (1987a). The liberal arts and sciences in the teacher education curriculum, In Carbone, M.J. & Wonsiewicz, A. (Eds.), *Excellence in teacher education through the liberal arts* (pp. 39-45). Muhlenberg, PA: Muhlenberg College.

Petrie, H.G. (1987b). Teacher education, the liberal arts, and extended preparation programs. *Educational Policy, 1*(1), 29-42. (Reprinted by the Nelson A. Rockefeller Institute of Government, State University of New York, No. 26 (Spring, 1987). Reprinted in Weis, L., Altbach, P.G., Kelly, G.P., Petrie, H.G., & Slaughter, S. (Eds.), (1989a). *Crisis in teaching: perspectives on current reforms.* Albany, New York: SUNY Press.)

Petrie, H.G. (1990). Reflections on the second wave of reform: restructuring the teaching profession. In Jacobson, S. & Conway, J. (Eds.), *Educational leadership in an age of reform* (pp. 14-29). New York: Longman.

Petrie, H.G. (1992a). Interdisciplinary education: Are we faced with insurmountable opportunities? In Grant, G. (ed.) *Review of Research in Education,18.* Washington, DC: American Educational Research Association. 299-333.

Petrie, H.G. (1992b). Knowledge, practice, and judgment, *Educational Foundations, 6*(1), 35-48.

Petrie, H.G. & Oshlag, R. (1993). Metaphor and learning. In Ortony, A. (Ed.), *Metaphor and thought,* Second Edition (pp. 579-609). New York, Cambridge University Press.

Petrie, H.G. (1995a). A new paradigm for practical research. In Petrie, H.G. (Ed.), *Professionalization, partnership, and power: Building professional development schools* (pp. 285-302). Albany, NY: SUNY Press.

Petrie, H.G. (Ed.). (1995a). *Professionalization, partnership, and power: Building professional development schools.* Albany, NY: SUNY Press.

Petrie, H.G. (1995b). Purpose, context, and synthesis: Can we avoid relativism? In D. Fournier (Ed.), *Reasoning in evaluation: Inferential links and leaps* (pp. 81-91). San Francisco: Jossey-Bass.

Petrie, H.G. (1998). From 'my work' to 'our work'. In Jacobson, S.L., Emihovich, C., Helfrich, J., Petrie, H.G., & Stevenson, R.B., *Transforming schools and schools of education: A new vision for preparing educators* (pp. 23-45).Thousand Oaks, CA: Corwin Press, Inc.

Popper, K. (1965). *Conjectures and refutations: The growth of scientific knowledge,* 2nd edition. New York: Basic Books.

Powers, W.T. (1973). *Behavior: The control of perception.* Chicago: Aldine.

Powers, W.T. (1998). *Making sense of behavior: the meaning of control.* New Canaan, CT: Benchmark Publications.

Scheffler, I. (1960). *The language of education.* Springfield, IL: Charles C. Thomas.

Scheffler, I. (1965). *Conditions of knowledge.* Chicago: Scott, Foresman.

Toulmin, S. (1963). *Foresight and understanding.* New York: Harper and Row.

Weis, L., Altbach, P.G., Kelly, G.P., Petrie, H.G., & Slaughter, S. (Eds.). (1989a). *Crisis in teaching: Perspectives on current reforms.* Albany, New York: SUNY Press.

Weis, L., Farrar, E., & Petrie, H. (Eds.). (1989b). *Dropouts from school: Issues, dilemmas and solutions.* Albany, New York: SUNY Press.

Weis, L., Altbach, P.G., Kelly, G.P., & Petrie, H.G. (Eds.). (1991). *Critical perspectives on early childhood education.* Albany, NY: SUNY Press.

Hugh Petrie
Professor Emeritus and Retired Dean of the Graduate School of Education
State University of New York at Buffalo

D.C. PHILLIPS

THE DEVELOPMENT OF A DISILLUSIONIST

The title above is a playful reference, not only to what I consider to be my main philosophical program – the shattering of illusions and delusions, particularly uncritical adherence (by others) to various of the great "isms" of our times – but also to the fact that ever since childhood I have had an interest in conjuring. In my more advanced years this hobby matured into using my ten-minute magic act as a vehicle for satirical comment upon the professional beliefs and commitments of my colleagues – I had discovered that one could get away with a lot so long as the criticism (explicit or implied) was dressed up as the humorous patter of a bumbling illusionist. I also learned the importance of quickly tweaking the audience's interest. Somewhere along the line I noticed that there had been a merging of styles between my avocation and my vocation. But I jump the gun.

I was born and raised in Melbourne, Australia; my environment was crammed with books and populated by colourful relatives of theatrical bent and with radical political proclivities. My father was an author, and a onetime vaudeville script-writer, although by the time I knew him his day job was as a civil servant; but through watching him I learned that writing was a hard and serious business. At school I managed to survive in a competitive system in which only a small percentage of an age-group made it through to twelfth grade (sixth form). Only a fraction of these survivors were selected to enter university, and I made it by the skin of my teeth. And so it was that, several months after my seventeenth birthday, in early March 1955, I entered the University of Melbourne as a candidate for a degree in the sciences (the academic year in the antipodes runs from March until November). I was equally interested in the humanities, but in the later years of high school I had been directed into the "science stream" – I had won a "secondary studentship" that carried a small cash award for the last two years of high school, but the enticement was that it also paid all fees plus a liberal living allowance if eventually I was admitted to university. The catch was, I had to agree that upon graduation I would train as a secondary school teacher – and furthermore I would go and serve for three years wherever in the State of Victoria the Education Department chose to send me! There was one further catch: although Australia was short of teachers in all high school subjects, there was a desperate shortage of teachers of mathematics and science, hence my being directed to specialize in this general area. As the idea of being a teacher appealed to me, and as the prospect of being able to afford a university education appealed even more, shortly before my fifteenth birthday I made the weighty decision to sign the studentship agreement; and thus it was that about two years later I was riding high, with my first check in my pocket and my first-year science textbooks under my arm.

L.J. Waks (ed.), Leaders in Philosophy of Education: Intellectual Self Portraits, 173–184.
© 2008 *Sense Publishers. All rights reserved.*

During my undergraduate years I took a variety of courses in vertebrate and invertebrate zoology, botany, physiology and biochemistry, cytology and genetics, physics, chemistry, and pure mathematics; my major field was biology, which I knew nothing about in my high school days. I also managed to fit in a year-long course in the history and philosophy of science that I imagined would be useful for me in my career as a high school teacher. With the benefit of hindsight, three aspects of this program stand out as being of great importance for my later intellectual/professional life as a philosopher. The first was the sense it gave me of the many forms of scientific inquiry, of the ways in which theory and field or laboratory work were interrelated, and of the precision with which scientific arguments were developed and measurements were made. (Traces of some of these influences can still be found in my most recent work; see Phillips, 2006.) My undergraduate experiences also made me receptive to Thomas Kuhn's concept of "normal science" when I met it more than a decade

---

PERSONAL FAVORITES

Books

Holistic Thought in Social Science (1976).
Visions of Childhood (1987), with J.F. Cleverley.
Philosophy, Science, and Social Inquiry (1987).
Perspectives on Learning (4th ed., 2004), with Jonas Soltis.
The Expanded Social Scientist's Bestiary (2000).
Postpositivism and Educational Research (2000), with Nicholas Burbules.

Essays and articles

Hierarchical theories of development in education and psychology (1975), with Mavis E. Kelly.
Popper and pragmatism: A fantasy (1975).
Kohlbergian moral development: A progressing or degenerating research program? (1978). With Jennie Nicolayev. (See also ch.14 of *Philosophy, Science, and Social Inquiry*.).
On describing a student's cognitive structure (1983). (See also ch.12 of *Philosophy, Science and Social Inquiry*.).
Was William James telling the truth after all? (1984).
Philosophy of education (1985).
The good, the bad, and the ugly: The many faces of constructivism (1995).
Coming to grips with radical social constructivisms (1997).
John Dewey's *Child and the Curriculum*: A century later (1998).
Muddying the waters: The many purposes of educational inquiry (2006).

---

later. (Later still I became annoyed by the widespread misapplications of Kuhn's work, by the uncritical acceptance of the relativistic aspects of it, and also by the lack of awareness on the part of many educational theorists of the great complexities involved in assessing Kuhn; see Phillips, 1987, especially ch.8. For the past thirty years or so I have been teaching a Stanford course "Popper, Kuhn and Lakatos", which undoubtedly has been my favourite, and during which I unashamedly draw on examples from my undergraduate studies.)

The second thing that had enormous impact on me was my exposure to the theory of evolution; what first impressed me was the way it served to bring order to what otherwise would have been an overwhelming mass of disconnected facts. The light-bulb flashed for me in an advanced course in vertebrate zoology and comparative anatomy; we were expected to remember the anatomy of a large number of different vertebrates, especially of the thorax and the intricate arrangement of the blood vessels and nerves and their relationship to the gills or lungs and also to the heart, and in the laboratory exam at the end of the year we had to perform a dissection of one of the systems of one of the species that had been studied. At first all was confusion in this course, with severe memory overload, until the instructor suggested we open Gavin de Beer's treatise *Vertebrate Zoology* (1951) at pp.284-5, where we found six diagrams – from fish to mammal – showing how the archetypal pattern of aortic blood vessels around the gill slits had gradually been modified in the course of the evolution of the higher types, as gill arches were lost and the lungs evolved. Suddenly the anatomical arrangements in the six vertebrate species depicted made sense, and the pattern of progressive development became crystal clear (although it was still complex)! The well-worn diagram from that text, with its mass of pencilled notes, is still one of my treasured souvenirs from my undergraduate days.

Thus began my lifelong interest in the theory of evolution and its impact on Western thought – my attraction to William James and John Dewey initially stemmed from this, as did my interest a little later in Jean Piaget and developmental and cognitive psychology; my master's thesis in education (in the early sixties, which became my first publication in an edited volume) explored the different ways in which Herbert Spencer and Dewey used evolutionary theory, and my subsequent work on holistic thought and systems theory had the same root. In general, as I later discovered, the theory of evolution had much the same impact on me as it had on Dewey and many others – I became a convinced naturalist in the philosophical sense, although as yet I did not know the term and certainly had only reflected superficially. (For a recent account of the spread of naturalism, see Phillips, 2000, ch.5.)

There is no doubt, however, that the third influence upon me in my undergraduate days turned my world upside-down. The course in history and philosophy of science – that I took more-or-less on a whim – covered several of the standard issues in philosophy of science, and devoted a great deal of time to the history of optics, and to Descartes. The instructor, Gerd Buchdahl, was the epitome of the disorganized scholar, and I fell under his spell immediately – how could one resist a man who came to class muttering "My wife is thinking of divorcing me, and she is citing Descartes as co-respondent!" One of the essays I wrote for him was on justifications of induction – no doubt a precursor of my lifelong interest in Popper, of which more later – and another was on operational definitions; on one of these he wrote "I have learned from you", which was a heady comment for an eighteen-year-old to receive, one that convinced me that my future lay along a philosophical path. Unfortunately, at the end of that year Buchdahl left Melbourne for a readership at Cambridge.

Upon graduation, as contracted, I entered the one-year teacher-training program in the Faculty of Education. I will pass over in silence my first exhausting classroom experiences. I was somewhat shocked by the pabulum served-up in some of the coursework, but enjoyed the course that surveyed the history of educational thought (Plato to Dewey, via Locke, Rousseau, Newman, Spencer, and others long forgotten) – this was the nearest thing to philosophy of education that was on offer. Dewey I found to be rather mysterious, and I could not see how the summaries to many of the chapters in *Democracy and Education* related to the body of the chapters. At the end of the year I was assigned to teach in a well-established middle class suburban high school that needed a biology teacher, and I spent three years there until I received promotion to a school on the outskirts of Melbourne, in a tough neighbourhood adjoining a migrant camp; I was just twenty-four, and found myself senior mathematics and science master, with the additional heavy responsibility of being the school's first-aid officer. I spent two challenging years there, and although my proficiency at staunching the flow of blood from cuts did not noticeably improve, I felt I really learned how to teach. In particular, the lesson that was emerging from my magic was reinforced at this "difficult" school – the secret was a Deweyan one, namely the importance of very quickly capturing the attention of the students/audience and engaging them in a relevant and interesting problem or mystery. (In later years I have been much mystified myself at philosophers who – for example – launch into a detailed analysis of the possible positions with respect to the body/mind problem, without first ensuring that their students actually *feel* the problem. It has always seemed obvious to me, since those early days, that if you don't appreciate the problem then you will not understand the possible answers.)

Intellectually the five years I spent teaching were very productive, for at both schools I was within convenient driving distance of the university. The Faculty of Arts (in which, of course, philosophy and philosophy of science were located) did not offer late afternoon or evening courses, but the Faculty of Education did, and so I decided to pursue further work there while I was teaching, specializing as much as possible in the history of educational thought. I converted my year of teacher-training into a second bachelor's degree by doing several years of evening coursework, and – having done well enough to enable me to proceed – I was admitted to the M.Ed program, which consisted entirely of writing a thesis. My topic was the one mentioned earlier, comparing Spencer's and Dewey's different use of evolutionary theory. I argued that Spencer used it quite mechanistically and stressed the role of natural selection; and furthermore he used it in domains (such as in a discussion of "the genesis of knowledge in the individual") where it was not obvious that it was applicable. On the other hand Dewey was more impressed by the role of chance variations and the novelties and unpredictable elements thus introduced into nature – culminating of course in the greatest novelty of all, human intelligence. I learned a lot through my wide background reading – but I learned a great deal more, and at first suffered a great deal of mortification, at the hands of my supervisor Barbara Falk. She was an Oxford-trained historian, and had mixed in circles with Gilbert Ryle, but she did not know much about my topic; however, she had the most incisive mind I have met, before or since, and almost without looking at my draft pages she could detect vagueness, obfuscations, ambiguities, beatings around the bush, and more stylistic sins than I care to remember. And she meticulously noted these in red ink, using straightforward prose along these lines: "this is bullshit", "this is a cop-out", "what is this supposed to mean", "this sentence has four possible interpretations....am I supposed to guess what you actually mean". For months I felt tears welling up when I received her feedback, but I persisted and gradually the red ink appeared less frequently. I owe her an inestimable debt (as, I believe, do my own advisees whom I persist in treating in the same manner!), and under her tutelage I not only finally learned how to write, but I came to see that formulating one's ideas vaguely was a form of hypocrisy – I had held many of my beliefs (like Descartes?) because they were not "clear and distinct", and if I wanted to avoid self-delusion I had to strive for the utmost clarity. On Barbara's suggestion, I took the time to carefully work through *An Introduction to Philosophical Analysis*, by John Hospers, and found that this gave me further tools to enhance the clarity and precision of my writing, not to mention my thinking!

My thesis was well-received, and was awarded the Freda Cohen Prize (Phillips, 1966). With the support of one of my examiners, D.A.T. Gasking, a logician and former student of Wittgenstein's (and chair of Melbourne's Department of Philosophy) I applied to, and was accepted by, two doctoral programs – one in the Philosophy Department in the Institute of Advanced Study at the Australian National University, where I would work with the historian of philosophy and chairperson, John Passmore. But for family reasons I accepted the offer of a handsome fellowship at Melbourne, where (unusually) I had two supervisors – Barbara Falk from Education and Douglas Gasking's wife Elizabeth, from History and Philosophy of Science. (Passmore later served as one of the external examiners of my doctoral dissertation.) In 1964 there was no doctoral coursework in Australia (which followed the British system); instead, I was supposed to spend three years or more writing a dissertation that would then be examined by one person internal to the university and two who were experts in the topic and who would come from "somewhere else in the world". But I felt that before writing I needed to fill-in some of the enormous gaps in my philosophical background, and during the first two years I took a number of year-long courses and seminars in philosophy and philosophy of science. Meanwhile my topic evolved, and eventually became *Organicism and its Influence on the Philosophical and Educational Writings of John Dewey*. Essentially I analysed a group of holistic ideas that were current in the late nineteenth-century (the best known of which are "the whole is more than the sum of the parts" and "the parts of an organic whole are dynamically interrelated or interdependent"); I showed these were derived from Hegel's "principle of internal relations" (Phillips, 1970; 1976, ch.1), and I went on to discuss their influence on Dewey – for example, his horror of "dualisms" in part stemmed from his view that they artificially divided aspects of a "whole" and set these up as separate entities (Phillips, 1971). A few years later I expanded the scope of these ideas to cover among other things systems theory and functionalism, and thus was born *Holistic Thought in Social Science* (1976), which was published in the UK and the USA, with an Italian translation in 1980.

It was while I was working on this doctoral dissertation, during an advanced seminar I was taking in philosophy of science in 1966 or 1967, that another important milestone in my intellectual development was reached – for it was then that I read Karl Popper's *Conjectures and Refutations* (1965), relatively shortly after its publication. I had met Popper's philosophy of science briefly before, but this book had an enormous impact on me. The clarity and vigour with which a non-native speaker of English could write simply amazed me, as did the way in which he lucidly (and interestingly) dealt with many of the great problems of philosophy. Even the book's title struck me as masterful, capturing in three words the essence of his thought. I became an instant fan, and although over the years the problems have become more apparent to me, the attraction of his work remains. Popper reinforced in me the lessons about writing and thinking that I had learned from Barbara Falk – for he was explicit in stressing that clarity of expression is part-and-parcel with openness to criticism and "error-elimination", and hence is vital for intellectual progress. A decade or so later he wrote what is perhaps my favourite piece – a devastating critique of certain Continental philosophers who fostered in their students "a cult of un-understandability" and whose convoluted prose was (and is) often mistaken for deep scholarship, when in fact it was its abrogation – and he had the gall to publish it as the climactic chapter in a volume edited by sinners (Adorno et al., 1976)!

A few years after Popper had made this strong initial impression on me, I started to see close resemblances between much of his work and much of Dewey's, and I wrote a (fictional) dialogue between them that almost entirely consisted of their own words strung together in conversational mode. I submitted this piece first to the *British Journal of Philosophy of Science*, and Imre Lakatos (then the editor) wrote to me that he had much enjoyed it; subsequently however two reviewers, evidently fervent Popperians, expressed their indignation that anyone would be so misguided as to suggest there were parallelisms between Popper and ... that man! The essay appeared in *Educational Theory* (1975).

On several occasions over the years I was an "academic visitor" in Popper's department at the London School of Economics (the first was in 1972, a few years before my Popper-Dewey dialogue was published); and although Sir Karl had retired and was never a presence, the visits gave me opportunities to interact with Imre Lakatos and John Watkins. The latter helped me to get my book on holism published in the UK, and the former overwhelmed me – as he had done to so many before – with his magnetic personality, his drive, and his penchant for histrionics (and of course his intellect). I have a vivid memory of Imre, at one of the first departmental seminars I attended, interjecting in his heavy Hungarian accent, in the midst of a visitor's presentation, "Oh, Wittgenstein! He only said two things: one of these was trivially true and the other was trivially false!" To my eternal shame I cannot now locate the sheet of paper on which I wrote down the specifics of Imre's insight!

Many years later Popper made a brief visit to Stanford (to which he had donated his personal papers – a goldmine), and I spent a memorable Saturday morning with him, during which he railed at great length against former friends and students whom, he felt, had betrayed him by unfairly criticising his work. For a man whose philosophy stressed the importance of giving and receiving strong criticism, he obviously felt it was more blessed to give than to receive! He must have discovered that I did not believe that he had solved the classic epistemological problem of induction, for on his second visit to campus I was dropped from the guest lists to the various social gatherings, despite the fact that I was the only person on campus who taught a course based largely on his work.

But again I am jumping the chronological gun, and need to return to my doctoral-student years: Shortly before I had completed my dissertation, two significant events occurred. The first was the formation, by a small group of faculty members and graduate students, of the Philosophy of Education Society of Australasia (PESA) – the latter term denoting that some interested individuals came from New Zealand. I became a foundation member, and a few years later was elected Secretary-Treasurer, a position I held until my move to Stanford. The second event was the opening up of a job opportunity – a rare occurrence – and after due process I was appointed Lecturer (assistant professor) in Education at Monash University, Melbourne's second and very young and vibrant university. I could not have been luckier, for Monash had been founded at a time when there was a large pool of talented young scholars, in all fields, looking for academic positions – and as a result my colleagues were stimulating and cooperative, and the social interaction between us closely resembled the famous Monty Python skit about the "Philosophy Department at the University of Woollomooloo" and its irreverent "philosophers song". I learned a great deal about empirical educational research, and about theories of learning and the like, from these colleagues; and my co-teaching of a required course in history of educational thought with John Cleverley (an historian) not only helped me go deeper into topics in the history of ideas, but also led to us collaborating on a book first published in Australia and later, with some extensive revisions, by Teachers College Press under a new but informative title *Visions of Childhood: Influential Models From Locke to Spock* (1987). It was during my seven years at Monash that I wrote some papers on systems theory in the social sciences (these are holistic, and reproduce in modern guise the nineteenth-century ideas about wholes that I had discussed in my doctoral dissertation); and the section from my dissertation that analysed the Hegelian basis of these holist/organicist ideas appeared in *Journal of the History of Ideas* (1970). I also wrote several papers critiquing Paul Hirst's influential theory concerning "structure of knowledge"; he had argued that forms of knowledge differed along four dimensions, and using this as his analytic net had arrived at the conclusion that there were seven basic forms of knowledge (which was heaven-sent news for curriculum planners, as the high school typically had seven periods each day!). I argued that the four characteristics Hirst had used were not logically discrete, and I also provided examples to show that some forms of knowledge contained branches within them that had quite different "Hirstian" structures. (Later I expanded this work (Phillips, 1987, ch.11.) By this time my research trajectory seemed to be pointing in a number of different directions, a phenomenon that caused me to reflect on my role as a philosopher working in a School of Education. I decided that I had three general audiences, each of which occasionally I should try to address: professional colleagues in philosophy of education; colleagues in departments of philosophy; and non-philosophical colleagues in education and practitioners (and I thought of this last category as being wider than teachers, but also as including researchers in education and the related social sciences, evaluators, curriculum designers, policy-makers, and perhaps parents). As a rule of thumb I am still guided by this.

Late in my time at Monash I also began working on an essay with a young psychologist colleague. This collaboration stemmed from a faculty-lounge conversation about cognitive and social development in children, during which we discovered a shared scepticism about hierarchical stage theories of development and their underlying logic. This paper eventually became the first that either of us had published in the Harvard Educational Review (Phillips and Kelly, 1975); and no doubt it paved the way for my later sceptical treatment of the concept of "cognitive structure" (Phillips, 1983), and my writings about the structural defects in Piaget's theories (Phillips, 1978), and about the techniques used to avoid refutation in Lawrence Kohlberg's stage theory of moral development (Phillips and Nicolayev, 1978, in the course of which my co-author and I made use of the philosophy of science of Imre Lakatos, for it was an ideal tool for displaying the adjustments made to a research program over time as it confronted what appeared to be negative evidence). But completion of this first paper on what turned out to be an important intellectual path for me was delayed, for late in 1973 or early in 1974 a letter turned up out of the blue, with a Stanford return address, that inquired whether I would be interested in being considered as a candidate for a position on their faculty; the signatory was "Lee J. Cronbach". I immediately responded in the affirmative and put hierarchical theories on the back--burner, and thus began a series of sometimes harrowing events that led to my arrival, on Friday September 13, 1974, on the Stanford campus.

Again I was extremely lucky. Shortly after I had been offered the position at Stanford but was still at Monash, Lee Cronbach sent me a draft of the paper he was going to deliver when he was honoured with the gold medal of the American Psychological Association (it later appeared in the *American Psychologist*, as the famous "Beyond the Two Disciplines of Scientific Psychology", 1975). On the whole the content was new to me, but after several readings I was certain that I had detected an important logical flaw in the argument, and following much soul-searching I summoned enough courage to convey this to the rather daunting author (my concern was that I might have been so ignorant with respect to the material that I was quite mistaken about the existence of this flaw). But I was right, and Cronbach was delighted with my feedback, so delighted in fact that he wrote to invite me to join a group he was forming – the Stanford Evaluation Consortium (SEC) – the mission of which was to rethink the nature (purpose and methodology) of educational and social program evaluation. I arrived on campus in time to attend the second meeting of this group, and for several years I faithfully attended the two meetings a month, and gradually learned a great deal about evaluation and research design. The meetings were exciting, for Cronbach's reputation attracted social and behavioural scientists from around campus (usually there were twenty or more faculty at each meeting, and several amazing doctoral students), and often we had impressive visitors who presented papers or sought to get advice on an evaluation problem they were facing. After two or three years a group of eight of us, led by Cronbach, started meeting weekly to write a book based on what we were learning; this turned into a two-year commitment, but eventually the influential volume by Cronbach and Associates, *Toward Reform of Program Evaluation* (1980), was published. During this period the SEC spawned a training program, and upon his retirement Lee designated me as its director. I had moved from being a complete ignoramus to at least having a strong philosophical and methodological interest in the field; my thinking had been honed by countless intense interactions with Lee, who as an unrelentingly tough critic ran a very close second to Barbara Falk. After taking over the leadership of the training program I occasionally published on program evaluation issues, and with my colleague Milbrey McLaughlin (formerly a RAND-based evaluator and social scientist) I edited a NSSE Yearbook that celebrated what we rather arbitrarily identified as the twenty-fifth anniversary of the birth of the modern field of program evaluation. (In this volume we invited the intellectual giants of the field, such as Ralph Tyler and Michael Scriven, to revisit the issues in one of their classic essays that had helped to shape thinking during the past quarter century; Milbrey and I provided summaries of the relevant classic works (McLaughlin and Phillips, 1991.)

It is difficult to select highlights of my intellectual life since arriving at Stanford, as the environment is so rich and full of opportunities – almost everything has been a highlight! But I have been struck, on reflection, with how important chance events and opportunities have been in what I hope has been my continuing development as a scholar. Four things stand out as warranting brief comment. First, my colleague James Greeno (a philosophically-able cognitive psychologist) started a weekly interdisciplinary seminar on cutting-edge issues in the learning sciences (the "symbolic systems seminar"), to which I was invited. Over the years of my attendance the readings and discussions prepared me for co-authoring with the philosopher of education Jonas Soltis of Teachers College a small volume, aimed at undergraduates, *Perspectives on Learning* (1st. ed. 1985) – which now is in its fourth edition and has been translated into four languages. This book, rather like my one with John Cleverley on models of childhood, taps my interests in learning theories and history of ideas.

Second, at the surprise invitation of the Swedish educational researcher Torsten Husen, I had contributed a long entry (sixteen thousand words) on the field of philosophy of education to the first edition of the mammoth Pergamon Press reference work, *International Encyclopedia of Education* (1985). This gave me an entrée to Pergamon's education and social science editorial staff who evidently had liked my piece, and who used it for several years in their instructional brochure as the sole example when commissioning authors for their other encyclopedias.

Taking advantage of the opportunity, over the next few years I proposed several books based on various groupings of my published essays, the first of which surprised me by going through five printings (Phillips, 1987). The second – clearly aimed at protecting social scientists from philosophical "beasts" – came out in 1992, and eventually I updated it with a different publisher who did something that by then was impossible for Pergamon, namely, make it available in a (relatively affordable) paperback edition. This book had the most beguiling title of anything I have published: *The Expanded Social Scientist's Bestiary* (2000); it is the book I am proudest of, and it has been well-received by my wife, children, and the dozen or so friends and students who have read it.

Third, in the late 'nineties the American educational research community became concerned that the Federal Government was about to become draconian and would in future allocate educational research funding only to projects that were rigorously scientific, which was defined in terms of the use – and only the use – of randomised experimental designs, the so-called "gold standard" which of course excludes rigorous ethnographic or other qualitative work. The National Academies of Science had been brought into the fray, and its "working arm", the National Research Council, set up a panel to produce a report clarifying (and many hoped liberalizing) the nature of scientific research in education. I was invited to serve on this panel, and greatly enjoyed the experience of meetings and public hearings in Washington, and the sessions in which the panel members jointly worked on the report (NRC, 2002; parts of this report drew heavily from a monograph on postpositivism that I had authored with Nick Burbules – see Phillips and Burbules, 2000.). I did not enjoy the subsequent fallout, for the report (and its authors) were attacked from both left and right; I even had lively exchanges with friends who accused me of authoring things that were nowhere to be found in the report (which later they admitted never having read)! My longer-term response has been to write a number of essays making clear how bizarre the view of science is that underlies this funding policy; scientists do a great many things worthy of support other than conducting randomized experiments, as the work of Newton, Darwin, and William Harvey nicely illustrate. I have argued that it is fruitful to view the work of scientists as involving the construction of cases that support or warrant their claims, and these cases contain a variety of types of evidence and argument forms. For rhetorical purposes I labelled the construction of good cases as the "platinum standard" (see for example Phillips, 2006).

Finally, when I was giving some invited lectures in Australia on issues in philosophy of science and how these might be relevant to science educators, on one occasion my presentation was interrupted by a heckler from the audience who accused me of imposing my own usage of terminology upon everyone else – the word "gold" (which I had used in an example) could mean what anyone who used it wanted it to mean. Language was constructed by each user (which of course is partly right and partly wrong). This was my first and very unproductive interaction with a so-called "radical constructivist", and it prompted me to do a great deal of reading and reflecting on an ideology that, I discovered, had come to a position of dominance especially in the research and curriculum development communities in mathematics and science education. I wrote the first of several papers that have attempted to clarify and separate a number of different issues that are being run together under the label of "constructivism" (such as the construction of the public disciplines of knowledge, and on the other hand the personal cognitive construction of understanding that is involved in individual learning), and *"The Good, the Bad, and the Ugly"* appeared in *Educational Researcher* in 1995. It turned out to be my best-known work, cited over three hundred and twenty times, and I still harbour the dream of writing a book on the same topic. Maybe Clint Eastwood will play me in the film version that, I am confident, eventually will follow.

REFERENCES

Adorno, T., et al., (Eds.). (1976). *The positivist dispute in German sociology*. New York: Harper & Row.

Cleverley, J.F. & Phillips, D.C. (1987). *Visions of childhood: Influential models from Locke to Spock*. New York: Teachers College Press.

Cronbach, L.J. & Associates. (1980). *Toward reform of program evaluation*. San Francisco: Jossey-Bass.

McLaughlin, M. & Phillips, D.C. (Eds.). (1991) *Evaluation and education: At quarter century*, 90th NSSE Yearbook. Chicago: University of Chicago Press.

National Research Council. (2002). *Scientific research in education*. Washington, DC: National Academies Press.

Phillips, D.C. (1966). The idea of evolution in educational thought. In E.L. French (Ed.), *Melbourne studies in education 1965*. Melbourne, Australia: Melbourne University Press.

Phillips, D.C. (1970). Organicism in the late nineteenth and early twentieth centuries. *Journal of the History of Ideas, 31*, 413-432.

Phillips, D.C. (1971). John Dewey and the organismic archetype. In R.J.W. Selleck (Ed.), *Melbourne studies in education 1971*. Melbourne, Australia: Melbourne University Press.

Phillips, D.C. (1975). Popper and pragmatism: A fantasy. *Educational Theory, 25* (Winter), 83-91.

Phillips, D.C. (1976). *Holistic thought in social science*. Stanford: Stanford University Press; and London: Macmillan.

Phillips, D.C. (1978). The Piagetian child and the scientist: Problems of assimilation and accommodation. *Educational Theory, 28* (Winter), 3-15.

Phillips, D.C. (1983). On describing a student's cognitive structure. *Educational Psychologist, 18*(2), 59-74.

Phillips, D.C. (1984). Was William James telling the truth after all?. *The Monist, 67*, July, 419-434.

Phillips, D.C. (1985). Philosophy of education. In T. Husen and N. Postlethwaite (Eds.), *International encyclopedia of education*. Oxford: Pergamon Press.

Phillips, D.C. (1987). *Philosophy, science, and social inquiry*. Oxford: Pergamon Press.

Phillips, D.C. (1995). The good, the bad, and the ugly: The many faces of constructivism. *Educational Researcher, 24*(7), 5-12.

Phillips, D.C. (1997). Coming to grips with radical social constructivisms. *Science and Education, 6*(1-2), 85-104.

Phillips, D.C. (1998). John Dewey's *The Child and the Curriculum*: A century later. *Elementary School Journal, 98*(5), 403-414.

Phillips, D.C. (2000). *The expanded social scientist's bestiary*. Lanham, MD: Rowman & Littlefield.

Phillips, D.C. (2006). Muddying the waters: The many purposes of educational inquiry. In C. Conrad & R. Serlin, (Eds.) *SAGE handbook for research in education*. Thousand Oaks, CA: SAGE.

Phillips, D.C. & Burbules, N. (2000). *Postpositivism and educational research*. Lanham, MD: Rowman & Littlefield.

Phillips, D.C. & Kelly, M.E. (1975). Hierarchical theories of development in education and psychology. *Harvard Educational Review*, *45* (August), 351-375.

Phillips, D.C. & Nicolayev, J. (1978). Kohlbergian moral development: A progressing or degenerating research program? *Educational Theory*, *28* (Fall), 286-301.

Phillips, D.C. & Soltis, J. (1985). *Perspectives on learning* (1st edition). New York: Teachers College Press.

D.C. Phillips
School of Education and Department of Philosophy,
Stanford University

RICHARD PRING

FIDES QUAERENS INTELLECTUM

SCHOLASTIC BEGINNINGS

My first acquaintance with philosophy was in October 1955, after a four day journey to Rome (one did not fly in those days). The English College (Venerabile Collegio Inglese) had been founded in 1579 by William Allen, Fellow of Oriel College Oxford, in the Via Monserrato, just round the corner from the magnificent Piazza Farnese. Its aim was to train priests at a time when to be a priest in post-reformation England was punishable by death – and 44 of students of the College were so punished. The training in Rome was seven years, with one opportunity after three years to return to England for a three month holiday. Those first three years were devoted to the study of philosophy.

The lectures in philosophy were conducted in Latin at the Pontifical Gregorian University, staffed by the Jesuits. Latin was the *lingua franca* in a colourful and multinational student body, housed in national colleges and identified by the colour of their soutanes – the Germans and Hungarian College in scarlet, the Scots in purple, the Pio Latinos with green belly bands, the Americans with red belly bands, the English in black albeit with cats-fur broad brimmed hats (which I still possess), the French in large dirty boots to show their affinity with the workers (it was the period of 'worker priests'), and many other nationalities and colours. My letter home (18.10.55) reflects the bewilderment of a 17 year old, newly arrived and following a programme which had hardly changed for several hundred years.

> Life is very hectic here. Hardly a minute is left free. We rise at 5.25 a.m., meditation at 6.00, Mass at 6.30, breakfast 7.15, bell for the Gregorian at 8.00, first lecture at 8.25. During the course of the morning we have four lectures, each lasting 50 minutes. I have not yet been able to understand the lecture, but I am making great progress with Morandini who gives two lectures a day on Minor Logic and speaks in a very clear Latin. …. The fourth lecture is *historia philosophiae*. This is given by an Hungarian S. J., who speaks very quickly and in a Latin that has a queer accent, so that so far I cannot understand him. By the fourth lecture anyhow I am feeling very tired and I try to sleep.

This struggle to comprehend the mysteries of philosophy through the oral and written medium of Latin was not confined to Division II intellectuals like myself. Anthony Kenny, who was a student at the Venerabile from 1949 to 1956,

L.J. Waks (ed.), *Leaders in Philosophy of Education: Intellectual Self Portraits*, 185–200.

describes, in his *A Path from Rome*, the difficulty of a 'lingua franca' spoken by lecturers of many different nationalities, not only because of their distinctive accents, but because of their different idioms. For example,

> lecturers did not scruple to translate the idioms of their own tongue into Latin, leaving foreigners to make what they could of them Thus a Frenchman would talk of a far fetched interpretation of a Scripture text as being 'ad usum delphini', while an American would drawl 'haec theoria non tenet aquam'. (Kenny, 1985, p.46)

There was, indeed, a distinct hierarchy in perceived competence, as well as considerable bafflement from the English speaking students, as is clear from my letter home on 18th October, 1955 (slightly edited to save embarrassment):

> Evidently the English are renowned for being fairly dim, the Scotch are reckoned to be a little dimmer and the Americans, although hard-working, are the dunces.

I tried strenuously to overcome this problem, as is evident from my diary:

> Ut augeam capacitatem meam ad linguam latinam loquendam, intendo scribere hunc libellum in hac antiqua lingua. Ratio est sequens: passus sum magnum et gravem perturbationem cum, in universitate gregoriana, conatus sum questionem rogare, propter impossibilitatem quam studentes alteri experti sunt ad mea verba cognoscenda.[i]

On the other hand, there is a certain irony in the final sentence of that day's entry.

> Nocte ineunte, spectaculum factum est in collegio. Titulum vocabitur 'The Importance of Being Earnest'.

Upon arrival, we were immediately into Logica Minor taught by Fr. Morandini, in which we learnt the basic principles of syllogistic thinking which shaped the rest of the programme – bArbArA, cElArEnt, and so on. At the same time there was a course in the History of Philosophy taught by Fr. Korinek, S.J. I have vivid memories of my viva voce with this severe looking Hungarian as he cross-examined me in Latin on the two Greek philosophers, Parmenides and Heracleitus. 'explica mihi, si ens est et non-ens non est, quomodo ens factum est non-est'ii, he demanded. I cannot remember my reply but it was sufficient to get a pass *cum laude* in my first examination in philosophy.

The entire course in philosophy, apart from the Logica Minor, the History of Philosophy, and certain options, was divided into 100 theses covering Logica Major or Critica, Epistemolo-gia, Metaphysica, Ethica Generalis, Cosmologia, and Theologia Naturalis. Each thesis set out sharply the disputed issue (*quaestio disputata*), the background to it, the main *adversarii*, and then the syllogistic mode of approaching the thesis. That meant that there was a major premise, a minor premise, followed by *Ergo* (Therefore ..). In '*Ad premissam majorem*' and '*Ad premissam minorem*', justifications would be given, usually in terms of showing the errors of other philosophers. Just as in ethics *virtus stat in media*, so also *veritas*. And there was a constant finding the middle way between the rationalists (Descartes, Leibniz and Spinoza) and the empiricists (Locke, Berkeley and Hume), between the idealists (Hegel, Bradley, Green) and the 'naive realists'. In a memorable phrase which so succinctly anticipates some of the problems of postmodern philosophers of education, *objective quoad id quod concipitur, non autem quoad modum quo concipitur*[iii].

I found something attractive in this comprehensive and integrated view of the world – a 'descriptive metaphysics' within the tradition of what Etienne Gilson (1961) referred to as the 'perennial philosophy', rooted in Aristotle and indebted,

Books:

Personal and social education in the curriculum

Closing the gap: liberal education and vocational preparation

Philosophy of educational research 1st ed. 2000; 2nd ed. 2004)

Philosophy of Education: aims, theory, common sense and research (collected papers, 2004)

John Dewey: philosopher of education for the 21st century[i]

Articles:

Knowledge out of control', 1976

Education as a moral practice', Lawrence Kohlberg Memorial Lecture, in *Journal of Moral Education*, 30 (2) 2001

Victor Cook Memorial Lectures at the Universities of St Andrews, Aberdeen and Cambridge, 'Educational Aims: Liberal or Vocational?' and 'Educational Context: Monastery or Market Place?', reprinted in *The Cambridge Review*, vol. 115, no. 2324, November 1994.

Academic Respectability and Professional Relevance' inaugural lecture delivered before the University of Oxford on 8 May 1991, Oxford University Press, pp. 39, reprinted in Gordon, P. 'Inaugural Lectures'

The Virtues and Vices of an Educational Researcher', *Journal of Philosophy of Education*, Special Issue, 2001.

The 'False Dualism' of Educational Research', *Journal of Philosophy of Education*, (2), 2000.

as was pointed out, to the development of that tradition through the Arab philosophers Avicenna and Averroes, and the Jewish philosopher Maimonedes. I felt myself, therefore, in Rome, to be part of a far reaching (both in time and space) scheme of things, transcending vicissitudes of time and divisions of nationalities (it was only 10 years after the end of the war). Indeed, I was delighted to receive, from Stuart Hampshire in 1961, as the Rosa Morison Prize for Philosophy, Gilson's *The Christian Philosophy of St. Thomas Aquinas*, and *Insight*, by Bernard Lonergan, the best known professor at the Gregorian, as well as a signed copy of *Thought and Action*. Certainly it was a matter of *fides quaerens intellectum* rather than *intellectus quaerens fidem* which, theoretically at least, would be how most philosophers see their enquiries.

Of course, problems posed in this balanced way were not always easy to escape. One particular problem was reflected in my diary:

> There are many problems of our philosophy still left unsolved – some of them very fundamental. I find it hard to avoid pantheism.

To be a pantheist was somewhat uncomfortable in a seminary, and the difficulty needed to be resolved. The difficulty lay in reconciling the transcendence and the immanence of God, and it was inevitably tackled through the distinctively scholastic mode of enquiry. Looking back at my notes, I am intrigued by the subtle distinctions and critical analysis of the adversaries *(immanentisimus idealisticus sicut Brunschvicg* and *immanentissimus materialisticus sicut Feuerbach)* and by the final positive assertion of the thesis:

> non repugnat intellectum aliquem sub quibusdam conditionibus objectum sibi transcendens attingere posse, et talis est noster intellectus[iv].

Then followed a couple of pages of demonstration, *ex parte intellectus* and then *ex parte objecti*. Phew, I was able to continue with my studies.

That scholastic form of disputation (setting out rival positions) entered into our daily walks, as reflected once again in my diary

> There was an argument: can sleep be enjoyed? <u>Pro</u>: since one looks forward to it so much, although one is intimately acquainted with it over many years, it must be enjoyed. <u>Con</u>: since one is in a state of unconsciousness during sleep, one cannot enjoy it. A dilemma, and this is what we argued about it Castel Sant'Angelo gardens.

An excellent forthcoming book by Vivien Boland O.P., 2007, provides an extensive account of the distinctive pedagogical approach developed by the scholastics, not the least of whom was Aquinas, a pale reflection of which we received in Rome.

One of the options was that of modern British Philosophy, taught by Fr. Frederick Copleston, whose monumental eight volume *A History of Philosophy* remains a valued possession. The rule of the Gregorian was that all lectures had to be given in Latin, but Copleston found it difficult engaging with the subtleties of Austin's *How To Do Things With Words* or Russell's 'logical atomism' in the Latin language, and so each year, teaching only to an English speaking audience, he lectured in English ... until one year (not mine fortunately) a non-English speaking Portuguese insisted upon attending. Poor Copleston had to translate his explanations of illocutionary acts and performatives into Latin.

The final examination was an hour of oral disputation with four severe looking, black robed Jesuits (Italian, Spanish, Irish and French – each with his distinctive way of pronouncing Latin). They chose at random any four of the 100 theses which constituted the three-year course. Each student had to defend each thesis against the combined opposition who might assume the role of a Duns Scotus, a Descartes or an Occam. But I had been well prepared, spending weekends preparing in the ruins of Augustus' palace in the Forum or in the cool cloisters of San Onofrio on the Janiculum, and I finished with a *cum laude* and the Gregorian 'silver medal' for 1958, which merited the *bene merenti* from Pope Pius XII. However, not returning to collect it after the three months' vacation, I finally received it 30 years later.

And why did I not return? Partly it was fear – 'tu es sacerdos in aeternam secundum ordinem Melchisadech'. Partly it may have been my acquaintance with a particular philosopher, although the reference to me in Ben Rogers' (1999) autobiography of A.J. Ayer is somewhat exaggerated. But in the final year we had to write a dissertation – fortunately in our native language. Amongst the rows of ancient and Latin books in the college library, I discovered *Language Truth and Logic*. Had it been placed there by some disgruntled seminarian? It was a challenging book to read towards the end of a three year course which assumed that the mind, or *intellectus agens*, could penetrate mysteries beyond what could be immediately perceived or demonstrated by the principle of contradiction. And so I wrote my dissertation (*exercitatio practica*) on Ayer's emotive theory of values. Reading it again for the first time in 50 years I feel it wasn't too bad. But what is interesting about it is the struggle it reflects – the challenge it posed to a metaphysical form of thought with which I had previously felt comfortable. The only solution seemed to be to go and study under Professor Ayer.

COPING WITH THE 'PHILOSOPHY OF NONSENSE'[v]

I had a year to sort myself out; it was too late to apply for university entrance in 1958. I signed on at Sheffield Employment Exchange. Being literate, I was immediately hauled over the counter to help with the signing on – in the room immortalised in the film *The Full Monty*. I was seconded to the National Service medical examinations as an orderly, having failed the examination myself, but I was quickly returned to the Labour Exchange after I mixed up the urine tests. Thus showing myself to be practically incompetent, I applied to read philosophy at

University College London where A.J. Ayer was The Grote Professor of Mind and Logic. In preparation for the interview and already acquainted with *Language, Truth and Logic*, I read assiduously *The Problem of Knowledge*. By the time of the interview I felt better prepared for my oral with Ayer in English than I had been for my oral with Morandini in Latin. Perhaps I might have got another *cum laude*. The interview went well, and I was accepted.

It is necessary to say something about the department which Ayer had formed around him in the attempt to create a rival to Oxford. It included Bernard Williams, Richard Wollheim, and A.H.Basson (author of the Penguin book on Hume). Very soon, Ayer took the post of Wykeham Professor of Logic at Oxford, but was replaced by Stuart Hampshire. Ted Honderich had just arrived as a post-graduate student. The students were an eclectic and exciting group – there solely because of interest in philosophy: Jennifer Dawson, recently author of *The Ha Ha*, Robin the artist who wanted to understand a little philosophy and do two more paintings before he died, 6ft 4 inches Ken the West Indian journalist, Jenny whose frequent stretches during Williams' lectures on Plato produced convincing evidence that the sensible world was more than a mere shadow. (I expressed my devotion to Jenny on Wimbledon Common, only to be told that she was to be engaged to a vicar. Not much chance there for a failed Catholic priest.) The lectures-cum-seminars were thrilling; the weekends together – staff and students – at the Beatrice Webb House in Surrey, inspirational; the faltering efforts of undergraduates to write philosophy sympathetically heard. Ayer, and then Hampshire, despite their pre-eminence, saw teaching to be their first and foremost duty, an example which has stayed with me all my life. And their influence was immense, although it did have its funny side. The common room under the influence of Ayer was fairly silent due to the fact that only empirical and tautological statements were meaningful – and lack of interest in empirical truths was one reason for studying philosophy. Under Hampshire, everyone took five minutes to light their *gauloise* – each movement requiring a long pause as he or she gave birth to the next profound thought. It was there that I discovered Sartre, Camus, and De Beauvoir – but as leisure time reading, for philosophy as such had really stopped in France with Descartes, as in Germany with Kant. It was possible to take an option in Hegel, but that was not advised and it would be with Professor Findlay at Kings College in the Strand. Heidegger was treated as joke. And the corpse of Bentham, staring benignly from his glass box, replaced the picture of Blessed Ralph Sherwin as my inspiration.

It is fashionable now, especially in educational doctorates, to dismiss logical positivism as a superficial aberration, which however still casts a shadow over educational research. Hence, it becomes a duty of every research student to reject it as false as they espouse the 'qualitative paradigm'. That is a pity because there is much to be learnt from it, as there was for me in my acquaintance with Ayer. First, there is a need to examine carefully the logic of our language and to analyse the different usages of key words – to be aware of how we can be deceived by language if we are not careful. Second, what one says must be said with as much clarity as is needed in order to know what evidence would support or undermine a belief. The verification principle as defined by Ayer may be too narrow, but the meaning of a statement must entail some account of how it might be supported or negated by evidence of a certain sort.

Ayer's colourful life has been well portrayed by Ben Rogers' biography, and it is interesting to note that my two philosophical lives were brought together at his funeral. The only two philosophers present were Frederick Copleston, whose radio debate with Ayer on the existence of God remains a classic of philosophical reasoning, and Ted Honderich who succeeded Ayer (not immediately) as The Grote Professor of Mind and Logic.

JOINING THE 'GUARDIAN CLASS'

In 1962, tired of philosophy, I joined the Home Civil Service as an Assistant Principal at the then Ministry of Education in the previous home of MI6 in Curzon Street. This interlude (as it turned out to be) may not seem pertinent to a philosophical story. Only in retrospect do I now see it to have been crucial to my subsequent thinking and action. The Administrative Class Home Civil Service was an elite group with an entry of about 130 per year, recruited almost exclusively from Oxbridge (especially Greats and PPE) and the public schools. Having gone to neither (in common with one other who went to 'Min. of Ag.'), I at first found it a little awesome. Training consisted of 'devilling' for senior civil servants, a spell in private office with the Minister and an annual tea with the powerful Deputy Secretary, Sir Toby Weaver. In that way one learnt that the civil servant was not expected to know anything about what he or she was administering – that was the job of the professionals. One's job was to make sure the machinery of government worked – maintenance of schools, supply of teachers, appropriate legislation, etc. Dr. Marjorie Reeves, the medieval historian with whom I drank nearly every night in Oxford until she died four years ago, aged 98, told me that, when appointed to the Central Advisory Council for Education in 1947, she was told by the then Permanent Secretary, Redcliffe Maud, that the chief duty of a member of the Advisory Council was to be prepared to die at the first ditch as soon as politicians tried to get their hands on education. Government was there to assist citizens, voluntary bodies established by those citizens, and professionals who knew best how to promote their welfare – whether these be university academics, doctors, engineers or teachers.

This conception of the role of government came to a head in the establishment of the Curriculum Study Group and then the Schools Council. I was the Assistant Principal on the CSG, devilling for Derek Morrell, in effect the creator of and inspiration behind the Schools Council established in 1966. Derek Morrell's lecture to the College of Preceptors, *Education and Change*, remains a classical account of the problems of preparing young people for an unpredictable future, especially when there is little consensus in society as to what constitutes a worthwhile form of life – and that was in 1965-6! Morrell, the civil servant, reflecting upon the establishment of the Schools Council, speaks of the need to democratise the processes of problem-solving as we try, as best we can, to develop an educational approach appropriate to a permanent condition of change.

That democratisation required joint efforts between teachers, researchers, government and the community in defining the characteristics of change, sponsoring research, evaluating the results of such work, and recognising that

> freedom and order can no longer be reconciled through implicit acceptance of a broadly ranging and essentially static consensus on educational aims and methods (Morrell, 1966, p. 12).

The second Working Paper of the Curriculum Study Group, concerned with the humanities curriculum at a time when the school leaving age was to be raised and when the temptation was to keep young people engaged through vocational studies, spoke of a place on the curriculum where 'teachers could share their humanity with the pupils', and this Working Paper was the blueprint for Stenhouse's Humanities Curriculum Project, one of the most successful and philosophically based curriculum projects. Why philosophical? As with the Schools Council, it embraced a democratic understanding of problem solving - a recognition that one might arrive at divergent conclusions on controversial matters in a society where there was little ethical consensus, whilst at the same time one might avoid the trap of relativism. The role of the teacher was that of an authority on procedures and on the use of evidence rather than on the conclusions to be reached. It drew upon Richard Peters' distinction between aims and principles of procedure, especially principles which excluded certain ways of proceeding if one were to arrive at justified, though always provisional, conclusions (Stenhouse, 1975, p. 87-88). This essentially philosophical point was often misrepresented as when the 'role of the neutral teacher' was debated by the Royal Philosophical Society (see Brown, 1975), but it seemed to me to be crucial to understanding how values might be handled in the classroom where there is little consensus in society over controversial issues. And it became the basis of my Stenhouse Memorial Lecture at the British Education Research Association in 1992 and of the 13th. Lawrence Kohlberg Annual Memorial Lecture to the conference of the American Moral Education Society in 2000, 'Education as a Moral Practice'.

The work in the Curriculum Study Group, in the setting up of the new Certificate of Secondary Education examinations and in the establishment of the Schools Council, created a desire to be an active part of the new move towards a comprehensive system of education, and that commitment to comprehensive schools has remained.

TEACHER TRAINING, DOCTORAL STUDIES AND GOLDSMITHS COLLEGE

I left the Civil Service, therefore, to train to be a teacher at the College of St Mark and St John where I met the philosopher, Pat Wilson, who remains a lasting influence. Eventually we became colleagues at Goldsmiths College. Wilson read and lived John Dewey, and from that pragmatist position challenged many of the orthodox views about the aims of education which prevailed at the Institute of Education. His paper, 'In Defence of Bingo', 1967, was a challenging rebuttal of Richard Peters' argument for the intrinsic value of certain subjects or studies. His now forgotten book *Interests and Discipline in Education* (1971) stirred my interest in John Dewey, despite the rather supercilious rejection of his thesis at the Philosophy of Education Society Conference in 1969.

My training for teaching, though taken at the College of St. Mark and St. John, required me to go every Friday to lectures at the Institute of Education on the philosophy (Peters and Hirst), sociology (Bernstein), psychology (Walls) and history (Beales) of education. That whetted my appetite once again for philosophy, and I registered for doctoral studies, part-time under the University's philosophy board but supervised by Richard Peters.

Peters, as with the philosophers I met at UCL, gave as much priority to teaching as he did to his own scholarly work. Indeed, he even came to see me teach at my school in Kentish Town. What greater sense of duty to one's students could there be than that! I owed so much over the next few years to his criticism and support. My thesis was an examination of the ethical and epistemological implications of what was then a fashionable attempt to integrate the curriculum. A synopsis of it appeared in the *Proceedings of the Philosophy of Education Society of Great Britain,* and Peters selected it for his edited contribution to G.J.Warnock's series *Oxford Readings in Philosophy* in 1973.

CAMBRIDGE / LONDON COMMUTE

In 1971, I joined the Cambridge Institute of Education, working with Hugh Sockett on 'social education' – and also on my PhD. I became a neighbour of John Elliott and benefited from the perceptive and philosophically profound understanding of 'curriculum', 'teaching' and 'research' of the Stenhouse team at the Centre for Applied Research in Education at the University of East Anglia. 'Teachers as researchers', action research, democratic evaluation, and the key distinction between 'educational research' and 'research on education' were important innovations, grasped through the regular conversations over dinner with John Elliott.

But that was the period, too, when to live in Cambridge was a glorious thing – regular meetings and seminars with John Elliott (CARE), Hugh Sockett (Cambridge Institute of Education), David Bridges, Charles Bailey, Tony Scrimshaw (Homerton College) and Paul Hirst (newly elected Professor of Education at the University). Together we produced a series of books, *Social Education and Social Understanding* and *Values and Authority in Schools*, published by the University of London Press, which pulled together our deliberations. Later we continued our cooperation in producing a series for Open Books, mine entitled *Knowledge and Schooling*. Never before or since have I worked in so congenial and stimulating a group, with seminars in Hugh Sockett's thatched Elizabethan home on such subjects as equality and justice, whilst our wives made the sandwiches. But they, without the philosophical training, had greater insight into these concepts, and eventually rebelled. Then began, I think, my interest in the vexed relationship between thought and action, and the significance of 'doing' philosophy of education where there lacked either interest in or relevance to changing practice.

Therefore, I was delighted to be appointed in 1974 to the newly established Department of Curriculum Studies at the University of London Institute of Education, led by Professor Dennis Lawton. The reason for its establishment was that the study of the curriculum, and of the research into its development, required an integration of the so-called 'foundation disciplines'. I was to be the philosopher in a team of a sociologist (Dennis Lawton), a psychologist (Bill Gibby and later Maggie Ing) and an historian (Peter Gordon). These were exciting years with two spiritual homes – that of the Cambridge 'set', extending now along country roads to the creative curriculum development of CARE at Norwich, and that of the Institute of Education, with its extensive links into the impressive departments of philosophy, psychology and sociology. The intellectual debates between philosophers and sociologists over the nature and construction of knowledge extended into the bars around the Institute, and my 'Knowledge out of control', published initially in *Education for Teaching*, in response to Michael Young's *Knowledge and Control*, became quite a discussion point, evoking even a personal telephone call of gratitude from Basil Bernstein, whom I had exonerated from the errors within the book to which he had contributed. Re-reading it for its republication in the collection of papers published in 2004, I still find the argument correct, although it lacks the awareness of the wider philosophical landscape which the sociologists, not the philosophers, were introducing to the study of education, and which only later did I come to appreciate.

There is, however, a wider background to the creation of the new and interdisciplinary department with a focus on the curriculum. The 1970s saw the creation in Britain of a specifically educational degree – the B.Ed. The Honours level was usually a one year top-up to the practical Teachers' Certificate. This had to be 'academically respectable' – to be achieved only if the prevailing theory of education was replaced by systematic studies in the so-called 'foundation disciplines'. Posts were created in the philosophy of education in most, if not all, of the many colleges of education, then under the academic wings of university institutes of education. For example, under the academic supervision of the Institute of Education in London alone, there were about 30 colleges of education. On the other hand, curriculum questions could not be formed or solved within any one 'foundation discipline' – there was a need to see them through various interacting 'lenses', the integrating element being the practical questions themselves.

Professor Lawton is, along with Stenhouse, rightly seen as the founding father of Curriculum Studies within Britain, and I shall always remain deeply indebted to his wide understanding of the issues. With his encouragement, which remained long after I left the Institute for the University of Exeter, I produced what I thought was the right kind of philosophical text for the study of the curriculum, namely, in 1984, *Personal and Social Education in the Curriculum.*

OXFORD – A HOME FOR DITHERERS

From the Institute I went in 1979 to a Chair of Education at the University of Exeter, helping to see through the first merger between a university and a college of education (that of St Luke's). I loved Exeter a great deal – an excellent place to have a family, so near to sea and moors, and working with Ted Wragg. But eventually I was invited to apply for the newly established Chair of Educational Studies at the University of Oxford - the only Chair of any kind that had a Secretary of State on the appointing board. Fortunately, he, Kenneth Baker, sent a substitute.

I had decided I did not want the job. The whole interview, therefore, consisted in asking me why I did not want the job. It must be one of the few appointments ever made where the candidate was appointed because he lost the argument. But towards the end of the interview I told the chairman that 'I suppose I have dithered so long that I have disqualified myself from the post'. The quintessentially Oxford response from Professor Michael Brock, pro-Vice Chancellor, was that 'dithering is reason for being in Oxford, not for staying away'.

Of course, there is so much truth in that. Persuaded by the anti-foundationalists, I am constantly in a state of doubt, and decision-making is always on the best evidence, when 'best' gives little ground for certainty and often turns out to be misleading – a theme pursued in the recently edited book with Gary Thomas, *Evidence Based Educational Practice.* That theme has vast implications for philosophising about education, about the conduct of educational practice, about the conduct of educational research and about the formation of teachers. I would like to think that such justified dithering is reflected in the papers and books which I subsequently wrote, especially about the aims of education. These are scattered around in various places, but I particularly valued the opportunity to contribute to the series of Victor Cook Memorial Lectures, organised over several years, by Professor John Haldane, of the University of St Andrews, who brought them all together in 2004 in his *Values, Education and the Human World.* My two contributions to the lectures in 1995 were 'The Aim of education' and 'The Context of Education', reprinted in the *Cambridge Review*, delivered at the universities of Aberdeen, St. Andrews and Cambridge, juxtaposed with two lectures also given at those universities by Mary Warnock. The theme of those lectures was expanded in the book published in 1995, *Closing the Gap: Liberal Education and Vocational Preparation*, the philosophical ideas of which continue to inform the major review of education and training which I am presently leading for the Nuffield Foundation.

The Oxford department was rightly noted for its innovative Internship Scheme for the training of teachers, which involved an unprecedented partnership between university, schools and the local education authority – the creation of the exceptional partnership between my predecessor, Harry Judge, and the then Chief

Education Officer, Tim Brighouse. This required every member of the teaching staff to work in one of the internship schools on one day a week. I did this for 14 years, believing that, if philosophising about education was to make sense, it had to be based on regular and active experience of the classroom. In Oxford I have had the privilege of working with the best teacher educators anywhere, and I was as proud of the top ratings we received for the quality of our teacher training as I was of the grade 5 ratings which we finally achieved for our research. Indeed, if there were to be a choice between one and the other, I would have chosen the quality of our teacher education programme, for it was for that reason that the department was established in 1894. I argued that a department of education which was to sacrifice its commitment to schools in order to boost its research ratings would both betray its raison d'etre and ultimately undermine its own existence. As I pointed out in a recent paper, 2007a, 'Remember Chicago!'

The commitment to the comprehensive ideal, reflected in the publication of a series of lectures held in the Department and published under the editorship of Geoffrey Walford and myself (Pring and Walford, 1997), remained a central tenet of the Department of Educational Studies during the 14 years I was Director. This got me into not a little trouble. Some of the attacks on me, both public (from the Secretary of State at the Headmasters Conference) and private, were a cause of concern, especially after the headline in one paper said that 'Oxford snubs Eton'. Even at the North of England Conference, the Secretary of State, John Patten, expressed surprise that I was still here. But my reply that I would be around long after he had gone got the loudest applause. Being convinced of the arguments for a more egalitarian system, I felt I had to fight for those principles in practice. It is to the credit of a great university that it was prepared to support a Head of Department where he was able to argue for the policy he had adopted, even if that policy 'was likely to lose the university money'. Indeed, it was one of my proudest moments during the 14 years as Director of the Oxford department when the new Vice Chancellor, Colin Lucas, phoned me to say that ours was such an important department in the university, since, if universities fail to produce excellent school teachers, they undermine their own capacity for teaching and learning. I wonder how many Vice Chancellors expressed such support for their education departments, so often cast in the role of Cinderella.

However, the growing interest in Dewey also got me into trouble initially with Lord Keith Joseph who had been the formidable Secretary of State under Margaret Thatcher. When I was appointed to Oxford in 1989, one of my first responsibilities was to share a platform with him at a large conference at Wolfson College – and then to be seated next to him at dinner. After the soup, he asked if my name were Pring – a fact difficult to deny after 50 years. Having identified me, he accused me of being responsible for all the problems in our schools, the reason being that I had introduced teachers to John Dewey. The conversation continued until dessert, and then weeks later at the House of Lords. Later, however, he sent someone to talk to me at Oxford, convinced that Dewey had been misunderstood by those who saw him as the patron saint of child-centred education.

That, however, did not stop the mild persecution I suffered from those who, from the political right, wanted to trap me. I was visited by the Daily Mail who wanted to know if we taught John Dewey – the questioning ending when I said that the only child-centred educationalist the Department had appointed in recent times was Chris Woodhead. Then I was called for radio interview by Melanie Phillips. However, I believe that, under New Labour, Dewey's works are no longer on the Index of Forbidden Books, and my latest publication is an effort to demonstrate *John Dewey: the Philosopher of Education for the 21st Century.*

On the other hand, the University, despite its support for the professional work and commitment of the Department, did expect all its departments to get top grades in research. I inherited a department that was graded 2. It was important to build a research tradition on the department's excellence in teacher training, and I was here indebted to the pioneering thinking and research of Donald McIntyre, later to take up the Chair of Education at Cambridge. The integration of theory and practice has been a constant theme from my first paper to the Philosophy of Education Society in 1967, and it was the main theme of my inaugural lecture at Oxford in 1991, reprinted in Gordon, 1995.

It was important, in raising the research output and quality in the department, to create a cadre of research students where previously few existed. This we did through obtaining as many ESRC studentships as we could (ten in one glorious year) and in creating a research training programme with ESRC recognition. Philosophy of the Social Sciences was central to this programme, and my book, *The Philosophy of Educational Research*, arose from the seminars I led on that course. Fortunately, the Department moved from 2 to 4 and then to 5 in the next two Research Assessment Exercises. I was ready to retire.

RUNNING INTO THE TWILIGHT

Running a Department under such pressure left no time for sabbatical terms – I managed only one in the 32 years in a University. Books and papers had to be written at night, on trains and planes, and at weekends, children permitting – and 15 of these over a period of 32 years have been collected together in *Philosophy of Education: Aims , Theory, Common Sense and Research,* published by Continuum in 2004.

Even in 'retirement', I have had no time off. I was invited by the Nuffield Foundation to lead a six year, £1 million Review of the whole of education and training for England and Wales. This is exciting, a wonderful way to end one's professional life. And the philosophical training I have received is proving to be so important as we tackle *aims* of education, *quality* in education, *equivalence* between qualifications, *standards* within learning, assessment of *understanding*, organisation of *knowledge*, and so on. Indeed, as Wittgenstein said, 'My aim is: to teach you to pass from a piece of disguised nonsense to something that is patent nonsense' (Wittgenstein, 1958,1.464), and there is much disguised nonsense in educational policy and practice – a theme developed in my address to the 2006

Annual Conference of *Educational Review*, 'Reclaiming Philosophy for Educational Research' (Pring, 2007a).

I still run marathons – two or three a year, and I hope to have run 50 by the age of 80. That keeps me fit for another ten years' work. I have ambitions in that time: first, to complete the Nuffield Review and to see its recommendations enter into policy and professional practice; second, to complete the third edition of *Philosophy of Educational Research*, meeting the valid criticism of Dennis Phillips, namely, that it is not sufficiently rooted in examples of research; third, to complete the fruit of the Nuffield Review with a philosophical assessment of educational policy and practice since those exhilarating days in the Curriculum Study Group over 40 years ago - entitled *Training, Training and a Little Education*; finally, to return once again to the legacy of the Venerabile, namely, the interest in the religious basis of education, begun in papers I have published already but extended particularly through my work over 15 years with the Aga Khan University in Karachi and its Institute for the Study of Muslim Civilisations in London.

One of the most important books I have read in the last few years is that of the Chief Rabbi, Jonathan Sacks (2002), *The Dignity of Difference* – the first printing of which got him into not a little trouble. There Sacks argues for, not just respect for or tolerance of, others' beliefs, but also a serious attempt to understand and to learn from them. My summary of its main message – philosophical but of considerable practical significance in a troubled world – is that the thesis ('I have the truth and therefore my adversaries are wrong – 'heretics', etc.') and the antithesis ('No one has the truth – it is all a matter of different opinions') are reconciled in the synthesis, namely, that we possess only part of the truth, and that we approximate to the truth through recognising what is true in other traditions and in other people, and learn from them. In a sense, that is what Newman argued in *The Development of Christian Doctrine*.

Sacks' book, *The Politics of Hope*, arose out of the Victor Cooke Lectures, the Oxford sessions of which I organised in 1996. I can claim some credit for them, for in the Acknowledgements, the Chief Rabbi thanks Professor John Haldane of St. Andrews University for his intellectual support and Professor Richard Pring of Oxford University for his 'boundless and infectious enthusiasm'. I liked that. I read John Haldane's philosophical work with deep admiration, and I know I could never emulate it or that of so many others. But, as I run into the twilight, I retain my enthusiasm for my battle for the educational aims and ideals I have written about and fought for politically, especially the comprehensive and non-selective educational system. A telling quote in *The Politics of Hope* is taken from Jacob Neusner:

> Civilisation hangs suspended, from generation to generation, by the gossamer thread of memory. If only one cohort of mothers and fathers fails to convey to its children what it has learned from its parents, then the great chain of learning and wisdom snaps. If the guardians of human knowledge stumble only one time, in their fall

collapses the whole edifice of knowledge and understanding. (Sacks, 1997, p.173)

We all inherit different traditions through which we see and understand the physical, social and moral worlds we inhabit. Those traditions, at their best, have their own internal discourse of criticism, evolving, however, over time through dialogue with others. My constant preoccupation has been with the reconciliation of the tradition I have inherited with those of others which I have encountered and absorbed – and with the institutional framework, especially in schools, through which such an evolution of thinking can be public as well as private. Christian thinking was transformed through the great philosophers of the Middle East, Arab and Jewish, and they in turn were transformed through their contact with the inheritance of Greece. How can that be recognised and lead to further enlightenment in a world which is riddled with dogma and division?

NOTES

i   Translated from poor Latin to better English: 'In order to improve my capacity to speak in Latin, I am trying to write this diary in that ancient language. The reason is as follows: I suffered a serious fit of anxiety, when, at the Gregorian University I tried to ask a question, because the students found it impossible to understand what I was saying'. The irony referred to in the next paragraph might be roughly translated: 'In the evening, there was a play in the College. It was called 'The Importance of being Ernest''

ii   Translated: explain to me how, if a being exists and a non-being does not exist, that which is becomes that which is not'

iii   Translated: 'objective as far as that which is conceived, but not as far as the mode through which it is conceived'

iv   Translated: 'It is not repugnant that some kind of intelligence might, under certain conditions, be able to know the objects which transcend itself, and of such is our intellect'.

v   The subtitle of the chapter 'Language Truth and Logic' in Ben Rogers' book on A.J.Ayer.

REFERENCES

Boland, V. (2007). *Aquinas*. London: Continuum.

Brown, D.C. (Ed.). (1975). *Philosophers discuss education*. London: Macmillan.

Gordon, P. (Ed.). (1995). *The study of education: Inaugural lectures* – Volume 4. London: The Woburn Press.

Kenny, A. (1985). *A path from Rome*. London: Sidgewick and Jackson.

Morrell, D.H. (1966). *Education and change*. London: College of Preceptors

Pring, R. (1991). *Academic respectability and professional relevance*, Inaugural Lecture at the University of Oxford, reprinted in Gordon, 1995.

Pring, R. (2001). 'Education as a moral practice', 13th Lawrence Kohlberg Lecture, *Journal of Moral Education, 30*(2), and in Pring, 2004.

Pring, R. (2000). *Philosophy of educational research*, London: Continuum (2nd edition, 2004).

Pring, R. (2004). *Philosophy of education: Aims, theory, common sense and research*, London: Continuum.

Pring, R. (2007a). Reclaiming philosophy for educational research, *Educational Review*.

Pring, R. (2007b). *John Dewey: The philosopher for the 21ˢᵗ Century?* London: Continuum.
Pring, R. & Walford, G. (eds) (1997) *Affirming the comprehensive ideal,* London: The Falmer Press.
Rogers, B. (1999). *A.J. Ayer: A life,* London: Chatto and Windus.
Sacks, J. (1997). *The politics of hope,* London: Jonathan Cape.
Sacks, J. (2002). *The dignity of difference,* London: Continuum.
Stenhouse, L. (1975). *Introduction to curriculum development and research,* London: Heinemann.
Wilson, P.S. (1967). In defence of bingo, *British Journal of Educational Studies.*
Wilson, P.S. (1971). *Interest and discipline in education.* London: RKP.
Wittgenstein, L. (1958). *Philosophical investigations.* London: Blackwell.

EMILY ROBERTSON

THE VALUE OF REASON

EDUCATION AND OTHER INFLUENCES

I was born in the 1940s into a working class family in a small West Virginia town that strongly resembled Garrison Keillor's Lake Wobegon. While we didn't have a Lutheran church, we had twenty-two other protestant churches to make up for it. And we did have a Chatterbox Café. Neither of my parents completed high school. My father worked for the Norfolk and Western Railroad Company repairing track and performing other maintenance operations. My mother's work was our home, her extensive extended family, and our church. Early a bookish kid, I loved school. That's something I've often felt guilty about as I've listened to others explain how they rebelled against the educational system. My endorsement of school has sometimes felt like a defect in my character. But I know that for me the school opened doors to a wider world and I was grateful.

My happy experience with school led me to choose teaching as a career. I left West Virginia to attend a small church-related liberal arts college near Philadelphia. I found I couldn't choose between mathematics and English as a major and so I did both. The beginnings of the Civil Rights Movement and the assassination of John F. Kennedy were the public markers of my undergraduate era.

I stumbled upon philosophy of education as a field of study in the late 1960s. I was teaching mathematics at a suburban high school near Philadelphia, having recently completed my undergraduate degree, and needing to do graduate work to maintain my certification. I intended to do a master's degree in mathematics or mathematics education eventually, but in the meantime I registered for a few courses at Temple University. Among them was Tom Nelson's introduction to philosophy of education. Soon I was hooked. I remember feeling as if I'd discovered a name for a way of thinking that had been mine for a long time. I had had one course in philosophy as an undergraduate, but its historical approach did not attract me. I could understand the perspectives of competing philosophical systems, but I felt as if the field lacked a truth orientation and I couldn't quite see the point of studying the competing "schools." In the philosophy of education program at Temple, I was introduced to the analytic movement. Analytic technique appeared to me, as it did to others at that time, to provide a way to make progress on philosophical questions. I remember feeling that, for the first time in my education, I wasn't just learning what others had thought or discovered, but was able to bring my own ideas to the problems at hand. Only much later did I understand how lucky I was to be in a department that had five philosophers of education on the faculty.

L.J. Waks (ed.), Leaders in Philosophy of Education: Intellectual Self Portraits, 201–209.
© 2008 Sense Publishers. All rights reserved.

D.J. O'Connor's Introduction to the Philosophy of Education, the primary text in Tom Nelson's class, formed the base line for my understanding of philosophy of education. Scheffler's *The Language of Education* and *Conditions of Knowledge,* along with the essays in R. S. Peters' *The Concept of Education,* provided models of what good analytic work involved. Jim Macmillan and Paul Komisar were contributors to the then current debates about analyses of teaching, learning, and education. Jim McClellan, an analytic philosopher but also a self-described Marxist, located education in a wider political and social context. Paul Komisar interpreted Dewey's *Democracy and Education.* Temple was embroiled in student protest movements that fueled philosophic discussions about the true nature of education and the ways institutional structures could impede its realization. Protests against the Vietnam War and the Civil Rights Movement provided further resources for a re-examination of the educational system.

FAVORITES

More than words can say: Making room for the tacit dimension (1983).
Practical reasons, authority, and education (1984).
Moral education, subjectively speaking (1988).
Reason and education (1991).
Is Dewey's educational vision still viable? (1992).
Reconceiving reason (1995).
Teacher authority and teaching for liberation (1995).
The value of reason: Why not a sardine can opener? (1999).
Teacher education in a democratic society: Learning and teaching the practices of democratic participation (forthcoming).

All this was a heady brew for a young, small town woman fresh from an undergraduate experience at a Baptist college. I soon discovered that I wasn't in Kansas anymore when a biblical quotation I attributed to "Paul" in a conversation with other Temple students was taken to be a reference to some unfamiliar article by Paul Komisar. Jim McClellan was the first Marxist I'd ever knowingly met face to face. I finally learned from him less than ten years ago, not long before his death, that those guys I'd wondered about who were hanging around the Temple department were in fact Black Panthers that he was protecting in some way.

After completing a master's degree at Temple, life circumstances led me to move my studies to Syracuse University. There I worked with Tom Green, whose seminal papers on the concept of teaching I'd read at Temple, and Paul Dietl, whom Tom had recently recruited to philosophy of education from Temple's philosophy department. As a graduate assistant, I worked with Paul Dietl on his paper, "Teaching, Learning and Knowing." In it, he reviewed the substantial literature on whether there are "logical" connections between teaching and learning, including papers by Komisar and Green in Macmillan and Nelson's *Concepts of Teaching,* and developed his own argument for why teaching, learning, and knowing are conceptually connected. Paul Dietl was much more analytically oriented than Tom Green, despite the fact that Tom's *Activities of Teaching* was widely used to convey analytic technique to students. Rather than addressing problems internally generated by philosophical theory, Tom grounded his questions in ordinary experience. Not ethical theory, for example, but rather the problems of moral education claimed his attention. As a teacher, Tom liked to work through rich philosophical texts, such as Hannah Arendt's *The Human Condition* or John Rawls' *A Theory of Justice*. Reading through Rawls in a seminar with Tom was the origin of my subsequent interest in liberal political thought and its meaning for civic education.

Paul Dietl came to philosophy of education with a prior interest in philosophy of history that I came to share and later broadened into an interest in philosophy of social science. After Paul's untimely death in 1972, I began teaching his courses as an instructor while simultaneously completing my Ph.D. in the Syracuse Philosophy Department. At the same time, I married a Syracuse philosopher, thus making philosophy a family affair, acquired two stepsons, and had a daughter with my new husband. My dissertation, directed by Alexander Rosenberg, was finished before my daughter turned three. It was in the philosophy of social science and focused on the relationship between observer and participant accounts of social phenomena, using Peter Winch's and Emil Durkheim's views of social science as opposite poles. Drawing on the work on functional explanation in biology, I explored the prospects for functional explanations of social action that would wholly bypass participant accounts. I argued that any observer account of social action must ultimately be rooted in participant accounts.

This brief account of my education has focused on what my teachers taught me, but equally important were qualities of my teachers themselves. Despite Jim McClellan's frequent refrain of "seize the means of production and destroy the capitalist state," Jim was not in my experience doctrinaire. His fundamental commitment to rationality as a form of cooperative inquiry left his students free to think for themselves and make their own choices, even when they disagreed with his. Jim Macmillan and Paul Dietl shared a commitment to "hard-nosed" (as Jim frequently put it) philosophical argument, but they listened attentively and with great intellectual openness to what others said. They were never mean-spirited or motivated solely by the hope of showing up their intellectual opponents. But in the end, they said what they genuinely believed without fear or favor. Their intellectual integrity has been a model for me in my own professional life. Tom Green's groundedness in experience, his commitment to asking about the human point of the inquiry in question, serves as a test for my own work. None of them sought disciples: they were all interested in helping students learn to hum their own tunes, a stance I take with respect to my own students.

In addition to my education and my teachers, I believe that a primary source of my research interests has been my teaching and my colleagues at Syracuse. After completing my Ph. D., I was hired to fill Paul Dietl's position and I have remained at Syracuse ever since. I have been fortunate in holding a joint position in the Cultural Foundations of Education Department (CFE) and the Philosophy Department. In the Philosophy Department, I took over teaching philosophy of social science after Alex Rosenberg's departure, as well as teaching an undergraduate course in philosophy of education for Arts and Sciences students. In CFE, I had sociologists and historians as my colleagues, as well as Tom Green, who remained in the department until his retirement in 1993. My colleagues directed me toward sociological theory, feminist perspectives, history of education, and cultural studies. Further I was fortunate in being able to teach selected topics seminars in philosophy of education, usually to both philosophers and non-philosophers. Although there are tradeoffs, for me, the discipline of frequently teaching and discussing philosophical work with non-philosophers has had benefits. It requires focusing on what is really at stake from a human perspective. It highlights the value of examples and of stories that convey the point.

Early in my tenure at Syracuse, we formed a reading group called "Friends of Philosophy" that met on Friday mornings. In recent years, our reading group has expanded to include faculty and students from the University of Rochester and, most recently, from Cornell. Since for almost ten years, I was the only philosopher of education in my department, a not uncommon situation these days, forming regional alliances was an important strategy. At present, the Syracuse philosophy group has almost achieved parity with the Temple department of my experience, having added Professors Barbara Applebaum, Ken Strike, and Kal Alston in recent years. Both through my teaching and in departmental and reading group discussions, my horizons have expanded and my conception of philosophy of education has moved beyond O'Connor's minimalist account that I acquired in my early education at Temple.

MY WORK

The central core of my written work has focused on the elaboration and defense of the cultivation of rationality as a primary educational aim. My dissertation research and my teaching in the philosophy of social science led to an interest in debates about realism and anti-realism, objectivity and subjectivity, and how best to understand and explain human action. These questions in philosophy of social science intersected with questions in philosophy of education about the nature of knowledge and the aims of education. It may be that Israel Scheffler's account of teaching, encountered early in my studies at Temple, partially laid the foundation for this interest. Teaching, Scheffler (1960) said, requires teachers to submit themselves "to the understanding and independent judgment" of their students; to reveal their reasons for believing the claims they're teaching to their students and so submit them to the students' "evaluation and criticism" (pp. 57-59). Later Scheffler (1973) wrote that "rationality…is a matter of *reasons*, and to take it as a fundamental educational idea is to make as pervasive as possible the free and critical quest for reasons" (p. 62).

Some of my early publications explored rationality in the moral domain. Madhu Prakash and I (1983) examined Gilbert Harman's theory of metaethical relativism and its implications for education. In "Practical Reasons, Authority, and Education" (1984), I used the philosophical debate about "internal" versus "external" reasons to examine issues of teacher authority. My article on tacit knowledge noted the limits on making some forms of knowledge explicit in rules or decision procedures. The importance of acknowledging that judgment is not a totally rule-governed activity is a theme that has persisted throughout my work on rationality.

My more recent work has focused on interpreting and responding to what Richard Bernstein (1988) has called the "rage against reason" (p. 216). From the perspective of those who endorse a commitment to reason, reality and truth are independent of what human beings take them to be. Rationality involves believing and acting on the basis of reasons, i.e., considerations that speak in favor of the belief or action in question. Good reasons enhance one's prospects for arriving at true beliefs or strategic success of action. Education should centrally involve the development of rationality, including initiation to rational modes of inquiry and the knowledge gained through them, the ability to construct and criticize reasons, and the disposition to be guided by reasons in believing or acting. Rational assessment of inherited beliefs and traditions fosters individual autonomy and potentially emancipatory social and political change. By contrast, the critics argue: "Reality" is socially constructed; specific criteria of truth represent various regimes of power; the search for an objective standpoint through "rational" inquiry suppresses the legitimate perspectives of some, especially those who are dominated or oppressed; criteria for what is "rational" serve to maintain the power and privilege of dominant groups, who have constructed the criteria (not necessarily knowingly) in ways that serve their own interests. Education in the critics' view should centrally involve fostering the capacity and commitment to uncovering and combating privilege in individuals and in social structures in the interest of greater social justice.

I have attempted to reformulate and to defend rationality against its critics, while also learning from the challenges they present. The response to the critics takes place in two domains. On the one hand, there are the more narrowly philosophical debates spawning enormous literatures on realism versus anti-realism; relativism, particularly whether truth, reason, reality are relative to conceptual schemes; objectivity and subjectivity; and so on. On the other hand, there are attempts to locate these questions within broader moral and political domains, that is, to say what is at stake in these debates for everyday life and educational practice.

On the philosophical side, it's difficult to establish precisely what the target is of the attack on reason. Are we really being told that we should stop appealing to reasons in deciding what to believe or how to act? What are we to use in reason's place? Is the attack being made on theoretical or practical reason? Or is it what Habermas (1984) calls "communicative rationality," the effort at mutual persuasion through the exchange of reasons, that stands convicted (p. 10)? In "Reason and Education" I argued that reason's critics tend to hold a highly restricted, narrow view of reason as universal, impartial, abstract, limited to the manipulation of symbolic formulae or formalizable in algorithms, and thus as excluding particular, partial, and concrete perspectives of diverse human experiences. But conceptions of reason after the rejection of classical foundationalism and positivism acknowledge that rational forms of thinking do not have to be algorithmic or formulable in explicit rules or lead to infallibly true outcomes.

I've found particularly useful Putnam's (1982) view that reason must be understood as both "immanent" and "transcendent" (p. 8). The transcendent aspect of rationality as a regulative ideal expresses the goal of rational thought and action. Rational belief aims at truth, rational action at success, rational desire at the good, however these end states are defined. Embedded in the concept of rational judgment, then, is the assumption that some ways of forming beliefs or deciding how to act or what ends to seek are more likely to meet with success than are others. But the regulative ideal does not itself specify criteria of rational judgment; that is, it doesn't tell one how to determine which beliefs are true or what actions are best. It simply says, "Seek truth, etc. by the best available means." For actual guidance one needs to turn to particular immanent traditions of rationality. Thus determining what is rational at a given place and time is possible only by utilizing a concrete, established practice of rational thinking. Yet any such practice can itself be rationally criticized and that shows that reason cannot be wholly identified with any existing standards.

Thus to abandon the regulative ideal of rationality would require either rejection of the goals of rationality (truth, strategic success of action, a good life) or extreme skepticism about the claims of any forms of judgment (any immanent practices of rational thinking) to be better ways of reaching these goals. Of course, criticisms of particular immanent traditions of how to achieve rationality in belief, desire, or action are always possible, but this approach would not mean abandonment of the enterprise of seeking rationality in belief and action, but rather the formulation of new immanent conceptions of what rationality requires.

While in my earlier writing I was concerned to join the narrowly philosophical debates about reason, I later became interested in saying why a defense of reason matters for life and for educational practice. I have focused on the practices of rational persuasion as a way of considering the role such practices play in our ordinary lives. In "The Value of Reason—Why Not a Sardine Can Opener?" (1999) I considered the giving and receiving of reasons as a social practice with a distinctive phenomenology and then asked how our daily experience and political life would be altered in a world without that practice. I've argued that rational persuasion requires a number of dispositions including: a willingness to be shown wrong; a high regard for the value of truth in the particular context; a willingness to regard others as participants in inquiry; an acceptance of the relevant norms of rationality as fair; and a belief that the truth of the matter in question is independent of one's individual belief. I believe that rational persuasion involves a moral ideal. The commitment to rational persuasion transforms a disagreement into joint inquiry into truth rather than the imposition of one will on another. So the practices of rational persuasion are worth caring for if this form of human relationship has worth, and it seems clear that it does. However, I also argue in "The Value of Reason" that rational persuasion is not the only mode of relationship that it can be rational choose in a particular context. There are alternatives that can be rationally compelling in specific circumstances, such as: interest group politics; mediation and diplomacy; disruption; and love, loyalty, and identity politics. Thus I claim that engaging in rational persuasion involves a fundamental choice about the kind of human relationship it is reasonable to have in a particular context. I argue that reason's critics can sometimes be interpreted as making this point.

RECENT DIRECTIONS AND FUTURE PLANS

For the last five years I've been primarily an academic administrator, first as interim dean of the college and then as associate dean. When our Provost called me to ask me to serve as interim, I was visiting at Stanford for a term where I was teaching a seminar on the philosophy of higher education. I'd become interested in exploring contemporary challenges to traditional conceptions of the university. Among the issues are whether the university should be committed to the pursuit of truth and objective knowledge, whether it should be neutral toward contending political and social views, and whether it is increasingly operating with a market perspective that undermines its capacity to offer genuine education and to be a site of social criticism. I thought that in becoming dean I'd be able to investigate these questions first hand.

When Michael Katz asked me to give the Villemain Lecture at San Jose State University in 2005, I took the occasion to pursue the question of the university's role in the education of democratic citizens, a site where some of my questions come to a head. In that lecture I argued that citizens need the capacity to engage in the practices of rational persuasion, bargaining and negotiation, and social activism. I argued that the university properly contributes to the civic education of its students through teaching them the practices of rational persuasion and developing their capacities for social criticism. But, I further argued, in order to play its civic role, the university must protect its autonomy from dominant sources of power, whether governmental or economic.

When writing "The Value of Reason" I'd already begun to think about the role of rational persuasion in democratic life. And I continued to pursue the question, not only in the Villemain lecture, but also in a chapter on "Teaching and Learning the Practices of Democratic Participation" for the forthcoming *Handbook of Research on Teacher Education* (3rd edition), arguing that public school students, and therefore their teachers, need not only to be initiated, to the practices of rational persuasion, but also to learn how to negotiate their differences as citizens, and how to bring about change through social activism.

I'm about to step down from my administrative role and return to the faculty. I expect to continue to examine the contested ground of higher education. I also my interest in rationality. While I've written three papers and given talks on autonomy spaced throughout my career, I've not yet been sufficiently satisfied with what I've produced to share it with a wider audience.

It's been an interesting experience writing this essay. On reflection, it appears to me that the themes that have attracted and sustained my research are somehow near to who I am as a person rather than being simply the "puzzle solving" enterprise that Thomas Kuhn argued was part of normal science. A vocational counselor once said to me: "You try always to state the exact truth as you see it, thus you're likely to be misunderstood by most people for whom truth is only one aspect of reality." I've spent time trying to defend my views to those for whom other features of reality rank higher. But disagreement about the rank order of differing goods is a fundamental part of the human condition. I have been lucky to be part of a field that makes it possible to spend one's time in such pursuits.

REFERENCES

Arendt, H. (1958). *The human condition*. Chicago: University of Chicago Press.

Bernstein, R. (1988). The rage against reason. In E. McMullin (Ed.), *Construction and constraint: The shaping of scientific rationality* (pp. 189-221). Notre Dame, IN: University of Notre Dame Press.

Curren, R., Robertson, E., & Hager, P. (2003). The analytical movement. In R. Curren (Ed.), *A companion to philosophy of education* (pp. 176-191). Oxford: Blackwell.

Dietl, P. (1973). Teaching, learning and knowing. *Educational Philosophy & Theory, 5*, 1-25.

Dewey, J. (1916). *Democracy and education*. New York: The Free Press.

Green, T. F. (1964). A topology of the teaching concept. *Studies in Philosophy and Education, 111*(4), 284-320.

Green, T. F. (1964). Teaching, acting, and behaving. *Harvard Educational Review, 34*(4), 507-524.

Green, T.F. (1971). *The activities of teaching*. New York: McGraw-Hill.

Habermas, J. (1984). *The theory of communicative action* (Vol. 1, Reason and the rationalization of society) (Thomas McCarthy, Trans.). Boston: Beacon Press.

Macmillan, C.J.B. & Nelson, T.W. (Eds.). (1968). *Concepts of teaching: Philosophical essays*. Chicago: Rand McNally.

O'Connor, D.J. (1957). *An introduction to the philosophy of education*. London: Routledge & Kegan Paul.

Peters, R.S. (Ed.). (1967). *The concept of education*. London: Routledge & Kegan Paul.

Prakash, M. & Robertson, E. (1983). Ethical and metaethical relativism: A consideration of moral relativism and its implications for moral education. In D. Kerr (Ed.), *Philosophy of education 1982* (pp. 75-85). Normal, Illinois: The Philosophy of Education Society.

Putnam, H. (1982). Why reason can't be naturalized. *Synthese, 52*, 3-24.

Rawls, J. (1971). A theory of justice. Cambridge, Mass.: Belknap Press of Harvard University Press.

Robertson, E. (1983). More than words can say: Making room for the tacit dimension. In D. Kerr (Ed.), *Philosophy of education 1982* (pp. 95-105). Normal, Illinois: The Philosophy of Education Society, 1983.

Robertson, E. (1984). Practical reasons, authority, and education. In R. Roemer (Ed.), *Philosophy of Education 1983* (pp. 61-75). Normal Illinois: The Philosophy of Education Society.

Robertson, E. (1988). Moral education, subjectively speaking. In J. Giarelli (Ed.), *Philosophy of education 1988* (pp. 101-108). Normal, Illinois: The Philosophy of Education Society.

Robertson, E. (1991). Reason and education. In M. Buchman & R. Floden (Eds.), *Philosophy of education 1991* (pp. 169-180). Normal, Illinois: The Philosophy of Education Society.

Robertson, E. (1992). Is Dewey's educational vision still viable? In G. Grant (Ed.), *Review of research in education,* vol. 18. (pp. 335-381). Washington, DC: American Educational Research Association.

Robertson, E. (1995). Reconceiving reason. In W. Kohli (Ed.), *Critical conversations in philosophy of education: From theory to practice and back* (pp. 116-126). New York: Routledge.

Robertson, E. (1995). Teacher authority and teaching for liberation. In M. Katz (Ed.), *Philosophy of education 1994* (pp. 261-264). Urbana, Illinois: Philosophy of Education Society.

Robertson, E. (1996). Defending reason: The priority of rationality over ideology. In A. Neiman (Ed.), *Philosophy of education 1995* (pp. 363-371). Urbana, Illinois: The Philosophy of Education Society, 1996.

Robertson, E. (1999). The value of reason: Why not a sardine can opener? In R. Curren (Ed.), *Philosophy of education 1999* (pp. 1-14). Urbana, Illinois: The Philosophy of Education Society. [Reprinted in R. Curren (Ed.) (2007), *Philosophy of education: An anthology* (pp. 448-457). Oxford: Blackwell.]

Robertson, E. (forthcoming). Teacher education in a democratic society: Learning and teaching the practices of democratic participation. In M. Cochran-Smith, S. Feiman-Nemser, & J. McIntyre (Eds.), *The handbook of research on teacher education* (3rd edition). New York: Taylor and Francis.

Scheffler, I. (1960). *The language of education.* Springfield, Ill.: Charles C. Thomas.

Scheffler, I. (1965). *Conditions of knowledge.* Chicago: Scott, Foresman.

Scheffler, I. (1973). *Reason and teaching.* Indianapolis: Bobbs-Merrill.

Emily Robertson
Syracuse University

FRANCIS SCHRAG

THE ROAD TAKEN

CORNELL IN THE LATE FIFTIES

My adventures in philosophy of education began with an undergraduate philosophy major at Cornell in the late fifties. Cornell's philosophy department was a very exciting place to be at that time, having hosted Ludwig Wittgenstein for an extended visit not that long before. I asked Norman Malcolm, a disciple and friend of Wittgenstein, with whom I'd had a course in sophomore year, to be my advisor and he agreed. Malcom was a charismatic teacher, but if the word "charismatic" conjures up the image of a professor whose fluency and brilliance dazzle his audience, then I am misleading you. Malcolm was a big man, a Midwesterner, slow and deliberate of speech, His devotion to grappling with philosophical questions, and the intensity of his effort and concentration is what captured our attention. If one of us asked a question or raised an objection to something he'd said, sometimes he took several minutes before answering, pacing the room, his brows furrowed, his hand scratching his head as he appeared to be grappling with the point for the very first time. The excitement was in the process, and I was hooked.

I acquitted myself well in philosophy courses and was one of three students invited at the end of my junior year to work for an honors degree. I approached a young, highly thought of assistant professor with whom I'd had a course, asking him if he would be willing to supervise my proposed honors thesis on the feasibility of historical laws, and John Rawls accepted. We met for a tutorial every week: Rawls had a severe stammer; he had trouble, especially, with words beginning with "m" and one had to avoid letting this get in the way of appreciating the clarity of his thinking, as well as his enormous range and erudition. I recall one time he tried (with limited success) to explain quantum theory to me. Among my other teachers were Max Black, Georg von Wright, David Sachs, Keith Donnellan, and Frank Sibley, all important philosophers in the analytic tradition. Students were permitted to attend regular Friday evening seminars during which professors or invitees read papers, after which their work was subject to severe, sometimes withering criticism. It became a kind of entertainment for a while and a couple of students even brought dates along. Only then did the department close these gatherings to undergrads, excepting us three honors students.

Little did I know at the time that I was being indoctrinated into what philosophy was and how one went about it. The history of philosophy was largely irrelevant; real philosophers "did philosophy," and it often seemed to matter little what earlier thinkers had said. I recall asking Malcolm once during office hours whether we'd be reading Sartre and he said that I could read that on my own or in literature

L.J. Waks (ed.), Leaders in Philosophy of Education: Intellectual Self Portraits, 211–218.
© 2008 *Sense Publishers. All rights reserved.*

courses. I also recall that Malcolm did not encourage students to become academics; following the master, he felt philosophy was a calling, not a profession one selected from among other professions.

COLUMBIA AND CHICAGO

I mention all this because it was a soul-stirring time for me, making a deeper impact than my graduate studies a decade later at Teachers College and the Columbia philosophy department. When I entered Teachers College about 1966, after having taught in a variety of settings including a suburban high school and the U.S. military, the analytic movement was beginning to take over in philosophy of education. My advisor at TC, Jonas Soltis, was a very capable young philosopher who'd recently come from Harvard where he'd been trained by Israel Scheffler. Scheffler and the British philosopher Richard Peters were the leaders of the analytic movement in education, and Peters had persuaded some eminent British philosophers such as Gilbert Ryle and Michael Oakeshott to contribute to the anthologies he edited.

PERSONAL FAVORITES

Justice and the Family, (1976)
Social Science and Social Practice, (1983)
Back to Basics, (1995)

Soltis and other "young Turks" helped spread the notion at TC that the careful, rigorous analysis of educational language would provide the clarity needed for practical people to introduce much needed reforms into schools. Soltis, following Scheffler, also valued the American pragmatists, Dewey especially, and we were introduced to his thinking. When I went to the other side of 120th Street to take courses in the philosophy department, I noticed a big change from my Cornell days. The analytic movement was dominant, to be sure, (though I took a fine course on European philosophy taught by Robert D. Cumming), but the genre practiced at Columbia, derived less from the analysis of "ordinary language," favored by the Wittgensteinians and more from the version associated with the logician W.V.O. Quine. Dewey, once considered "the" American philosopher was a non-person so far as philosophy departments were concerned. There's a certain irony there as Quine considered himself a philosophical descendant of the pragmatists.

Most of the efforts of the analysts in education, inspired by Scheffler and Peters, were focused on reason and rationality and their roles in teaching and learning. Much ink was spilled (these were the days before computers when most of us still had fountain pens) in trying to determine whether teaching implied learning, what the meaning of "equality of opportunity" was, what was meant by "indoctrination," and how it differed from "education," and a few other questions. I wanted to write a dissertation on a topic not being discussed at all. I tried to answer the question: What, if anything, might be meant by the education of the emotions? My dissertation, typical of the time, was careful, plodding and dependent on the work of a couple of analytic philosophers outside education, but it led to at least one interesting paper, "Psychoanalysis as an Educational Process," arguing that the "talking cure" is better conceived as an educative than a medical process.

By the time I was a graduate student, I was married with two children and graduate school was more of a 9-5 job for me. I did, however, get caught up in the excitement of the '68 student revolt at Columbia. I was then teaching an undergraduate course in philosophy of education, hence eligible to join the faculty group who were trying to protect the students who'd taken over buildings from the police. I was called in the middle of the night to come to campus where a police action to clear the buildings was anticipated. I arrived in time to be caught up in the ensuing melee with police—fortunately no one was killed or seriously injured, though we later learned that one of the cops did incur a serious injury.

After my doctorate, my first job was at the University of Chicago. The TC chair, the eminent historian Larry Cremin made a call to the Chicago chair and they invited me for an interview. That's how things were done in those days. The Chicago Department of Education was home to some illustrious scholars such as Bruno Bettelheim and Benjamin Bloom, and two fascinating but quirky older philosophers, Harold Dunkel and Joseph Schwab. There were a couple of young scholars with whom I became friendly, especially Ian Westbury, with whom I had many good conversations, but overall I found the Chicago department stuffy and complacent.

During my first year or so in Chicago, my philosophical interests shifted towards social and political philosophy, inspired no doubt by the social turmoil of the sixties and seventies. The social ferment outside the academy awoke philosophy from its scholastic slumber and normative issues came to the fore once again. After the Black Power movement, there was beginning to be talk of women's liberation and children's rights, and I became interested in the status of children in schools, and in political and social philosophy. Some of my best work was begun at Chicago and then continued during my first years at the University of Wisconsin where I'd moved in 1972.

I might mention that while in Chicago I was recruited to serve on the dissertation committee of the first student who proposed to carry out an ethnographic study—under Philip Jackson—instead of the usual hypothesis driven empirical investigation. I was recruited to the committee because no other educational researcher in the department would sign on.

From the point of view of my philosophical development, a great advantage of the move to Wisconsin was that I now had a joint appointment in the philosophy department, and I began to interact with some of the philosophers in an informal way. Where there had been little collaboration or interest in each other's work at Chicago, this was not the case at Wisconsin. I was invited to join an interdisciplinary study group interested in psychoanalysis that met informally at participants' homes to discuss texts of interest. This was one of the richest experiences I've had. The group varied over the nine or so years we met monthly, but regulars included a couple of practicing analysts, a professor of comparative literature, one in the law school who was also an analyst, myself and another philosopher with expertise in European philosophy. We had wine and cheese and exciting discussions in an atmosphere marked by conviviality and mutual respect. I mention the group because newcomers to the academy often think that it is full of such contexts and occasions, but the truth is that they are very rare. If you should be fortunate enough to find such a group, nurture and cherish it.

It was still a time of intellectual and social transformation—only later did we realized that the "revolution" was much shallower and much less pervasive than we in campus settings experienced. In addition to almost weekly colloquia, the philosophy department had the custom of having profs attend each other's seminars. I recall, for example, that shortly after Rawls' *Theory of Justice* was published, Marcus Singer offered a semester's seminar on the book. Several of us younger faculty attended, and we went through the chapters very carefully.

WORK ON CHILDREN AND THE FAMILY

During the decade of the 1970s, I wrote a number of articles dealing with children's status and these are not only among the best things I've ever written, but probably those that have had the most influence—note I did not say a lot of influence. Let me spend a bit of time on these.

As has become much clearer today, the images of the world embedded in most Anglo-American political and social theory is that of stable, isolated polities populated by able, adult men. So my question was: how, conceptually, do children fit into this world, and what, if any implications might this have for how we educate them? There were several articles in this series, published in both education and philosophy journals. I'll mention a few: first "The Right to Educate" which appeared in *School Review* in 1971, then "The Child's Status in the Democratic State," published in *Political Theory* in 1975, "The Child in the Moral Order in Philosophy" in 1977 and "Justice and the Family" in *Inquiry* in 1976. In the first article, I was trying to figure out who had the right to educate children. I canvassed earlier political philosophers' responses to the question, and showed that the assumption of parental rights over children, however "natural," was not based on very convincing arguments. My own answer was that there were completing claims by the state and the local cultural group—at that time the Yoder case, soon to be decided by the Supreme Court, was much discussed—which were also legitimate. In other words, no agent had exclusive rights over children.

In the articles on democracy and paternalism, I showed that defences of the autonomy and full citizenship of adults were not easy to reconcile with the subordination of children. I was not an advocate of children's rights—after all I had children of my own-- and I recognized the silliness of extreme views regarding children's liberation that were abroad at the time. What my articles did reveal, however was that the arguments of political and social theorists intended to embrace every adult while at the same time excluding every child were far from satisfying. Very recently, in the wake of a spate of sophisticated analyses by political philosophers of the nature and justification for democracy, in "Children and Democracy: Theory and Policy" (2004), I returned to this theme once more, showing the weaknesses in the arguments of those few philosophers who did not simply assume the exclusion of children but tried to defend it. Here I tried to link up my philosophical reasoning with empirical evidence showing that children's exclusion from the franchise was damaging to children's interests, and I suggested a couple of practical ways of insuring that children's interests and stake in the polity were not overlooked by legislators. I consider the piece a good example how philosophical reasoning embedded in a context of empirical fact can provide a basis for advancing policy initiatives.

I think my article on "Justice and the Family" (1976) is the single article I'm proudest of. In the first part of the article, focussing on Robert Nozick's then recent book defending the minimal state, I showed that accounts of justice that paid no attention to equality of opportunity were fatally deficient. I then argued the limitations of Rawls' famous *A Theory of Justice* for considering the family by constructing a thought experiment in which parents follow Rawls' difference principle rather than giving preference to their own children. The question I then addressed was what, exactly was lost, under such a scenario and the general point that emerged was that the family provided goods related to intimacy that differed from the "respect" which the state owed each citizen, goods which only the family could supply. I say this article is one I'm proudest of for two reasons: Though carefully argued, it was written with a bit of flair and is, I would guess, one of the few, if not the only article on Rawls and Nozick to quote Sigmund Freud and Martin Buber. The second reason is that the article is the acknowledged ancestor of a line of work a generation later. In their acknowledgements to "Parents' Rights and the Value of the Family," which just appeared in *Ethics*, Harry Brighouse and Adam Swift thank me for "Justice and the Family," "which inspired the argumentative strategy of the current article." [i]

THE SOCIAL SCIENCES AND EDUCATION

At the end of the seventies, I experienced a crisis of confidence. I felt I'd said all I wanted to say about children and saw ethics and social philosophy as barren. Meta-issues were beyond my interest or competence and normative theories must, I felt, must either accord with common sense or be considered wildly implausible. There were exciting developments taking place in philosophy of science, where issues deriving from the work of Thomas Kuhn, Imre Lakatos, and others were attracting a lot of attention. It also happened that the philosophy of science and epistemology wing of the department was very collegial and professors not only attended each others' seminars but held evening discussions on texts of mutual interest. I joined this group, sat in on Fred Dretske's seminar on Kuhn and tried to retrain myself as a philosopher of the social sciences. Dretske became my philosophical hero. His ability to cut to the heart of an issue and to express difficult ideas clearly and accessibly was amazing. Dennis Stampe, Elliott Sober, and Berent Enc were in this group and occasionally I'd join them for lunch in the cafeteria. Since my primary affiliation was in the school of education, I was something of an outsider, but they welcomed me. Conversation was almost always

215

about philosophy. What really impressed me was they were not looking to score points against each other (or anyone else), nor vying for honor or publicity, but trying to find the right answers.

Gradually, I developed an insight that evolved into several articles taking a similar line. Among these were "Knowing and Doing" (1981) and "Social Science and Social Practice" (1983). As in the case of most of my best work, what was (somewhat) original was the question I asked: If the natural sciences had led to enormous transformations of technology, why weren't the social sciences doing the same thing? My answer was interesting, because counter-intuitive. Advances in psychology had not led to practical breakthroughs (in pedagogy, for example) not because psychology was still waiting for its Newton, but because we humans were already such effective teachers. The argument was based on a realist view of science enunciated by Rom Harré that scientists discover new powers in nature, which blaze new trails for technology, but that no such powers had been discovered by social scientists. The reason, oddly enough, is that we understand humans better than inanimate nature because live in a social world that we have made. The idea goes back to Vico, an opponent of Cartesianism.

SCHOOLING

It might appear from what I've so far written that my focus and intellectual interests were abstract and philosophical, far from the world of schools. This is a partial view that I should now correct. Though many of my courses were cross-listed between the philosophy department and the department of educational policy studies, I also taught classes primarily for future teachers, classes that did not have a philosophical focus, and as a former teacher myself, I was very interested in schools and tried to reach audiences that were primarily concerned with schooling. My primary appointment was in the school of education, and I was fortunate to be part of a very congenial department. My scholarly work was immensely enriched by informal contact with historians and sociologists of education, with such scholars as Carl Kaestle, Michael Olneck, and Mary Metz as well as with my congenial philosophical partner in the school of education, Daniel Pekarsky.

Let me, therefore, say a few words about my two books. The first one, *Thinking in School and Society*, looked at the nature of thinking and the nurture of thinkers, moving out in concentric circles from a focus on the individual mind as understood by psychologists to the classroom, and beyond to the workplace, polity, and television. I think the most original part of the book lay in its analysis of why serious, thinking is rarely found in conventional classrooms.

The analysis contrasted the conditions and demands of the school classroom with those found in the scientific laboratory. The classroom, I argued, lacked most of the features required for thinking, and for a good reason—the freedom and absence of routinization required by scientific investigators would invite disorder in the classroom.

In *Back to Basics: Fundamental Educational Questions Reexmained* (1995), I tried to bring my philosophical thinking about education to bear on the questions of what schools are for, what makes teaching difficult, whether schools could change radically, who ought to control schooling, and others. Writing as clearly and vividly as I knew how, I hoped to reach a broad audience because I felt that philosophers of education were remiss in writing mostly for each other. The spirit of the work is largely Deweyan, arguing that what educators need to focus on is neither inculcating facts nor training skills but fostering in students two key dispositions: caring about the evidence regarding whatever matter they confront, and maintaining a desire to go on learning.

Although the sprit of the book is Deweyan, that does not mean that I endorsed Dewey's positions or conclusions. For example, where Dewey held out the hope of radically restructured schools, I argued that after decades of failed experiments, we needed to realize that this was a utopian aspiration and to understand why. In the chapter on teaching, which I especially liked, I explained why teaching was so difficult, yet at the same time unlikely to be advanced by scientific research in psychology or education.

The last piece I'd like to spend a bit of time on is my presidential address to the Philosophy of Education Society, entitled "Perfectionism and Equality: The Liberal Educator's Dilemma" (2005). I faced a considerable challenge in writing this piece: because my work had ranged from topics in ethics and political philosophy to those in epistemology and philosophy of the social sciences, I wanted my presidential address to somehow establish a connection between these normally separated spheres. My argument was that we liberal (in two senses) educators face a tension between our loyalty to the best work in the fields we teach and to the equality of all citizens. The tension resulted from the fact that the best, be it in physics or poetry, is often inaccessible to all but the strongest students. In the main part of the address, I enunciated a number of seductive challenges to the notion that there really was a hierarchical dimension to cultural achievements, whether in physics or poetry, rebutting each of them. But I showed that recognition of that hierarchy, far from propelling us into an elitist posture, ought to intensify our concern for social justice.

As I look over my vita, I see that I have published articles on a very wide range of topics, among them: political liberalism and religion, Marxism, politics and curriculum, Michel Foucault, feminist science, positivism, egalitarian grading, and high stakes testing. One of the joys of philosophy of education, I have always felt, lays in the opportunity to move around in the world of scholarship and inquiry, to explore new fields, new questions. Although recently retired from teaching, I'm pursuing a number of new writing projects.

CONCLUSION

When I was a graduate student in philosophy of education, I believed that we philosophers were doing important work clearing the ground of intellectual rubbish that prevented educational reconstruction. This was a time when the disciplines of history, sociology, philosophy, and anthropology were believed to have important contributions to make in reforming our schools. Today, I perceive the voice of the philosopher to have largely been drowned out by that of the policy wonk, often one trained in economics or other forms of "scientific" research. Unfortunately his or her discourse is laden with dubious philosophical assumptions which need to be brought to light and criticized. This is a role philosophers are well suited to, but they must learn to speak intelligibly to broader audiences if they are to have some impact.

I began this retrospective with my undergraduate immersion in philosophy. A half century later, I still admire the intensity of the search for philosophical truth. Over the years, I've come to realize that analytic philosophy is often arid and scholastic, but it embodies a craftsmanlike appreciation for a well made argument that is, if anything, more valuable in an age of hype, self-promotion and bullshit.

NOTE

 Brighouse and Swift, p.80.

REFERENCES

Brighouse, H. & Swift, A. (2006). Parents rights and the value of the family. *Ethics, 117*(1), 80-108.

Schrag, F. (1971). The right to educate. *School Review, 79*(3), 359-378.

Schrag, F. (1972). Psychoanalysis as an educational process. In Mary Anne Raywid (Ed.), *Philosophy of Education 1972* (pp. 285-297). Studies in Philosophy and Education. Edwardsville, IL.

Schrag, F. (1975). The child's status in the democratic state. *Political Theory, 3*(4), 441-457.

Schrag, F. (1976). Justice & the family. *Inquiry 19*(2), pp.193-208.

Schrag, F. (1977). The child in the moral order. *Philosophy, 52*(2), 167-177.

Schrag, F. (1981). Knowing and doing. *American Journal of Education, 89*(3), 252-282.

Schrag, F. (1983). Social science and social practice. *Inquiry, 26*(1), 107-124.

Schrag, F. (1988a). *Thinking in school and society*. New York & London: Routledge.

Schrag, F. (1988b). Response to Giroux. *Educational Theory, 38*(1), 143-144.

Schrag, F. (1995). *Back to basics: Fundamental educational questions reexmained*. San Francisco: Jossey Bass.

Schrag, F. (2004). Children and democracy: Theory and policy. *Politics, Philosophy & Economics, 3*(3), 255-262.

Schrag, F. (2005). Perfectionism and equality: The liberal educator's dilemma. In Chris Higgins (Ed.), *Philosophy of education 2004* (pp. 1-11). Urbana IL: University of Illinois Press.

Francis Schrag
University of Wisconsin - Madison

HARVEY SIEGEL

IN SEARCH OF REASONS

EARLY DAYS

I came to philosophy of education late, but to philosophy quite a bit earlier. Indeed, I didn't become aware of the existence of philosophy of education as an academic specialization until the end of my undergraduate days.

My introduction to philosophy came by way of consideration of the 'Design Argument' for God's existence, put forward by our Rabbi in response to my demand for some reason to believe in God's existence, when I was 13. My father had died that year, and in accordance with traditional practice I went to synagogue with my older brother Jack to recite the prayer of mourning twice a day – early in the morning, before school, and again at dusk – for a year. That experience, and of course the death itself, prompted serious doubt; the argument was the Rabbi's way of responding to it. The result, in my case, was two-fold. First, the argument's weakness was clear – even my thirteen-year-old self was easily able to recognize its weaknesses, and I quickly realized that, if this was the best that could be offered in its defense, in the face of human suffering and death, God's existence was doubtful in the extreme. Second, I got my first glimmer of the power of logic and reasoning (and, as I eventually realized, of philosophical analysis) to address such questions, and of (philosophical) arguments to answer them. In the event, I became both an atheist and an aspiring philosopher. In my high school years I continued down this road, guided by my older sister Sue, then a college student who passed along her philosophy books – esp. the novels and plays of Sartre and other existentialists – and discussed them with me.

UNDERGRADUATE STUDIES AT CORNELL

When I began at Cornell in 1970, I declared philosophy as my major, but all I knew about it was my informal exposure to the design argument and my familiarity with some existentialist literature. But I got lucky. My Introduction to Philosophy course my first semester was taught by Jaegwon Kim, then a young professor at Michigan visiting Cornell that year. The small seminar gave lots of opportunity for discussion, and Kim's friendly, engaging teaching style was encouraging, and his enthusiasm for the subject matter infectious. By the end of that course I was hooked, and never again seriously entertained the possibility of pursuing any other academic subject or career. Lucky indeed!

My experiences in philosophy courses at Cornell were mixed. I didn't enjoy Allen Woods' survey course on History of Modern Philosophy, and almost failed Nicholas Sturgeon's advanced undergraduate seminar in ethics, which I took

L.J. Waks (ed.), Leaders in Philosophy of Education: Intellectual Self Portraits, 219–228.

before I was ready for it. But I loved Robert Stalnaker's courses in philosophy of language and philosophy of science, and other courses in logic, epistemology, and other areas of philosophy. I also enjoyed some very engaging courses in political theory taught by the Straussians Werner Dannhauser and Allan Bloom, though I didn't know at the time who Leo Strauss was or what his influence on them meant. I did an honors thesis on Rawls under the direction of Richard Miller, which was not a great success. My main influence at Cornell, however, was Max Black, who kindly let me attend his graduate seminars on decision theory and on von Wright's new book *Explanation and Understanding*. These were very exciting intellectual experiences for me, and solidified my interests in epistemology and philosophy of science. Black also became a kind of mentor, and he shared stories about his teacher Wittgenstein, his early philosophical days in England, and his subsequent philosophical experiences in the U.S. and elsewhere. We also talked a fair amount of philosophy outside of class. We stayed in sporadic contact for the remainder of his life.

When I first arrived at Cornell the philosophical issues and themes that most engaged me were broadly existentialist, but I quickly realized that my interests involved issues more systematically treated in the 'analytic' tradition, and I followed those interests. In one of the philosophy of science courses I took we read Israel Scheffler's *Science and Subjectivity*. I was very taken by it, and my interests in issues involving the nature, power and convicting force of reasons, the character of rationality, the possibility of objectivity, etc., began to crystallize at that time. It was then that I first thought systematically about going to graduate school and pursuing a professorial career. Up to that point I had not given serious thought to such a career; worse, conversations with the Cornell graduate students made me well aware of the abysmal job market in philosophy at that time (early 70s). But there was nothing I wanted to do more than philosophy, and I thought that if I could get in a few more years doing it before circumstances forced me to join the 'real world,' I would. When the time came to apply to graduate programs, I wrote to Scheffler, expressed my admiration for his book and

---

PERSONAL FAVORITES

"What Is the Question Concerning the Rationality of Science?" (1985)

Relativism Refuted: A Critique of Contemporary Epistemological Relativism (1987)

Educating Reason: Rationality, Critical Thinking, and Education (1988)

"Justification by Balance" (1992)

"What Price Inclusion?" (1995)

"Naturalism and the Abandonment of Normativity" (1996)

"Instrumental Rationality and Naturalized Philosophy of Science" (1996)

Rationality Redeemed?: Further Dialogues on an Educational Ideal (1997)

"Multiculturalism and the Possibility of Transcultural Educational and Philosophical Ideals" (1999)

"Relativism" (2004)

"Truth, Thinking, Testimony and Trust: Alvin Goldman on Epistemology and Education" (2005)

"Epistemological Diversity and Educational Research: Much Ado about Nothing Much?" (2006)

---

my desire to pursue related topics, and asked about the possibility of working with him as a graduate student. He kindly wrote back and explained that of course I could apply to the Harvard Philosophy graduate program; or I could apply to a combined philosophy/philosophy of education program that he ran, housed bureaucratically in the Graduate School of Education (HGSE). That was the first time I encountered the phrase 'philosophy of education.' My first reaction was not positive. But as I began to learn more about the subject, and saw that the philosophical issues in which I was most interested were also relevant to the philosophical study of education, I warmed up to the idea. First passes through Scheffler's *Conditions of Knowledge, The Language of Education* and *Reason and Teaching* – books I studied much more seriously after I began graduate school – not only persuaded me that I could pursue those issues in the context of the philosophical study of education, but kindled an interest in the subject, and persuaded me of the interrelationships among and the mutual relevance of epistemology, philosophy of science, and philosophy of education. This understanding of these sub-disciplines of philosophy has stayed with me, and has led me over the years both to complain repeatedly about the isolation of philosophy of education from work done by denizens of departments of philosophy, and to encourage those denizens to take seriously philosophical issues concerning education. (On the latter, see Siegel 2008)

In any event, being convinced that I would never be admitted to Harvard's graduate program in philosophy, in the end I applied to Scheffler's joint program, was lucky enough to be accepted, and my future course was set – though it took quite a while to get settled.

GRADUATE STUDIES AT HARVARD

Harvard was incredibly exciting philosophically. At HGSE I took two of Lawrence Kohlberg's courses on moral development/education, an excellent course on Piaget and developmental psychology taught by Carol Feldman, and a small handful of others. But the majority of my coursework was taken in the philosophy department. My first semester I took an ethics course with Roderick Firth, and the infamous PHIL 140 – W.V.O. Quine's basic logic course, for which *Methods of Logic* was the text. Time passed, and in the fall of my second year I was scheduled to serve as T.A. for Scheffler's philosophy of education course. A few days before the semester began, the lead T.A. for PHIL 140 called: one of the scheduled T.A.s had to withdraw, all the other philosophy graduate students were committed elsewhere, and was I willing to be a T.A. for PHIL 140? I was committed to serve as T.A. for Scheffler, but he would have none of it: "You can T.A. for me any time, but you won't get the opportunity to T.A. for Quine again." He released me from my commitment (I T.A.'d for him the following year), and I joined the T.A. team for PHIL 140. Despite having done well in the course when I took it the previous year, I was in well over my head at first. But the other T.A.s – and Quine himself during our weekly meetings – helped pull me through. Several of the undergraduate students in my section understood the material better than I

221

did; I learned from them more than they learned from me. Quite an experience! But it did give me the chance to get to know Quine a bit; contrary to reputation, he was quite friendly (as were Goodman, Putnam, and the other 'big names') and remained so during interactions at conferences and such over the years.

I also took Quine's *Word and Object* seminar – another staple of the Harvard graduate curriculum – and courses with Hilary Putnam, Michael Friedman, Warren Goldfarb, and several others. My first published paper was written first for Putnam's seminar in philosophy of science. Regrettably, I never had the opportunity to take courses with either Rawls or Nozick, though I got to know the latter a bit in later years. When my coursework was completed and I was working on my dissertation, I was able to sit in on Nelson Goodman's last seminar before he retired. The topic of the seminar was the manuscript of what became *Ways of Worldmaking*. Goodman did not share the manuscript with us, but rather read from it for a time and then opened the floor for discussion. It was a tremendously stimulating (though somewhat maddening) experience. The price for permission to audit was presenting a paper to the seminar comparing Kuhn's and Goodman's versions of relativism. Goodman approved of my way of distinguishing the two versions and agreed with my criticisms of the former, but not with my criticisms of the latter. In the fullness of time pieces of my presentation found their way into print, along with other papers/chapters on Goodman. This was an important event in the development of my thinking about relativism, a topic on which I have written quite a bit. Of course there are many doctrines that go by the name 'relativism,' and it is important to be clear on the position being considered. Once clarified, my general view is that there can be no coherent assertion and defense of relativism, because any such assertion and defense requires 'absolutist' presuppositions. As such, relativism succumbs to the standard self-refutation arguments first articulated by Plato; one can 'defend' relativism only by giving it up. (On Goodman, Siegel 1984; on relativism more generally, Siegel 1986, 1987, 2004)

Courses on Piaget and Kohlberg at HGSE combined nicely with work in the philosophy department to generate a serious interest in *naturalized epistemology*: what is the relation between psychology and epistemology, or, more broadly, between science and philosophy? Are these areas to be sharply distinguished or viewed as merging into one another? Can epistemological questions be informed, or even resolved, by the results of scientific inquiry? I pursued these issues in several papers during graduate school, including one for Quine's seminar, of which he most definitely did not approve. But my interest in this cluster of issues grew, and for a time I thought seriously about making this the topic of my dissertation. In the end I opted for a different topic, but I've continued to teach courses on and write about naturalized epistemology/philosophy of science over the years, and hope to publish a book on the topic in due course. My line is that a thoroughgoing naturalism in epistemology – either of the sort (often attributed, correctly or not, to Quine) that eliminates epistemic normativity, or the sort that reduces it to instrumental (and so naturalistically accessible) efficacy – fails fully to account for that normativity, and so fails as a meta-epistemological account of the normativity of epistemology. (Siegel 1995, 1996, 1996a)

Instead of addressing naturalized epistemology in my dissertation, I chose to write about *Kuhn's Philosophy of Science and Science Education*. In it I continued to develop my critique of epistemological relativism and began to address questions concerning rationality in general and the rationality of science in particular, and wrote for the first time about science education. All these topics have remained on my post-dissertation agenda (Siegel 1985, 2001, 2002, 2004b).

Contact with Max Black at Cornell provided a sense of connection to Wittgenstein and British philosophy more generally. At Harvard the connections to the recent philosophical past were even stronger: Quine was of course a philosophical intimate, critic and heir of Carnap; Putnam was a student of Reichenbach; Goodman and Scheffler were close colleagues of the New York pragmatists as well as the positivists. They were the clear descendents and, in important ways and despite substantial disagreements, the designated heirs of the preceding generation of philosophers, who themselves profoundly shaped the course of twentieth century philosophy. And of course they all made signal contributions to philosophy themselves. It was a heady experience to spend time as a voyeur in that intellectual milieu.

Scheffler was a terrific supervisor: there when I needed him and exceedingly helpful and conscientious, but strongly encouraging, as he was with all his students, of my finding my own voice. He was and remains an inspiring mentor and a constant source of support, encouragement, and philosophical guidance. (It will come as no surprise that he and I see eye to eye on many philosophical matters, though I've never been inclined to embrace his Goodman-inspired view of epistemic justification (Siegel 1992), or to share his sympathetic view of pragmatism in epistemology.) It was at his suggestion that I submitted my first paper to PES in 1976, where I found a community that has been a source of friendship and stimulation from then to now. His learnedness and philosophical ability were and continue to be surpassed only by his care, concern, and kindness. He is the very model of a *mensch*.

Several of the chapters of the dissertation found their way eventually into print, and put me squarely on the 'publish or perish' path so central to life in the academy. These publications straddled philosophy and philosophy of education, and for a while it was unclear which path (if either) my career would follow. I was lucky enough to emerge from graduate school with an offer to teach the latter at the University of Nebraska – my only job offer. So in 1977, brand new EdD in hand, off I went to Lincoln, Nebraska. (I should say a word about that degree. Although most of my course work at Harvard was in the philosophy department, Scheffler's joint program was housed in the GSE. At Harvard only the Graduate School of Arts and Sciences can award the PhD. The GSE can award only the Ed.D. So that's what I got. For many years I was embarrassed about it, and tried to hide it; when people assumed that I had a Ph. D., I didn't correct the mistaken assumption. Lately, though, I have come to regard it as a sort of badge of honor, having secured a career in philosophy despite it. Strange what people find worth worrying about...).

EARLY LIFE IN THE PROFESSION

Lincoln turned out to be my only experience teaching in a School of Education. I taught introductory courses in foundations of education (my first non-trivial exposure to the non-philosophical foundational disciplines) and philosophy of education, and some upper-level courses in the latter. I liked my colleagues there, but never quite adjusted to Midwest culture (though I still enjoy telling stories about my experiences of football Saturdays, when the stadium became the third-largest city in the state, filled with people dressed head to toe in red, and of visiting local homes complete with rooms completely decked out in red, right down to the toilet seats), and after three years took a leave of absence in order to take a non-tenure-track position teaching philosophy courses at Sonoma State University in northern California. In the end I never returned to Nebraska, preferring non-tenure-track life in philosophy in California to tenure-track life in philosophy of education in Nebraska. Naturally I wanted to return to the tenure track, but that would take several more years.

In both places I wrote a lot, both because there was a lot I wanted to say and because I thought it the only way to get back on the tenure track. My time at Sonoma State was significant in several ways – besides the chance to live in Berkeley/Oakland and to get to know that wonderful part of the world – two of which are worth mentioning here: the chance to meet people in philosophy and education while serving as a visiting scholar in the school of education at UC-Berkeley, and my introduction to the world of critical thinking.

Being at that point very career-oriented and frustrated by my lack of prospects for tenure, I spent a fair amount of time cultivating relationships with Berkeley faculty. This led to quite a few dead ends, but conversations with Marcia Linn led to a co-authored and rather atypical (for me) publication on 'post-formal reasoning', and a chance encounter with Elliot Turiel led to my becoming an expert witness for the State of California in its infamous evolution/creationism trial, which led to my only publication in *Phi Delta Kappan* (although I never got to testify; for the full story see Siegel 1981). Hanging around the philosophy department and sitting in on the occasional seminar (e.g., Donald Davidson's on relativism, which eventually led to Siegel 1987, ch. 2) led to the opportunity to serve as visiting associate professor of philosophy during the summer of 1986. (I served in the same capacity at Stanford that same winter.)

At Sonoma State I had a teaching load of 4, and occasionally 5, courses/semester. A staple course was Critical Thinking. At the time that department was chaired by Richard Paul, who was just becoming a prominent expert on that subject and who instituted an annual summer conference on critical thinking. Working with Paul, teaching those courses, and getting to know the many philosophers, informal logicians and argumentation theorists who routinely attended the conferences were all instrumental in my focusing on the nature of critical thinking and its relation to rationality. This was a very productive period for me, resulting eventually in the writing of *Educating Reason* (Siegel 1988). That publication, along with my experiences at Sonoma State, had a major influence on my subsequent career trajectory, and since then I've continued to participate in the critical thinking/informal logic/argumentation theory communities.

After three years at Sonoma State, I was still searching for a tenure-track appointment. Finally, I was offered and accepted a tenure-track associate professor of philosophy position in the department of humanities at Michigan Technological University on Michigan's Upper Peninsula. I enjoyed my brief time there, although I wasn't fond of the small size of the community, the remoteness of the location, or the 240 inches of snow (the average amount) that fell during my one winter there. That February I was lucky enough to interview for a position in philosophy at the University of Miami. Leaving those 240 inches of snow and arriving to find palm trees swaying in the sunny, 80 degree breeze, I had barely hit the tarmac before telling myself that "if they make me an offer, I'm coming!" They did, I did, and I've been at Miami ever since. It took seven years, but finally I found academic security and a congenial department in which to work and grow philosophically. (One indication of that congeniality: I was interviewing for a position in philosophy of science. During the interview, I was asked whether I intended to continue to work in philosophy of education. I answered that I hoped to continue to do that, though also to continue to work in philosophy of science and epistemology, and hoped that it wouldn't be a problem to do so. The collective reaction was that as long as I did the latter, it would be quite all right to pursue the former as well. I don't think that many departments at the time would have responded in that way. In the intervening 20+ years my colleagues have always been supportive, if occasionally uncomprehending, of my desire to continue to work in philosophy of education. I teach the subject only rarely – twice in the last decade – but have continued to write in it steadily.)

MIAMI

During my year at MTU I applied for and was awarded a John Dewey Senior Research Fellowship to write the book that became *Educating Reason*. But Miami wouldn't let me take the year immediately; they were worried that if I delayed for a year the Dean might revoke the line. So I went to Miami for one academic year before spending a fellowship year in Berkeley and then returning to Miami. My early years there were highly congenial: fine colleagues, the chance to teach graduate students, and a young but ambitious private university. Three years after arriving I was awarded tenure, and the following year promoted to full professor. Both *Relativism Refuted* and *Educating Reason* appeared in print around that time.

Eventually it was time for my first sabbatical, and in 1990-91 my family and I spent a very happy semester in Amsterdam, where I served as visiting professor at the University of Amsterdam and gave a seminar on argumentation, followed by several months in Yorkshire. While in Amsterdam I was encouraged by my new

Dutch friends and colleagues Jan Steutel, Wouter van Haaften and especially Ben Spiecker to apply for a recently advertised chair in philosophy of education at the University of Groningen. While I didn't get that position, the man who did, the eminent historian of education Jeroen Dekker, magnanimously invited me to visit on a regular basis. Thus began a five-year stretch as visiting professor of philosophy of education there; my family and I spent five consecutive, very enjoyable and enriching summers in and around Groningen.

Like many academics, I was horrified by the prospect of administration, and did my best to avoid it. Our department was fortunate to have had a string of able and conscientious chairs. However, in 1999, the then-chair became ill and passed away, and it was my turn, so, reluctantly, I became department chair. This proved to be an eye-opening experience. I had been to that point pretty much ignorant of the ways of academic administration. It didn't take long to appreciate the importance of Deanly support for departmental flourishing, and I spent a lot of time cultivating and maintaining Dean- and Provost-level support for the philosophy department. Happily, my colleagues were uniformly talented and productive scholars, and when changes in the senior administration brought to campus a new emphasis on climbing the rankings and becoming an increasingly powerful research university, philosophy was well placed to take advantage of university resources and ambitions, and we've been able over the last few years to bring several excellent philosophers to the department. Although quite time-consuming and distracting, I've found department-building engaging and satisfying (perhaps to my shame). Of course the administrative aspects of the job – the 'administrivia' – are not fun, but mostly tolerable and occasionally even useful.

Despite this distraction, I have managed to continue to do philosophy, including philosophy of education. In the '90s I became increasingly preoccupied with the efforts of others to draw deep epistemological lessons from the varied phenomena and related theory appearing under the label *multiculturalism*. In the end I wrote a series of papers on various aspects of multiculturalism, seeking to show that one can and should embrace the moral and political imperatives of multiculturalism, while rejecting the relativistic and other noxious epistemological views often thought to follow from it. The main issue here, I think, is this: it is a mistake to think that once the possibility of a 'transcendental,' Gods-eye point of view is given up, relativism or anything like it follows. It is correct that such a possibility should be rejected: there is no 'view from nowhere' – at least, none accessible to the likes of us. There is no alternative to judging from the perspective of the conceptual scheme we happen to occupy, and this will of course reflect our particular cultural/gendered/racial/etc. locations. Nevertheless, we can gain critical perspective on those judgments; we are not prisoners of our conceptual schemes, and this is sufficient to keep open the possibility of rational, objective judgment. A God's eye point of view is not available, but neither is it necessary for the satisfaction of these epistemological desiderata. (Siegel 1995a, 1997, Part 2, 1999, 2001, 2002, 2006, 2007)

Like much of my work, this bit of it straddles epistemology, philosophy of science, and philosophy of education; I continue to view these sub-disciplines of philosophy as interacting and mutually enhancing. They also converge on and inform questions usually thought to fall into the nearby domains of informal logic, argumentation theory, and science education. I also continue to work at the intersection of epistemology and philosophy of education. (Siegel 2005)

SOME CONCLUDING THOUGHTS

As should be clear by now, most of my publications have been aimed at audiences of philosophers and philosophers of education. Unlike many philosophers of education, I have spent relatively little time trying to speak to teachers, administrators, policy makers or non-philosophical educational researchers/scholars. So besides the *Phi Delta Kappan* article from long ago already mentioned, I should note that I've also written a bit about the educational dangers of high-stakes testing – an interest inspired by long friendships with Don and Barbara Arnstine and Jim McClellan, all three of whom were passionate about the subject and far more aware of the nature and extent of those dangers than I will likely ever be (Siegel 2004a), 'epistemological diversity' and educational research (Siegel 2006), and the field as a whole, for the interested non-specialist (Siegel 2007a).

While happy to have made some small efforts in that direction, I continue to think that philosophy of education is first and foremost a branch of philosophy, that it is most unfortunate that historically contingent events have conspired to locate its practitioners primarily in schools of education rather than departments of philosophy, and that philosophers of education would do well to focus more on advancing the intellectual agenda of the field and less on efforts to improve educational practice. (Of course these are not incompatible or even entirely distinguishable, and they are both noble and worthy enterprises.) In my ideal world philosophy of education would take its place among the other areas of applied philosophy researched and taught in departments of philosophy. This is as far as I can tell a minority opinion in the community of philosophers of education, and I am content, until my ideal world is realized, to be a member of the loyal opposition on the point.

REFERENCES

Siegel, H. (1981). Creationism, evolution, and education: The California fiasco. *Phi Delta Kappan*, *63*(2), 95-101.

Siegel, H. (1984). Goodmanian relativism. *The Monist*, *67*(3), 359-375.

Siegel, H. (1985). What is the question concerning the rationality of science? *Philosophy of Science*, *52*(4), 517-537.

Siegel, H. (1986). Relativism, truth and incoherence. *Synthese*, *68*(2), 225-259.

Siegel, H. (1987). *Relativism refuted: A critique of contemporary epistemological relativism*. Synthese Library, Volume 189. Dordrecht: D. Reidel Publishing Company.

Siegel, H. (1988). *Educating reason: Rationality, critical thinking, and education*. Philosophy of Education Research Library. New York and London: Routledge.

Siegel, H. (1992). Justification by balance. *Philosophy and Phenomenological Research*, *52*(1), March, pp. 27-46.

Siegel, H. (1995). Naturalized epistemology and 'first philosophy'. *Metaphilosophy*, *26*(1), 46-62.

Siegel, H., (1995a). What price inclusion? In A. Neiman (Ed.), *Philosophy of education 1995* (pp. 1-22). Urbana: Philosophy of Education Society.

Siegel, H. (1996). Naturalism and the abandonment of normativity. In W. O'Donohue & R. Kitchener (Eds.), *The philosophy of psychology* (pp. 4-18). London: Sage.

Siegel, H. (1996a). Instrumental rationality and naturalized philosophy of science. *Philosophy of Science, 63*(3), Supplement (PSA 1996 Proceedings, Part 1), pp. 116-124.

Siegel, H. (1997). *Rationality redeemed?: Further dialogues on an educational ideal.* New York: Routledge

Siegel, H. *(1999).* Multiculturalism and the possibility of transcultural educational and philosophical ideals. *Philosophy, 74,* 387-409.

Siegel, H. (2001). Incommensurability, rationality and relativism: In Science, culture, and science education. In P. Hoyningen-Huene & H. Sankey (Eds.), *Incommensurability and related matters* (pp. 207-224). Boston Studies in Philosophy of Science). Dordrecht: Kluwer.

Siegel, H. *(2002).* Multiculturalism, universalism, and science education: In search of common ground. *Science Education, 86*(6), 803-820.

Siegel, H. (2004). Relativism. In I. Niiniluoto, M. Sintonen, & J. Woleński (Eds.), *Handbook of epistemology* (pp. 747-780). Dordrecht: Kluwer.

Siegel, H. (2004a). What ought to matter in public schooling: Judgment, standards, and responsible accountability. In K. A. Sirotnik (Ed.), *Holding accountability accountable: What ought to matter in public education* (pp. 51-65). New York: Teachers College Press.

Siegel, H. (2004b). Rationality and judgment. *Metaphilosophy, 35*(5), 597-613.

Siegel, H. (2005). Truth, thinking, testimony and trust: Alvin Goldman on epistemology and education. *Philosophy and Phenomenological Research, LXXI*(2), 345-366.

Siegel, H. (2006). Epistemological diversity and educational research: Much ado about nothing much? *Educational Researcher, 35*(2), 1-10.

Siegel, H. (2007). Multiculturalism and rationality. *Theory and Research in Education 5*(2), 203-223.

Siegel, H. (2007a). The philosophy of education. *Encyclopaedia Britannica Online,* <http://search.eb.com/eb/article-9108550>; print version in press

Siegel, H. (Ed.). (2008). *Oxford handbook of philosophy of education* (in press).

Harvey Siegel
Department of Philosophy
University of Miami

JONAS F. SOLTIS

THE JOURNEY OF A TEACHER
On the Frontiers

THE BEGINNINGS

As far back as I can remember, I always wanted to be a teacher. As a youngster in elementary school, I remember frequently "playing school" with my neighborhood children and I was always the teacher. Later, during WW II, as a twelve year old member of our local boys group, I became their "master sergeant". Tired of playing cowboys and Indians, we decided "War" would be a better game to play. I decided we needed some "military learning" to play it well. So I taught my little group map reading skills, marching and arms drills, and because they wanted to play "paratroopers", I set out to teach them how to jump off a small box, land on their feet, and tumble forward to ease the impact of their landing. For graduation, I had them jump off the much higher chicken coop roof, land on an old car seat with springs and continue to tumble forward rolling up onto a standing position. Out of seven boys, only one sprained an ankle and one broke a finger. I then realized that teachers don't always succeed, but I still wanted to be a teacher.

Later on in secondary school, taking Latin my first year, I felt that the "memorization approach" was not only boring, but wasn't very successful at producing learning in our class. So that summer, I tried to produce a better teaching approach by imitating classic comics. For Caesar's Gallic Wars, I tried creating a comic strip of action figures with the Latin on the top of each picture and English at the bottom. I didn't get too far, but I showed my started project to my second year Latin teacher who said, "Very interesting!" and then proceeded to teach Cicero with the good old memorization approach. I realized then how hard it is for teachers to seek better learning strategies and change their ways, but I still wanted to become a teacher.

After high school, while in the Air Force, I served as an instructor and education counselor. That's where I found philosophy. I don't know how or why, but I found myself wondering almost daily about how we know the truth about anything. I got the bright idea to look up "truth" in the card catalogue at the library and started reading all the books that dealt with the concept of truth. My new found epistemological curiosity served me well in the years to come. After my discharge, I became a philosophy major and in 1956, after enjoying the mental challenges of philosophy as an undergraduate, I completed my B.A. degree with Distinction in Philosophy at the University of Connecticut. I then enrolled in a two year Master of Arts in Teaching Program at Wesleyan University to pursue my dream of becoming a teacher. (There weren't many jobs for philosophers in the classifieds

L.J. Waks (ed.), Leaders in Philosophy of Education: Intellectual Self Portraits, 229–240.
© 2008 *Sense Publishers. All rights reserved.*

in those days anyway.) My MAT major was history and I was being prepared for secondary school teaching in history and social studies. I practice taught in a suburban junior high school and interned full time for a half year in an inner city high school. I enjoyed all my courses in both history and education, but best of all was a seminar on John Dewey's education writings. I had studied Dewey as an undergraduate philosophy major at U Conn, but never was introduced to his educational thought. Upon graduation from Wesleyan, I applied for a number of secondary teaching posts, but also happened upon the notice of a position at a branch of the University of Connecticut as Registrar and Instructor in History and Philosophy. I applied and was offered the post. After teaching at the college level for two years, I was sure I wanted to continue on for a doctorate in philosophy of education so that I could continue teaching at that level and also continue my central interest in teaching and still be a philosopher. Luckily, I was recommended for a scholarship at the Harvard Graduate School of Education by one of my MAT Dewey seminar professors, Reginald Archambault, and was accepted.

PERSONAL FAVORITES

Books

Seeing, Knowing, and Believing, (1966)
An Introduction to the Analysis of Educational Concepts (1968)

Edited Book

Philosophy and Education: Eightieth Yearbook of the National Society for the Study of Education, 1981

Co-Authored Books

Approaches to Teaching (With Fenstermacher, 1985)
The Ethics of Teaching (With Strike, 1985)

Article

Education and the Concept of Knowledge, 1981

I didn't know much about the formal field of philosophy of education at that time, because, except for Dewey, all my work in philosophy had been in the traditional branches of that field, e.g. epistemology, metaphysics, ethics, aesthetics, etc. But having found Dewey's philosophical writings on education at Wesleyan, I was sure that advanced work in philosophy of education was the best way for me to combine my love of philosophy and fascination with epistemology with my desire to be an educator. I soon found out, however, that philosophy of education was not regarded by many if any academic philosophers as a legitimate sub field of their discipline.

REVOLUTIONS

But some things happened around mid century that helped to set philosophy of education on its path toward legitimacy. The whole field of education itself was often treated as a second class citizen in institutions of higher learning in the U.S. and a movement began in the whole field to attempt to gain legitimacy, rigor, and acceptance as a scholarly field. Most often the way chosen to attain this state was by using scientific method in educational research to test and ground assertions about the educational processes of teaching and learning. Social science paradigms were also used to study and investigate the social dimensions of schooling. In this way, the various academic disciplines were put to the task of legitimating educational scholarship. Philosophy, it seemed, would have to contribute in a similar way.

In fact, in 1964 after completing my Harvard degree and becoming an assistant professor at Teachers College, Columbia University, I found myself in a department then called The Foundations of Education but soon to be changed in name to the Department of Philosophy and the Social Sciences. My Teachers College department was already well along into the revolution taking place in schools of education that were now seeking to hire young scholars from various academic fields to use their disciplines to study and teach about various dimensions of the phenomenon of education.

But now back to my Harvard experience. In 1960 I arrived at the Harvard Graduate School of Education and Israel Scheffler was my advisor and mentor there. He was a young philosopher of education, but also had a joint appointment in the Harvard Philosophy Department where he taught a course in the relatively new field of philosophy of science and in doing so, he gained his stamp of legitimacy as a philosopher. As a doctoral student, I quickly found that the field of philosophy of education was also undergoing its own revolution at that time. The major way philosophy of education had been organized and taught in the 1940s and 1950s was by a "schools of philosophy" approach i.e. Realism, Idealism, Essentialism, Experimentalism et al. (See the NSSE Yearbooks, Philosophies of Education (Brubacher, 1942) and Modern Philosophies and Education (Brubacher, 1955).) Students were taught the basic beliefs regarding the nature of truth, reality, and the good life of each school of philosophy and were supposed to choose which position best suited them as a broad philosophical framework for thinking about the aims of education, the curriculum, the relation of school to society, et al. They were then expected to do their work in the real world of schooling guided by their chosen philosophy of education.

But around mid century, another revolution, this time in academic philosophy was taking place and it would eventually help a new generation of philosophers of education to challenge the "schools approach". In my own intellectual journey in philosophy, I mark it by Gilbert Ryle's publication of The Concept of Mind (1949), but there are other markers one can point to that signal a major change in academic philosophy, most notably the work of Ludwig Wittgenstein (1953). This so called analytic movement was marked by the avoidance of asking and answering the big questions of existence, purpose, being, truth, and the good, and directed at a careful examination of the language and concepts we use to make sense of the world.

Scheffler was trained as a first generation analytic philosopher and had already published *The Language of Education* (1960) when I arrived at Harvard. At this time, he was teaching a course called Philosophy of Education that was really about how we use the term knowledge and what we mean by various and different kinds of knowledge, e.g. facts, skills, theories, values, etc. that soon was to become his book, *The Conditions of Knowledge* (1965). He became recognized as one of the leaders in the United States of the analytic movement in philosophy of education that included in its ranks such philosophers as Paul Komisar, James McClellan, Robert Ennis, and B.O. Smith. R.S. Peters, a well known and respected philosopher of education at the University of London in England, played much the same role there. Scheffler invited Peters to teach for a year at Harvard and I had the opportunity to take a seminar with him on the topic, soon to be his book, *Ethics and Education* (1966). At that time he was probably best known for his paper, "Must an Educator Have an Aim?" (1959). Thus I was totally immersed in the analytic approach to philosophy of education at its earliest beginnings.

In fact, I used much of the analytic approach in my dissertation later to become my first book, *Seeing, Knowing, and Believing: A Study in the Language of Visual Perception* (1966). In it, I was able to blend my interest in epistemology with my concerns regarding teaching and learning. Perception, sense data, the given, etc. was where epistemologists most often began when questioning the basis for empirical knowledge. I began my book by trying to show how what we have learned and believe enters into our visual perceptions of the world not just as sense data or the given, but as enhancements to our seeing. For example, someone who has studied Greek culture sees so much more when viewing an ancient urn in a museum than the young child on a field trip who sees only an old jug. A teacher brings a globe into a Kindergarten classroom. The children see a multi colored ball that would roll if put on the floor. The teacher sees the earth and its many features. Soon the children will see the globe as she does as they learn many things about this representation of the earth. My book also treated the phenomena of misperception, illusions, how false beliefs affect perceptions, et al. Never did I get to solve 'the Problem of Truth,' however.

I was also fortunate at Harvard with my MAT in history to serve as course assistant to Visiting Professor Lawrence Cremin in his Harvard summer session course in the history of U.S. education. He had taught and developed this course at Teachers College, Columbia University and was putting the finishing touches on it for publication as a book, *The Transformation of the Schools* (1961), which was a history of the progressive education movement in the United States and won the Bancroft prize in history in 1962. This experience gave me another perspective on the history of the field of philosophy of education and brought me back to my fascination with Dewey and his legacy in the real world of schooling. One thing happened that summer that I shall always remember. Cremin was a brilliant lecturer and always asked his doctoral students to give one of the lectures in his classes to help them prepare to be teachers themselves. So he asked me if I wanted to give a lecture and I, realizing not only his brilliance, but that I was on sabbatical from history while studying philosophy said, "Sorry, I don't think I can do it anywhere near as well as you".

THE IDEA OF FRONTIERS

After completing my course work at Harvard, I went back to the Wesleyan MAT program to teach philosophy of education for two years while finishing my dissertation and then was invited by Cremin to apply for the post of philosopher of education at Teachers College. I got the job and remember asking Cremin, who was then head of the foundations department, what courses I would be expected to teach beside the basic introductory course in philosophy of education. He replied, "What courses would you like to teach?" I said that I hadn't looked in the catalogue to see what courses Teachers College offered in philosophy of education and he said, "Good. This is Teachers College, the leading graduate school of education in the world. Our task is to be at the frontiers of our fields and to develop courses and books that educators need today or will need tomorrow and not just initiate them into yesterday's writings". "Wow!" I felt myself saying. Then he asked, remembering my Harvard summer school reluctance to give a lecture, "But can you teach?" I blushed and said, "Yes, I've been doing it since I was a kid". I was given a very light course load with the expectation that I would eventually increase it to a standard load by inventing and developing new courses. It was a demanding yet exhilarating experience and through the years many of my publications came out of the courses I developed and taught at Teachers College.

One of the first things I did, imitating Scheffler, was to go to the graduate school philosophy department at Columbia and talk to the chairperson about the possibility of my doing a joint Teachers College/Philosophy Department course on John Dewey. I couldn't believe that at Columbia where Dewey spent most of his academic career after Chicago and earned his reputation as one of America's foremost philosophers that there was no course on Dewey's philosophy in either the Foundations or Philosophy departments. I was granted permission to offer a course on Dewey that every other year changed its focus to a different part of Dewey's corpus that spoke to one of the sub fields of philosophy, e.g. social philosophy, aesthetics, ethics, etc. for philosophy graduate students. I then used alternate years to teach a seminar on his work in philosophy of education for Teachers College students that I was pleased that some of my previous graduate students in the philosophy department came over to take. I remember myself having spent a whole semester of independent study reading Dewey's major works as an undergraduate without ever being asked to read in his philosophy of education and I was pleased to be able to fill that gap for these graduate students in philosophy. Out of my many years of teaching this course came my entry on John Dewey in The Encyclopedia of Education (1971), and I would like to think, my election to the presidency of The John Dewey Society in 1990.

But my first really new course at TC was an examination of the newer work in analytic philosophy of education. In a short time I eased back on using mostly the work of other contemporary analytic philosophers because their work was often over the heads of people who wanted to be educational practitioners and not philosophers. So I decided to develop my own way of teaching the skills of analysis to my students most of whom would never become philosophers of education, but would be teachers, administrators, curriculum specialists, et al. I firmly believed that learning analytic thinking skills would serve them well in whatever capacity they took on as educators. My second book came out of that course and was called *An Introduction to the Analysis of Educational Concepts* (1968). It was translated into German in 1971 and Chinese in 1995.

In it and even more fully in the second edition (1978, reprinted in 1985), I tried to teach not the results of various analyses of different educational concepts by other philosophers, but rather, the skills of doing analysis itself. So the book contained many exercises and reflections on three particular forms of analysis. I invented a schema to identify and name what I called the generic type, differentiation type, and conditions type analysis and visually, as well as verbally, described the steps one needed to take to be successful at each type of analysis. In my Introduction to the book, I noted that Dewey once said, there is all the difference in the world between thinking and thought. Thinking is an activity, a vital process full of adventure and excitement; thought is the end of this process. It is the end of thinking. I knew that too often students are asked to fill their baskets with the thoughts of others to be stored and used (if at all) in the future. They seldom engaged in the rigor and excitement of the thinking process itself. I decided that my book should invite students to engage in the adventure of thinking and developing the skills of conceptual analysis so they could begin and continue to think about their craft in philosophically appropriate ways.

For philosophy of education majors, I next developed a course, Contemporary Philosophy of Education, to give them a sense of the history of the late 19th and early 20th century development of the field. No book came out of this, but lots of good background for my Philosophy of Education Society presidential address, "Philosophy of Education: Retrospect and Prospect" (1976), my Introduction to the NSSE Yearbook, Philosophy and Education (1981), and a special issue of the Teachers College Record, Philosophy of Education since Mid-Century (1979) that was also published as a book by Teachers College Press (1981a).

Basically, by this time in my career during the 1970s, I had come to the conclusion that the field of philosophy of education had evolved sufficiently in its new directions to be ready for some cohesive overview of it to be conceived, constructed, and presented to educators. Fortunately, I had the opportunity to do just that when I was asked to serve as the editor of a new NSSE yearbook on philosophy of education continuing the tradition of doing such yearbooks as was done in 1942 and 1955. I decided to title my NSSE yearbook not Philosophy of Education, but *Philosophy and Education* (1981b) because I wanted to offer a new way to look at how philosophy and education were related. Besides chapters in the yearbook demonstrating philosophical thought about curriculum and teaching, there were other chapters showing how the sub fields of philosophy could illuminate some educational topics of genuine interest to practicing educators. I chose epistemology for myself and recruited others to do chapters in the sub areas of aesthetics, logic, ethics, social philosophy, philosophy of science, and metaphysics. Harry Broudy, at that time highly respected philosophy of education elder wrote the opening chapter, "Between the Yearbooks" (pp. 13-35) providing a very good overview of the ways in which the field changed and evolved in the 40s, 50s, 60s, and 70s.

Returning now to my description of my development of new courses at Teachers College, I turned to philosophy of science. Seeing the field of educational research seeking to become more legitimate by using the methods and techniques of science and the social sciences and having taken Scheffler's course in philosophy of science at Harvard, I thought a course in Philosophy of Science and Educational Research would be useful to the many doctoral students in various departments at Teachers College. Fortunately I received a U.S.O.E. post doctoral fellowship in educational research for a free year of study for that project and spent most of my time sitting in on relevant graduate courses at Columbia's Graduate School of Arts and Sciences such as Nagel's philosophy of science, Barber's philosophy of social science, Harris' history of anthropological thought, and Robert K. Merton's sociology and then finished the year at the Center for Behavioral Sciences at Palo Alto. I returned to Teachers College having mapped out the outlines of my new course determined over the next three to five years to do a book in this new field.

A NEW WAY TO TEACH

But while I continued to develop and teach the course, an event happened that would change the course of my writing plans and even changed the way to teach philosophy of education to pre and in service teachers. I had been on the search committee for a new director for Teachers College Press and we selected Tom Rotell whom I got to know as an informal advisor to the Press. One day he asked me why the Press had no basic textbook in philosophy of education and I replied that the field was in transition and that there was no single approach that most would take as the way to teach introductory philosophy of education. Moreover, I reported that many professors were using multiple books and anthologies of recent work to teach such a course and that a single textbook for all seemed to go against the grain of the reality of the field at that time.

The incident bothered me and nagged me for weeks and I finally said to myself there ought to be a way to overcome the complexity of diverse approaches being used and taught in the field and so I set myself to try to move to the next frontier by inventing a new way to teach philosophy of education. Diversity wasn't the only problem, however. In trying to become more scholarly and academic, the writing in philosophy of education was often more abstract and removed from the world of practice than most pre service teachers could handle. Too often, we professors of philosophy of education heard from our students that our theory and their practice didn't connect.

So I thought if nothing else, a basic text in philosophy of education needed to be written in a style suitable for the neophyte and not, as most were at this time, attempts to make the field more scholarly and academic. Moreover, I felt that the text ought to aim directly and engagingly at getting students to think about their everyday work as teachers from various philosophical perspectives rather than aim at them learning various theories and then applying them to practice in the future. And finally, I thought that short multiple texts so much in vogue at the time would be better than a single heavy text so that some or all of them could be used in a basic course.

So I took the four "common places" of education i.e. teaching, learning, curriculum, and school and society and made each a focal point of one of four books that later were titled: Approaches to Teaching (1986), Perspectives on Learning (1985), Curriculum and Aims (1986), and School and Society (1985) and I called the set the Thinking About Education series. I took my idea to Tom Rotell at the Press and he said, "Go for it!"

I realized then that it was going to be an impossible project for one person and that there were good people in the field who knew one of these areas better than I did so I set out to recruit four co-authors to work with me on the series who were willing to use the down to earth format/style I had envisioned and would demonstrate for them how I expected our book(s) to get pre and in service educators to think about their practice. I was fortunate to recruit Gary Fenstermacher for the teaching volume, Denis Phillips for learning, Decker Walker for curriculum, and Walter Feinberg for school and society. As I began my work with each co-author, I laid out a draft first chapter for our book that would demonstrate the kind of down to earth style I was looking for and then we each began to sketch out the main ideas we wanted to treat in our book. We shared the writing and rewriting and I served as overall final editor trying to make the series complementary and cohesive as a set of short related texts.

In the teaching book, Fenstermacher and I identified, named, and described via vignettes three distinct approaches teachers use. We called them the executive, the therapist (later the facilitator), and the liberationist approaches. The executive was more of a managerial type concerned with the production of learning and its assessment. The therapist/facilitator was more concerned with the individual student and his/her development. And the liberationist was focused on freeing the mind of ignorance and false beliefs via the study of the liberal arts and sciences. Walker and I dealt with basic problematic areas in curriculum such as the aims of education, the structure of subject matter, reform, changes in curriculum, the idea of a general education, and meaningful learning experiences, etc.

In School and Society, Feinberg and I examined how schools function as socializing agents. We identified three major ways and called them the functionalist, the conflict theorist, and the interpretivist approaches. The functionalist socialized students to fit in and function as a productive member of their society. The conflict theorist saw society as a conflict of classes with students being taught their place in society via the hidden curriculum. And the interpretivist saw schooling primarily as bringing students into a culture of shared meanings and shared norms.

In the learning book, Phillips and I treated various learning theories, i.e. classical theories, behaviorism, Gestalt, Piagetian developmental theory, cognitive and disciplinary strategies, and modern cognitive science based theories asking our readers to use them to make sense of various concrete examples of learning in actual school based activities in classrooms. In all the books, we each committed ourselves to engage our readers in philosophical thinking about actual situations in each of these various dimensions of education.

THE ETHICS FRONTIER AND THE BIRTH OF CASE STUDIES

Meanwhile in 1981, I received an invitation from the Hastings Center Institute of Society, Ethics, and the Life Sciences to do the keynote address for a conference they were planning on the place of ethics in teacher education. I responded saying I'd be happy to attend the conference, but was afraid I had nothing to say because to the best of my knowledge little if anything was being taught anywhere in U.S. colleges of education about the ethics of teaching. As evidence for the truth of this, I went to our library and took 100 catalogues, two from each state, one private and one public off the shelf to examine to see if there were any courses in education with ethics in their title or course description. I found three out of 100!

I attended the conference, gave this bad news to the philosophers of education in attendance and in small groups we turned this revelation to thoughts and discussions about how we could bring ethics to the education of educators. There I met an old acquaintance, Kenneth Strike, whose writings on ethical issues on education were well known and highly respected. Ken was teaching at Cornell and we agreed that we would go back to our colleges and try to develop a course in the ethics of teaching sharing together what we might learn in our individual efforts and hopefully write a textbook on the subject. We also agreed that the course should not be a teaching of traditional ethical theories book, but one that would speak meaningfully about the kinds of ethical problems that arise in schools. Upon my return to Teachers College, I went to Tom Rotell and told him I would like to expand my *Thinking About Education* series to five books, but there was a problem. He asked what it was. I said, "I'd like to include a textbook in the series for which there are no courses on the subject". I explained what Strike and I were about and he said, "Go for it!"

As I approached my first attempt to put together a new course on the ethics of teaching, I remembered that one of the ways that business schools taught MBA candidates to think about various business problems bringing in appropriate ideas and theories was via case studies. I thought this also might be a promising way to bring ethical theory down to earth in the style I was developing for the series. I wondered if anyone used case studies extensively in philosophy of education courses and so I sampled a number of textbooks and found little or no evidence that this had been done even though I did find some uses of case methods in doctoral dissertations in physical education and home economics in the 30s and 40s.

When I developed the first case studies in my new ethics course, I saw immediately the value of this approach in starting with a real world situation/dilemma and then bringing various philosophical distinctions, theories, and ideas to help people deal with their resolution of the situation. In that way, theory was immediately and meaningfully linked to practice. I then took my idea of starting each chapter with cases to my four co-authors of the *Thinking about Education* series' books. I wrote some sample cases for each book and told them that this was the style that I would like us all to adopt to reach practitioners. They were all enthusiastic and so the case studies approach to the *Thinking about Education* series was launched. As of this writing well over a million copies have been sold in English and over half a million in translations in German, Spanish, Norwegian, Korean, Japanese, and Chinese. The five books in English are now in their fourth editions (2004). Not long after the series was published, Ken Strike invited me to coauthor with him and his colleague, Emil Haller, a book called The Ethics of Educational Administration (1988, 1998, 2005) that followed the series style and format and now is in its third edition. In it we treated such topics as equal educational opportunity, honesty, integrity, multicultural/racial diversity, personal liberty, freedom of expression, due process, assessment and evaluation, etc. using the case study approach.

In my last years at Teachers College I was asked to teach a seminar for the Klingenstein Foundation special program for independent school heads. One thing I always included in it even though I changed other things was the ethics of teaching and the ethics of school administration. One of the seminar participants, Bongsoon Zubay, headmistress of the Berkeley Carroll School, found herself excited when she came up with the idea of engaging her whole school in a program aimed at raising ethical awareness and moral reflection. She contacted me and asked if I would serve as a consultant to help her and her staff explore ways to do that. I agreed and we knew early on that we not only had to convince the staff that ethics should have a place in the school, but more importantly we had to convince the parents that we were not teaching "religion" or taking their place in instilling ethical values in their children. To get the staff involved, we got them together with some students and gave them some case studies to discuss on such topics as cheating, punishment, due process, equal treatment of students, parents' rights, etc. When the session was over and Zubay consulted with her staff, she found them to be enthusiastic about making ethics a year long theme for all grades (K-12) and sharing their experiences with each other in general assemblies.

Now the parents; I was a little nervous being the main speaker at parents' night introducing the idea of raising ethical awareness in the whole school as the year's pervasive theme. But I decided that rather than defend such a practice abstractly, I'd take a page from my series style and I began my talk as I stood at the blackboard by asking the parents to help me compile a list of ethical values and moral characteristics that they as parents hoped their children would acquire as they grew up to become educated adults. The list grew by leaps and bounds. We filled two blackboards with such things as honest, kind, generous, respectful of others, just, fair, et al. As we began to run out of steam and space, I asked them if there were any values that any of them thought should be removed because that value doesn't fit with their religious views or their conception of what an ethical

238

person is. There was silence. I told the parents that it was these sorts of values that we hoped to emphasize in the various activities planned for the whole school effort that year. The program was so successful that it was extended for two additional years. When it was over, Zubay asked me if we could write a book describing the three year project so that others in either independent or public schools might consider doing a project like it and base it on the many case studies that were created for discussion during that period by teachers, administrators, students, and parents. We did it and the book was titled, *Creating the Ethical School: A Book of Case Studies* (2005).

JOURNEY'S END?

Finally, I offer one last memory. In 1979 when I was giving my inaugural lecture as the newly appointed William Heard Kilpatrick Professor of Philosophy and Education at Teachers College, Lawrence Cremin, then the President of TC introduced me. My lecture was on "Education and the Concept of Knowledge" later to be reworked and published as my chapter by the same name in the 1981 NSSE yearbook. When I finished to a nice round of applause, Cremin came over to me and whispered, "Boy, you sure can teach!" I knew he meant "lecture", but I also knew that I had some pretty good ideas about what teaching really is.

So that's pretty much the rendering of my journey in philosophy of education in the 20th century with even a few more books and new editions coming out here in the early 21st century. I also continue to serve as Series Editor for the Teachers College Press' *Advances in Educational Thought* series. Now I leave it to the new generation of philosophers of education and readers of this book to develop the field in the 21st century in positive directions. My efforts at it in my lifetime engaged me in a wonderful teaching and learning journey on many frontiers. Remember, at the beginning of this essay I said I always wanted to be a teacher and now it seems even in my retirement through my various books, I'm still teaching! I am grateful for the opportunity to have lived the life of a teacher and a philosopher of education.

BIBLIOGRAPHY

Broudy, H. S. (1981). Between the yearbooks. In J. F. Soltis (Ed.), *Philosophy and education: Eightieth yearbook of the National Society for the Study of Education* (pp. 13-35). Chicago, IL: University of Chicago Press.

Brubacher, J. S. (Ed.). (1942). *Philosophies of education: Forty-first yearbook of the National Society for the Study of Education, Part I.* Chicago, IL: University of Chicago Press.

Brubacher, J. S. (Ed.). (1955). *Modern philosophies and education: Fifty-fourth yearbook of the National Society for the Study of Education, Part I.* Chicago, IL: University of Chicago Press.

Cremin, L. A. (1961, 1962, 1964). *The transformation of the schools: A history of the progressive education movement.* New York, NY: Knopf.

Feinberg, W. & Soltis, J. F. (1985, 1992 (2nd ed.), 1998 (3rd ed.), 2004 (4th ed.)). *School and society.* New York, NY: Teachers College Press.

Fenstermacher, G. & Soltis, J. F. (1985, 1992 (2nd ed.), 1998 (3rd ed.), 2004 (4th ed.)). *Approaches to teaching.* New York, NY: Teacher College Press.

Peters, R. S. (1959). Must an educator have an aim? In R. S. Peters (Ed.), *Authority, responsibility and education.* London: George Allen and Unwin Ltd.

Peters, R. S. (1966) . *Ethics and education.* London: George Allen and Unwin Ltd.

Phillips, D. C. & Soltis, J. F. (1985, 1992 (2nd ed.), 1998 (3rd ed.), 2004 (4th ed.)). *Perspectives on learning.* New York, NY: Teachers College Press.

Ryle, G. (1949). *The concept of mind.* London: Hutchinson.

Scheffler, I. (1960). *The language of education.* Springfield, IL: C. C. Thomas.

Scheffler, I. (1965). *The conditions of knowledge.* Glenview, IL: Scott, Foresman.

Soltis, J. F. (1966). *Seeing, knowing and believing: A study in the language of visual perception.* London: George Allen and Unwin Ltd. and Reading, MA: Addison-Wesley Publishing Co.

Soltis, J. F. (1968, 1978 (2nd ed.)). *An introduction to the analysis of educational concepts.* Reading, MA: Addison-Wesley Publishing Co. Reprinted (1985), Lanham, MD: University Press of America. German translation (1971), Dusseldorf: Pedagogisher Verlag Schwaan. Chinese translation (1995), Taipei, Taiwan: Wu-nan Book Co. Ltd.

Soltis, J. F. (1971). John Dewey. In L. C. Deighton, *The encyclopedia of education.* New York, NY: Macmillan.

Soltis, J. F. (1975). Philosopy of education: Retrospect and prospect. In R. Pratte (Ed.), *Philosophy of Education 1976.* Urbana, IL: The Philosophy of Education Society and the University of Illinois Press.

Soltis, J. F. (Ed.). (1979). Philosophy of education since mid century. *Teachers College Record,* 81(2).

Soltis, J. F. (Ed.). (1981a). *Philosophy of education since mid-century.* New York, NY: Teachers College Press.

Soltis, J. F. (1981b). Introduction. In J. F. Soltis (Ed.), *Philosophy and education: Eightieth yearbook of the National Society for the Study of Education, Part I.* Chicago, IL: University of Chicago Press.

Soltis, J. F. (1981c). Education and the concept of knowledge. In J. F. Soltis (Ed.), *Philosophy and education: Eightieth yearbook of the National Society for the Study of Education, Part I.* Chicago, IL: University of Chicago Press.

Strike, K. A. & Soltis, J. F. (1985, 1992 (2nd ed.), 1998 (3rd ed.), 2004 (4th ed.)). *The ethics of teaching.* New York, NY: Teachers College Press.

Strike, K. A., Haller, E. and Soltis, J. F. (1988, 1998 (2nd ed.), 2005 (3rd ed.). *The ethics of school administration.* New York, NY: Teachers College Press.

Walker, D. F. & Soltis, J. F. (1986, 1992 (2nd ed.), 1998 (3rd ed.), 2004 (4th ed.). *Curriculum and aims.* New York, NY: Teachers College Press.

Wittgenstein, L. (1953). *Philosophical investigations.* New York, NY: Macmillan.

Zubay, B. & Soltis, J. F. (2005). *Creating the ethical school.* New York, NY: Teachers College Press.

Jonas F. Soltis
William Heard Kilpatrick Professor Emeritus of Philosophy and Education,
Teachers College, Columbia University

KENNETH A. STRIKE

CONFESSIONS OF A SUBLIMATED CLERIC

I often advise graduate students that a thesis is best written twice, once from beginning to end and once from end to beginning. I will begin by taking my own advice. As I look over my career several things stand out:

1. Intellectually my career feels more like a series of (mostly) fortuitous accidents than a planned research program. Few of my intellectual twists and turns were planned. At the same time, I have had some enduring commitments that have helped me to deal with the vicissitudes of fortune productively, and my work has threads that weave through it.

2. To do philosophy of education well one must stay grounded in both philosophy and in education. Philosophers need frequently to ask themselves, "Is the problem I am working on a real problem? And "Would people working in education view this problem as a problem?" If the answer to these questions is "No" this is not a decisive fact about what one is doing, but it should be worrisome. One of the fortuitous accidents that shaped my thinking was that at one point in my career I was dragooned into teaching education law. I found that not only did I enjoy this, but that looking at a problem through both a legal and a philosophical lens was intellectually stimulating and helped to keep me grounded. Also my closest colleagues have not been philosophers. I have profited greatly from listening to lawyers, economists and sociologists about issues of mutual interest. And I have discovered the problems that have most engaged me in their treatment of educational issues.

3. I remain an unrepentant egalitarian liberal. Among the reasons are that liberalism has, more than other traditions, been open enough to adapt to circumstances and to learn from its critics. The ideologies of the right, I think to be largely excuses for plutocracy. I have a better opinion of the left, particularly the critical theory of people such as Habermas and Young, but I find that much of what passes for leftist scholarship these days condemns the left to obscurity and irrelevance.

4. Community is important and is all too often not naturally occurring. This is true both for the intellectual life of a scholar and for the education of children.

Now let's begin at the beginning.

COLLEGE AND GRADUATE SCHOOL

I began my undergraduate experience in 1961 at Wheaton College with the expectation that I was going to be a clergyman. This aspiration disappeared as I discovered that the convictions of the conservative denomination in which I was

L.J. Waks (ed.), Leaders in Philosophy of Education: Intellectual Self Portraits, 241–249.

raised were doubtful. I majored in philosophy because someone suggested that it was a suitable background for theological studies. I came quickly to love it. Off to graduate school at Northwestern (1965).

I did not go to Northwestern to study philosophy of education. I had seen an ad for a joint program in philosophy and philosophy of education and had mentioned in my application that I might be interested in this. When I showed up I found that the generous financial package I had accepted was predicated on my participation in this joint program. I was advised that the program was largely in the philosophy department and that such work as I might be expected to do in education would be modest and painless. Both of these turned out to be true. In addition the study of education helped to sublimate my clerical aspirations.

PERSONAL FAVORITES

On the expressive potential of behaviorist language (1974).

Toward a Moral Theory of Desegregation (1981).

Educational Policy and the Just Society (1982).

Professionalism, democracy and discursive communities: Normative reflections on restructuring (1993).

On the construction of public speech: Pluralism and public reason (1994).

Centralized goal formation and systemic reform: Reflections on liberty, localism and pluralism (1997).

Schools as Communities: Four Metaphors, Three Models, and a Dilemma or Two (2000).

Community, the Missing Element of School Reform: Why Schools Should be More Like Congregations than Banks (2004).

Small Schools, Size or Community? (2007).

Ethical Leadership in Schools: Creating Community in an Environment of Accountability(2007).

Schools as Communities: A Third Way Toward School Reform (forthcoming).

Northwestern's philosophy department was dominated by people whose interests were in continental philosophy. I read Sartre, Heidegger, and Husserl. While I did fine, I found this genre of literature willfully obscure and not particularly illuminating – although I doubt I could have said what it was that I wanted illuminated. However, Northwestern had recently hired Henry Veatch, a well established Aristotle scholar, and three young "analytic" philosophers. These people along with Joe Park who was then the philosopher of education in the school of education (and who was a wise and kind man to whom I will always be grateful) were my mentors. One of the young philosophers was Hugh Petrie who had an interest in philosophy of education. He provided a useful model of how it could be done responsibly and well. Veatch helped me to discover that I was an Aristotelian by temperament if not always by conviction.

Apparently I am viewed by some as an analytic philosopher. I have never thought of myself in this way. I found the analytic preoccupation with language interesting, but constraining, and the set of papers in philosophy of education that emphasized the analysis of concepts such as "teach" or "learn" tedious. From Wittgenstein I learned to respect the contingency of language, but the uses to which ordinary language philosophy were put in education did not seem to capture what the latter Wittgenstein was actually about. The best expression of my (somewhat) Wittgensteinian view of language is a paper in *AERJ* entitled "On the expressive potential of behaviorist language" where the emphasis is not on the analysis of concepts, but on what can and cannot be said with the vocabulary of behaviorist psychology. Much of import about human life cannot be said. Or so I argued. What can and cannot be said with a particular vocabulary and how languages structure problems and direct one's theoretical gaze are enduring concerns for me.

Northwestern, at the time, had no one who focused on political philosophy or ethics and offered no courses that emphasized these areas. These enterprises had been killed off in much of Anglo American philosophy by logical positivism. As I moved through my graduate career, I found that I was not really very pleased with either the continental philosophy or the analytic philosophy that was available. I wanted something with more human significance.

I resolved this dilemma first by taking my studies in philosophy of education more seriously than I had expected to and by emphasizing the philosophy of the social sciences. These projects seemed both stimulating and of human significance. I did, however, find much of the literature in philosophy of education intellectually depressing. At the time philosophy of education was organized into clubs with names like "pragmatism" and "realism." It seemed like half the papers in *Educational Theory* had (or could have had) titles like "The Implications of the philosophy of Philosopher P for education" and at least half the members of the profession seemed to think that the writings of John Dewey were divinely inspired. (Yes, there is a bit of hyperbole in this.)

WISCONSIN

I left graduate school with what I think was a good intellectual tool kit – I think my training in the philosophy of the social and behavioral sciences has served me well in interacting with empirical research in education and my study of analytic philosophy had sharpened my mind- but without much intellectual direction. My first job was at the University of Wisconsin where I had a joint appointment in Philosophy and Educational Policy Studies. At the time this seemed like my dream job. Its importance, however, was that I found an intellectual direction there. I started in 1968. The student revolution had not reached Northwestern, but it was in full bloom at Wisconsin. Students regularly claimed that the educational system was oppressive and called on me to either agree or to rebut the charge. Not only that, they pressed me to justify my own privilege and position. In my very first class (a section of Introduction to Philosophy with about 250 students) a young man asked me if I intended to lecture. I said I thought I might, but asked him what else we might do. His response was that "we" want to vote on the curriculum. (The consent of his classmates did not seem required for this announcement.) I asked how one might structure such a vote. He said that I would have to tell them enough about philosophy so that they could vote intelligently. Opening my note book, I said, "Fine. It will take about a semester." He looked about, noted a few smirks appearing on his peer's faces, and stormed out, slamming the door. Wisconsin was often like this.

A second factor was the chair of the philosophy department, a brilliant man with a reputation for justice untempered by mercy. One day he called me and announced that since I was a philosopher of education I obviously knew something about political philosophy. Hence I was going to help prepare and grade the part of the qualifying exam that dealt with political philosophy and ethics. I did not feel it was prudent to disabuse him. Hence a crash course in political philosophy.

The result of the Wisconsin environment and my rapid self tutoring in political philosophy was that I found a set of problems that engaged me and a body of literature that provided the tools to engage these problems. Some of my early writing emphasizes questions of intellectual liberty and authority – the kinds of questions Wisconsin students regularly pressed on me. There was a particularly helpful interaction between some of J.S. Mill's arguments about intellectual liberty and some views of Kuhn and Toulmin and I began to have some useful ideas about the ways in which "received ideas" have authority in education that were much influenced by Kuhn's views on the role of paradigms in the education of scientists. My first paper dealing with legitimate authority was "Philosophical reflections on *Tinker v. Des Moines*" in which these themes are developed. They come to full flower in my second book, *Liberty and Learning*. Prior to this engagement with political theory, I had been mining my thesis for articles. I dropped this effort (not a good idea for career building). Most of my subsequent work has been focused on questions of legitimate authority, equality of opportunity, and religious liberty. I have written on student rights, desegregation, affirmative action, school finance, and democracy in schools. My first book, *Educational Policy and the Just Society,* provided an early and somewhat integrated statement of my views on some of these issues that was rooted in my version of egalitarian liberalism. This book was deeply informed by Rawls's *A Theory of Justice.*

Much of its argument I would still stand by. I am unrepentant about my commitment to egalitarian liberalism. In retrospect, however, what I find of interest about this book is that it has the seeds of some ideas that have become more important in my recent work. There I argued that the schools of liberal democracies, because of their commitment to neutrality among conceptions of the good, had difficulty "educating" because (as I would now say it) a coherent view of a good education requires a commitment to at least a partial conception of human flourishing. This idea (which expresses a latent Aristotelianism) has morphed into the claim that good education needs schools that are coherent communities. In one recent work, "Schools as Communities: Four Metaphors, Three Models, and a Dilemma or Two," I have explored several metaphors for schools as communities: families, guilds, polities, and congregations. I have also explored a dilemma to which this emphasis on community leads. Insofar as the coherence and cohesiveness of a school community is linked to a substantive conception of what is educationally worthwhile, a school will not be neutral among competing conceptions of the good; nor can it be fully inclusive. This dilemma is developed and explored in two papers: "Can schools be communities? The tension between shared values and inclusion" (1999), and "Is Liberal Education Illiberal?" (2004). The idea that schools should be democratic communities is developed in "Liberty, democracy, and community: Legitimacy in public education" (2003). If there is a solution to this dilemma it is to have schools that are committed to both the core values of liberal learning and to building democratic communities.

I have also done a fair amount of work on school reform. My interests in this area have generally been to expose and discuss the moral and political norms implicit in various proposals for school reform. In "Professionalism, democracy and discursive communities: Normative reflections on restructuring" (1993) I worry about the undemocratic potential of the claims that teaching is a profession, and in "Centralized goal formation and systemic reform: Reflections on liberty, localism and pluralism" (1997) I worry about the illiberal potential in systemic reform. These papers along with "On the construction of public speech: Pluralism and public reason" (1994) are also steps in the development of a democratic conception of school community.

I currently teach a class entitled Democracy and Educational Policy. This class takes a tour through major issues of educational policy since *Brown V. Board of Education*. I try to appraise them through the lens of what I call constitutional essentials – the constitutive principles of liberal democracy – liberty, equality, democracy. I end with an appraisal of *No Child Left Behind* and argue that its central problem stems from its roots in *A Nation at Risk*. *ANAR* launched the standards movement and focused the attention of policy makers on educational productivity and human capital formation. It also moved attention away from the issues of inequality, the policy focus that had

FAVORITES BY OTHER AUTHORS

Coleman, J. S. (1974). Youth: Transition to adulthood. Chicago, IL: University of Chicago Press.

Kuhn, T. (1970). The Structure of Scientific Revolutions. Chicago: University of Chicago Press.

MacIntyre, A. (1981). After virtue. Notre Dame, IN: University of Notre Dame Press.

Mill, J. S. (1859/1956). On Liberty. New York: The Bobbs-Merrill Company, inc.

Rawls, J. (1971). A Theory of Justice. Cambridge, MA: Harvard University Press.

Rawls, J. (1993). Political Liberalism. New York: Columbia University Press.

dominated education since *Brown*. (In "Toward a moral theory of desegregation" (1981) I argue that the disassociation of educational productivity from equality begins in judicial interpretations of *Brown* that see desegregation concerned with equal citizenship more than with equal opportunity. Among other things this interpretation permits significant racial isolation in American schools so long as the racial imbalance is *de facto* rather than *de jure* and regardless of the consequence of racial isolation for the education of minority children. This decoupling of educational productivity from social equality is expressed by *NCLB's* emphasis on school-only solutions to achievement gaps (to which inequality has been reduced) and goes a long way towards explaining why current efforts at school reform are unlikely to succeed at either raising achievement or closing achievement gaps.

CORNELL

I left Wisconsin in 1971 to take a position in the Department of Education at Cornell. I found this a productive move. Cornell's department was small, and I had a number of good colleagues and friends in areas such as economics, sociology, and science education who helped expand my intellectual horizons (as well as teaching me to canoe, fish, and enjoy martinis). Somewhere during the 29 years I spent at Cornell, I developed my interest in the idea of community. I would reconstruct the roots of this interest as follows: One of the works that has been most important to my intellectual life was Rawls's *A Theory of Justice*. This work provided tools both to refine my own thinking and to address problems of interest. An illustration is some papers I have written about school finance. One such issue is how one thinks about balancing need against ability to profit as criteria for allocating resources. Rawls Second Principle of justice, especially the Difference Principle, suggests useful ways to think about this. I develop this in "The ethics of resource allocation in education: Questions of democracy and justice."

Theory had a fruitful dialogue in my head with two other books. The first was Alisdaire McIntyre's *After Virtue* along with other communitarian critiques of liberalism. These critiques produced two quite different reactions in me. The first was that their critique of liberalism was largely wrong. McIntyre's primary reason for claiming the liberalism had failed (because there are conflicting interpretations) struck me as less than credible. Michael Sandel's claim in *Liberalism and the Limitations of Justice* that Rawls's has an unencumbered self seemed to me to be based on an erroneous reading of the text. As Rawls notes, the original position where agents choose not knowing who they are, is a thought experiment, not a description of human nature. Indeed, it is a device to discover principles of justice for people who are variously encumbered in a society characterized by durable pluralism. At the same time, I thought that McIntyre's discussions of some of the ills of modern societies and his idea of a practice (complex and coherent activities with their own internal goods and excellences) suggested that liberal theorists had not taken the role of community in human life seriously enough. People learn by being initiated into communities that sustain practices. It is this initiation that makes them who and what they are. Liberalism has not denied this, but it has not made much of it either. I began to look for a more community friendly interpretation of liberalism and to construct a somewhat communitarian reading of Rawls (one I think *Political Liberalism* largely confirms). At some point into this mix of ideas came James Coleman's work. Coleman persuaded me that community has structural and material conditions as well as cognitive and affective ones. *Youth Transition to Adulthood* makes much of age segregation as well as formal education institutions as barriers to intergenerational socialization. Much of Coleman's later work develops these themes.

This mix of ideas has become important to me in thinking about school reform. I have always been distrustful of the standards movement because of the way it decoupled questions of equity and productivity. But as the standards movement morphed into systemic reform and the accountability movement typified in *NCLB*,

I have become increasingly convinced that its troubles go deeper than a perverse view of equality. We are asking the wrong questions, and, until we ask better ones, we are not likely to succeed in creating better schools. The core modern debate about reform has been whether government management or quasi-markets is the most likely path to educational productivity. We think about reform in terms of incentives, resources, and techniques. We need to ask more questions about creating good communities and non-alienating environments.

For the last decade I have been feeling my way towards a view of school reform rooted in the idea of community. It has two ideas at its heart. The first is that the central problem for school reform to deal with is alienation. Students, especially high school students, do not care much about learning what adults wish to teach them. This fact is not just about the poverty of what adults want to teach, it is also about the poverty of the outlooks that shape how youth are likely to appraise what adults want them to learn. When school reformers recognize this at all they are inclined to respond with incentives for productivity. This is largely a mistake. The cure for alienation is not bribery or threats. It is community.

The second idea is that there is an intimate connection between learning and belonging. Education is (mostly) initiation into practices. Practices are sustained by communities. The relationship is dialectical. People are motivated to learn because they want to belong to the communities of those who care for and about them. But what they learn transforms them so that they become members having the perspective of their community. This is true about food, religion, carpentry and physics. These themes are developed in "Community, the Missing Element of School Reform: Why Schools Should Be More like Congregations than Banks" (2004).

The small schools movement has sniffed out some of this. But some of its advocates have made two key errors. They have substituted "personalization" for community. This disconnects learning and belonging. Second, they have identified scale as the crucial element that enables schools to achieve personalized environments. These are both half truths. Personalization is a good thing, so are small schools. But scale is neither necessary nor sufficient for community. Personalization roots community in a network of caring relationships, but misses the importance of shared purpose. This argument is made in "Small Schools: Size or Community?" (2007).

RECENT YEARS

There are two more autobiographical parts to my thinking about community. After my almost 30 years at Cornell I spent three years as a department chair at a major state university. I found the experience both unpleasant and disturbing. The university (unlike Cornell which is run much as I think universities should be run) was authoritarian and bureaucratic. Several of its senior administrators were the personification of arrogance. The university knew how to alienate people. Moreover, I found the bureaucracy of the state educational system to be dominated by careerism, cronyism, and deceit. (I must add that I also met many kind, competent, and good people who sometimes were able to temper the excesses of these institutions.) This experience has awakened a kind of latent Calvinism in me. I don't think that the sins of this place were particularly original, but they seemed pervasive. Any theory of community has to deal with human nature and cannot rest on the assumption that people are naturally and routinely altruistic. It must also note the extent to which leadership sets the tone for an institution. One expression of this concern has been that my most recent book, *Ethical Leadership in Schools: Creating Community in an Environment of Accountability* (2007) includes a discussion of the ethics of accountability which focuses on gaming the system in response to accountability requirements.

Since 2003 I have been at Syracuse University as a part time faculty member trying to ease my way into retirement (without much success). In the SU environment I have talked with and read the works of people who talk a lot about inclusion and who worry about racism and exclusion in ways that are different than the ways that I have learned to think of them. I have not, heretofore, considered the genres of scholarship that their views are rooted in seriously. In part, I suspect that one reason is that this literature often engages in gratuitous and erroneous liberal bashing. (Apparently even among those who write about inclusion the desire to exclude can be strong). However, at SU I have met several kind, decent, and intelligent people who write on matters of inclusion. They have persuaded me that a theory of community needs a conception of inclusion that gives special place to the weakest and most disadvantaged among us.

Community involves a web of themes to be developed and integrated. I have been trying to get them together into a good book on the topic. The operating title of this is *Schools As Communities: A Third Way Toward School Reform* and it is under contract with TC Press. This book has been coming along more slowly than I would like, partly because it occurs at the intersection of many paths and is hard to thematically organize. I hope to finish before I fully retire, which (hopefully) will be soon, and before my interest in this project is overwhelmed by my growing passion for environmental ethics. But that is the story of my next life.

Let me end with the fact that my working life has been shaped by a loving wife who for 40 years has kept me grounded and (possibly) sane, and by having raised two children who successfully navigated the public school system to become competent, successful, and good people. I have learned much from them, especially about what is really important.

REFERENCES

Coleman, J. S. (1974). *Youth: Transition to adulthood*. Chicago, IL: University of Chicago Press.
Kuhn, T. (1970). *The structure of scientific revolutions*. Chicago: University of Chicago Press.
MacIntyre, A. (1981). *After virtue*. Notre Dame, IN: University of Notre Dame Press.
Mill, J. S. (1859/1956). *On liberty*. New York: The Bobbs-Merrill Company.
National Commission on Excellence in Education. (1983). *A nation at risk*. Washington, D.C.: U.S. Department of Education.
No Child Left Behind Act of 2002: Executive Summary. U.S. Government Department of Education. Available: http://www.ed.gov/nclb/exec-summ.html

Rawls, J. (1971). *A theory of justice*. Cambridge, MA: Harvard University Press.

Rawls, J. (1993). *Political liberalism*. New York: Columbia University Press.

Sandel, M. (1982). *Liberalism and the limits of justice*. Cambridge, England: Cambridge University Press.

Strike, K. (1974). Philosophical reflections on *Tinker v. Des Moines. Philosophy of Education, 30*, 397-410.

Strike, K. (1974). On the expressive potential of behaviorist language. *American Educational Research Journal, 11*(2), 103-120.

Strike, K. (1981). Toward a moral theory of desegregation. In J. Soltis (Ed.), *Philosophy and education: Eightieth yearbook of the National Society for the Study of Education* (pp. 213-235). Chicago: University of Chicago Press.

Strike, K. (1982). *Educational policy and the just society*. Urbana: University of Illinois Press.

Strike, K. (1982). *Liberty and learning*. Oxford: M. Robertson.

Strike, K. (1988). The ethics of resource allocation in education: Questions of democracy and justice. In Monk, D. & Underwood, J. (Eds.), *Microlevel school finance: Issues and implications for policy* (pp. 143-180). Cambridge, MA: Ballinger.

Strike, K. (1993). Professionalism, democracy and discursive communities: Normative reflections on restructuring. *American Educational Research Journal, 30*(1), 255-275.

Strike, K. (1994). On the construction of public speech: Pluralism and public reason. *Educational Theory, 44*(1), 1-26.

Strike, K. (1997). Centralized goal formation and systemic reform: Reflections on liberty, localism and pluralism. *Educational Policy Analysis, 5*, 11. URL http://olam.ed.asu.edu/epaa/v5n11.html

Strike, K. (1999). Can schools be communities? The tension between shared values and inclusion. *Educational Administration Quarterly, 35*(1), 46-70.

Strike, K.A. (2000). Schools as communities: Four metaphors, three models, and a dilemma or two. *Journal of Philosophy of Education, 34*(4), 617-643. [This paper was the keynote address for the Philosophy of Education Society of Great Britain, Spring 2000.]

Strike, K.A. (2003). Liberty, democracy, and community: Legitimacy in public education. In W.L. Boyd & D. Miretzky (Eds.) *American Educational Governance on Trial: Change and Challenges*. Chicago: University of Chicago Press, 37-56.

Strike, K.A. (2004). Community, the missing element of school reform: Why schools should be more like congregations than banks. *American Journal of Education, 110* (3), 215-232.

Strike, K.A. (2004). Is liberal education illiberal? Political liberalism and liberal education. In C. Higgans (Ed.), *Philosophy of Education 2004* (pp. 321-330). Urbana: Illinois State University, Philosophy of Education Society.

Strike, K.A. (2007a). Small schools, size or community? (forthcoming).

Strike, K. (2007b). *Ethical leadership in schools: Creating community in an environment of accountability*. Thousand Oaks, CA. Corwin Press.

Strike, K. (forthcoming) *Schools as communities: A third way toward school reform*. TC Press.

Toulmin, S. (1972). *Human understanding*. Princeton, New Jersey: Princeton University Press.

Kenneth A. Strike
Syracuse University

LEONARD J. WAKS

THE MAKING OF A SCHOOLING AND
TECHNOLOGY SKEPTIC

SCHOOLING

I was frequently in a fog at school; I did not take well to classroom learning and did not connect well socially. Moreover, I sensed quite early that there was something fraudulent about schooling. After Russia got the bomb in 1949, we were shown movies of the total devastation of Hiroshima and then directed to 'take cover' under our desks at the sound of an air raid siren. I refused. How, I wanted to know, would a school desk protect me from the devastation we had just seen? When no answer was forthcoming, I wouldn't budge!

The fog persisted throughout High School. Math and science were easy and straightforward enough, but I was baffled by humanities subjects. Why were we compelled to read Dickens' *Great Expectations* (in both eighth and eleventh grades!!) when everything I read on my own (e.g., Keroauc's *On the Road*, Steinbeck's *Of Mice and Men*) had so much more vitality? Why, in a community surrounded by Spanish language speakers, were we taught Spanish by a teacher who could not speak Spanish? Why, in the American history class of our integrated school, were we asked to take Virginius Dabney's *Life Magazine* article (1958) justifying Southern resistance to school integration, so seriously? Why were all of my questions and concerns handled so defensively and greeted with such hostility?

I relied on music and poetry to lift my fog. Miles Davis, John Coltrane, Charlie Mingus, and Thelonius Monk played frequently in the New York clubs in the late 1950s and those below the drinking age (18) could sit in designated non-drinking areas. Monk's music, in particular, engaged me with its iconoclastic style and the transcendent beauty of his original melodies and mind-bending improvisations. Allen Ginsburg and other beat poets were also on the scene, and I read them as well as the poetry and stories of William Carlos Williams and others who influenced them.

In my senior year of high school I decided to become a philosopher. Based on such models as Sartre, Camus and Russell, I took a philosopher to be a social and cultural critic whose thinking lifted mental fogs, exposed fraudulence, and pointed to ways of living more freely. When I asked my father, a school principal, to provide a more precise definition, he suggested that we read the article about philosophy in the *Encyclopaedia Britannica*. When that didn't clear things up, we went to the bookstore and I selected Marjorie Greene's *Dreadful Freedom* because of its appealing title and its cover art -- a man having a panic attack. Greene began by explaining the philosophy of existentialism -- existence preceded essence. My dad and I pored over the text with a dictionary for hours before admitting defeat.

L.J. Waks (ed.), Leaders in Philosophy of Education: Intellectual Self Portraits, 251–268.
© 2008 *Sense Publishers. All rights reserved.*

My fog magically lifted when I entered Queens College, CUNY. In a freshman course, *Introduction to Contemporary Civilization in the West*, one of the early readings was Book Six of Plato's *Republic.* The image of the cave and the ascent to reality hit me like a bolt of lightening! The cave was just like school! Monk's music and beat poetry were glimpses into Reality – the true, good and beautiful. After that I was completely hooked on philosophy.

THE UNIVERSITY OF WISCONSIN

In my sophomore year, 1961, I transferred to The University of Wisconsin in Madison to study philosophy more seriously. The first semester I took Ethics with Marcus Singer, Aesthetics with Eugene Kaelin, and elementary logic. Singer devoted most of his lectures to the ethical theories of Kant and Mill, and to his own theory, in which the generalization argument ("what if everyone did that?") was central. Singer lectured even in the section of the course devoted to contemporary moral issues, and discouraged questions. In Kaelin's course, however, the whole idea was to "do philosophy" together. Kaelin covered a few classical aesthetic concepts and theories in the opening weeks, but most of his lectures provided tools for analyzing arguments and vocabulary for talking about works of art. Even though the class had more than a hundred students,

---

PERSONAL FAVORITES

Book

Technology's School: The Challenge for Philosophy (1995)

Articles

Non-behavioral goals: Investigating the validity of the two-defect argument (1973)
Freedom and desire in the Summerhill philosophy of education (1975)
Educational objectives and existential heroes (1975)
Three contexts for philosophy of education: intellectual, institutional and ideological (1988)
Emptiness (1995)
Experimentalism and the flow of experience (1998)
Post-experimentalist pragmatism (1998)
The Continuum of means-ends and the reconciliation of science and art in the later philosophy of John Dewey (1999).
How globalization can cause fundamental curriculum change (2003)
Globalization, state transformation and education (2006)
The concept of fundamental educational change (2007).

---

he encouraged and even enjoyed give and take. The end of the course involved students' philosophical analyses of art works, styles and movements. I gave a presentation on the aesthetics of modern jazz, donning a T-shirt proclaiming "Bird Lives" for the occasion.

The department was dominated by analytic philosophers, and soon I was initiated into that manner of philosophical work. One of my favorite teachers was

Fred Dretske, who, like Kaelin, conducted all his classes as cooperative inquiries; his own articles and book chapters were included as texts along with other contemporary works, and he encouraged students mercilessly to criticize his formulations. I took his classes in philosophy of language and philosophy of perception; for the latter I wrote a term paper on 'unconscious perception' in which I argued that the standard cases were neither instances of unconsciousness nor perception. In addition to philosophy I minored in history, studying with several of Wisconsin's famous cultural historians. This came in handy later on.

I stayed on at Wisconsin for graduate school, beginning my studies in January 1964, just as U.S. involvement in Viet Nam was escalating. I loved philosophy but it troubled me that what we were studying seemed irrelevant to pressing real world problems related to the war, technology and the environment. My fellow graduate student Peter Goldstone said that if I wanted to solve *real* problems I should go into politics. Philosophers, he said, worked on *philosophical* problems.

This was all part of an endless grad student discussion about what philosophy was and about how to conduct oneself as a philosopher. The consensus view was that one should read the main journals, find problems of interest, apprentice oneself to a professor working on them, and learn to join the discussion. I held the quite different view that one should take on contemporary 'real world' problems that one found troubling, think very hard about them in ways guided by the philosophical tradition, and contribute to their resolution in communications to professional and public audiences. Today I would regard the opposition between these positions as overdrawn, and would urge a pluralistic common ground.

I had taken philosophy of education from Donald Arnstine as an undergraduate. The textbooks, including the Brubacher yearbooks of 1942 and 1954 on the various "isms" and Dewey's *Democracy and Education*, seemed hopelessly opaque, but I was impressed by Dewey's effort to develop educational ideas specific to his era and situate them in the history of thought. I considered that this might be a worthwhile lifetime project. Having neither a clear sense of the emerging problem set nor a set of ideas relevant to it, I filed the idea away for future reference.

In graduate school I specialized in ethics and social philosophy, and also took several courses in contemporary epistemology and logic. In addition to Fred Dretske, the teachers who influenced me most were the political philosopher Gerald MacCallum and the polymath William Hay, who eventually became my thesis director. Like many other Wisconsin graduate students, I was deeply influenced by the ethical theorist A. Philips Griffiths, who visited Wisconsin several times in the 1960s. A colleague of Richard Peters at Birkbeck College, Griffiths was a co-author with Peters of "The Autonomy of Prudence" (1962), and one of the few analytic philosophers at the time who shared his interest in education.

I was a teaching assistant every semester, teaching logic, ethics, or introduction to philosophy. I also continued to read a lot on my own about 20th century Anglo-American philosophy, including most of the available volumes in the Library of Living Philosophers series edited by Paul Arthur Schilpp (the much awaited volume on Carnap appeared in 1963), the Carus lectures, and the two-volume collection of personal essays by American philosophers that served as an important inspiration for the current volume (Adams and Montague, 1962/1930). Like most of the other grad students I at least skimmed every fresh issue of such leading journals as *Ethics* and *The Philosophical Review*. My favorite philosophers at that time were Clarence I. Lewis (*Mind and the World Order, An Analysis of Knowledge and Valuation*),[i] who had died during my first semester in graduate school, and Georg Hendrick von Wright (*Norm and Action, The Varieties of Goodness*). Wittgenstein had a large though often indirect influence on all of us. Thomas Kuhn's *The Structure of Scientific Revolutions* had recently been published and its institutional, historically grounded, view of knowledge, which owed much to Wittgenstein, was beginning to challenge empiricist epistemology. Peter Winch's *The Idea of a Social Science* was also influential. I greatly admired all of this work but did not find in it specific models for what I wanted to do.

ANTI -TECHNICSISM

I got my first glimpse of something I *did* want to do shortly after I entered graduate school. I needed a minor field and chose Educational Policy Studies, in part because I could amass the necessary credits in philosophy and history of education, subjects I had already developed a taste for as an undergraduate.

When I signed up for my minor, the educational historian Merle Borrowman, who had supervised an undergraduate project I had undertaken on the history of the Wisconsin philosophy department, asked what I wanted to do in educational studies. I had already read some philosophy of education in such journals as *Educational Theory* and thought that most of it was truly awful. I had also read Scheffler's *The Language of Education* and the collection of essays on analytical philosophy of education edited by B. O. Smith and Bob Ennis (1962), and while I saw that analytical work of that sort as absolutely essential for the future health of philosophy of education, and I greatly admired Scheffler's work, I knew I didn't want to do anything quite like it. I also saw that analysis was an inadequate programmatic base for a philosophy of education capable of coming to grips with the emerging problematic situation of war, technology and the environment, a view I was to proclaim as chair of the 'analytical session' of the Philosophy of Education Society in 1969 and in "Philosophy, Education and the Doomsday Threat" (1969).

I told Borrowman that I might eventually endeavour to frame up some pertinent educational notions for our time. He asked whether this work have 'an empirical reference point', cautioning that that education faculty expected educational scholarship to have one. He gave the example that ideas for educational practice should be considered as hypotheses about means to empirically measurable ends. I flashed on those deadening school drills I had suffered. Comparing them with philosophy classes where arguments were followed wherever they led, I immediately thought that this business of specific measurable ends for education was the stupidest idea I had ever heard. I knew immediately that my work would have something to do with challenging it.

I prepared a not terribly successful doctoral dissertation on *Understanding as an Educational Aim*, the overall gist of which was that while 'understanding X' as an aim was not typically meant as a measurable objective, it was nonetheless a perfectly good move in the actual language game of stating aims. I included a naïve chapter on Dewey's means-ends continuum and theory of educational aims, as discussed in *Democracy and Education*. I published a chapter on "Knowledge and Understanding as Educational Aims" (Waks, 1968) in a special issue of *The Monist* on philosophy of education, arguing that the familiar distinction between knowledge and understanding as educational aims was problematic because standard analyses of knowledge all included a condition (e.g., *justified* belief) that *implied* understanding.

EARLY PROFESSIONAL LIFE

I left graduate school armed with three analytical tools: a model of philosophical clarity, an appreciation for formal logic as a tool for assessing logical validity (and as a fascinating subject in its own right), and a method for analyzing the multiple and interconnected meanings of words in various practices or 'language games'. I was still searching for a style of Anglo-American philosophy combining both the Anglo and American features.[ii] I had, however, identified my initial philosophical goal -- "exposing the irrationality of technical rationality."

I found a first philosophical model in Boyd Bode, an esteemed pragmatist philosopher who left professional philosophy for educational studies so that he could deal directly with real problems. I saw the chapters (originally journal articles) of his *Modern Educational Theories* (1927) as similar in spirit to the articles I wanted to write. Bode did not confine himself narrowly to the literature of philosophy of education; he was simply a very good *philosopher* thinking hard about problems arising across the educational landscape.

Eugene Kaelin assisted in getting me a tenure track position in philosophy at Purdue. In my two years there I taught undergraduate ethics, social and political philosophy, and American philosophy, as well as a graduate seminar on the later philosophy of Dewey and another, more original one, on the theory of revolutionary change, in which I explored parallels between fundamental changes in scientific, cultural, and social-political realms. I was appointed to the American Studies faculty and team taught several courses in American Studies. My efforts to link up with education, however, were soundly rebuffed by those I contacted in the education college.

After two years at Purdue I accepted a joint appointment in philosophy and education at Stanford. I taught undergraduate ethics and conducted graduate seminars on the theory of value (Lewis and Von Wright), and again on the theory of revolutionary change. I also developed a course on philosophy, education and society. I continued thinking about technical rationality, and what seemed like its opposite -- the do- your-own-thing Summerhill philosophy of free schools. Such schools were popping up all over the country at that time, and Pacific High School, close to Stanford campus, provided me with first hand experience.

I had read Summerhill in the early 1960s. While attracted to the open climate, so different from that of my own high school, I wondered where great teachers like Eugene Kaelin fit in. Neill had said that teaching did not matter much. My experiences at Pacific High School added to my concerns. Freed from compulsory classes, most Pacific students seemed utterly without direction, lost in a fog! Some concentrated on drugs and sex and radical political protest, but to my eye they did so not because they were driven by unconscious needs but because nothing else on offer was all that appealing. Neill had argued that attractive alternatives to what youngsters *really* wanted to do would only lead to confusion, suppressed desire, and neurosis. My experience at Pacific demonstrated the opposite: confusion and neurosis resulted not from attractive learning opportunities but from their *absence*. In "Freedom and Desire in the Summerhill Philosophy of Education" (Waks, (1975), I exposed a logical fallacy in Neill's underlying argument for the Summerhill philosophy, and relied on it to account for its emotional attractiveness and surface plausibility as well as its ultimate rational invalidity.

TEMPLE UNIVERSITY

Despite the seemingly ideal combination of philosophy and education in my Stanford position, the joint appointment was stressful because the expectations of the two colleges conflicted, and the large number of non-philosophy courses, required by the education doctoral program and my senior colleague in philosophy of education made it hard to train my education graduate students in philosophy. After three years I followed Bode's lead and in 1971 accepted Paul Komisar's offer (no application, no interview) to come to Temple's college of education.

Temple in the early 1970s was analytical philosophy of education central. Jim McClellan, Paul Komisar and Robert Holtzman, the three senior faculty members, had all studied at philosophy of education at Illinois. Peter Goldstone, my grad student colleague at Wisconsin, had just arrived. I became the fifth full time philosopher in an unusually bookish, scholarly group. We waited anxiously for each issue of *The New York Review of Books*, discussed the reviews in the hallways with our grad students, and even read many of the reviewed books together.

Three new factors were at play when I started at Temple. First, Ivan Illich had just published his article on de-schooling in the *New York Review of Books*. Illich was no foe of teaching, learning, or even schools. His target was *schooling*, the compulsory subjection of young people to limitless years of age-graded, pre-sequenced curricula. This he saw as conditioning learners for life-long dependence on pre-packaged experiences,

---

FAVORITES WRITTEN BY OTHERS

Boyd Bode, Modern Educational Theories (1927)
John Dewey *School and Society*,(1900)
-------- *Democracy and Education* (1916)
Eugen Herrigel *Zen in the Art of Archery* (1953)
Ivan Illich, *Tools for Conviviality* (1974)
Plato *Apology, Crito, Republic*
D.T. Suzuki *The Field of Zen* (1970)

---

thus making recognizable learning opportunities scarce and leaving people not more but less intelligent. His argument to this effect in *De-Schooling Society* and *Tools for Conviviality* I still find entirely convincing. My broader assessment of Illich's philosophy of education is found in Waks (1991b).

Second, my loathing for technicist means-ends reasoning led naturally to an interest in Zen. I was too conventional to see Zen fitting directly into my philosophical research, but every so often I stocked up on Zen books, called in sick, and retired to my bed to read. I particularly admired Herrigel's *Zen in the Art of Archery* (1953) and D. T. Suzuki's *The Field of Zen* (1970).

Third, I started designing educational encounters based on anti-technicist principles. Artists, I reasoned, learn through their creative acts, but what they learn depends on their unique creative trajectories. *That* they learn in significant ways through their art is predictable, but *what* they learn is neither predictable nor generalizable. I set out to design and lead courses of structured encounters with the arts that were rich with this sort of *non-specific* learning potential. These soon became very popular with Temple students and took up much of my time. Kenneth Maue's *Water in the Lake* (1979) later became something of a model for that work.

In my research I continued to work on problems with technical rationality. Ken Strike and Hugh Petrie published important articles on behavioral objectives (Strike, 1974; Petrie, 1975) focusing on the limits of behavioral language. My line was somewhat different; for me the problem was not limits in the *language* of measurable ends, but the very *conception* of educational *action* (and many other forms of human action, and especially inter-action) as the taking of means to specific ends. Behaviorism simply added a second set of fallacies on top of those inherent in technicism, a view I developed in "Educational Objectives and Existential Heroes" (Waks, 1975), a paper I started to write in the summer of 1969.

I had also become convinced that the underlying logic of the standard *argument* in support of technicist means-ends reasoning in education, though persuasive in practice, was deeply flawed. That argument went like this: "if you don't state your ends in measurable terms, you will know neither what you are aiming at nor whether or not you have succeeded. Thus, failure to state your ends in this way is irrational." I called this the 'two defect' argument. In "Non-Behavioral Goals: Assessing the Two Defect Argument" (1973) I showed that this argument only retains plausibility if "knowing what you are aiming at' is taken tacitly to *mean* "having a measurable objective" and if "knowing you have succeeded" is taken to imply "*measuring* your results against your objectives" But as there were good non-technicist ways of making sense of the language of aims and evaluation, as I had argued in my dissertation, the two-defect argument begged the question.

I also started to explore the idea that the specious rationality of technical logic and the specious freedom of Summerhill were related. My thinking, no doubt influenced by Wittgenstein, went something like this:

First, suppose that in considering teaching and learning you bracket out or hide from view the background of social and educational institutions. You would then be considering a new, different, and greatly impoverished form of life. Someone undertaking to teach in such a world would start off without the normative

257

direction inherent in the institutions that had been bracketed out, and so would indeed need some specific objective at every step to know what he was aiming at. In reality, of course, any 8 year old can, without any specific aims, do a plausible imitation of teachers, because they have already incorporated the relevant institutional norms. Only the trick of hiding the background institutions made it seem necessary to have specific aims in order to know what you were doing.

Now, suppose someone like Neill, blinded by this trick, wrongly accepted that only specific learning objectives could get *teaching* going, but rightly believed that this sort of teaching would be lifeless and would nullify the agency of learners. That person might then say that there was something else in such a world that could at least get some *learning* started, and that was the *basic, institutionally unconditioned needs and wants* of learners, such as desires for sex in explicit or sublimated forms. From this starting point the Summerhill philosophy could be derived. Remember that in such a picture the very natural desires of students to be initiated into institutionalized practices of their society are hidden by the disappearing trick: the background institutions and their practices had been bracketed out. Once we bring them to light, however, initiation into them can be seen as the most *obvious* candidate for what students want, and the idea that by providing attractive pathways into these practices we are deflecting learners from what they *really* want loses all plausibility.

This thinking influenced both "Educational Objectives and Existential Heroes" and "Freedom and Desire in the Summerhill Philosophy of Education," but I never developed this connection between technicist and Summerhill logic into an article.

TECHNOLOGICAL SOCIETY

By 1974 it was clear to me that educational technicism was more than just a logical mistake but something utterly sinister. Jacques Ellul's *The Technological Society* (1964) had argued that technical rationality, the straight line adjustment of means to ends without consideration of contextual factors, has such an enticing simplicity that it attracts people, eclipses their capacity for more complex forms of thought, and then, like a mental disease, drives them in all sorts of blind, irrational directions, with vast destructive results on the surrounding contexts. (My assessment of Ellul on technical rationality in human services and education can be found in Waks (1989). Harry Braverman's *Labor and Monopoly Capital* (1974), on the other hand, saw a kind of twisted acquisitive logic behind the madness of technical rationality: capitalist owners and managers seek to reduce human labor to rationalized means in order to rob workers of their productive knowledge and skill and to reconstruct it under their own power. The goal is not the stated one of efficiency, but external control over work processes. The fact that socialist bureaucrats also embraced this sort of work rationalization, however, convinced me that it was alluring not only to capitalists but to anyone seeking domination.

This idea could readily be extended to the control of teaching and other service professions. While the contracting out of educational services to corporations had not yet become standard practice, the control of the intimate details of teaching and learning by the state itself troubled me no less. If state bureaucrats could dictate measurable objectives for teaching, they could also adjust the official success levels of those measures at will, and thus arbitrarily reject any teaching, no matter how successful on its own terms, as 'inefficient'. They could then replace professional teachers and long-established educational practices by 'more efficient means' such as proletarianized teachers following a scripted manual, or computers with artificial intelligence. In this way they could gain complete control over the behavior of teachers and students - a true night of the living dead!

Just then many states started moving in exactly that direction. The Pennsylvania state department of education introduced a plan ("Project 81") to have all classroom instruction planned and evaluated according to specific, measurable learning objectives. Education courses at the tertiary level, in turn, would have to be aimed at specific learning objectives correlated with teachers' efficiency in producing their learning objectives in elementary and secondary education. A minor bureaucrat visited Temple to explain this regime, and all of our objections were met by persistent reiterations of the "two defect" argument. As Ellul had predicted, once her mind had been bitten by the technicist bug her capacity, indeed, her tolerance, for more complex forms of reasoning had completely evaporated.

I prepared a critique of Project 81 (Waks, 1995/1974) and hand-delivered it to the project director in the State Capitol, Harrisburg, who politely thanked me for "my input on her outputs." She was clearly indifferent to the project's rational basis, pushing specific learning objectives simply because that was what mid-level bureaucrats were doing right about then. Fashion, not faulty reason, was driving the insanity, although the fashion no doubt reflected deep processes in society. Solving real world problems with philosophy suddenly seemed very much more daunting.

RETRENCHMENT

I was promoted to Professor in 1978, on the basis of letters from external reviewers Israel Scheffler, Richard Peters and Hugh Petrie. The satisfaction was not long-lived, as by then things had deteriorated seriously at Temple. Jim McClellan had left for SUNY Albany. Strong graduate students no longer arrived, as jobs in philosophy of education had dried up. More seriously, Temple experienced a sharp drop off in undergraduate applications because of a decrease in the national college-age cohort and the de-industrialization of Philadelphia. Rumors of imminent faculty retrenchments circulated. The teacher education program replaced our philosophically inspired 'foundations of education' course with a course of their own, in order to increase their "credit generation" statistics. Over night our department's students, and our trust and conviviality, vanished.

At the height of my despair over these developments a student missionary handed me a Good News Bible. I took it to bed along with my Zen books, found it full of philosophical insight. This led naturally to reading the Hebrew Scriptures, which I found even more philosophically illuminating. I gradually came to the view that there are important insights in religion, broadly understood, and not just in Zen, that can not be translated into secular understandings, a position subsequently developed in "Functionalism and the Autonomy of Religion" (Waks, 1985). My own religious thinking developed along the lines of the so-called 'perennial philosophy' or what Philip Kitcher (2007) has recently dubbed "spiritual religion", the view that the great world religions share certain ideas that distinguish them from secular world views *as* religious, and that these ideas are in some sense better or truer than their secular counterparts.

In 1979 Temple's college of liberal arts initiated a required humanities sequence, *The Intellectual Heritage Program*, consisting of two courses, *The Ancient world* and *The Modern World*. Teaching in the IHP allowed me to fill my work load after foundations courses vanished, and to think and teach about many philosophical topics. It also forced me finally to develop a coherent story line about the history of civilization. The *Ancient World* course in particular provided further opportunity to think about links between philosophy and religion. From this I later developed an article on "Emptiness" (Waks, 1995) in which I argued that despite superficial cultural differences, the ideas of Socratic ignorance, Christian poverty and Buddhist emptiness were more or less philosophically equivalent.

Thinking that a pink slip would come from the retrenchment effort, and needing to prepare for a new career, I entered a doctoral program in applied social and organizational psychology in 1979. It included courses on T-groups, research methods in small group psychology, organizational consulting, group counselling, and workshop and conference management. I also took several courses on psychopathology and neurology, and earned a professional certificate in psychotherapy. My dissertation was a study of my anti-technicist creativity workshops, and I later published a programmatic article from it on "Laboratory Education in the Creative Process" (Waks, 1988).

SCIENCE-TECHNOLOGY-SOCIETY & TECHNOLOGICAL LITERACY

I received the long-expected pink slip at the end of 1981, and my Temple job finally terminated in 1983. I opened a workshop and seminar business and my first offering was a workshop course on 'The Love of Wisdom,' billed as a 'personal, practical course in philosophy, with readings from philosophical classics and the scriptures of the great world religions'. Surprisingly I had almost 20 students in my first workshop, many of whom also sought philosophical counselling from me, making me a pioneer in the now established field of 'philosophical practice'.

The following year, just as I was completing my psychology dissertation, Madhu Prakash introduced me to Rustum Roy, director of Penn State's Science, Technology and Society (STS) program. Rustum, a prominent materials scientist and radical Christian theologian, was then leading a national effort to close the two cultures divide by introducing techno-science content into humanities education and vice versa. Rustum's friend Ivan Illich and his band of roving scholars made the STS program a home base. Robert Rodale, editor of *Prevention*, was also on the faculty. Carl Mitcham, founder of philosophy of technology as a recognised academic discipline, joined us a couple of years later. Just as Temple had been analytical philosophy of education central in 1971, Penn State was technology criticism central in the 1980s! I was once again in the right place at the right time.

Rustum Roy hired me to teach courses for the STS program on technology and values (cross-listed with philosophy), which eventually became open colloquia, with as many visitors from the community in attendance as students. But he was particularly interested in my organizational background and he assigned me to take charge of a national conference he was planning for STS, supported by a grant he obtained from the National Science Foundation. He situated me in the office next to Ivan Illich. I became a regular at Illich's frequent symposia and dinner parties.

As 'technological literacy' had become a buzz word in the wake of *A Nation at Risk*, I sought to re-appropriate the term for our interdisciplinary technology criticism crusade, and named the conference "The National Technological Literacy Conference (TLC)." I sought and received sponsorship from the National Science Teachers Association, The National Council for the Social Studies, and the International Technology Education Association, among other groups, and formed working relations with their leaders. Based on my background in organizational studies, and guided by a magical sheet of paper someone handed me entitled "39 steps to a perfect conference" I designed and managed a national award winning program drawing about a thousand attendants annually.

As program chair of the TLC I acquired a magic telephone. U.S. Senators, TV personalities, corporate CEOs and prominent social and political activists returned my phone calls. Robert Rodale, Ivan Illich, Carl Mitcham and Jeremy Rifkin were among our primary advisors. Just about everyone invited to speak accepted, and surprisingly, many celebrities actually contacted us and volunteered their time. The first conference received coverage on the front page of *USA Today's* business section. I subsequently designed the South American Technological Literacy Conference in Brasilia, gave keynote addresses or short courses on STS and technological literacy in Belgium, Denmark, Argentina, Puerto Rico, Spain and Scotland, consulted on interdisciplinary education for many two and four year colleges, conducted NSF-sponsored Chautauqua courses on interdisciplinary college science teaching, and with Mitcham, co-directed a National Council for the Humanities summer institute for college teachers on the philosophy of technology and wrote the first philosophy of technology entry for the *Encyclopedia of philosophy* (Mitcham and Waks, 1996) and on my own, the entry on education in the *Encyclopedia of science, technology and ethics* (Waks, 2005). I gathered some of my philosophical papers in a volume in Mitcham's monograph series on philosophy of technology under the title *Technology's School* (Waks, 1995). Most of my publications during my years at Penn State, and many of them subsequently, however, have focused on issues of interdisciplinary science and technology education, educational technology, and technological literacy that are somewhat tangential to the philosophy of education, narrowly conceived. Selected examples include (Waks 1987, 1991a, 1991b, 1991c; 1993, 1998b, 2001b, 2006b). My programmatic statement on technological literacy is (Waks, 1987). My Illich-inspired reservations about STS and other forms of "green studies" in the school curriculum are expressed in (Waks, 1991c).

EDUCATION IN GLOBAL NETWORK SOCIETY

When I was forced to leave Temple in 1983 despite my status as a tenured full professor, the university had been placed on an AAUP blacklist for violating the academic freedom and tenure provisions of the academic code of ethics. By 1992 Temple was ready to make peace with the AAUP, and soft money for STS and technological literacy was drying up, so I returned to Temple. As the foundations of education department had been eliminated I was assigned to the department of educational leadership and policy studies (ELPS), in which there was neither a program in policy studies nor a single course in philosophy of education. I resumed teaching in the Intellectual Heritage Program, eventually becoming Associate Director of the program. In 1996 the education college Dean asked me to chair the ELPS department, and as I moved back into the department I began to teach history of education (which remained on the books as an 'American Culture' core option), and resumed full time research work in philosophy of education.

Two issues led me to re-focus my research studies: the up-coming 100th anniversary of Dewey's epochal *The School and Society*, and the growing attention being paid to globalization and its social impacts. Globalization provided an opportunity for framing up ideas on educational commonplaces including teaching, learning, subject matter, setting, and social context, parallel to those in *The School and Society* and *Democracy and Education*, for 'global network' society.

Re-Reading Dewey and Pragmatism

I have aimed to provide a fresh reading of Dewey's ideas and their fit with the emerging global network society, following Dewey's template in *School and Society*, by first raising sociological questions about contemporary trends in society and education, and following these with philosophical questions about how best to respond to and modulate these trends in a new educational synthesis.

On the theoretical side I have critiqued both the "new scholarship on Dewey" and the re-appropriation of Dewey's legacy by Richard Rorty. In "Experimentalism and the Flow of Experience" (Waks, 1998a) I argue that contrary to new readings of Dewey by Robert Westbrook and many others, the emphasis on science throughout his works is not merely a rhetorical device to catch the pro-science wave of his time, but rather is logically essential to his experimentalist philosophy. In "Post-experimentalist Pragmatism" (Waks, 1998c) I argue that Rorty's reformulation of Dewey's pragmatism, which eliminates this emphasis on science and method, is logically inconsistent with Dewey's experimentalism and actually incapable even of generating coherent answers to the questions Dewey addressed. The challenge faced by a contemporary public philosophy, I argue, lies in framing up a system of public ideas as grounded in experience and evidence as those generated via Dewey's experimental logic, while also appealing to postmodern sensibilities that are sceptical of science. In "The Means-Ends Continuum and the Reconciliation of Science and Art in the Later Philosophy of Dewey" (1999a) I provide a comprehensive account of Dewey's continuum concept, based on a review of his various formulations throughout his body of work, in order to explain Dewey's novel conception of the complementary relationship between science and art that might mitigate postmodern concerns about science.

On the practical side, in "John Dewey and Progressive Education 1900-2000: *School and Society* Revisited in the Global Network Era" (Waks, 2003) I identify three educational problems addressed by Dewey that arise in new ways in the global network era: the technologically-mediated nature of contemporary experience, the postmodern character of current ethnic and cultural diversity, and the call for educational reconstruction involving non-state actors and agencies.

"Experience and (Computer-Mediated) Education" (Waks, 2001) takes up the first of these. It starts by noting Dewey's insistence, in *The School and Society* on the primacy, for learning, of immediate experience with the natural world, and raises the question whether his theory provides grounds for rejecting computer simulations of natural events as acceptable replacements. I argue that his four criteria of miseducative experiences in *Experience and Education* provide such grounds. "Re-reading Democracy and Education Today: Dewey on Globalization and Multicultural Education" (Waks, 2007) takes up the second. Situating *Democracy and Education* in the context of the nationalism that generated WWI, I explain that work as laying out the design of a program to promote cosmopolitan cooperation across difference through carefully structured learning activities. This approach requires that representative members of different subgroups are in school under the same roof, a condition that is rapidly disappearing in our current situation of school privatization and resegregation. "Brown, Common Citizenship and the Limits of Curriculum" (Waks, 2005) takes up the third question. Building on Dewey's approach in *Democracy and Education*, I argue that narrowly curricular solutions are largely irrelevant to education for equal citizenship when schools are segregated and unequal. I conclude that only a trans-district, metropolis-wide educational network incorporating state and non-state schools and home schooled children can effectively and legally address the problem of privatization and resegregation, by establishing means for bringing young people from all groups in the metropolis together periodically for common face-to-face significant learning experiences, and then supplementing these experiences through computer-network-based distributed learning at various local sites. Those experiences best adapted to preparing young people for work and social action in the age of computer networks, I argue, are not narrowly 'curricular'. That is, they are not organized as predetermined, pre-sequenced subject matters directed at specific learning aims. Rather they set learners to contend with unstructured problems requiring the use of multiple knowledge and experience bases and streams of on-line real-time information, with unpredicted outcomes. As I argue in "Project Method in Post-Industrial Education (1997) this calls for a new, more nuanced concept of 'project method' than Kilpatrick's, which Bode (1927) thoroughly demolished.

The Post-Globalization Educational Situation

In thinking about the post-globalization situation, I have started with these questions: What *is* 'fundamental' educational change? Will globalization cause fundamental educational change and usher in a *new* education? And if so, how? Will new models of rational action, teaching and learning, and educational organization, specific to the global network age, replace the dominant models of the industrial age? What will be the role of the state and non-governmental organizations in operating educational agencies in the emerging, post-globalization organizational structure? Assuming that private, for-profit universities, charter schools and home-schooling were all components of this emerging structure, why is the state willing to devolve operational responsibility for education to diverse non-state providers? And how might democratic publics best respond to these social and educational trends so as to modulate them in the interest of justice and human flourishing? Here is a summary of my thoughts:

In "The concept of fundamental educational change" (Waks, 2007) I argue that fundamental change is change at the *institutional* level, that is, as change in the *norms* that *authorize* the practices of educational organizations. Contrary to the well-known formulations of Larry Cuban, Michael Fullan and others, changes in *organizations*, regardless of their magnitude, are not fundamental unless they result from the need to bring practice into accord with new institutional norms. Thus fundamental change takes place as members of society come to think of education in new ways in response to changing conditions, thus generating new institutional norms, not as the result of 'change agents' manipulating educational organizations.

In "Citizenship in Transition: Globalization, Technology and Education" (Waks, 1995) I argue that as new learning formats and organizational models emerge in the era of global networks, we should expect them to reflect the models of rational action of the information age in the same way that technical means-ends reasoning model reflected the age of industrial production.

In "How Globalization Can Cause Fundamental Curriculum Change" (2003) I argue that specific barriers to fundamental change identified by such organizational theorists as Larry Cuban and Robert Dreeben, such as the institutional categories in the public's mind that induce it to reject innovations, have been undermined by recent migration trends and the new global distribution of labor, making fundamental change, and in particular change from a dominant state system to a loose network of public and non-government providers, *possible*.

In "Globalization, State Transformation and Education" (2006) I then address the question: why might the state be willing to cede operational control of education to non-government providers? I argue that while the modern nation state had traditionally relied on state educational systems to shore up its power bases, its continued control of educational systems now actually *weakens* the administrative, symbolic, and economic power bases of the post-globalization nation state. State education systems, I argue, cannot fulfil the inherent promise they make to students or their families of providing diploma holders access to advantageous social and economic positions. So, rather than bearing responsibility for this failure, state actors are happy to pass it on to non-state actors appealing to postmodern ethnic identities. Ethnic communities, having been given 'schools of their own', cannot then hold the state accountable for continuing social and occupational inequalities.

How then can we make the educational provisions in the emerging network society more just and beneficial than they have been under recent neo-liberal regimes? In "The Concept of the Networked Common School" (2004) I begin to lay out a framework for public metropolitan education networks assigning new roles to regional agencies capable of serving all young people across municipal and school district lines through both in-person, significant non-curricular learning and distributed learning through computer information networks. I am now working to clarify and expand this framework and connect it with actual organizational developments and new opportunities in the field, including charter schools formed by regional school district consortia and regional cyber schools.

INTUITION

I will close with brief comments about two other themes in my work: intuitive practical thinking, and the social uses of philosophy.

The first of these, intuition, I associate closely with the anti-technicist emphasis that runs through my work. The problem with all technicist approaches in such practical arts as teaching, consulting, psychotherapy and medical healing is that the practitioner brings to each situation a deep fund of practical knowledge, learned through direct experience, which extends well beyond anything explicitly formulated in technical maxims or rules of thumb. Michael Polanyi refers to this knowledge as *tacit*. Practitioners rely on this knowledge to orient themselves, to take account of contextual factors bearing on right action in particular circumstances and to sense through feeling various factors of the situation that might not be picked out by the practical categories inhering in the explicit rules and maxims they apply. The acquisition of tacit or intuitive knowledge of this sort strikes me as lying at the heart of practical training. To restrict practitioners to the use of standard rules of practice, to the adjustment of predefined means to predefined ends, nullifies this component of their training.

John Dewey took this sort of thinking as central to all arts (see his essay, "Qualitative Thought, (LW 5, 243-263), and Jim Garrison has recently helped us to see just how important it is in his system of ideas (Garrison, 1997). This kind of thought is also exhibited in the immediate awareness spoken of in Zen. One difficulty in getting a handle on intuitive thinking in practice is that the inherited philosophical concept of an "intuition" as either a sensory impression or a lucky guess bears almost no connection to it. In my paper "Intuition in Education: Teaching and Learning without Thinking" (2007) I offer an alternative account of "intuition" along the way to explaining its proper place in teaching and learning. I have also been exploring intuitive perception of persons as wholes, that is, perception that goes beyond the sort of reductive categorization used in e.g., educational, psychological or medical assessment. When a student or client says that a practitioner relates to him or her "as a person not a number" this is what they have in mind. In "Two Types of Interpersonal Listening" (in preparation) I contrast listening to others by way of categorizing their responses vs. listening in a direct or immediate, intuitive manner. Borrowing a term from religious contemplation, I label the former type of listening as *cataphatic* and the latter as *apophatic*. The role of apophatic listening in education is straightforward: the speakers apprehended in this manner feel "heard" and thus valued, and this positive valuation opens further avenues of action for them. One of my future projects is to develop a more complete account of the super-intelligence that draws readily on tacit or intuitive thought, side-stepping institutional and inner psychological constraints.

THE SOCIAL USES OF PHILOSOPHY

My early conviction that philosophy should be contributory to society has persisted. In "Three Contexts of Philosophy of Education: Intellectual, Institutional, and Ideological" (1988) I argue for a qualified pluralism in philosophy of education, contending that philosophical communications of different types, addressed to different kinds of audiences in different contexts, must meet different and often conflicting standards of evaluation. While communications in each of the three contexts are valuable and no one type is primary, the entire body of communications in the field is rightly held to practical account. If the enterprise as a whole has no practical value it can not sustain its social support and deserves to perish. As Richard Pring reminds us in his chapter, "Remember Chicago!" In "Public Philosophy and Social Responsibility" (1992), I construct a clear sense for the term "public philosophy" differentiating it from both popular philosophy and academic philosophy of an applied nature addressing public issues, and connecting it to communications between philosophers and members of democratic publics and social movements.. Finally, in "Public Intellectuals and Interdisciplinary Studies" (1997a) I argue that the role of public intellectuals situated in normatively-driven interdisciplinary programs such as ethnic or gender or environmental studies is not to prescribe ideas to social movement actors, but rather to recover and clarify insights embodied in historical and contemporary communications and re-construct them as usable instruments for the thinking and decision-making of those actors themselves.

Meanwhile I have recently accepted the chair of the Commission on Social Issues of the John Dewey Society, and am currently dialoguing with the commission and general membership to determine how best to use philosophy and the resources of Dewey Society to address pressing real world issues of our time.

NOTES

[i] Only the 'valuation' section appealed to me. Despite his pragmatist leanings, Lewis remained an empiricist in the theory of knowledge, with a strong commitment to the distinction between analytic and synthetic propositions. Having absorbed Quine's holism, expressed in "Two Dogmas of Empiricism" in From a Logical Point of View, I found these aspects of Lewis's thought implausible.

[ii] Morton White's *Toward Reunion in Philosophy* promised such an approach, but I found it disappointing.

REFERENCES

Adams , G. & Montague, W. (1962/1930). *Contemporary American philosophy: Personal statements*. New York: Russell & Russell (original publication 1930).

Bode, B. (1927). *Modern educational theories*, NY: MacMillan.

Dabney, V. (1958) Virginia's peaceable, honorable stand: A noted Richmond editor explains why South's responsible leaders oppose all integration of schools. *Life Magazine* September 22.

Garrison, Jim (1997). *Dewey and Eros: Wisdom and desire in the art of teaching*. New York: Teachers College Press.

Herrigel, E., (1953). *Zen in the art of archery*. New York, NY: Pantheon Books

Kitcher, P. (2007). *Living with Darwin: Evolution, design, and the future of faith*. New York: Oxford University Press.

Maue, K. (1979). *Water in the lake: Real events for the imagination*. New York: Harper & Row.

Petrie, H.G. (1975). Can education find its lost objectives under the street lamp of behaviorism? In Smith, R. (Ed.), *Regaining educational leadership: essays critical of PBTE/CBTE* (pp. 64-74). New York: Wiley.

Strike, K. (1974). On the expressive potential of behaviorist language. *American Educational Research Journal, 11*(2), 103-120.

Suzuki, D. T. (1970). *The field of Zen; contributions to the Middle Way, the journal of the Buddhist Society*. New York: Harper & Row.

Waks, L. (1968). Knowledge and understanding as educational aims. *The Monist, 52* (1), 104-119.

Waks, L. (1969). Philosophy, education and the doomsday threat. *Review of Educational Research, 39*(5), 607-621.

Waks, L. (1973). Non-behavioral goals: Investigating the validity of the two-defect argument. *Curriculum Theory Network, 4*(1), 37-42.

Waks, L. (1975). Freedom and desire in the Summerhill philosophy of education. In D. Nyberg (Ed.), *The philosophy of open education* (pp. 195-208). Routledge and Kegan Paul.

Waks, L. (1975). Educational objectives and existential heroes. In Smith, R. (Ed.), *Regaining educational leadership: Essays critical of PBTE/CBTE* (pp. 87-103). New York: Wiley.

Waks, L. (1985). Functionalism and the autonomy of religion. *Teachers College Record, 87*(1), 271-276.

Waks, L. (1987). A technological literacy credo. *Bulletin of Science, Technology and Society, 7*(1), 357-366.

Waks, L. (1988). Three contexts for philosophy of education: Intellectual, institutional and ideological. *Educational Theory, 38* (2), 167-174.

Waks, L. (1989). The oil in the machine: Human technique in technological society. *Research in Philosophy and Technology, 9*, 155-170.

Waks, L. (1991a). The new world of technology in American education: A case study of policy formation and succession. *Technology in Society, 13*(1), 233-253.

Waks, L. (1991b). Technological literacy for the new majority. In S. Majumar (Ed.), *Science education in the United States: Issues, crises, priorities* (pp. 446-483). Philadelphia: Pennsylvania Academy of Science.

Waks, L. (1991c). Science-technology-society education and the paradox of green studies. In P. Durbin (Ed.), *Europe, America and technology: Philosophical perspectives. Philosophy and Technology, 9*, 247-257.

Waks, L. (1991d). Ivan Illich and *Deschooling Society*: A reappraisal. In P. Durbin (Ed.), *Europe, America and technology: Philosophical perspectives. Philosophy and Technology, 9*, 57-73.

Waks, L. (1992). Philosophers and social responsibility in technological society. In J. Pitt & E. Lugo, (Eds.), *The technology of discovery and the discovery of technology*, Society for Philosophy of Technology, and reprinted in *Technology's School*.

Waks, L. (1993). Science-technology-society as an academic field and a social movement. *Technology in Society, 15*, 399-408.

Waks, L. (1995a). Emptiness. In J. Garrison & A. G. Rud (Eds.), *The educational conversation: Closing the gap* (pp. 85-95). Albany NY: SUNY Press.

Waks, L. (1995b). *Technology's school: The challenge for philosophy.* Westport, CT: JAI Press.

Waks, L. (1996a). Citizenship in transition: Globalization, technology and education. *International Journal of Technology and Design Education, 6,* 287-300.

Waks, L. (1996b). Environmental claims and citizen rights. *Environmental Ethics, 18,* 133-148.

Waks, L. (1997a). Public intellectuals and interdisciplinary studies. *Research in Philosophy and Technology, 16,* 61-72.

Waks, L. (1997b). The project method in post-industrial education, *Journal of Curriculum Studies, 29*(4), 391-406.

Waks, L. (1998a). Experimentalism and the flow of experience. *Educational Theory, 48*(1), 1-19.

Waks, L. (1998b). Four basic questions about high-tech education. *Technology in Society, 20*(3), 275-286.

Waks, L. (1998c). Post-experimentalist pragmatism. *Studies in Philosophy and Education, 17*(1), 17-28.

Waks, L. (1999a). The continuum of means-ends and the reconciliation of science and art in the later philosophy of John Dewey. *Transactions of the C. S. Peirce Society, 35*(3), 595-612.

Waks, L. (1999b). Reflective practice in the design studio and teacher education, *Journal of Curriculum Studies* 31 (3), 303-316.

Waks, L. (2001a). Computer-mediated experience and education. *Educational Theory, 51*(4), 415-432.

Waks, L. (Ed.). (2001b). *Philosophy of Design, Design Education, and Educational Design.* Special Issue of the *International Journal of Technology and Design Education, 11* (1).

Waks, L. (2003a). How globalization can cause fundamental curriculum change. *Journal of Educational Change, 4*(4), 383-418. Reprinted in H. Lauder, P. Brown, & A. Halsey (Eds.). (2006), *Education, globalization, and social change* (pp. 835-851). Oxford: Oxford University Press.

Waks, L. (2003b). John Dewey and progressive education 1900-2000: *School and Society* revisited in the global network era. Chapter 16 in G. Spadafora, ed., *John Dewey: Una nova democrazia per Il XX! seccolo,* Rome: Anicia, 231-245 (in Italian English translation of this volume is in preparation at Southern Illinois Press).

Waks, L. (2004). The concept of the networked common school. *E-Learning, 1*(2), 317-328.

Waks, L. (2005). Brown v. Board, common citizenship, and the limits of curriculum. *Journal of Curriculum and Supervision, 20* (2), 94-128.

Waks, L. (2005b). Education in science, technology and ethics. In C. Mitcham, C. (Ed.), *Encyclopedia of science, technology, and ethics.* Detroit: Macmillan Reference USA.

Waks, L. (2006a). Globalization, state transformation and education: Will bureaucratic standardization or postmodern diversity prevail? *Studies in Philosophy and Education, 25*(5), 403-424.

Waks, L. (2006b). Globalization and the renewal of technological literacy. In J. Dakers (Ed.), *Defining technological literacy: Towards an epistemological framework* (pp. 275-296). New York: Palgrave Macmillan.

Waks, L. (2007a). Re-reading *Democracy and Education*: John Dewey on globalization and multi-cultural education. *Education and Culture. 23*(1), 27-37.

Waks, L. (2007b). The concept of fundamental educational change. *Educational Theory, 57*(3), 277-295.

Waks, L. (2007c). Intuition in education: Teaching and learning without thinking. In D. Vokey (Ed.), *Philosophy of Education 2006.* Normal, ILL: Philosophy of Education Society, 379-388.

Waks, L. (in preparation). Two types of interpersonal learning. In S. Haroutunian-Gordon & L. Waks (Eds.), *Listening in context: Challenges for Teachers.*

Leonard J. Waks
Temple University

JOHN WHITE

THE CENTRALITY OF WELL-BEING

BEGINNINGS

It probably all started with my father. He came from a respectable working-class family in the East End of London, won a scholarship to a grammar school in the First World War, and left it at 16 to work in a commercial firm. Two things stand out. First, listening with him to the Brains Trust around the end of the Second World War and sharing some of his intellectual excitement, if not his grasp of the arguments, as the philosopher C.E.M. Joad and his co-discussants unpicked the latest theory of the nature of time or wrestled with the justification of democracy. And second, during the general election campaign of 1945, his going out at night to paint 'Vote Labour' slogans on the local roads.

I find it hard to say, more specifically, when I first became interested in philosophy of education. There are signs, perhaps, in the left-wing, existentialist sentiments of the journals I began writing in embarrassing mid-Victorian prose from the age of nineteen. Five years later, in 1959, my essay about my first teaching practice as a trainee history teacher contained comments like 'Am I sure that the subject I am teaching them is essential to their development? ...What habits and attitudes is it fostering? ...What are thinking, habits, attitudes, emotions, instincts, feelings? The words come up in my self criticism, but are left quite undefined.'

Roger Wilson, Professor of Education at Bristol University in my training year, told me in a frank but kindly way that my ideas were promising but half-baked. He suggested that if I taught in London, I should get in touch with a good friend of his – and fellow-Quaker – Richard Peters, who had just launched a joint BA degree in Philosophy and Psychology at Birkbeck College, London University. This was – and still is – a college for mature students studying part-time in the evening.

I met Peters – who a few years earlier had been a colleague of Joad's at Birkbeck – and signed up for his new degree while teaching history and French in a secondary school in east London. Philosophy and philosophical psychology became absorbing in their own right. The interest in getting clear about fundamental matters, which in an uninformed way had been part of my psyche for years, now became all-enthralling.

I shifted to teaching liberal studies part-time in technical colleges so as to give me more time for philosophy. In the final year of my degree, 1965, my contract at Battersea College of Advanced Technology was not renewed for the next academic year and I was out of a job. Peters, now at the Institute of Education, was building up his team of philosophers of education and I applied successfully to join it.

L.J. Waks (ed.), Leaders in Philosophy of Education: Intellectual Self Portraits, 269–278.

So I came into the discipline by chance. I might well have found myself instead applying fruitlessly for posts in epistemology, or, if professionally luckier, researching some technical issue in the philosophy of action. Who knows what might have been?

PERSONAL FAVOURITES

Books:

White, J. (1973) *Towards a Compulsory Curriculum* London: Routledge and Kegan Paul

-------- (1979) *Philosophers as Educational Reformers* (with Peter Gordon) London: Routledge and Kegan Paul

------- (1982) *The Aims of Education Restated* London: Routledge and Kegan Paul

------ (1990) *Education and the Good Life* London: Kogan Page

------ (1991) *A National Curriculum for All* (with Philip O'Hear) London: Institute for Public Policy Research

------- (1997) *Education and the End of Work* London: Cassell

------- (1998) *Do Howard Gardner's Multiple Intelligences Add Up?* London: Institute of Education

------ (2002) *The Child's Mind* London: RoutledgeFalmer

------ (2005) *The Curriculum and the Child* London: Routledge

Articles:

------- Intelligence, Destiny and Education: the ideological roots of intelligence testing London: Routledge (2006a)

------- 'Multiple invalidities?' in Schaler, J. A. (ed) *Gardner Under Fire: A Rebel Psychologist Faces His Critics* Chicago, Ill.: Open Court Publishing Company (2006b)

------- What schools are for and why IMPACT 14, Philosophy of Education Society of Great Britain (2007a)

My first published papers in philosophy of education were on indoctrination and on teaching creativity. The initiative for these came not from me but from Richard Peters. His project at the time was a comprehensive investigation of central educational concepts and he enlisted several of us in this task.

Gradually, I began to work on things that came more from the heart. Big, sprawling things like the shaping of a fairer society, in which personal freedom was a central value. Like other young people welcoming in a new era of socialism after thirteen years of Conservative power, I was eager for radical change. Education was key to this. This thought had been present in the solitary wrestlings of my journal entries. Now it had behind it not only seven years' teaching experience, but also training in philosophy. This helped to give it stiffening.

The Labour government of 1964 favoured comprehensive education. This in my view needed a common curriculum. Until that time, academic schooling was only for an élite selected for grammar schools partly by intelligence tests. The rest had something more intellectually denuded, more fitting for a life of manual work.

I explored the idea of a defensible common curriculum first in a number of articles in the weekly *New Society* and spelt it out at book length in *Towards a Compulsory Curriculum* (TCC) (1973).

In one way this last was an attempt to define my own position vis-a-vis those of Richard Peters and my other colleagues Paul Hirst and Robert Dearden. Like all of

In one way this last was an attempt to define my own position vis-a-vis those of Richard Peters and my other colleagues Paul Hirst and Robert Dearden. Like all of them, I was in favour of an intellectually demanding curriculum, based not on conventional subject divisions but on logically distinctive areas of understanding. Unlike all of them, I did not find this basis in Hirst's 'forms of knowledge' theory, but in what seemed to me at the time a radically new departure (...but which now looks more like a variation on the Hirstian theme).

I also thought there should be a state imposed curriculum in place of the autonomy that schools then had. If the tradition of socially divided curricula was to go, its replacement had to be centrally enforced.

This was one of the themes in the book that persisted into later writings. Another had more to do with philosophy. My journal philosophisings had obsessed about how best to live, individually and communally. When I began my philosophy degree, I took it for granted that it would help me sort things out. What else could a degree in philosophy be for? By the end of the course, philosophy of life had receded in my priorities and interrelated fascinations of metaphysics, epistemology, and philosophy of language had come to the fore. But gradually, after the degree was over, the ethical interest won through again.

PERSONAL WELL-BEING AND PERSONAL AUTONOMY

My first philosophy teacher at Birkbeck had been Richard Peters. He taught me – inspirationally – history of ethics and philosophy of mind. He spoke to my confusions, since he, too, was fascinated by ideas of what human beings are and how they should live. Around the time he left Birkbeck for the Institute of Education, in 1962, he co-published an article with A P Griffiths called 'The autonomy of prudence' (Griffiths and Peters 1962). This created little stir, but was of great interest to me. Most writings in ethics at that time were about morality. The latter was patently a relevant topic for anyone, like myself, interested in how we should live. But morality was only half the story. However decently I (or anyone else) lived, I still faced choices about what I was to do. Taking a moral framework for granted, what was a fulfilling life *for me* (or anyone)?

Although Mill, Sidgwick and Moore had written on this, Griffiths and Peters's paper was the only contemporary treatment of it I knew. A little later, in 1966, Peters developed its central, Kantian, idea in an educational direction in his celebrated chapter of *The Ethics of Education* on 'worthwhile activities'. Although the Kantian argument did not seem to me to work, I considered the topic itself – personal fulfilment – to be pivotal in justifying the school curriculum. TCC was the first of many shots – continuing to this day – at spelling out the nature of personal well-being and showing how curriculum activities can promote it.

I have just talked about *justifying* the school curriculum. Looking back from 2007, this seems an odd word to use. It is as though the academic curriculum is in some sense a fixture and reasons have to be given for showing why it is right that it be a fixture. This reflects how many of us in our field thought about education in those days. We took for granted that moving away from a divided educational

271

system to a comprehensive one meant giving ordinary, non-grammar, children the academic schooling from which they had been excluded. The philosophical task, so it seemed to us, was to provide a valid rationale for such a programme.

After 1973 I became less interested in this justificatory project and more in getting at the fundamental aims on which a defensible common education could be based – without pre-commitment to the kind of curricular vehicles which might best further them. *The Aims of Education Restated* (AER) shows where I was at in 1982. In TCC I had bracketed off moral aims of education so as to concentrate on those to do with the good of the pupil. In AER I felt readier to take both on board, and to deal with their interrelationships. Economic aims, and their links with the two aims mentioned, also came into the picture.

My views on interconnexions between personal well-being and morality had meanwhile been deepened by a co-authored book with a historian of education colleague on the educational ideas and influence of T.H.Green and other British Hegelians, called *Philosophers as Educational Reformers* (White 1979). Acquaintance with Hegel, aroused by Charles Taylor's *Hegel* of 1975, further distanced me from Peters's Kantian approach to ethics. It helped me eventually to locate myself within a broadly Aristotelian tradition. This deepened during the 1980s, especially after the publication of MacIntyre's *After Virtue* in 1981.

Meanwhile my treatment of the good of the pupil in AER still had to depend largely on my own resources. Soon after I wrote it, in 1986, two seminal works on personal well-being were published: Joseph Raz's *The Morality of Freedom* (see especially chs 12 and 14); and James Griffin's *Well-being*. I incorporated insights from them in my 1990 book *Education and the Good Life* (EGL), but in AER, as in TCC, I was still making what seemed to me later the mistake of writing personal autonomy into personal well-being. This came out in my account of the good of the pupil in terms of 'post-reflective-desire-satisfaction'. In other words, those of one's experiences and activities contribute to one's flourishing which, having reviewed all major possibilities, one chooses to pursue for their own sake. This assumes that the chooser is an autonomous person, able to reflect on a wide range of possible ends. But it overlooks the point made by Raz that people can flourish or fail to flourish not only in liberal societies like our own, where autonomy is a central value, but also in societies where one's major goals are laid down for one by custom or authority.

In EGL, as in AER and TCC, while still advocating the promotion of the pupil's personal autonomy, I was also still arguing that personal well-being is a subjective matter in the sense that it depends on the desires of the individual. All attempts I had seen to show that it is something objective, culminating in Richard Peters's theory of worthwhile activities, had seemed to me flawed. This was not only of academic interest, since it raised the possibility, if not the likelihood, of pupils' being brought up, misguidedly, to believe that certain activities, the pursuit of intellectual activities, for instance, are intrinsically valuable for any human being and so for themselves.

The main shift in my thinking on personal well-being since 1990 has been to question *both* the individualistic-subjectivist *and* the objectivist approaches in favour of a largely culturally-dependent (but not culturally relativist) account. For instance, enjoying Mozart's music can contribute to one's well-being. This value is independent of any individual's desires, but not of human desires more generally. It is a value dependent on a certain culture – it did not exist before the eighteenth century. At the same time listening to Mozart is still a worthwhile activity, even though the princely culture that produced it has long since faded away: the value is not relative to that culture. For more on this see White 2005, ch12; 2007b. Joseph Raz's more recent writings like *Engaging Reason* (1999) and *The Practice of Value* (2003) have been a main inspiration here.

I have also been interested in exploring possible specific components of well-being, always with applications to educational aims in mind. The place of knowledge in education and in well-being is discussed in TCC chs 2, 3, 6, AER ch2, EGL ch7. In all my writings on the subject, I have pressed the cause of altruism in various forms as an obviously desirable educational aim. But is it a necessary feature of the personally fulfilling life and so already covered in aims to do with the pupil's own well-being? Can there be a flourishing life without art or aesthetic experience? In a secular world, do we need for our flourishing some awareness of a cosmic framework to our lives? What is the place of work in the good life? What room is there for patriotism? For recognition? Essays on nearly all these themes can be found in my *The Curriculum and the Child* (2005 chs 9-13). A book length treatment of work and well-being is my *Education and the End of Work* (1997). My interest in art and aesthetic experience is indebted to Ray Elliott, who taught me ethics and aesthetics at Birkbeck and later became a colleague in Richard Peters's department. Ray was the profoundest philosopher I have known and the one most catholic in his sympathies. His insights into the subject and his critical assessments of my own work have been a valuable, and often chastening, part of my philosophical development.

PHILOSOPHICAL POLICY CRITIQUE

A few years after I had joined Richard Peters' unit in 1965, I remember Richard telling me of a conversation he had had with Brian Simon, the leading historian of education of the time and left-wing champion of the new comprehensive school system. 'I see you have a sport in your department, Richard', Simon is reported to have said, referring to myself.

What he had in mind were my political interests. They came out in my views about the control of the school curriculum. I first floated the idea of a shift from professional to political control in an article in *New Society* in 1969. This was during Harold Wilson's Labour government. The state had to step in to ensure a decent – academically demanding – curriculum for all.

TCC spelt out this notion further. Throughout the 1970s I continued refining the arguments for state curriculum control, also taking advantage of my history degree to find out why state control over most schools' curricula was *abandoned* in the 1920s (White 2005, ch.5). I was pleased in 1976 when the Callaghan Labour government embraced the idea that the school curriculum was no longer to be a 'secret garden' in which only professionals could wander. But I was a little less delighted when Labour lost power to Margaret Thatcher in 1979 and her administration intensified the pressure for political control.

There is an irony here. The National Curriculum created under Thatcher in 1988 extended the curriculum of the grammar school to the whole state school population, from five to sixteen. No problem then, of working class children being sold short by being chained to low-status programmes. Did not the National Curriculum realise the vision I had had since the 1960s?

Far from it! My views on what the government could legitimately impose had become sharpened over the years. By the 1980s it was clear to me, influenced as I was by the work of Patricia White, that the central argument for a shift to political control went back to the nature of democracy. Teachers have no more right than any other section of the citizenry to determine what the aims of education should be. Since this topic is closely bound up with what kind of society is desirable, it is a political matter on which all of us should in principle have an equal voice. Where teachers *should* have privileged powers is in determining how aims are best realised in the specific circumstances in which they work, i.e. in more detailed curriculum planning and pedagogy. Only they are in a position to know what works best here (White 2005, chs 6, 7).

The trouble with the 1988 National Curriculum was that the government got things precisely the wrong way round. It laid down in great specificity a curriculum and assessment arrangements based on traditional grammar school subjects, but said next to nothing about what this whole complex system was *for*. It ignored its own legitimate remit as a democratic authority and vastly encroached on that of teachers. Much of what I have written on the topic since that time – beginning with EGL in 1990 – has revolved, in different ways, around this constitutional blemish.

By 1988, as I said above, I had become less interested in the components of the timetabled curriculum and more in a defensible set of aims. If children were being sold short, it was not because they were not getting an academic curriculum, but because, on the contrary, they *were* getting an academic curriculum when no valid reasons had been given why this was desirable. It was imposed in 1988, it seems, out of respect for tradition alone, but there was no guarantee that what might or might not have been appropriate for a small minority of middle-class children in the mid-nineteenth century was suitable for children from every background living in the twenty-first.

Since the early 1990s I have been increasingly involved in working with UK policy-making bodies on the idea of an aims-based school curriculum, one, that is, which sees traditional school subjects as just one kind of vehicle among many possible ones for realising well-thought-out aims. In 1991 I co-authored *A National Curriculum for All* for the left-wing think tank, the Institute for Public Policy Research (IPPR). The appearance in 1999 of the first official set of national aims in the country's history alongside the National Curriculum subjects led to work with the Qualifications and Curriculum Authority (QCA) on how far there was a good match between the new aims and the detailed statutory requirements in these subjects. As I showed in my edited collection *Rethinking the School Curriculum*

(2004a: chs 1, 2, 14), for most subjects there was a gross mismatch. This is scarcely surprising, since the National Curriculum subjects predated the aims and already had their own internal *modi vivendi,* orientated for the most part towards specialist expertise in their own area, rather than towards wider purposes. Mathematics, for instance, is widely assumed to be a subject of central importance in the curriculum, but its credentials as regards its more abstract elements are open to question (White 2005, ch 16). I have discussed more recent government moves towards an aims-based curriculum in *What schools are for and why* (2007a).

This last publication is an IMPACT booklet. IMPACT is a topical policy-focussed series produced by the Philosophy of Education Society of Great Britain. I was its first editor, in 1999-2000, and responsible for its first half dozen or so publications – on hot topics ranging from assessment to performance-related pay for teachers. I have always enjoyed this kind of work. In the 1980s I contributed to many of the Bedford Way Papers published by the Institute of Education, producing philosophical critiques of current policies on the school curriculum, headteacher training, teacher education, and education in a pluralist society. In the 1990s, in other policy-related Institute publications, I critiqued arts education in schools, the teaching of history, the school effectiveness movement, mathematics in the curriculum, and the future of the national curriculum.

I have always seen work in our discipline as stretching on a gamut between abstract investigations in general philosophy at one end and, at the other, issues of the day requiring conceptual clarification or the unearthing of assumptions. In my own case, I have constantly shifted back and forth along my personal gamut, now exploring in an academic journal the meta-ethics of personal well-being, and now, in a newspaper article, degutting the British government's campaign for 'personalised learning' or its Gifted and Talented Strategy. I have always wanted philosophy of education to cut ice. As a branch of applied philosophy, it is a handmaiden to the education service just as medical ethics is to the health service. Both applied fields can occupy this role while observing a proper philosophical rigour and objectivity. Spending one's time as a philosopher of education reading papers at exotically-located international conferences on the scarcely-educationally-relevant ideas of the latest cult philosopher seems to me professional corruption.

PHILOSOPHY OF MIND AND PHILOSOPHICAL PSYCHOLOGY

Richard Peters was my first teacher of philosophy of mind. I remember those early weeks at Birkbeck in autumn 1960, struggling with Ryle's *The Concept of Mind*. Whether Richard's Quakerism was a factor or not, he taught partly by silence. He would throw us a question like 'What is consciousness, then?' and sit patiently puffing on his pipe for the several minutes (it seemed) for some brave participant – never me – to limp out an answer.

David Hamlyn, Richard's colleague at Birkbeck, deepened and broadened my understanding of philosophy of mind. I came to see connexions with central issues in epistemology and metaphysics previously unknown to me. Both men were also among pioneers in the new field of the philosophy of psychology, which draws on philosophy of mind to explore the soundness of theories in psychology. While Peters was fascinated by the whole history of psychology from Plato to Freud and Skinner, Hamlyn's particular interests were in the psychology of perception, behaviorism and, a little later, Piaget's developmentalism. It was partly through his work on Piaget that Hamlyn also became a major contributor to philosophy of education. In very many ways he was also a major influence on my own work in particular.

Politics, as often, also came into the picture. In the 1960s the 11+ exam was still standardly used for secondary school selection and opposed by campaigners for comprehensive education. Since intelligence testing was a key part of the 11+, I focused on the concept of intelligence most closely associated with it. I located what seemed a critical weakness. Written into it was the assumption that we each have our own individually differing ceilings of intellectual ability beyond which we cannot progress. It was this assumption that provided a rationale for 11+ selections. I argued that it is neither verifiable nor falsifiable, thus placing it, following Popper, outside the realm of science (White 2005, ch1).

Although I had taught courses on philosophy of mind throughout my career, I did not write much on the topic before the millennium apart from a paper on the education of the emotions that presented an alternative account to Richard Peters's more austere, Kantian, interpretation (White 2005, ch2). In *The Child's Mind* in 2002 I expanded and updated in a more popular form my lecture material on philosophy of mind applied to education.

By that time Howard Gardner's theory of 'multiple intelligences' had become enormously influential in school reform. I wrote a critical monograph on it in 1998 called *Do Howard Gardner's Multiple Intelligences Add Up?* and followed this up with a fuller critique in White 2006b. I agreed with Gardner in rejecting the centrality of the logico-linguistic intelligence traditionally associated with the IQ, but found no sound basis for his more many-sided categorisation.

I knew that the traditional view of intelligence found in Cyril Burt went back to the eugenic ideas of Francis Galton. But I had no idea what its earlier history was. This led me into a historical exploration of the origins of intelligence testing in *Intelligence, Destiny and Education* (2006a). Here I tested out the hypothesis that, since, as I discovered, virtually all the pioneers of intelligence testing in Britain and in the USA were from Dissenting or Puritan stock, some of these origins may lie in the early thought world of radical Protestantism. Linking my two interests, intelligence and the school curriculum, I also argued in the book that the traditional academic curriculum may well have roots in the same soil.

CHRISTIAN LEGACIES

Religion has become more salient in my interests in the last few years. This has nothing to do with death being not far round the corner. Religious ideas are the mystifications I've always thought them to be. For this, too, I should thank my father for first setting me on the sceptical path.

I have become increasingly aware of the continuing and often unnoticed influence of Christian ideas from Britain's past on today's largely secular society. Sometimes, as in the present Thatcher-to-Blair period of our politics, there have been overt attempts to shore up a decaying creed via Christian-biased legislation about the content of religious education and via the encouragement of faith schools and faith-based academies. Some of my recent writings (e.g. White 2004b) have questioned whether we need religious education as a separate subject; suggested that it should avoid ethical recommendations about how we should live; and pressed for religious assumptions, eg about the existence of God, not to be taken for granted but to be openly and fairly discussed.

The less noticeable residues of Christian belief are intellectually more fascinating. I have explored these, as I have said, as they affect contemporary views about the mind of the learner, and about the school curriculum. They come into my book on the centrality of work in our society and in related attitudes inculcated into school children. The work ethic we owe to the puritan-dissenting strand of our history is still powerful (White 1997, ch1). They come, too, into the way we conventionally think about how we should live and about how this matter should be taken up in schools. There has been a tendency to over-moralise the topic and at the same time to separate personal fulfilment too discretely off from moral obligations and to play it down (White 1990, ch 3). I see this tendency as a legacy of an age when mortal life was based on our duties towards God and personal fulfilment, if it existed for any of us at all, could only be in the life hereafter. Bernard Williams's work, not least his *Ethics and the Limits of Philosophy,* as well as Nietzsche's writings such as *The Genealogy of Morals*, have helped to open my eyes on these issues. They have helped me to understand the dominance of moral philosophy in British ethical writings in the earlier part of my career and the lack of interest in personal well-being. I have mentioned this above.

CONCLUSION

So much for the past. What of future plans? It will be good to go back to personal well-being and explore it in more depth. As in the past, theoretical enquiry may occasionally have to yield to practical involvement and I may find myself caught up in philosophical policy critique. Beyond this, I have nothing more specific in mind. I prefer things to be open in this way. It's part of what I understand by a flourishing life. For me, that is. Not everyone will want it.

REFERENCES

Griffin, J. (1986). *Well-being.* Oxford: Clarendon Press.
Griffiths, A.P. & Peters, R.S. (1962). The autonomy of prudence. *Mind, LXXI.*
MacIntyre, A. (1981) *After virtue.* London: Duckworth.
Nietzsche, F. (1887). *On the genealogy of morals* (Ed. Kauffmann, W.). New York: Vintage, 1968.
Peters, R.S. (1966). *The ethics of education.* London: Allen and Unwin.
(1986) *The morality of freedom.* Oxford: Clarendon Press.
Raz, J. (1999). *Engaging reason.* Oxford: Clarendon Press.

Raz, J. (2003). *The practice of value.* Oxford: Clarendon Press.

Ryle, G. (1949). *The concept of mind.* London: Hutchinson.

White, J. (1973). *Towards a compulsory curriculum.* London: Routledge and Kegan Paul (TCC).

White, J. (1979). *Philosophers as educational reformers* (with Peter Gordon). London: Routledge and Kegan Paul.

White, J. (1982). *The aims of education restated.* London: Routledge and Kegan Paul (AER).

White, J. (1990). *Education and the good life.* London: Kogan Page (EGL).

White, J. (1991). *A national curriculum for all* (with Philip O'Hear). London: Institute for Public Policy Research.

White, J. (1997). *Education and the end of work.* London: Cassell.

White, J. (1998). *Do Howard Gardner's multiple intelligences add up?* London: Institute of Education

White, J. (2002). *The child's mind.* London: RoutledgeFalmer.

White, J. (Ed.) (2004a). *Rethinking the school curriculum.* London: RoutledgeFalmer.

White, J. (2004b). Should RE be a compulsory school subject? *British Journal of Religious Education, 26*(2).

White, J. (2005). *The curriculum and the child.* London: Routledge.

White, J. (2006a). *Intelligence, destiny and education: The ideological roots of intelligence testing.* London: Routledge.

White, J. (2006b). Multiple invalidities? In Schaler, J. A. (Ed.), *Gardner under fire: A rebel psychologist faces his critics.* Chicago, Ill.: Open Court Publishing Company

White, J. (2007a). *What schools are for and why.* IMPACT 14, Philosophy of Education Society of Great Britain.

White, J. (2007b). Wellbeing and education: Issues of culture and authority. *Journal of Philosophy of Education, 41*(1).

Williams, B. (1985). *Ethics and the limits of philosophy.* London: Fontana.

John White

PATRICIA WHITE

FROM FEMALE ANATOMY TO CIVIC VIRTUES

BEGINNINGS

First came the passion for education. I was brought up in a terrace house in a working class district of Bristol by a father who was a motor mechanic and a mother who was a shop assistant. We had coal fires, gas lighting, no bathroom, an outside toilet and three books: *The Illustrated Family Doctor*, by a General Practitioner, *The New Illustrated Universal Reference Book* and *The New English Dictionary*. Apart from a writing pad, most often used for writing notes to school, it had no writing paper. Going first to a state primary school and then, after passing the 11+ examination, to a state secondary school gave me interests and enthusiasms which transported me into a new existence. No question then about my future career. If a state education system could do this, I wanted to be part of it.

After a degree in German, I trained as a teacher. From the first day teaching was a joy. My classes were relatively small and as the only German teacher in the school I was teaching at all levels. I enjoyed the enthusiasm of the eager language learners and the intellectual challenge of discussing Kafka, Schiller, Hölderlin and Heine with students preparing for university entrance examinations and only a few years younger than myself.

But then a small cloud appeared over this Eden which was to put me on the path to work in philosophy of education. More accurately, it was not a cloud but the female upper arm. In the girls' school in the country town where I was working, the new headteacher announced in the summer of 1960 that staff must wear frocks with sleeves that covered the upper arm at least to the elbow. What was the problem? The reason given was that the female upper arm was the ugliest part of the female anatomy and must be covered. This was one of a number of rules delivered *ex cathedra*. (Another was that girls should stand in assembly hands by their sides with palms facing inwards. Palms facing outwards indicated mental illness.) This latest rule had a life-changing effect on me. It led me to think about the institution of the school, the basis of the headteacher's authority, the legitimate area of the school's control over its students and staff, the state's control over schools.

LEARNING AND TEACHING PHILOSOPHY OF EDUCATION

In 1962 I asked Roger Wilson, who was the professor of education at Bristol where I had done my teacher training, to suggest the best place to pursue these questions. He suggested the University of London's Institute of Education where a new professor, Richard Peters, had just been appointed. This man was going to bring

L.J. Waks (ed.), Leaders in Philosophy of Education: Intellectual Self Portraits, 279–288.

the kind of depth and rigour into educational studies I was seeking. Reading educational theory books in preparation for the course, I began to wonder if Roger Wilson was right. They seemed either to specialise in a kind of refined preachy woolliness or to give accounts of what the Great Philosophers had said about education. Would the Diploma in Philosophy and Sociology of Education I was about to embark on really be that different?

PERSONAL FAVOURITES

Books

Beyond Domination: An Essay in the Political Philosophy of Education, 1983

Civic Virtues and Public Schooling: educating citizens for a democratic society 1996

Philosophy of Education: Major Themes in the Analytic Tradition (With Paul H Hirst) 1998

Papers

Education, Democracy and the Public Interest. In R S Peters (Ed.) *The Philosophy of Education*, Oxford, Oxford University Press, 1973

'Having a Voice and Getting a Hearing: an educational perspective on free speech in a plural society' *Studies in Philosophy and Education* , volume 15, 1996, 201-208

'Gratitude, Citizenship and Education' *Die Zeitschrift für Pädagogik. 38. Beiheft,* 1998, 241-250

'Political Education in the Early Years: the place of civic virtues' *Oxford Review of Education*, Vol. 25, Nos. 1 & 2, 1999, 59-70

'Educating Investors: an exploration in virtue ethics' In Jürgen Oelkers and Max Mangold (Eds.) *Demokratie, Bildung und Markt*, Bern, Lang-Verlag, 2003

'Political Forgiveness and Citizenship Education' In Rita Casale and Rebekka Horlacher (Eds.) *Bildung und Öffentlichkeit,* Weinheim und Basel, Beltz Verlag, 2007

It certainly was. I entered a different world. Richard Peters often said he aimed to replace mush with mesh. For me this is just what he did. His courses went beyond the standard ethics and political philosophy courses then taught in university philosophy departments. Starting with the traditional discussions of intuitionism, emotivism, utilitarianism, he located this material intellectually in relation to his own developing position on the appropriate ethical and social framework for education. This he later set out in *Ethics and Education.* In parallel courses, and in lively interaction with the class, Paul Hirst forged a conception of the place of philosophy in educational studies, and developed an epistemologically based foundation for curriculum development (Hirst 1965a, b). This was the soon to be hotly contested forms of knowledge theory, which much later still underwent a radical reassessment by its author (Hirst, 1993). I was by now head of a German department in a London school and studying at the Institute in the evenings. It was exhilarating to be in Peters' and Hirst's classes as each step of the arguments they were developing came under challenge, often by one or other of them as they sat in on each others' classes. Views which withstood this intense scrutiny would provide, I thought, the framework I was seeking for my school practice. This would not be some invincible structure to last for my whole teaching career, but a rationally revisable one. For this, as Hirst and Peters stressed, clarity was essential. It was praise indeed when Richard Peters said to me that the best thing about my seminar paper was that it was so clear he could see exactly where it was wrong.

Two significant influences came from the US. With Kingsley Price's *Education and Philosophical Thought* I discovered that treatment of historical philosophers' views on education need not take the form of 'stories'. Their views could be deftly analysed and assessed. Jane Roland Martin's paper 'On the Reduction of "Knowing That" to "Knowing How" intrigued me. I pored over it for hours. Aside from the content, it was important to me that here was a *woman* doing this kind of forensic analysis which actually had a real bearing on education. In Britain in the early 1960s, as far as I was aware there were no women working analytically in philosophy of education. While the US influences came from writings, a third influence, from the UK, depended very much on personal contact. An important counterpoint for me to the 'London line', as it later came to be called, was Peter Winch's courses in ethics and epistemology at Birkbeck College. I was lucky enough to be in a class with half a dozen other students with the man who had just written *The Idea of a Social Science*. Even more significant for me, though, than Peter Winch's challenging of the idea of an ethics like Peters' based on principles, was being in his classes and experiencing his deeply serious attitude to ethics and his tenacity in argument. Often a whole class would be spent on one point as he dealt with the objections of a single student.

Looking at my work in school from these new perspectives helped me to get the intellectual grasp on the aims and content of education I had been wanting. But I was not the only one persuaded of the benefit of philosophical understanding for teachers in schools. With the aim of achieving a wholly graduate teaching profession in Britain, the government established the Bachelor of Education degree. This included the disciplines seen as foundational in educational studies – sociology, philosophy, psychology and history. Peters now had the task of providing courses in philosophy of education to equip college teachers to teach the new B. Ed. degree. As well as a special government-funded one year Diploma course, he had developed, with Paul Hirst, an MA in Philosophy of Education. Students took a core seminar in philosophy of education and two 30 week courses chosen from a number of options, including ethics, epistemology and metaphysics, political philosophy and philosophy of mind. For this Peters needed to expand his teaching team and I was invited to join the staff. At the time I was in Year 1 of a joint Sociology and Philosophy of Education MA programme. I was torn because I enjoyed my work in my East End school and was about to become deputy head. On the other hand the idea of joining this dynamic staff which promised to contribute substantially to the theoretical foundation I felt any education system needed was too attractive an opportunity to pass up. I joined the Institute staff in 1965.

With Stanley Benn, Peters had recently written *Social Principles and the Democratic State* and his MA Political Philosophy course was in part based on the topics of the book and in part dealt with the great classical political philosophers, Plato, Aristotle, Hobbes, Locke and Mill. When I finished my MA Richard Peters decided that I should take over this course whilst he taught the educational courses.

281

Given that the course could not be exhaustive in its coverage, in selecting topics I was keen to make political philosophy relevant to the concerns of those working in education. This was not easy. Political philosophy had been pronounced dead in the 1950s and even in 1962 the editors of the Second Series of *Philosophy, Politics and Society* could not yet 'proclaim the resurrection [of political philosophy] unreservedly and with enthusiasm' (Laslett and Runciman, 1964, p. vii). The great flowering of late twentieth century work in the subject was only just beginning.

I decided that the course should focus on issues and problems of democratic theory. The first part of the course drew relevantly on the classics of political philosophy to this end, whilst the second part tackled the issues and problems head on. As the work of political philosophers like Barry, Rawls, Nozick and Dworkin began to emerge in papers and chapters, so it began to figure in the course. Soon the course began to cover topics like rights, civil disobedience, political violence, positive discrimination, the public interest, fraternity as a political value. Rawls' idea of justice as fairness was discussed and dissected several years before its appearance in book form. This was to the surprise of some colleagues who wondered why I was not focussing on 'mainstream' notions of justice and equality. The 'dirty hands problem' turned out to be surprisingly relevant to educational policy making. Walter Feinberg, a visiting scholar at the Institute at the time, sat in on some of these classes in the mid-1970s and we would continue the discussion as we walked to Goodge Street tube station, putting and countering arguments until we got on our separate trains.

THE PUBLIC INTEREST AND POLITICAL EDUCATION

The first fruit of the grafting of my educational questions on to my developing understanding in political philosophy was a paper on 'Education, Democracy and the Public Interest.' It sprang from a general scepticism at the time about whether in a large pluralistic democracy there *could* be any policies in the public interest. Construing this as a policy which benefits every member of a given public under the description 'member of the public', I argued that there could be at least one such policy in a democracy, namely an appropriate political education. Paul Hirst, arguing persuasively for a broad education in all the forms of knowledge, had suggested that insofar as one was pursuing a liberal education the criterion for choosing particular content in the various forms would be the extent to which any given content exemplified that form (Hirst, 1965b, p133-4). If one had political education in mind, however, I argued, one would choose those items (for instance, statistics in mathematics, parts of sociology in social science) which would help children to understand the democratic society in which they were growing up. Political education would in this way be pegging the forms of knowledge to the actual context of schooling. I did not anticipate that this concern with political education in a democracy would be the focus of my work for the next 40 years or so.

Through the 1970s I continued to write papers connecting work in political theory to questions of political education and citizenship. Broadly speaking, I argued that political education should begin in the first school and that teacher education should take this into account by preparing all teachers for their responsibilities. I attempted to counter possible fears about indoctrination and, whilst sketching out a plan for the long-term, made suggestions about how we might proceed from where we were. But since the Great Education Debate of 1976-7 in the UK came and went with scarcely a mention of political education, it was hardly surprising that my academic papers did nothing to raise its profile. It was heartening at least that in 1974 Bernard Crick, then Professor of Politics at Birkbeck College, was also arguing the case for political education and forging with colleagues *A Programme for Political Education* based around the idea of political literacy (published in 1978 with related papers as *Political Education and Political Literacy*). Broadly in agreement with its emphasis on conceptual development, John White and I produced a constructive critique. We felt that in its first formulation the *Programme* had remediable defects – amongst other things little attention to the aims of political education and economic understanding, and a rather individualistic slant. But the lively academic debate notwithstanding, the time for citizenship education as a serious contender for a place in school was still a long way off.

In retrospect, although frustrating at the time, the lack of interest in political education had some advantages because I continued throughout the 1970s to plough my own furrow and follow ideas where they led. This culminated in *Beyond Domination: An Essay in the Political Philosophy of Education*, in 1983. This had grown out of my ten years of teaching political philosophy and set out from the assumption that any discussion of education had to be placed in a political context. If that was a democratic context, then that would have an effect on the organisation and content of education, which would itself be subject to continuing democratic debate, discussion and revision. The first chapters set out basic democratic principles and explored in some detail the kind of institutions needed to realise these, not least democracy in the workplace – another topic whose time had

---

FAVOURITE WORKS OF OTHERS

The philosophers below, and especially the works mentioned, have been major influences.

Aristotle, *Ethics*

Benn, Stanley I (1988) *A Theory of Freedom*, Cambridge, Cambridge University Press (book based on earlier papers)

Hirst, Paul H (1965b). Liberal Education and the Nature of Knowledge. In R. D. Archambault (Ed.) *Philosophical Analysis and Education*, London, Routledge & Kegan Paul

MacIntyre, Alasdair, (1981) *After Virtue: A Study in Moral Theory*, London, Duckworth

Midgley, Mary (1980) *Beast and Man, The Roots of Human Nature,* London, Methuen 1980

Williams, Bernard (1972) *Morality*, London, Penguin

Williams, Bernard, (1985) *Ethics and the Limits of Philosophy*, London, Fontana Paperbacks

not yet come! It concluded with three chapters on: political education, the case for an appropriate training for head teachers – my early pre-occupation with arbitrary power was still with me – and a consideration of parents' educational rights and duties. The idea of questioning parents' rights over their children's education seemed almost eccentric at the time, something which only some out of touch educational theorist would think worth discussing. But that was soon to change.

POLICY CRITIQUE

During the 1980s I began to contribute, in academic papers as well as publications accessible to a wider public, to the informed critique of the Conservative government policies mounted by philosophers and other colleagues. These contributions grew out of my developing views about what a civic education in a democracy required. In my contribution to *Lessons before Midnight*, a pamphlet which called for public education about nuclear issues, I argued that there were compelling reasons why a political education in school should directly tackle these. The argument, drawing on the writings of philosophers like Bernard Williams and Stanley Benn, countered charges that this would inevitably involve indoctrination and/or unnecessarily frighten children who would not be likely to understand the issues anyway, (charges more fully critiqued in White 1988). It claimed that it was both possible and desirable.

Another pamphlet, *The Quality Controllers*, drew attention to the government's impoverished notion of 'quality' in its plans to improve the quality of teacher education. In our paper John White and I attacked what we saw as the re-tread conception of in-service work implicit in the government's plans. (In those days a cheap alternative to buying new tyres for your car was to have them remoulded, in effect the tread replaced.) As against this, as well as offering teachers courses to hone their skills, we argued that in-service education could help them take a broader view of their work. We listed as examples seven areas of beliefs – epistemological, social, psychological, political, ethical, metaphysical, and educational – where teachers might have taken-for-granted assumptions that could benefit from critical examination. For this kind of fundamental reflection, we argued, teachers needed time. Keeping teachers hard at work at the chalk face with no time for reflection was no way to ensure quality in education in a democracy. Once again these were ideas whose time had not yet come – and, 20 years later, have not yet come in UK government circles.

'Parents' Rights, Homosexuality and Education' was an attack on a Conservative government policy which sought to make sure that homosexuality was not 'promoted' in school. The paper drew on Michael Ruse's work in refuting the view that sexual orientation could be swayed by teaching, because evidence suggested it was given, not chosen. Further, it claimed that civic education in a democracy should be concerned about the flourishing of *all* citizens, including gay citizens, and not least gay students in school. This paper was part of a continuing commentary on the nature and place of parents' rights over the education of their children – an issue now firmly in the educational spotlight. It was followed by

'Parental Choice and Education for Citizenship'. This highlighted some of the problems in being a good parent and a good citizen in a society in which the right of parents to determine their children's education was coming to be regarded as a key element in the access to schools.

CIVIC VIRTUES

Beyond Domination and the policy papers I wrote in the 1980s focussed on the values and the institutions needed for national government and in the workplace, including the educational workplace, to make a society more democratic. Connectedly, the political education I argued for was concerned to promote greater understanding of this conception of democracy. But this and the related notion of democratic education, I came to realise, lacked a crucially important element, namely the array of dispositions needed to *be* a democratic citizen. Without the disposition to work the democratic institutions in the right spirit, ineptitude at best, corruption at worst, was inevitable. The kind of dispositions democratic citizens needed had to be identified and discussed. Dispositions relating to social justice, autonomy and tolerance are virtually definitive of democracy and had been much worked over in political philosophy. I turned my attention to others – hope and confidence, self-respect, self-esteem, courage, honesty, trust, decency, and later being prepared to give people a hearing, and gratitude (White, 1996a,b 1998a). The thing about these dispositions, I discovered, was that the relevant personal virtues could not simply be translated into the public sphere. In this arena they acquired a particular democratic aspect, as *Civic Virtues and Public Schooling* (1996a) tries to show. For this reason the school, as a public institution outside the family, is well suited to foster these democratic dispositions. To do so requires careful attention to teacher attitudes in the classroom and to the structure of the school.

As I worked on civic virtues, I benefited enormously from conversations with Ray Elliott, a retired colleague, known for his original and perceptive work in aesthetics, ethics and philosophy of education. The paper on "Self-Knowledge and Education,' which he contributed to the collection I edited on *Personal and Social Education,* is an immediately accessible introduction to his work. It draws on subtle interpretations of philosophical (Nietzsche, Hegel, D W Hamlyn) and literary sources to offer profound insights to the teacher in the primary and secondary classroom.

SHOWCASING THE SUBJECT

For a few years after 1996 my work on the virtues slowed almost to a standstill, because a publisher with the idea for a collection of published work in philosophy of education from about 1950 onwards invited me to be one of the editors. So with Paul Hirst as co-editor I began reading a phenomenal amount of work from all parts of the globe. From this we eventually selected the items which filled the four volumes of *Philosophy of Education: Major Themes in the Analytic Tradition.* It was particularly gratifying to make accessible important work – six papers from

Ray Elliott, for instance – which was not easily available. Considering how best to organise it as a resource for scholars in philosophy of education as well as other disciplines alerted the editors to those areas, like the political aspects of education, where there was a wealth of material as well as to others, like Volume II 'Education and Human Being,' where in recent years there had been little activity. Would the gaps inspire new work?

BACK TO THE VIRTUES

Returning to work on civic virtues I was aware that following recent ethnic conflicts around the world there were calls for political forgiveness. Indeed Archbishop Tutu had written a book with the title *No Future without Forgiveness*. Should the encouragement of political forgiveness, in certain contexts at least, be part of civic education? To tackle this question, I needed to look at the notion of personal forgiveness. The more I read of the vast philosophical literature on this, the more I puzzled over the question of whether there was a need for this practice. It seemed to me to involve at least two assumptions that I found ethically questionable: that there is a hierarchical relationship between victim and offender such that offenders were beyond the pale, and also that it was appropriate for offenders to spend ethical energy on seeking forgiveness: was this not self-indulgent? The idea of a duty of forgiveness perhaps made sense if you were within a Christian or some other religious framework, but could it be a duty for non-believers? I attempted to argue for more differentiated attitudes to wrong-doing amongst which forgiveness was an optional possibility.

Turning to political forgiveness, it seemed to me that even a most carefully argued case for its possibility and desirability (Govier, 2002) failed to show either. Whatever the case may be in the personal context, in the political arena the notion made far too many unwarranted assumptions, and, I argued, should be abandoned. It was not, as often presented, a matter of either forgiveness or revenge. There was a panoply of other possibilities for reconciliation between previously warring groups. These latter should have a place in civic education.

If political forgiveness was then to drop out of the civic education agenda, perhaps virtues connected with investing should come on to it. I had always been concerned with the need for attention to economic matters in civic education and an understanding of exercises of power in its overt and covert aspects. In *Educating Investors: an Exploration in Virtue Ethics* I argued an active investigation of investing would take in both.

'LIVE' PHILOSOPHY

This account of my writings and people who have influenced me presents a misleading picture in one way. It suggests that texts have been my exclusive inspiration. That is far from the case. For me the most exhilarating form of philosophy is the 'live' version. It has been a huge privilege over the years to sit in on classes given by Miles Burnyeat, David Hamlyn, Ted Honderich, and John

Passmore, and to attend lectures/seminars by some of the many philosophers who have passed through London. Given my interests, Alasdair MacIntyre, Susan Mendus, Mary Midgley, Martha Nussbaum, Bernard Williams are notable amongst these.

I talked earlier about ploughing my own furrow when there was little interest in civic education. In recent years that has changed. In my work I have been greatly heartened and encouraged by the knowledge that two other people in our field – until recently in two different continents from me – are pursuing the very philosophical aspects of civic education which seize my imagination. Eamonn Callan and Penny Enslin produce incisive, insightful, enviably interesting work. The opportunity for a 'live' exchange with them is a huge intellectual treat.

Research supervision has also always been a joy – from my first doctoral student, Robin Barrow, to my current ones. Professionally, there is nothing so exciting for me as settling down to a session of argument and counter-argument where the thesis-writer and I are seeing how far this argument can be pushed or precisely why it won't do. I am keen to see what turns on it and why it matters for a certain conception of education or some particular educational policy.

WORK IN PROGRESS

My current project is a philosophical investigation of the recently introduced citizenship tests in Britain for those wishing to become British citizens. My interest is in seeing what assumptions are being made about citizenship and how far those are compatible with the values and practices of a democratic society.

REFERENCES

Benn, S. I. (1984). Deterrence or appeasement? Or, on trying to be rational about nuclear war. *Journal of Applied Philosophy*, *1*(1), 5-20.

Benn, S. I. & Peters, R. S. (1959). *Social principles and the democratic state.* London: George Allen and Unwin.

Callan, Eamonn. (1997). *Creating citizens: Political education and liberal democracy.* Clarendon Press.

Crick, B. & Porter, A. (1978). *Political education and political literacy.* London: Longman.

Elliott, R. K. (1989). Self-knowledge and education. In Patricia White (Ed.), *Personal and social education: Philosophical perspectives*, Bedford Way Paper. London: Kogan Page.

Govier, Trudy (2002). *Forgiveness and revenge.* London: Routledge.

Hirst Paul H. (1965a). Educational theory. In J. W. Tibble (Ed.), *The study of education.* London, Routledge & Kegan Paul.

Hirst, Paul H. (1965b). Liberal education and the nature of knowledge. In R. D. Archambault (Ed.), *Philosophical analysis and education*, London, Routledge & Kegan Paul.

Hirst, Paul H. (1993). Education, knowledge and practices. In Barrow Robin and White Patricia (Eds.), *Beyond liberal education: Essays in honour of Paul H. Hirst.* London, Routledge.

Laslett, P. & Runciman, W. G. (1962). *Philosophy, politics and society: Second Series.* Oxford: Basil Blackwell.

Martin, Jane Roland (1961). On the reduction of 'knowing that' to 'knowing how'. In B. Othanel Smith & Robert H. Ennis (Eds.), *Language and concepts in education*, Chicago, Rand McNally & Co.

Peters, R. S. (1966). *Ethics and education.* London: Allen and Unwin.

Price, Kingsley. (1967). *Education and philosophical thought.* Allyn and Bacon.

Ruse, Michael. (1988). *Homosexuality*. Oxford: Basil Blackwell.

White, Patricia. (1973). Education, democracy and the public interest. In R. S. Peters (Ed.), *The philosophy of education*. Oxford: Oxford University Press.

White, Patricia. (1977). Political education in a democracy: The implications for teacher education. *Journal of Further and Higher Education, 1*(3), 40-55.

White, Patricia. (1983). *Beyond domination: An essay in the political philosophy of education*. London: Routledge.

White, Patricia. (1984). Facing the nuclear issues: A task for political education. In The Bishop of Salisbury et al., *Lessons before midnight: Educating for reason in nuclear matters*. Bedford Way Paper. London: Institute of Education University of London.

White, Patricia. (1985). 'Improving quality through INSET' (with John White). In Frances Slater (Ed.), *The quality controllers: A critique of the white paper 'Teaching Quality'*. Bedford Way Paper. London: Institute of Education University of London.

White, Patricia. (1988). Countering the critics. In David Hicks (Ed.), *Education for peace: Issues, principles and practice in the classroom*. Routledge.

White, Patricia. (1989). *Personal and social education: Philosophical perspectives*. Bedford Way Paper. London: Kogan Page.

White, Patricia. (1991). Parents' rights, homosexuality and education. *British Journal of Educational Studies, 39*(4), 398-408.

White, Patricia. (1994). Parental choice and education for citizenship. In Mark Halstead (Ed.), *Parental choice and education*. London: Kogan Page.

White, Patricia. (1996a). *Civic virtues and public schooling: Educating citizens for a democratic society*. Advances in Contemporary Educational Thought Series. New York and London: Teachers College Press.

White, Patricia. (1996b). Having a voice and getting a hearing: An educational perspective on free speech in a plural society. *Studies in Philosophy and Education, 15*, 201-208.

White, Patricia (with Paul H. Hirst). (1998a). *Philosophy of education: Major themes in the analytic tradition* (four volumes: I Philosophy and Education; II Education and Human Being; III Society and Education; IV Problems of Educational Content and Practices). London: Routledge.

White, Patricia (1998b). Gratitude, citizenship and education. *Die Zeitschrift für Pädagogik. 38. Beiheft*, 241-250.

White Patricia. (2002). What should we teach children about forgiveness? *Journal of Philosophy of Education, 36*(1), 57-67.

White, Patricia. (2003). Educating Investors: An exploration in virtue ethics. In Jürgen Oelkers & Max Mangold (Eds.), *Demokratie, Bildung und Markt*. Bern: Lang-Verlag.

White, Patricia. (2007). Political forgiveness and citizenship education. In Rita Casale & Rebekka Horlacher (Eds.), *Bildung und Öffentlichkeit*. Weinheim und Basel: Beltz Verlag.

Williams, Bernard. (1982). How to think sceptically about the bomb. *New Society*, 18 November.

Winch, Peter. (1958). *The idea of a social science and its relation to philosophy*. London: Routledge and Kegan Paul.

Patricia White
Institute of Education,
University of London

CHRISTOPHER WINCH

COMPLEXITY, CONTESTATION AND ENGAGEMENT

INTRODUCTION

I studied Philosophy as an undergraduate at Leeds University in a very distinguished department that included Peter Geach and Roy Holland, between 1967 and 1970. This formative period at Leeds oriented me to the analytic tradition in Philosophy, but with a predisposition to Wittgenstein's later work and to a particular view of conceptual analysis that did not suppose that there is one and only one correct account of a concept or family of concepts. I acquired a lasting interest in the philosophy of language, in epistemology, the philosophy of the social sciences and political philosophy at this point which have informed my work over the years. After pursuing postgraduate research for a couple of years, I worked in Further Education and then qualified as a primary schoolteacher. For over eleven years I worked as a primary schoolteacher in and around the Leeds area of Yorkshire in England, eventually becoming acting head of a small Church of England First School. This was a time when I learned the reality of education in a class-based society in which educational success counted for very little for many parents and their children and where, sadly, it was all too easy for schools to avoid their responsibility for providing a decent education for everyone. Educational theory seemed to conspire in this view, by providing a rich array of theories to explain why working class children were, on the whole, unlikely to achieve much at school. While studying to be a teacher, I came across the work of Basil Bernstein, the sociolinguist, and my background in linguistic philosophy, together with my interest in educational achievement, led me to wonder whether a philosophical critique could be applied to the assumptions underlying Bernstein's theories concerning educational achievement, which seemed to provide a spurious explanation for the failure at school of children from the lower working class. Some years later, I developed my interest in Bernstein in a more systematic way by undertaking a PhD on his sociolinguistic theses. At this time, I also came to appreciate the importance of literate culture in the lives of different groups of people and of the effect that it had on school success.

During this period, I was fortunate enough to meet Philip Pettit, who was at that time a youthful Professor of Philosophy in the Department of Interdisciplinary Human Studies at Bradford University. Philip's interests were, and are, diverse and his interest in educational theory led him to persuade me to register as a part-time PhD student at Bradford under his tutelage, in order to cast my thinking about language and educational achievement into a more systematic form. This proved to be a good move and I flourished in the Bradford Department and emerged with a PhD on Bernstein's sociolinguistics and the philosophical assumptions about

L.J. Waks (ed.), Leaders in Philosophy of Education: Intellectual Self Portraits, 289–300.

rationality that lay behind it several years after registering. I was, however, still very committed to primary schoolteaching and had to face the difficult choice of pursuing my career in that field or of taking an academic post. In the few years after gaining my PhD, I also managed to publish several articles on aspects of the PhD study, most notably on the conceptual underpinnings of verbal deficit theory, as the family of accounts of the relationship between language and educational achievement were called. Working in this area inevitably involved close engagement with the empirical studies that underpinned such theories and thus to an understanding of methodology in sociolinguistics and sociology. It seemed to me then, and still does now, that conceptual and empirical questions need to be carefully distinguished but that once having done so, it is often possible to assess empirical claims within a particular conceptual framework in which those claims can be understood.

While, like my father, Peter Winch, sceptical of much of the empirical work that has been carried out in education and the social sciences, and suspicious, in particular, of the all too frequent attempts to build grand theories on the basis of flimsy empirical evidence, I nevertheless did not take the view common in Philosophy of Education, that nothing useful can be known about education through empirical research. In fact I am proud to say that I am one of the relatively small number of philosophers of education who has carried out empirical research projects and my experience of doing this has convinced me that philosophers have an important role to play in the planning and carrying out of high quality empirical work in education. This role should stem from their ability to conceptualise problems, to think strategically about how to answer research questions, and a relatively high awareness of the advantages and disadvantages of different approaches to data collection and scrutiny.

MOST IMPORTANT PUBLICATIONS

Books

Language, Ability and Educational Achievement (1990)
Quality and Education (1996)
The Philosophy of Human Learning (1998)
Key Concepts in the Philosophy of Education (1999)
Education, Work and Social Capital, (2000)
Philosophy and Educational Policy: (2004)
Education, Autonomy and Critical Thinking, (2005)

Articles

'Cooper, Labov, Larry and Charles' (1985)
'Reading and the Process of Reading' (1989)
'Education Needs Training' (1995)
'Listian Political Economy: Social Capitalism Conceptualised?' (1998)
'Work, Well-being and Vocational Education' . (2002)
'Die Entwicklung kritischer Rationalität als pragmatische Aufgabe der Erziehung (2003)
What Do Teachers Need to Know About Teaching? (2004) '
Vom Erlenen der Tugenden bei der Arbeit (2006)

Over the years, my work has covered four related themes: *Language and Education, Learning and Knowledge, Policy and Accountability,* and *Vocational Education.* These themes have been relatively little explored in the Philosophy of Education and I see my contribution as having considerably extended and enriched the discussion of these themes and as having provided a platform for future work by others in these areas. Although Philosophy of Education is a subject with origins in ancient Philosophy, it has gained a place as a distinct branch of Philosophy in the relatively recent past and is still in the position of gauging the scope of its interests within the broader field of Philosophy, and also in those aspects of human activity that impinge on education. Noteworthy amongst these is the rise of the social sciences from the Seventeenth Century onwards. Furthermore, developments with Philosophy more generally have an impact on the concerns and techniques employed within the Philosophy of Education. This is particularly true of Epistemology, the Philosophy of Mind, Ethics, and Political Philosophy and, to a lesser extent, the Philosophy of Language. The areas in which I work reflect these broader developments in Philosophy, but also their relationship to the rise of the social and human sciences and to the development of Education as a mass activity funded by the state. These last two developments have a very important connection, since it is the perceived need by the state to provide a rationale for its educational activities in terms of the findings Psychology, Linguistics, Economics and Sociology that has driven many of the developments in modern education. It hardly needs mentioning that these subjects themselves, as empirical disciplines, are a relatively recent offshoot from philosophical discussion and have significant, and often contested, philosophical presuppositions.

At the same time, we should not forget that Philosophy of Education has its own distinct subject matter, namely the preparation of human beings for life, through learning. As Vico pointed out in *The New Science*, all human societies, however different they are from each other, express in some way our finite biological existence through social institutions connected with birth, reproduction and death. These are categories that shape our understanding of and enquiry into human life. Vico might have added that all societies have to bring up and prepare their young for life in their societies and that this preparation does not cease with biological maturity, because of the complexity of both of individuals and the societies in which they live. This is the categorical aspect of Education in its broadest sense, which has long been a major concern of the Philosophy of Education.

One of the fascinating and complex features of Philosophy of Education is that not only does it have this categorical side to its enquiry, but it has always been involved in more normative kinds of investigations, although historically the two are not usually kept distinct. Indeed, one of the complaints made against the discipline is that very often the normative enquiry masquerades as the categorical, giving Philosophy of Education and inbuilt conservative bias. The categorical investigation concerns universal features of education, irrespective of time, place and culture. Normative investigations, by contrast, concern what *ought* to be part of education in a particular society and epoch. In my view, these are distinct, jointly necessary and closely related aspects of the discipline that need to be pursued, but philosophers of education need to keep the distinction between them constantly in mind in pursuing their enquiries and to be cautious about the scope of their claims, particularly when they are engaging in normative enquiries. This distinction has an important methodological consequence for those working in the broadly analytical tradition within the discipline. Although the categorical aspects of the concept of education and those concepts related to it are contested (otherwise it is difficult to see how there could be a categorical enquiry within the Philosophy of Education), the normative aspects of those concepts are, to use and adapt W.D.Gallie's phrase, *essentially contested*, that is, since they express a particular ethico-political stance, they are of their nature going to be disputed by those who do not share such commitments. Indeed, it is often the case, as Gallie himself pointed out, that there may well be difficulties in mutual understanding of concepts with apparently the same scope, but issuing from different traditions or points of view. This does not mean that conceptual analysis is not an appropriate approach to normative enquiry in Philosophy of Education, but rather that it needs to be self-conscious about its engagement and consequently about its scope and limits as a type of enquiry. It is worth pointing out that this was a position towards which the *doyen* of twentieth century British analytical Philosophy of Education, Richard Peters, was himself moving towards at the close of his academic career.[i] In this sense, I regard my work as being in the mainstream of the British analytic tradition in method if not always in substantive claims.

LANGUAGE AND EDUCATION

My earliest work in the Philosophy of Education was much concerned with the application of the social sciences to educational issues, something of which I had had direct experience in my early work as a primary schoolteacher. My PhD thesis discussed the concept of rationality that underpinned Bernstein's sociolinguistic theses and suggested that the Bernsteinian model worked better with the contrast between spoken and written language than it did with the distinction between different kinds of speech. Basil Bernstein had developed, in the 1960s, a highly influential account of how the language of working class communities was ill-adapted to educational purposes. This thesis arose in the context of the decline of intelligence quotient theories as an account of the phenomenon of low working class educational achievement but maintained an ambiguous relationship with such theories, while at the same time seeking to supplant them. I argued that Bernstein's claim, when carefully examined, was that one kind of language variety, the so-called 'restricted code' was not equipped with the syntactic and semantic resources to express rationality. I argued, drawing on the work of Jonathan Bennett on rationality, that although Bernstein's claims were, broadly speaking testable, they were also implausible and the evidence that he and his associates presented did not support those claims. More positively, I argued that, drawing on a conceptual analysis of the differences between written and spoken forms of language, part of the explanation for class-based differences in educational achievement was to be found in the importance played by literacy in the lives of different communities.

This claim is supported by empirical studies and is now widely accepted and taken account of in practical initiatives to improve literacy (Mackay 2006).

I later developed a critique of the concept of intelligence used by psychometrical theory, suggesting that conceptions of abilities needed to be related to action, rather than to a postulated innate quality. A significant part of educational success, therefore, had to be conceptualized in terms of ability to master various kinds of activities and could not be adequately determined through a test in

FAVORITES WRITTEN BY OTHERS

Baker, G.P., Hacker, P.M.S. (1984) *Language, Sense and Nonsense*, Oxford, Blackwell.

Dearden, R.F. (1984) *Theory and Practice in Education*, London, Routledge.

Dent, N. (1988) *Rousseau*, Oxford, Blackwell.

Wittgenstein, L. (1953) *Philosophical Investigations*, Oxford, Blackwell

the way in which IQ theories suggest. These ideas about IQ theory and about Bernstein's work were eventually published as *Language, Ability and Educational Achievement* (1990); this was the first volume by a British author in the North American series 'Philosophy of Education Research Library'. I also wrote various articles on these topics in the second half of the 1980s, which included an exchange with David Cooper over the interpretation of one of the most prominent of the anti-Bernsteinian studies, 'The Logic of Non-standard English' by William Labov, first published in 1969 (Cooper 1984, Winch 1985). This concerned the kinds of interpretation that one is entitled to make of transcribed oral evidence and the inferences that one can validly make from such interpretations. I argued, following Grandy, Hollis and others that the presumption should be that one's informants be counted as rational in both practical and argumentative senses unless the evidence to the contrary was overwhelming.

I went on to carry out further work on the theme of language and education and wrote about the issue of whether standard English should be part of the then emerging English National Curriculum at the end of the 1980s, distinguishing between different senses in which a standard language should be considered as a norm and also carried out empirical work on the 'Creole Interference Hypothesis' with my colleague John Gingell in the early 1990s. The Creole Interference Hypothesis made the claim that the use of creole in domestic circumstances constituted a barrier to the acquisition of a written standard, such as standard English. The claim involved some ambiguities about alternative hypotheses and the work that we carried out was a refutation on empirical grounds of the hypothesis. Once again, however, conceptual work on the nature of the claims of the hypothesis needed to be carried out before empirical work was conducted.

POLICY AND ACCOUNTABILITY

From the early 1990s onwards, I was interested in policy issues and educational accountability. These concerns dated from my early experiences as a teacher working in the British state education system. I came to think that the response of Philosophy of Education to these issues was unduly negative and defensive and probably did not take sufficient account of social and political developments both in the UK and globally. I connected this concern with accountability to a traditional theme in British Philosophy of Education, 'What makes an education a good education?' Both these strands were brought together in *Quality and Education* (1996), which also contained substantial philosophical discussion of other topics such as assessment, markets in education and inspection. The book developed the view that the categorial concept of education as a preparation for life underdetermines particular conceptions of education. Judgments about the quality of education thus need to relate to the conception of education being considered. In this sense, the argument can be seen to be taking forward ideas about the contested nature of educational concepts that Peters had already expressed in 1982. *Quality and Education* was a book on a 'classical' theme in the Philosophy of Education, which dealt with topics already much discussed over the centuries, such as the values and aims that underpin education, the notion of a standard, pedagogy and the concept of a curriculum. It also sought to situate a discussion of these universal topics within contemporary policy debates and to link these debates with traditional concerns. It thus dealt with public accountability, assessment, including the assessment of the contribution that schools make to pupils' learning, equality and diversity, markets in education, inspection and the democratic governance of public education. The book thus contributed to a growing literature in Philosophy of Education that draws on debates arising from the revival of analytic political philosophy over the last 50 years.

Although the book arose from concerns within the British context, at least part of my intention was to open up the variegated nature of the issue of 'good education' in complex societies, where such contestation is inevitable. One of the most gratifying aspects of this book is that this intention seems to some extent to have been fulfilled, with attention paid to the arguments in countries such as India, South Africa and Australia. The book excited debate with Professor James Tooley (an internationally well-known advocate of markets in education) on the role of markets in educational quality, resulting in further publication on this issue, as well as a debate (in articles written with John Gingell), with Andrew Davis and John White on assessment, on school effectiveness and work on inspection generally and school inspection in particular.

LEARNING AND KNOWLEDGE

Like most contemporary Philosophers of Education, my work has generally been sceptical of the large-scale claims of empirical researchers in education, particularly those that have had such a large impact on educational policy and practice. This scepticism was apparent in my earlier work on Bernstein and the IQ theorists. The concept of learning is fundamental to the Philosophy of Education and has not always received the attention that it deserves. David Hamlyn had, in 1978, published a book on the concepts of learning and development, much influenced by the work of Wittgenstein, *Experience and the Growth of Understanding*, which to me was an inspiration for further work in this area. This led to *The Philosophy of Human Learning* (1998), which was concerned, among other things, with large-scale learning theories and their influence on educational practice. I developed a philosophical account of learning that took account of the normative and practice-related character of human activity and which provided a contrast with the Cartesian and Neo-Cartesian approaches that currently enjoy a great deal of influence and which have led to would-be comprehensive theories of learning such as cognitivism, with its representationalist assumptions, and developmentalism. I argued that Cartesian, Neo-Cartesian, Empiricist and Rousseauian approaches all adopted an essentially solitary approach to learning, which assumed that it could be understood solely in terms of individual minds, rather than in a social milieu, and that this view was erroneous. Particularly significant in this respect was the debate between Rush Rhees and Norman Malcolm on the one hand and Peter Hacker and Gordon Baker on the other concerning the nature of Wittgenstein's critique of private languages. My argument was that we cannot make sense of the notion of an ab initio rule-governed private language and hence of ab initio solitary learning in a normative context. Given, this, many of the assumptions of contemporary learning theories are untenable, with the notable exception of the Vygotskian tradition.

The book also developed a major critique of psycholinguistic and developmental accounts of learning and examined the implications of the general thesis for language learning, later learning and learning in religious, moral and aesthetic contexts. It made a significant contribution to discussions both within and beyond Philosophy of Education, being the first major essay in this area since Hamlyn's. Also connected with this work were articles on Rousseau on Learning and on representationalism and learning. International interest in this work was shown for example in the use made of it by commentators such as Paul Hager (one of the leading philosophers of education in Australia) and debate arising from commentary by Jim Mackenzie, also in Australia.[ii] Hager has used some of my ideas in his own work on new paradigms in learning theory and Mackenzie has acknowledged the importance of the critique of representational theories presented in the book.

VOCATIONAL EDUCATION

An interest in learning and the diversity of ways of learning, which had been present in my earliest work, together with a growing interest in the political dimension of education, led me into a concern with the Philosophy of Vocational Education, again an area in the subject which has traditionally received relatively little attention. To me, however, it is one of the most exciting areas of the subject, made even more alluring by the fact that, until recently, it has attracted relatively little attention. Vocational education is a treasure trove for philosophers, due to the range and complexity of the subject matter that it deals with. The relationship between propositional and practical knowledge, the concepts of action and judgment, the role of work in the pattern of human life, ethics and occupations and the nature and purpose of economic activity are all important parts of its remit. It is a terrain which Philosophers of Education are just beginning to explore and to which they have the potential to make a huge contribution. I started to carry out work on different aspects of vocational education from the early 90s onwards. First, its aims and its relationship with liberal education; second, the ways in which work and preparation for work were manifested in different societies and their relationship with a worthwhile human life; third, to learning in practical contexts and finally, to the detail and progression of programmes of vocational and professional education. These topics all received extensive treatment in *Education, Work and Social Capital* (2000), a major study of vocational education which looked at the significance of education from a social capital perspective, where the emphasis on economic strength is derived from the concept of *productive powers* of an economy, or its potential for production, a concept derived from the work of the economist Friedrich List. Within such a conception, human resources, including distributed knowledge and collective ways of learning become important in assessing economic strength, and vocational education must be oriented to these.

This work also led to a successful bid for an ESRC funded seminar series on the aims, values and history of vocational education for which I was the fund holder, with Linda Clarke of Westminster University, between 2002 and early 2004. One of the distinctive features of this programme was the range of international contributors; the series adopted an international and comparative treatment of vocational education, paying particular attention to the major West European countries, the United States and Australia. This has resulted in the edited book, *Vocational Education: philosophical and historical perspectives* (2007).

CURRENT AND FUTURE WORK

Connections with Work in Germany

In 1999 I was invited to join a German-speaking colloquium on the role of critique in education by Professor Dietrich Benner of the Humboldt University and the leading figure in German Philosophy of Education, which ran until 2002. I was the sole British contributor to this series. I started to work on aspects of civic education from this period. Of particular interest was the debate about autonomy as an aim of education, which had been a concern of Robert Dearden from the late 1960s onwards and has been a prominent feature of the work of John White in the UK. Latterly, the theme has been developed on both sides of the Atlantic as a response to the political theory of, in particular, John Rawls and, latterly, Joseph Raz. Raz's contention that autonomy is a necessary condition for leading a worthwhile life in the kind of liberal market societies that we inhabit seems broadly right. It is not a condition for a worthwhile life *per* se. I had, for some time, been concerned with the role that rationality played in autonomous decision-making and with the claim that autonomy had to be, in some sense, rational in order to be worthwhile. This view naturally led to a concern with the role that critical rationality in general and critical thinking in particular played in the development of rational autonomy, about which there was already a considerable literature, produced particularly in North America.

At the same time, I wished to follow through on Raz's claim that autonomy, if it is to be constitutive of worthwhile lives, must involve the capacity to make, not merely informed, but also worthwhile choices. At the same time, we live in societies in which the idea of what constitutes a worthwhile choice undergoes debate and change. The interplay between the education system and the evolution of society's views about this is a complex question which I tried to unpick in *Education, Autonomy and Critical Thinking* (2005) which defends weak autonomy as an educational aim, and which also tries to spell out the scope and limits of critical rationality in general and critical thinking in particular, in relation to education. This work includes not only a detailed survey of the available literature (see also book contribution 2), but also that on critical thinking in education. Although these topics have been much discussed, they have not before been brought together in such an explicit and systematic way. This study, just published, is therefore intended to be a major contribution to two interlinked debates in Philosophy of Education, one on the development of autonomy and one on the development of critical thinking as an educational aim. The views developed in this book also mark a realisation that the categorical concept of education is not quite as thin as I used to think. In particular, education needs to involve learning, understanding, and acculturation, as opposed to material preparation for life. Furthermore, and crucially for the argument concerning autonomy, it also involves preparation for a worthwhile life. It makes little sense to prepare someone for a non-worthwhile adult life. However, this does not mean, as some analytical philosophers have thought, that there is no such thing as bad education. Different individuals may have different views about what constitutes a worthwhile life, either for them or for other people. As suggested, in complex and critical societies such as ours, the concept of worthwhilensss generally and what is worthwhile for particular individuals or groups, is constantly contested.

I thus started to develop relatively unexplored themes in this literature. This involved a discussion of the weak/strong autonomy distinction (a topic that had not, until then, received much attention), a linking of earlier discussions about language use with discussion of citizenship and autonomy, and further discussion of the linkage between critical rationality and autonomy. This work has resulted in publication in English, as well as German, of the work of the Benner-led colloquium. The work also appeared in Italian. I was responsible, with Professor Frieda Heyting, of Amsterdam University, for ensuring that this work received an audience in the English-speaking world, leading us to co-edit a special edition of the *Journal of Philosophy of Education*, which is also appearing in book form in which the contributions were translated into English by Professor Heyting and myself.

Working within the German context has made me aware of another aspect of conceptual analysis within the Philosophy of Education, namely cross-cultural and cross-language conceptual variation. Oswald Hanfling, in his 'Philosophy and Ordinary Language' (1998) argued that the generally common nature of the human form of life led to a common conceptual framework, albeit with local variations, arising from the universal nature of human needs. This thesis, with its affinity with Vico's *New Science* is one that I find attractive. At the same time, it is not so clear that the universal aspects of human experience do lead directly to a common set of concepts as Hanfling seems to suggest. This is particularly apparent in an examination of the educational and epistemic concepts in the German language which show considerable variation with those embodied in English. Much recent work has been carried out on the concept of *Bildung*, in English but there is much less on, for example, the way in which knowledge, both propositional and practical, differs from   English usage. Even the work on Bildung fails to do justice to the concept, in particular to its relationship with occupational engagement as found in the *Bildungsromanen* of Goethe and Keller and to its role over a person's lifetime as in the Humboldtian concept of *allgemeine Menschenbildung* (Benner 2003).

More Recent Developments

The work that I am currently doing is to a large extent concerned with practical knowledge and education. I am thus currently consolidating my work on practical knowledge, with particular reference to its relationship with professional and vocational education, drawing on previous work and pulling various topics together. My particular current concern is with the nature of practical knowledge and whether or not it is a species of propositional knowledge. I am preparing a critique of the Stanley and Williamson thesis that all know-how is a species of propositional knowledge by arguing that such an account cannot explain how considerations of skill and expertise are a feature of know-how, but not of propositional knowledge. I do not argue that know-how is completely independent of propositional considerations, since I wish to maintain that applied theoretical knowledge is very important for many kinds of professional and technical activity. I am also concerned with the moral aspect of practical knowledge and the need to avoid separating its technical from its moral dimension The nature of the knowledge base of the teaching profession is a further concern of this project. My current aim is to review the literature on the concept of expertise and to develop an understanding of what the implications are for vocational education in particular. My current thinking on this subject is that an account of knowing how is required that is sufficiently distinct from, while related to, propositional knowledge. Furthermore, such an account must satisfy Ryle's requirement that one be able to apply evaluative concepts to purposive action. One cannot apply evaluative concepts to propositional knowledge in the same way, which seems to constitute a fatal weakness for accounts that attempt to assimilate knowledge how to knowledge that. It is also a problem for accounts of practical knowledge that assimilate it to mastery of forms of practical inference, which are conceptually distinct from the actions that may or may not issue from such inferences.

At the same time, there are also problems with Ryle's account as it is developed in *The Concept of Mind*. Briefly, Ryle appears to exclude the possibility of the application of propositional knowledge to action as part of the judgment that precedes or accompanies action. This implies that there is little room for the role of propositional knowledge generally and theoretical knowledge in particular in vocational and professional education. This claim seems, in turn, to be inaccurate in terms of professional education and also in terms of vocational education as it is carried out in countries such as Germany, where mastery of a *Beruf* is considered to require ability to apply theory to practice. Unless such forms of education are based on a philosophical mistake, and I do not think that they are, we require a philosophically satisfactory account of how this is the case which is rich enough to account for the novice/expert distinction as well as those characterisations of experience and ability that lie between these poles. This is unlikely to be a unified account, given the range and diversity of human action, but the conceptual territory is still, I think, in need of significant mapping.

The implications for qualification systems and, in particular, for European equivalences in vocational qualifications are also a major concern and I am currently working with Linda Clarke and Michaela Brockmann on a Nuffield Foundation funded study of the European Qualification Framework and the conceptual and linguistic problems that lie behind such an attempt to harmonise educational qualifications across different systems and cultures. We are particularly concerned with the different ways in which epistemic, labour and educational concepts vary across the different North European countries and the tensions that implementing a nominally independent framework may give rise to. Philosophy of Education can have a distinctive contribution to make to studies that embody value and conceptual issues as part of their research questions and this study is an example, as is the very important investigation, led by Richard Pring, into the nature of 14-19 education in England, also funded by the Nuffield Foundation, a study to which I also make a considerable contribution.

Concluding Remarks

Although Philosophy of Education in some form has been around for thousands of years, to me it feels like a landscape, large tracts of which philosophers have left unexplored. To adapt Goethe's Mephistopheles, the eternal tree of life has ensured that theory need not become grey. Changes in human life impact on systems of upbringing and education, and pose new issues for philosophers of education to engage with. At the same time, the oldest questions concerning the relationship between education and worthwhile life, the relationship between knowledge and learning and moral education, to name three, remain as important as ever.

NOTES

i R.S.Peters (1981) Ch.3 'Democratic Values and Educational Aims', in *Essays on Educators*, London, Routledge.

ii J. Mackenzie (2001), 'Representation and Learning: reply to Winch' Educational Philosophy and Theory ref. See also D. Beckett, P. Hager (2002) *Life, work and learning*. London: Routledge.

REFERENCES

D. Beckett & Hager, P. (2002). *Life, work and learning.* London: Routledge.

Benner, D. (2003). *Wilhelm von Humboldts Bildungstheorie.* Weinheim and Munich: Juventa Verlag.

Bennett, J. (1964). *Rationality.* London: Routledge.

Cooper, D. (1984). Labov, Larry and Charles, *Oxford Review of Education, 10*(2), 177-192.

Gallie, W.B. (1956). Essentially contested concepts, *Aristotelian Society Proceedings,* NS, Vol. lvi, March 1956.

Hamlyn, D. (1978). *Experience and the growth of understanding.* London: Routledge.

Hanfling, O. (1998). *Philosophy and ordinary language: The bent and genius of our tongue.* London: Routledge.

Labov, W. (1972). The logic of non-standard English. In Giglioli, P-P., *Language and social context* (pp. 179-215). London: Penguin,

MacKay, T. (2006). *The West Dunbartonshire Literacy Initiative.* West Dunbartonshire Council.

Mackenzie, J. (2001). Christopher Winch on the representational theory of language and its pedagogic relevance. *Educational Philosophy and Theory, 33*(1), 35-56.

Peters, R.S. (1981). Ch. 3, Democratic values and educational aims. In *Essays on educators.* London: Routledge.

Ryle, G. (1949). *The concept of mind.* London: Hutchinson.

Vico, G. (1968). *The new science.* Ithaca: Cornell University Press.

Winch, C. (1985). Cooper, Labov, Larry and Charles. *Oxford Review of Education, 11*(2), 193-200.

Winch, C. (1989). Reading and the process of reading. *Journal of Philosophy of Education, 23*(2), 303-316.

Winch, C. (1990). *Language, ability and educational achievement.* New York, London: Routledge, Chapman, Hall.

Winch, C. (1995). Education needs training, *Oxford Review of Education, 21*(3), 315-326.

Winch, C. (1996). *Quality and education.* Oxford: Blackwell. (Also published as a special edition of the *Journal of Philosophy of Education, 30*(2), 1996.)

Winch, C. (1998). Listian political economy: social capitalism conceptualised? *New Political Economy, 3*(2), 301-316.

Winch, C. (1998). *The philosophy of human learning.* London: Routledge.

Winch, C. (1999). *Key concepts in the philosophy of education.* London: Routledge (with John Gingell).

Winch, C. (2000). *Education, work and social capital.* London: Routledge.

Winch, C. (2002). Work, well-being and vocational education. *Journal of Applied Philosophy, 19*(3), 261-271.

Winch, C. (2003). Die Entwicklung kritischer Rationalität als pragmatische Aufgabe der Erziehung (The development of critical rationality as an educational aim) in special edition of the *Zeitschrift für Pädagogik* on critical rationality and education edited by D. Benner, 46, April 2003, pp.13-32.

Winch, C. (2004). What do teachers need to know about teaching? *British Journal of Educational Studies, 52*(2), 180-196.

Winch, C. (2004). *Philosophy and educational policy: A critical introduction* (with John Gingell). London: Routledge.

Winch, C. (2005). *Education, autonomy and critical thinking.* London: Routledge.

Winch, C. (2006). Vom Erlenen der Tugenden bei der Arbeit: Contribution to *Festschrift for Dietrich Benner', 'Perspektiven Allegemeiner Pädagogik'* edited J. Bellman, J. Ruhloff (Learning the Virtues at Work), Weinheim and Basel: Beltz Verlag.

Christopher Winch
King's College, London

APPENDIX A

EMILY ROBERTSON

REMEMBERING TOM GREEN

Thomas Franklin Green was educated at the University of Nebraska and at Cornell University, where he received his Ph.D. in philosophy in 1952. The early fifties was not a good time for securing positions in philosophy. Tom began his career as an instructor in ethics and classical philosophy at the School of Mines and Technology in Rapid City, South Dakota, where he stayed for three years. I didn't know until his daughter Sara spoke at his memorial service that he also worked in the Reptile Gardens at Rapid City. Apparently, the family has pictures of Tom with big snakes around his neck to prove it. According to Sara, the salary at the School of Mines required supplementing for a family with two children and a third on the way; hence the part-time job working with snakes. Tom was also a traveling salesman during this period, selling something called a "Baby Butler," which was a combination high-chair and card table. I suspect this was not exactly the beginning he had mind as a student of Norman Malcolm and Max Black. But in 1955, he moved to Michigan State University as assistant professor of humanities, eventually becoming associate professor of education there. In 1964, Tom was recruited to Syracuse University to join the newly founded program in Cultural Foundations of Education. He was with us at Syracuse for 29 years until his retirement in 1993.

Tom published 5 books, 3 monographs, and more than sixty articles and chapters. He was President of the Philosophy of Education Society, a member of the National Academy of Education, both a Guggenheim and a Whitehead Fellow at Harvard, a senior research fellow at Princeton Theological Seminary, and a Fellow of the National Institute of Education. He was selected to deliver both the John Dewey Lecture for the Dewey Society and the American Association of Colleges of Teacher Education and the DeGarmo Lecture for the Society of Professors of Education. He received the Outstanding Achievement Award in Education from the John Dewey Society. He lectured at dozens of universities in the United States and abroad. Not bad for a snake handler and convertible furniture salesman!

Tom's contributions to philosophy of education and educational policy and practice were wide-ranging and hard to characterize, if that means classifying them in some way. He approached philosophy with a love of the deep questions about human life entertained in theology and with an unusual (at least for a philosopher) interest in empirical data and what they reveal about our social structure and what we really value. His first book, *Work, Leisure, and the American School* (1968), was written at a time when "futurists" were predicting that eventually there

L.J. Waks (ed.), *Leaders in Philosophy of Education: Intellectual Self Portraits*, 301–304.

wouldn't be enough work to go around due to technological innovation and so education needed to prepare people for a life of leisure. Tom challenged that construal of the problem. He used the occasion to examine the ideas of work and leisure rooted in American culture. He drew on Hannah Arendt, classical philosophy, and the religious idea of a "calling" to ask "whether and in what respects they [our ideas of work and leisure] are either functional or dysfunctional in relation to our world and therefore in relation to the process of growing up into our world" (p. 7).

His first publications to gain national attention were analyses of the concept of teaching that later became part of his book *The Activities of Teaching (1971)*. That book was widely used in the United States and elsewhere to convey analytic technique to students in philosophy of education. This is a somewhat ironic fact, given that Tom's focus was never really on analytic technique. In the preface to *Work, Leisure, and the American School*, he expressed his lack of interest in what he called "the mock war of 'king-on-the-mountain'" played among competing schools in philosophy of education (at the time, these included realists, pragmatists, idealists, and existentialists). In contrast, he praised the "analytic path" for its "patient, piece-meal, and cumulative search for clarity." However, he cited as its principal defect its omission of questions of practical importance to educators. He worried about the danger that the search for clarity would wind up "providing answers to questions that nobody is asking" (pp. viii-ix).

Tom *was* concerned about questions of practical importance concerning public policy in education. As a Fellow at the National Institute of Education, a consultant to planners of a new community in Rochester, New York, a consultant to the Organization for Economic Co-operation and Development, and within his own church, he thought about ways to structure educational systems that would serve learners of all ages. These interests found their expression especially in Tom's seminal book, *Predicting the Behavior of the Educational System* (1980). In this work, Tom explored what he called the "practical rationality" of the educational system, which must be taken into account, he argued, in any attempt to construct policy *for* the system.

Tom's final book was *Voices, The Educational Formation of Conscience* (1999). At the time of his death, he was working on a related book, with the working title of *Walls*, foreshadowed in his DeGarmo Lecture, "Public Speech" (1993). *Voices* explored the formation of conscience within a community of belief. *Walls* was to have explored the construction of the public sphere by people whose consciences have been formed elsewhere. How is the one created from the many? And how does the conscience formed in a particular community find expression in the public realm?

What, if anything, holds all these projects together except that they were authored by the same person? Tom himself described his own approach to philosophy as "unwrapping the ordinary." The "ordinary" as that which lies closest to hand is usually overlooked, he held. But "the ordinary unwrapped can surprise us. The medium of our thought...can become the object of our thought, and when that happens, then philosophy has entered, not as someone else's text, but as our own.....The worldly significance of any philosophical project will be found in the way it connects to the ordinary. If it addresses the questions that are posed to ordinary men and women by the events of everyday life, and does so in a way that aids in their interpretation and adds to insight, then it is significant" (Green, 1991, pp. 86-9).

For me, there are two important aspects of Tom's connection to ordinary experience. First, experience is the *source* of the problems Tom chose to explore. In many academic areas, including philosophy, the problems are often internally generated within the discipline. In his DeGarmo lecture, Tom noted that there have been 500 years of debates over the principles of the liberal state and the nature of distributive justice. These debates have generated a vast literature in moral and political theory. But Tom didn't begin thinking about the problem by immersing himself in that literature. His interest was the result of some experiences he had in talking with high-level civil servants in Washington about moral problems and about what led them into the civil service. Tom discovered that, for many of the best, the foundation for their service was laid in the formation of their characters and consciences within the communities of belief and memory in which they grew up.

Second, Tom never lost sight of the problem and its home in ordinary experience as he theorized about it. Tom dumbfounded us all once in a seminar on moral education when he asked, "Before you read this literature, what *was* the problem you had about moral education?" Many of us were ashamed to admit we couldn't remember. Or perhaps we'd never had such a problem in the first place. I think it's because Tom's work had that connection to ordinary experience that his written work has had wide appeal beyond the profession of philosophy of education and it was also part of his impact as a teacher.

Of course, the value of "unwrapping the ordinary" depends on the significance of what the "unwrapping" reveals. Tom had an extraordinary capacity for seeing things in a new light. Time and again he could surprise you with his slant on things. His work was remarkably creative and generative; it opened up new possibilities for thought and action.

Tom's contributions as a citizen of Syracuse University were substantial. In everything he did, Tom worked to establish connections, whether between the School of Education and other Syracuse University schools and colleges, or among researchers, practitioners, and policy makers. One of his final contributions to the University was to fund a lecture at Syracuse by Richard Rothstein, a former education columnist for the New York Times and author of the recent book, *Class and Schools: Using Social, Economic, and Educational Reform to Close the Black-White Achievement Gap.* Tom designed Rothstein's visit to engage, not only the school of education, but also the S.I. Newhouse School of Public Communications and the Maxwell School of Citizenship and Public Affairs. During the question period, I listened to a doctoral student from the Maxwell School talk about how valuable she found this event and how rare it was in her experience that people were talking about important matters across professional and disciplinary boundaries. And I knew Tom hadn't lost a beat. He loved nothing better than a good conversation, which is why we honored him at Syracuse by naming a seminar room after him.

I was Tom's student and eventually his colleague and friend for over 30 years. I knew him to have been not only a scholar but also a man of faith, a fine clarinet player and lover of music, an excellent ball room dancer, a gentleman farmer, husband of Rosemary Cass Green for 56 years, a father of four, and grandfather of 9. I learned from his sister at his memorial service that as a ten-year-old he liked to sit on the roof of the family house with his feet in the rain gutters. Somehow that bit of iconoclasm seems a portent of future contribution. He was known among his students for certain aphorisms that I discovered at his memorial service he shared with his children as well. "When human beings learn something, their normal reaction is to laugh," he frequently said. And, he added, that proves Aristotle's claim that the exercise of theoretical wisdom is the highest form of happiness-- which, of course, led us all to laugh. Speaking of the proverb, "Do your duty though the heavens fall," Tom said, "If the heavens are *really* going to fall, maybe you should reconsider."

John Dewey once said of his own life: "One of the conditions of happiness is the opportunity of a calling, a career which somehow is congenial to one's own temperament. And I have had the sheer luck or fortune to be engaged in the occupation of thinking; and while I am quite regular at my meals I think that I may say that I had rather work—and perhaps even more play—with ideas and thinking than eat. That chance has been given me" (Dewey, 1981, p. 420). Thomas Franklin Green had such a chance and he used it to improve our thinking about education. He died in Syracuse on December 20, 2006. We will miss his frequent chuckle, his insight into the human condition, and his talent for surprising us by unwrapping the ordinary.

REFERENCES

Dewey, J. (1981). *The later works, 1925-1953* (Vol. 5: 1929-1930) (Jo Ann Boydston, Ed.). Carbondale, Edwardsville: Southern Illinois University Press.

Green, T. F. (1968). *Work, leisure and the American schools.* New York: Random House.

Green, T. F. (1971). *The activities of teaching.* New York: McGraw-Hill.

Green, T. F. (1980). *Predicting the behavior of the educational system* (with the assistance of D. P. Ericson and R. H. Seidman). Syracuse, NY: Syracuse University Press.

Green, T. F. (1984). *The formation of conscience in an age of technology* (the John Dewey lecture, 1984). Syracuse: Syracuse University/The John Dewey Society.

Green, T. F. (1991). Unwrapping the ordinary: Philosophical projects. *American Journal of Education, 100*(1), 84-105.

Green, T. F. (1993). *Public speech* (the 18th Charles DeGarmo lecture of The Society of Professors of Education). San Francisco, CA: Caddo Gap Press for the Society of Professors of Education.

Green, T. F. (1999). *Voices: The educational formation of conscience.* Notre Dame, IN: University of Notre Dame Press.

Rothstein, R. (2004). *Class and schools: Using social, economic, and educational reform to close the Black-white achievement gap.* New York, NY: Teachers College Press.

Emily Robertson
Syracuse University

APPENDIX B

PAUL H. HIRST

PHILOSOPHY OF EDUCATION IN THE UK

The Institutional Context

EDUCATIONAL STUDIES IN THE 1940S

Although modified by wartime regulations, in the early 1940s there were in the UK two distinct ways of training to be a schoolteacher. One was to study in a university for a bachelors degree in a subject relevant to the school curriculum and then take a one year teacher training course at a University Department of Education (UDE) for the Post-Graduate Certificate in Education (PGCE) which included some academic study of education and some practical training in schools. The other route was to train at a College of Education (publicly or privately established) for three years taking a combined course of academic studies in subjects relevant to the school curriculum and education plus practical training in schools, receiving at the end the College's own Certificate in Education. Most major universities had no undergraduate studies in education but an entirely postgraduate UDE which offered a PGCE course, some more advanced courses for Postgraduate Diplomas and opportunities for Masters and Doctoral study. All Colleges of Education offered a Certificate in Education course and most advanced courses for serving teachers. Public funds were available to all those taking such courses. The quality control of the courses in the Colleges was dependent on each institution having them regularly inspected by Government officers, known as Her Majesty's Inspectors of Schools (HMI), and judged to be 'fit for purpose'. There was no external control over any university work in education and much freedom was given to the institutions within this system.

NATIONAL DEVELOPMENTS: THE MCNAIR REPORT 1944

In 1944 a Government established Commission made a Report (The McNair Report) recommending that the qualifications of every College of Education should be brought under the supervision of some local university, each major university establishing for that purpose an Institute of Education (UIE) for the Colleges in its area. It was also proposed that these Institutes would act as centres for short and advanced courses for serving teachers in the area. In keeping with this Report, each major university in due time established an Institute of Education of this nature alongside its already well established Department of Education.

L.J. Waks (ed.), Leaders in Philosophy of Education: Intellectual Self Portraits, 305–310.

TOWARDS AN ALL GRADUATE PROFESSION: THE ROBBINS REPORT 1963

Some 15 years after the implementation of the McNair Report, a major Government Commission was asked to investigate the whole provision of Higher Education in the UK and part of its brief was to examine the status of the Colleges of Education and their relationship with their universities. The outcome was that in 1963 the Robbins Report recommended that all the Colleges of Education should redevelop their courses in arrangement with their local universities so that all three year students would be awarded an Ordinary Bachelor of Education degree and students taking a fourth year would go on to receive an Honours Bachelor of Education degree. The aim was to create eventually an all graduate profession of schoolteachers, recruitment to which would begin in some five years time. Nothing was spelt out in the Report concerning the character of the necessarily new courses in educational studies that would be needed, but once the Report was accepted by Government a major National Conference on the nature of the educational studies was convened by The Universities' Council for the Education of Teachers (UCET: See later). The proceedings of that conference, chaired by J. W. Tibble, were later published in book form as *The Study of Education* (1966), its papers having considerable national significance, particularly that on 'Educational Theory' by Paul H. Hirst and that on 'The Philosophy of Education' by Richard S. Peters. In the following years many excellent College courses in educational studies were developed, some achieving considerable sophistication in the level of their academic study of education within distinct disciplinary areas.

MERGER OF COLLEGES INTO UNIVERSITIES AND POLYTECHNICS

Following the full implementation of the Robbins proposals, various financial and institutional developments provoked a radical national change in the situation of all the Colleges of Education. Over a period of some years they all ceased to exist as distinct Colleges, being either fully merged into their related universities or combined with other colleges to develop into new universities. With these changes it of course became a nonsense to have in any one university both a Department of Education and an Institute of Education, each dealing with educational studies and teacher training. As a result, all universities integrated these functions into a single School or Faculty of Education with a major teaching force working across a wide range of educational studies from initial undergraduate and short course work to Ph.D. supervision linked to much externally funded educational research. The upshot of these developments is thus that all formal study of education is now in universities and in Faculties or Schools of Education. But it should be noted that in this development most undergraduate study of education is within B Ed degree courses which are directed at initial teacher education and is therefore heavily directed to practical teaching issues. Only one university in the UK, Cambridge, provides the possibility for undergraduates to study education solely as a strictly academic subject within their first degree programme.

THE UNIVERSITIES' COUNCIL FOR THE EDUCATION OF TEACHERS (UCET)

For the purposes of effectively contributing to the work of the 1944 McNair Commission, the Heads of the then existing University Departments of Education constituted themselves into a standing working-party to look after their own academic and institutional interests. They later also had to take on the initiative in their own universities for carrying out the Commission's recommendations by establishing the new Institutes of Education. The new Heads of those Institutes then formed a parallel standing working-party for their own mutual support in the development of their new responsibilities. When in due time it was clearly important for these two working-parties to collaborate closely, they were amalgamated to form a permanent consultative and advisory body of the Heads of all University Departments and Institutes of Education, taking the name of The Universities' Council for the Education of Teachers (UCET). This body has no official public standing in relation to any Government bodies though it has significant national influence in everything to do with teacher education and training. It has no direct political or 'trades union' interests and is a completely voluntary, strictly professional group with primarily academic and related institutional concerns. UCET has had no role whatever in quality assurance regarding staff in Faculties and Schools of Education. HMI, as inspectors of courses, were the only public national assurance body until 1994 (See later). There has never been any direct quality control of staff in university-based education programs.

THE UNIVERSITY OF LONDON INSTITUTE OF EDUCATION

Throughout all these developments from the 1940s the Institute of Education in London has always been in a unique position. The University of London is a huge institution formed of numerous big colleges like smaller universities within it and early in the 20th Century it established a separate kind of college to devote itself entirely to the training of teachers and the study of education much as if it were the Department of Education for the whole University. It soon had hundreds of students and scores of staff. It happened to call itself the Institute of Education and has kept that name. It appointed from the start Directors with very strong academic qualifications devoted to the serious academic study of education even if at first its main task was providing the PGCE year for graduates wanting to go into schoolteaching. In 1920 the first Director, Sir Percy Nunn, published a strongly philosophical book 'Education: Its Data and First Principles'. The second Director made senior appointments specifically in the psychology of education and the history of education. With the McNair Report sociology of education was soon recognised by a distinct appointment and the first Professor of Philosophy of Education, Louis Arnaud Reid, was appointed in 1947. Though the McNair report suggested each University should establish a new 'Institute of Education' alongside its existing 'Department of Education' the University of London simply added to its already existing Institute all the new functions of taking on the Colleges of

Education in the area to oversee all their teacher training courses. No one seems to have been daunted by the task of thus taking on the academic oversight of 25 Colleges of Education and the formal, if not the executive, academic responsibility for thousands of students. Such a development made the Institute far and away the most powerful centre in the UK for the study of education and enabled it to appoint many extra faculty members working in distinct educational disciplines.

When, following the Robbins Report of 1963 on the whole of national Higher Education, all this vast empire of teacher education work in all the Colleges of Education became elevated to work for the Universities' own degrees, the need to stiffen the academic nature of this work in the Colleges became a most serious matter and the whole question of the nature of the study of education at such a level became the cause of much heated dispute.. In 1964, within months of the appearance of the Robbins Report, Richard Peters was appointed to succeed Professor Reid in the Chair of Philosophy of Education and immediately began to play a central part in the reshaping of educational studies not only in the Institute's own taught programmes but in those in all the attendant 25 Colleges of the Institute as well. He had already a formidable reputation as an academic philosopher and he threw himself readily into helping the Institute sort out the academic and institutional demands of the Robbins recommendations.

PHILOSOPHY OF EDUCATION

Education was a respectable discipline in many universities and particularly at the Institute of Education in London (see above) long before Richard Peters came on the scene. E.g. Psychology of Education and History of Education were widely accepted. However Richard Peters was responsible for first establishing Philosophy of Education as a respectable area of study both amongst those working in Education nationally and amongst academic philosophers in general. He came to the task from being the Head of an academic department of Philosophy and Psychology in a College of the University of London and a sabbatical year spent with Israel Scheffler in Harvard. He found me already on the Institute staff having worked briefly in philosophy of education under Louis Arnaud Reid. Peters and I immediately began to work in the closest collaboration with him in charge. The development of work for us with existing lecturers in the Colleges of Education, now having to teach degree work in philosophy of education as a result of the new Robbins Report developments, produced a great demand for us to create philosophy of education in the contemporary analytical mode and to add new staff at the Institute fully qualified in academic philosophy. John White was one such appointee. Patricia White became a student with us and eventually a member of the staff. Other universities and colleges then started recruiting people to teach the subject as a distinct area, spurred on by the demands of the Robbins Report. The Philosophy of Education Society of GB was established in 1964 after a number of conferences run by the Institute of Education for lecturers in universities and Colleges of Education with Richard Peters as Chairman and myself as Secretary. Papers given at the Conferences and at London Meetings of the Society were first published as Society Proceedings in 1966. The publication later became a general journal run by the Society under the title of the *Journal of Philosophy of Education*.

EPILOGUE: THE IMPOSITION OF GOVERNMENTAL CONTROL

Following the changes of the post-Robbins Report period, the whole development of Education Studies in UK universities went well until the advent of a Conservative Government under Margaret Thatcher in the 1980s. The liberalism of educational developments in schools, which had long had great freedom under only loose inspectorial governmental control by HMI, was suddenly fiercely attacked and blamed for economic and social ills. State control over schools and a compulsory National School Curriculum were legislated. Tight control over teacher education in universities began with severe curtailment of finance for both in-service courses and for educational research, both of which were henceforth to be used almost exclusively in the service of politically determined educational policies. HMI for the first time now started to exercise a real power of quality control over teacher education courses in universities and a 1994 Education Act established a Teacher Training Agency for their detailed control under compulsory regulations. These restrictions, insisting on the direct practical relevance of all educational courses, have led to the near demise of all courses concerned specifically with the disciplines of educational theory within British universities. Recent Labour Governments have done nothing whatever to liberalise this situation. UCET has proved an impotent voice of protest and professional bodies like The Philosophy of Education Society of GB and the British Educational Research Association have achieved little by their efforts. Philosophy of Education like all the other 'disciplines' thus now survives in Faculties and Schools of Education only by living off its ever decreasing academic capital within an almost universally unsympathetic political climate. It is kept going by providing just Masters Degree courses and opportunities for research degree work to students able to pay the full tuition fees from their personal resources, and contributing where possible to practically orientated courses whose leaders appreciate the significance of philosophical issues for their work. In the best interests of serious educational research and the proper development of educational practices in schools it is to be hoped this myopic attention to just the immediacies of educational practices themselves will soon be cured and philosophy, like all the other disciplines, be again given its rightful place in the properly professional theory and practice of education.

REFERENCES

McNair Report. (1944). *Teachers and youth leaders.* London: H.M.S.O.
Nunn P. (1920). *Education: Its data and first principles.* London: Edward Arnold.

Robbins Report. (1963). *Higher education.* London: H.M.S.O.
Tibble J. (Ed.). (1966). *The study of education.* London: Routledge.

Paul Hirst
University of Cambridge

Printed in the United States
125942LV00002B/39/A